THE G8, THE UNITED NATIONS, AND CONFLICT PREVENTION

This innovative and forward looking work examines the Genoa summit agenda with a view to strengthening international conflict prevention institutions and identifying and analyzing economic early warning indicators. It devotes particular attention to the Italian contribution and approach and the ways in which it can be effectively implemented following the summit. The first book to compare the role of the G8 and the United Nations in conflict prevention and human security, *The G8, the United Nations, and Conflict Prevention* will be essential reading for academics, government officials and members of the business and media communities.

T0299962

The G8 and Global Governance Series

Series Editor: John J. Kirton

The G8 and Global Governance Series explores the issues, the institutions, and the strategies of the participants in the G8 network of global governance, and other actors, processes, and challenges that shape global order in the twenty-first century. Many aspects of globalisation, once considered domestic, are now moving into the international arena generating a need for broader and deeper international co-operation and demanding new centres of leadership to revitalise, reform, reinforce, and even replace the galaxy of multilateral institutions created in 1945. In response, the G8, composed of the world's major market democracies, including Russia and the European Union, is emerging as an effective source of global governance. *The G8 and Global Governance Series* focusses on the new issues at the centre of global governance, covering topics such as finance, investment, and trade, as well as transnational threats to human security and traditional and emerging political and security challenges. The series examines the often invisible network of G8, G7, and other institutions as they operate inside and outside established international systems to generate desired outcomes and create a new order. It analyses how individual G8 members and other international actors, including multinational firms, civil society organisations, and other international institutions, devise and implement strategies to secure their preferred global order.

Also in the series

The New Economic Diplomacy
Edited by Nicholas Bayne and Stephen Woolcock
ISBN 0 7546 1832 3

Governing Global Trade
Theodore H. Cohn
ISBN 0 7546 1593 6

New Directions in Global Political Governance
Edited by John J. Kirton and Junichi Takase
ISBN 0 7546 1833 1

New Directions in Global Economic Governance
Edited by John J. Kirton and George M. von Furstenberg
ISBN 0 7546 1698 3

The New Transatlantic Agenda
Edited by Hall Gardner and Radoslava N. Stefanova
ISBN 0 7546 1780 7

Guiding Global Order
Edited by John J. Kirton, Joseph P. Daniels and Andreas Freytag
ISBN 0 7546 1502 2

The G8, the United Nations, and Conflict Prevention

Edited by

JOHN J. KIRTON
University of Toronto

RADOSLAVA N. STEFANOVA
Istituto Affari Internazionali and European University Institute

Routledge
Taylor & Francis Group

LONDON AND NEW YORK

First published 2004 by Ashgate Publishing

2 Park Square, Milton Park, Abingdon, Oxon OX14 4RN
711 Third Avenue, New York, NY 10017, USA

Routledge is an imprint of the Taylor & Francis Group, an informa business

First issued in paperback 2016

Copyright © 2004 John J. Kirton and Radoslava N. Stefanova

The authors hereby assert their moral right to be identified as the authors of
the work in accordance with the Copyright, Designs and Patents Act, 1988.

All rights reserved. No part of this book may be reprinted or reproduced
or utilised in any form or by any electronic, mechanical, or other means,
now known or hereafter invented, including photocopying and recording,
or in any information storage or retrieval system, without permission in
writing from the publishers.

Notice:
Product or corporate names may be trademarks or registered trademarks,
and are used only for identification and explanation without intent to infringe.

British Library Cataloguing in Publication Data
The G8, the United Nations, and conflict prevention. - (The
  G8 and global governance series)
  1. Group of Eight (Organization) 2. United Nations 3. Pacific
  settlement of international disputes 4. Conflict management
  5. Security, International
  I. Kirton, John J. II. Stefanova, Radoslava
  327.1'7

Library of Congress Control Number: 2003112236

ISBN 978-0-7546-0879-0 (hbk)
ISBN 978-1-138-25660-6 (pbk)

Transfered to Digital Printing in 2009

Contents

Contents vii

List of Tables

List of Figures

List of Contributors

Sir Nicholas Bayne, KCMG, is a Fellow at the International Trade Policy Unit of the London School of Economics and Political Science. As a British diplomat, he was High Commissioner to Canada from 1992 to 1996, Economic Director at the Foreign and Commonwealth Office from 1988 to 1992, and Ambassador to the Organisation for Economic Co-operation and Development from 1985 to 1988. He has published numerous articles and books, including *Hanging In There: The G7 and G8 Summit in Maturity and Renewal* (Ashgate, 2000); he is also co-author, with Robert Putnam, of *Hanging Together: Co-operation and Conflict in the Seven Power Summits* (Harvard University Press, 1987) and, with Stephen Woolcock, of *The New Economic Diplomacy: Decision-Making and Negotiation in International Economic Relations* (Ashgate, 2003). Sir Nicholas also contributed to, among others, *New Directions in Global Economic Governance: Managing Globalisation in the Twenty-First Century* (Ashgate, 2001) and *New Directions in Global Political Governance: The G8 and International Order in the Twenty-First Century* (Ashgate, 2002).

Lorenzo Bini Smaghi is Director General for International Relations at the Italian Ministry of the Economy and Finance. He represents Italy in various international forums, in particular as G7 Finance Deputy. Before joining the ministry, he worked in the Bank of Italy's Research Department, and as head of the Policy Division and Deputy Director General for Research of the European Central Bank in Frankfurt. Dr. Bini Smaghi a graduate of the Catholic University of Louvain and the University of Chicago.

Robert Fowler is Canada's Ambassador to Italy, where he is also accredited as High Commissioner to Malta, Ambassador to Albania and San Marino, and Ambassador and Permanent Representative to the United Nations organisations based in Rome. Prior to his appointment as Ambassador to Italy, he was Canada's Ambassador to the United Nations in New York from 1995 to 2000, including during Canada's 1999/2000 term as a member of the United Nations Security Council. In July 2001, Mr. Fowler was asked by the Prime Minister to plan and organise the 2002 G8 Summit in Kananaskis, and was appointed Jean Chrétien's G8 Personal Representative (Sherpa) and his Personal Representative for Africa. In September 2002, Mr. Fowler returned to Rome to resume his duties as Ambassador to Italy, while remaining Personal Representative of the Prime Minister for Africa. Mr. Fowler has held various senior positions in Ottawa, including Executive Assistant to the Under-Secretary of State for External Affairs; Assistant

Secretary to the Cabinet (Foreign and Defence Policy) at the Privy Council Office advising prime ministers Pierre Trudeau, John Turner, and Brian Mulroney on foreign, defence, and development policy issues; Assistant Deputy Minister for Policy at the Department of National Defence; and Deputy Minister of National Defence.

Diana Juricevic is in her final year of a combined J.D./M.A. in Economics at the University of Toronto's Faculty of Law. A member of the G8 Research Group, she participated in the group's activities at Okinawa 2000 and Genoa 2001. She is currently conducting policy research for Médecins Sans Frontières and served as editorial assistant for the *Faculty of Law Review*. A resident Junior Fellow at Massey College at the University of Toronto, she is also an accomplished artist.

John J. Kirton is Director of the G8 Research Group, Associate Professor of Political Science, Research Associate at the Centre for International Studies, and a Fellow of Trinity College at the University of Toronto. He is the principal investigator of the University of Toronto's Centre for International Studies project on 'Strengthening Canada's Environmental Community through International Regime Reform' (EnviReform). He is co-editor of *The G8's Role in the New Millennium* (Ashgate, 1999), *Shaping a New International Financial System: Challenges of Governance in a Globalizing World* (Ashgate, 2000), *Guiding Global Order: G8 Governance in the Twenty-First Century* (Ashgate, 2000), *New Directions in Global Economic Governance: Managing Globalisation in the Twenty-First Century* (Ashgate, 2001), and *New Directions in Global Political Governance: The G8 and International Order in the Twenty-First Century* (Ashgate, 2002). As co-editor of Ashgate's Global Finance series, he is co-editor (with Michele Fratianni and Paolo Savona) of *Sustaining Global Growth and Development: G7 and IMF Governance* (Ashgate, 2003) and *Governing Global Finance: New Challenges, G7 and IMF Contributions* (Ashgate, 2002). He received his Ph.D. from the Johns Hopkins University School of Advanced International Studies.

Ella Kokotsis is the Communications Co-ordinator at the Independent Electricity Market Operator and is Director of Analytical Studies for the University of Toronto's G8 Research Group. She served on the National Round Table on the Environment and the Economy's Task Force on Foreign Policy and Sustainability in preparation for the 1995 G7 Halifax Summit, and has prepared commissioned policy papers for the Canadian Centre for Foreign Policy Development at the Department of Foreign Affairs and International Trade. Author of *Keeping International Commitments: Compliance, Credibility, and the G7, 1988–1995* (Garland, 1999), Dr. Kokotsis holds a Ph.D. in International Relations from the University of Toronto.

Frank E. Loy was Under Secretary of State for Global Affairs for the United States from 1998 to 2001. He served in the Department of State in two previous administrations, including appointments as Director of the Bureau of Refugee Programs from 1979 to 1981, with personal rank of Ambassador, and Deputy Assistant Secretary for Economic Affairs from 1965 to 1970. From 1981 to 1995 he was President of the German Marshall Fund of the U.S. He also holds many years of experience in the business sector, including having served as Senior Vice-President for International Affairs of Pan American World Airways and practising corporation law with O'Melveny & Myers. A founding member of the Institute of International Economics, Mr. Loy has served as chair of numerous nonprofit boards, including the Environmental Defense Fund (now Environmental Defense). In 1996, he was a visiting lecturer in International Law and Policy at the Yale Law School. Mr. Loy received his B.A. from UCLA and L.L.B. from Harvard University.

David M. Malone became President of the International Peace Academy in 1998, when he took leave from the Canadian foreign service. He was Canada's Deputy Permanent Representative at the United Nations, with rank of Ambassador, and chaired the negotiations of the UN's Special Committee on Peacekeeping Operations. He has also served as Director General of the Policy, International Organizations, and Global Issues Bureaux in the Canadian foreign and trade ministry. Within the Canadian foreign ministry, he co-ordinated Canadian participation in G7 summits from 1986 to 1988 and again from 1989 to 1990, and was a member of the Canadian delegation to the G7/8 summits between 1981 and 1995. He is an Adjunct Professor of Law at New York University and a visiting professor at the Institut des Études Politiques in Paris. His most recent book, *Unilateralism and U.S. Foreign Policy: International Perspectives* (Lynne Rienner, 2003), was co-edited with Yuen Foong Khong. He contributes frequently to scholarly journals, to the *International Herald Tribune* and *The Globe and Mail,* and to other publications.

Pierluigi Montalbano is a post-doctoral fellow in International Economics at the Department of Political Science of the University of Rome 'La Sapienza' and Scientific Co-ordinator of the Research Unit of IPALMO (Institute for Relations between Italy and the Countries of Africa, Latin America, and the Middle East). He has conducted studies on trade integration and international macroeconomic policy, with particular attention to the European Union and the central and eastern European countries. He is currently involved in a research project on trade and socioeconomic vulnerability being carried out by the Global Development Network in co-operation with the World Bank and in the Network on Conflict, Peace, and Development Cooperation of the Development Assistance Committee of the Organisation for Economic Co-operation and Development.

Kristiana Powell is a doctoral candidate in the Department of Political Science (International Relations) at the University of Toronto, and worked as a researcher and writer on security issues for the University of Toronto's G8 Research Group. She is also currently working as a Peace and Security analyst with Project Ploughshares in Waterloo, Ontario.

Reinhardt Rummel is the deputy head of the European Integration Department at the Institute of International Relations and Security in Berlin, where he deals with foreign policy and security questions for the European Union. He has held teaching positions at the University of Paris III, at Munich University, and at the Johns Hopkins University Bologna Center. As a visiting scholar, he has worked with the Center for International Affairs at Harvard University and with the Woodrow Wilson Center for International Scholars in Washington DC. From 1997 to 2001, he was director of the Conflict Prevention Network (CPN), a community of academic institutions, nongovernmental organisations, and independent experts who assist the European Union's institutions in peacebuilding, conflict prevention, and crisis management. He is also a founding member of Conflict Prevention Associates (CPA) based in Brussels. His most recent publication, 'From Weakness to Power with ESDP?', appeared in *European Foreign Affairs Review* (Winter 2002/2003). Dr. Rummel holds an M.A. in economics from Munich University, a degree in political science from the University of Paris I, and a doctorate from Tübingen University.

Mario Sarcinelli is Chairman of CERADI-Research Centre for Enterprise Law, lecturer in international monetary economics at the Faculty of Statistical Sciences of the University of Rome 'La Sapienza' and at LUISS Guido Carli University in Rome. He has served as Deputy General Manager of the Bank of Italy as well as Director General of the Italian Treasury and, for a brief appointment, Minister of Foreign Trade. He has been Vice-President of Operations for the European Bank for Reconstruction and Development in London, as well as chair of the publicly owned Banca Nazionale del Lavoro. In 2000, the Inter-American Development Bank appointed him to the External Review Group for assessing the role of the bank in the private sector. He has published extensively on economic, monetary, financial, and fiscal topics, both in Italian and in English, and is a regular contributor to *Il Sole-24 ORE*.

Radoslava N. Stefanova is a Professor of International Relations at the American University of Rome. She is completing her Ph.D. dissertation entitled "Conceptual Dimensions of Conflict Prevention: Assessing Possible Applications in Europe" at the European University Institute in Florence, Italy. From March to November 2002 she was a research analyst with the International Crisis Group's Kosovo office. Before that she was, for more than five years, Head of the South-East Europe programme of the Istituto Affari Internazionali (IAI). For two years she was also a co-director of the IAI's Transatlantic Programme. Her main areas of expertise are conflict management and peacebuilding, and NATO and EU enlargement and reform. She has published many book chapters and articles on these topics. She holds graduate degrees in international affairs from the Johns Hopkins Paul H. Nitze School of Advanced International Studies and from the Norman Paterson School of International Affairs of Carleton University, Canada. She received her undergraduate degree from the American University of Paris, *summa cum laude*.

Gina Stephens is a doctoral candidate in the Department of Political Science at the University of Toronto and a research assistant on the project 'Strengthening Canada's Environmental Community through International Regime Reform' (EnviReform).

Roberto Toscano is Italy's ambassador to Iran. Until 2003, he was Head of Policy Planning at the Italian Ministry of Foreign Affairs and chaired the Organisation for Economic Co-operation and Development's Development Assistance Committee network on conflict, peace, and development co-operation. As a career diplomat, he has served in a number of other posts (Chile, USSR, Spain, United States, as well as at Italy's Permanent Mission to the United Nations at Geneva). He holds a degree in law from the University of Parma and an M.A. from the School of Advanced International Studies at Johns Hopkins University, which he attended as a Fulbright fellow. In 1987–88 he was a Fellow at the Center for International Affairs of Harvard University. From 2000 to 2003, he was a visiting professor of international relations in the Department of Political Science at LUISS University in Rome. He is the author of books and articles (on human rights, peacekeeping, conflict prevention, ethics and international relations) published in Italy, the U.S., France, and Spain.

Umberto Triulzi is Professor of Political Economy in the Department of Political Science at the University of Rome 'La Sapienza' and Director General of IPALMO (Institute for Relations between Italy and the Countries of Africa, Latin America, and the Middle East). He is an advisor to the Italian Ministry of Foreign Affairs, and a member of the Italian Economists Association and of the Advisory Board of the Center for Economics and Law of the Market at the University of Rome 'La Sapienza'. He is currently involved as a senior expert in the Network on Conflict, Peace, and Development Co-operation of the Development Assistance Committee of the Organisation for Economic Co-operation and Development and in the research project on socioeconomic vulnerability being carried out by the Global Development Network in co-operation with the World Bank.

Preface and Acknowledgements

This book, the eleventh in Ashgate Publishing's series on the G8 and Global Governance, continues a tradition begun in 1998 of using the annual G8 Summit as a catalyst for an edited volume that explores the central themes in the emerging dynamic of global governance. The first volume, *The G8's Role in the New Millennium*, was produced on the basis of the 1998 Birmingham G8 Summit. It focussed directly on the role of the G8 as it began its new era with Russia as a virtually full member, as a system with a rapidly expanding array of ministerial level institutions, and one with a new, highly domestic agenda that included such new challenges of globalisation as financial supervision, employment, and crime. The 1999 Cologne Summit, taking place as the 1997–99 global financial crisis and the 1999 NATO humanitarian intervention in Kosovo were ending, inspired two volumes. The first, *Shaping a New International Financial System: Challenges of Governance in a Globalizing World*, took an economic and political economy approach to the central issues confronting the global economic community. The second, *Guiding Global Order: G8 Governance in the Twenty-First Century*, continued this economic exploration, but broadened the concern to embrace a wide range of political and international institutional issues and perspectives, including the defining, highly political question of war and peace. This volume also looked directly and comprehensively at the role of the G8 itself in shaping a new international order as the twenty-first century began. The 2000 Okinawa Summit also generated two volumes, with an economic and political-security focus respectively. The first, *New Directions in Global Economic Governance: Managing Globalization in the Twenty-First Century*, examined emerging trends in the governance of the 'new economy', international finance, and international trade. The second, *New Directions in Global Political Governance: The G8 and International Order in the Twenty-First Century*, extended the G8 and Global Governance series directly into the domain of international security, in both its classic and newer forms.

This present volume continues, in a refined fashion, the Cologne pattern of producing twin summit-inspired volumes covering the economic and the political-security dimensions of global order respectively. Beginning with the 2001 Genoa Summit, the economic activity of the G7/8 has been explored in annual volumes, focussed on finance, in a partner book series on Global Finance, with Michele Fratianni, Paolo Savona, and John Kirton as series editors. That series has produced two volumes — *Governing Global Finance: New Challenges, G7 and IMF Contributions*, based on the 2001 Genoa G7 Summit and the work of the G7 finance ministers forum that year, and *Sustaining Global Growth and Development: G7 and IMF Governance*, based on the finance, productivity, macroeconomics, and international development activities of the G7 and G8 at the 2002 Kananaskis Summit and throughout that year.

This volume represents the political-security contribution to this annual, summit-based, exploration of the major issues of global governance and the work of the G7/8. But it extends the tradition in several ways. First, it embraces in a single volume the political-security agenda and activity of two G8 summits and years — Genoa 2001 and Kananaskis 2002 — and their legacies at a third — Evian 2003. Second, it singles out a major component of the G8's political-security agenda — conflict prevention — with comprehensive relevance to the entire political-security, and indeed economic, sphere. Third, it selects for this specific focus a new issue of G8 interest and involvement, in order to chart more clearly how the G8 can take up, and in part create, new issue areas and principles for its own agenda, as well as for the global agenda, and thus provide leadership to the wider world. Fourth, in part as a consequence of this concern with global leadership, this volume deals directly with the G8's work as it interacts and compares with the work of other major international institutions, notably the broadly multilateral United Nations and the regional European Union. Fifth, this volume takes the series to the heart of the G8's post–11 September 2001 political-security preoccupation with fighting terrorism and socioeconomic development in Africa, Iraq and elsewhere, by addressing the earlier, deeper root causes from which terrorism and other forms of violent conflict can flow.

This volume has its origins in several activities. The first is a policy conference that took place at Canadian and Italian initiative in Rome on 16 July 2001, under the sponsorship of the G8 Research Group based at the University of Toronto, the Italian Istituto Affari Internazionali, and Italy's Centre for Advanced Military Studies (CeMISS), with the financial support of the German Marshall Fund. This conference, on 'Conflict Prevention and Human Security? What Can the G8 Do?' examined the performance and potential of international institutions, notably the G8, the United Nations, and the European Union, in preventing conflict and promoting human security. Substantively, the conference focussed on the Genoa Summit agenda with a view to strengthening international institutions involved conflict prevention, and to identifying and analysing economic early warning indicators; it also considered the Italian contribution and approach, the ways they could be effectively implemented following the Genoa summit, and the G8's performance and potential in upholding human security world-wide, through poverty reduction and economic development. The conference aimed at encouraging discussion and debate among G8 insiders, expert outsiders, and the interested public in the critical period immediately preceding the G8 foreign ministers meeting in Rome on 18–19 July 2001 and the G8's Genoa leaders meeting later in July. The dozen presenters and 100 participants, from all G8 regions, came from academic circles, the policy-making community (including diplomats and past and present G8 negotiators), developing countries and relevant international organisations, and the media. In its programme and participants, the conference emphasised continuity with the forthcoming Italian-hosted Genoa Summit and subsequent Canadian-hosted Kananaskis Summit. All the chapters in this volume, save for that of Gina Stephens and Kristiana Powell, are extensively revised and updated versions of papers first presented at the Rome conference.

The second activity on which this volume is based is the University of Toronto's Centre for International Studies project on 'Securing Canada's Environmental Community Through International Regime Reform' (the EnviReform project), financed by the Social Sciences and Humanities Research Council of Canada, through its strategic grant programme on 'Globalisation and Social Cohesion in Canada'. John Kirton serves as principal investigator of this project, in which Nicholas Bayne, Gina Stephens, and Kristiana Powell have participated. The project examines the links among trade, environment, and social cohesion that, in the G8's work and in the real world, are integrally related to the task of conflict prevention.

The third activity is the project on 'After Anarchy: Co-operation, Coherence, and Change in the G8 Concert', based at the University of Toronto's Department of Political Science and also financed by the Social Sciences and Humanities Research Council of Canada. John Kirton, Ella Kokotsis, and Gina Stephens are involved in this project.

The fourth activity enriching this volume is a public policy seminar, held in Tokyo, on 10 June 2002, on 'The Prospects for the Canadian G8 Summit'. Organised by Shinichiro Uda, Director of the G8 Research Group's Tokyo office, and co-sponsored by the G8 Research Group and the Canadian Embassy in Tokyo, with the support of the Canada-Japan Society, the Japan-British Society and the LSE International Social Economic Forum in Japan, this event at the Nippon Press Centre brought together presenters from all three G8 regions of Asia, North America, and Europe with leading policy makers and thinkers from Japan. It allowed for an in-depth exploration of the Genoa Summit's legacy and the prospects for the Kananaskis Summit that lay ahead, in the light of the terrorist attacks on North America on 11 September 2001. John Kirton's contributions to this volume benefited from his paper and the dialogue at this event.

The fifth supporting activity was a conference on 'Sustaining Global Growth: Prosperity, Security, and Development Challenges for the Kananaskis G8'. It was mounted by the Research Group on Global Financial Governance, a joint venture of the Guido Carli Association and the G8 Research Group, and by the University of Calgary, with the financial support of the Government of Canada, the University of Calgary, and the Social Sciences and Humanities Research Council of Canada through the EnviReform project. Held at the University of Calgary on 22 June 2002, in the immediate lead-up to the 2002 Canadian-hosted G7/8 Summit in nearby Kananaskis, this conference assembled a dozen scholars, practitioners, and policy makers from all G7 regions to present papers in an intense, day-long interchange with 75 expert colleagues and interested citizens. The chapters by John Kirton, Nicholas Bayne, and Ella Kokotsis have been enriched by the papers they presented at this conference and the discussions taking place during this event.

Most broadly, this volume has benefited from a July 2000 conference in Berlin, organised by the German Stiftung Wissenschaft und Politik. It represented the first focussed examination, by scholars and policy practitioners, of the G8 and the UN's respective roles in global peace and security as a whole. Inspired by Germany's leadership in the G8's political-security and conflict prevention work in 1999, when

Germany served as host of the G8, this conference produced a valuable book, edited by Winrich Kühne with Jochen Prantl, titled *The Security Council and the G8 in the New Millennium: Who Is in Charge of International Peace and Security?* John Kirton and David Malone presented papers at this conference, which helped stimulate their contributions to, and the creation of this current book.

This volume combines the talents of leading scholarly authorities and senior policy practitioners from all G8 regions (Europe, North America, and Asia), and from virtually all G8 countries. Emphasis has been given to including contributions from the policy community, and from countries and from intergovernmental and nongovernmental institutions outside the G8, notably the United Nations, European Union, and UN-focussed International Peace Academy. They each play a central role in the task of conflict prevention. Contributors come from a wide array of academic disciplines, scholarly fields, and professional communities, including political science, security studies, economics, and development. Several contributions come from senior professional practitioners involved, from Genoa through Kananaskis and into Evian, in guiding the work of the G8 and other intergovernmental institutions in conflict prevention. In addition, many of the other authors have experience within many of the core governmental and intergovernmental institutions at work in governing the international community or have served in senior advisory capacities. With this wide variety of theoretical perspectives, analytical approaches, policy experience, and critical judgement, the collection combines the insights of scholars and practitioners to produce a rich assortment of insights and conclusions. Yet all authors share a basic belief that preventing conflict and promoting human security is a compelling cause for the global community, and that the G8 along with other leading international organisations can make an important contribution to this complex and critical challenge.

Acknowledgements

In producing this volume, we have enjoyed the exceptional support of those who have contributed in many different ways. Within the government of Italy we are grateful to Giuliano Amato, President of the Council of Ministers of the Italian Republic at the time we prepared our Rome conference, and to Francesco Olivieri, Valerio Astraldi, Roberto Toscano, Massimo Leggieri, and their colleagues in Italy's G8 teams. Our debt extends to the Canadian government, and within it in particular to Robert Fowler, Canada's outstanding Ambassador to Italy and Personal Representative of Prime Minister Jean Chrétien for the G8 and Africa, to his deputy in Rome, Malcolm McKechnie, and to their colleagues at the Canadian Embassy in Rome — Nathalie Dubé, Véronique Lebel, and Kwahar Nassim. At headquarters in Ottawa, Randolph Mank and Stéphane Jobin have been constant sources of vital intellectual enrichment and practical support. Paul Meyer and Deanna Horton at the Canadian Embassy in Tokyo and Julie Audet in Ottawa have made much valued contributions as well. We further appreciate the willingness to take a major role in our project and book of two members of the G8 Research Group's Professional Advisory Council and Special Advisory Council: Nicholas Bayne and David Malone.

We are grateful for the essential financial and in-kind support for this volume and its supporting activities to several organisations: the German Marshall Fund of the United States; the Social Sciences and Humanities Research Council of Canada to the EnviReform and After Anarchy projects at the University of Toronto; the Canadian government through its embassies in Italy and Tokyo, headquarters in Ottawa, and G8 Summit Office in 2002; the Government of Japan (in regard to the June 2002 Tokyo conference); and the G8 Research Group and its loyal members and alumni and alumnae.

We are particularly indebted to the Italian sponsors of our conference in Rome. The Istituto Affari Internazionali and its president, Stefano Silvestri, and his staff took care of the scientific organisation of the conference. The Military Centre for Strategic Studies and Director General Carlo Bellinzona, under the auspices of the Centre for Advanced Defence Studies of the Italian Ministry of Defence, provided the splendid facilities in which the conference took place. At the IAI, Natalie Champion was a model of tireless efficiency and co-operation in making the many physical arrangements required for our venture.

In Toronto, we appreciate the support of the *Toronto Star*, which accredited John Kirton, Nicholas Bayne and other members of the G8 Research Group for the G8 foreign ministers meetings in 2001, 2002, and 2003, in order to help observe at first hand the G8's unfolding conflict prevention programme.

We owe a special word of thanks to Madeline Koch, the managing director of the G8 Research Group, whose managerial and editorial skills were essential in helping organise the conference and ensuring that initial thoughts and rough drafts were transformed into a polished integrated book. More broadly, we note with deep appreciation the indispensable contribution of Gina Stephens, the Co-ordinator of the G8 Research Group, of Sandra Larmour, the Director of Development of the G8 Research Group, of Helen Walsh, Director of G8 Online 2002, of Michael Rollason of RBC Dominion Securities, of Jason Wong of the Government of Ontario, and of Shinichiro Uda, Director of the G8 Research Group's office in Japan.

At the University of Toronto, we are grateful to President Robert Birgineau, former Vice-President Heather Munroe Bloom, Vice-Provost Carolyn Tuohy, Patrick Gutteridge, Judy Noordermeer, and their colleagues for their full co-operation in assisting the G8 Research Group with arrangements for President Amato's visit on 29 March 2001, and for their constant support of the G8 Research Group over the years. We also acknowledge the continuing support of our colleagues at the Centre for International Studies: its director, Professor Louis Pauly, who oversees the G8 Research Group's research activities, and Professor Peter Hajnal, who assumed the essential task of securing the anonymous referees who reviewed our draft manuscript and who collectively approved it for publication. We owe much to the comments of those referees, whose often trenchant but always supportive comments have been fully taken into account. At Trinity College, we acknowledge the critical support of provost Margaret MacMillan and former provost Tom Delworth, as well as bursar Geoffrey Seaborn, who manages the G8 Research Group's accounts, head librarian Linda Corman, who oversees the development of the G8 Research Library Collection, and Professor Robert Bothwell, Co-ordinator of the International Relations Program. At the Department of Political Science, Professor Robert Vipond, the Chair, and Professor Ronald Deibert have provided constant encouragement. At the University of Toronto Library, chief librarian Carole Moore, internet director Sián Miekle, and project manager Marc Lalonde have been indispensable.

As always, we reserve a special word of thanks for Kirstin Howgate at Ashgate for recognising the virtue of producing this volume and for working so effectively with her colleagues, Irene Poulton, Amanda Richardson, and Maureen Mansell-Ward, and with appropriate understanding, to ensure the smooth adoption and timely publication of the manuscript. Finally, we acknowledge the patience and support of our families as we laboured to convert raw drafts into publishable text. We are ultimately most indebted to the alumni of the G8 Research Group and to our students and others at universities throughout the world interested in the work of the G8, that of other international organisations and the challenging cause of preventing conflict and promoting human security. They provided a constant source of inspiration and constructive criticism as we pursued our work. It is to this next generation of scholars on the G8, global governance, and conflict prevention that we dedicate this book.

John J. Kirton and Radoslava N. Stefanova
July 2003

List of Abbreviations

ACP	African, Caribbean, and Pacific group of states
AIS	automatic identification systems
APEC	Asia-Pacific Economic Cooperation
API	advance passenger information
APR	Personal Representative (of a G8 leader) for Africa
ASG	Afghanistan Support Group
AU	African Union
BTWC	Biological and Toxic Weapons Convention
CAC	collective action clause
CBRN	chemical, biological, radiological, and nuclear
CCL	contingent credit line
CCWC	Convention on Certain Conventional Weapons
CFSP	Common Foreign and Security Policy
CivPol	civilian policing
COP6	Sixth Conference of the Parties (of the United Nations Framework Convention on Climate Change)
CPDC	Network on Conflict, Peace, and Development Co-operation
CPN	Conflict Prevention Network
CPOM	Conflict Prevention Officials Meeting
CSD6	Commission on Sustainable Development, Sixth Session
CSR	corporate social responsibility
CTC	Counter-Terrorism Committee
DAC	Development Assistance Committee of the Organisation for Economic Co-operation and Development
DDR	disarmament, demobilisation, and reintegration
Dot Force	Digital Opportunities Task Force
DPKO	Department of Peacekeeping Operations (of the United Nations)
ECAs	export credit agencies
ECHO	European Community Humanitarian Organisation
ECOMOG	Economic Community of West African States Monitoring Group
ECOSOC	Economic and Social Council (of the United Nations)
ECOWAS	Economic Community of West African States
EDIFACT	Electronic Data Interchange for Administration Commerce and Transport
ESDP	European Security and Defence Policy
EUPM	European Union Police Mission
FAO	Food and Agriculture Organization
FATF	Financial Action Task Force

FDI	foreign direct investment
FEWS	food early warning system
FIVIMS	Food Insecurity and Vulnerability Information and Mapping Systems
FSAP	Financial Sector Assessment Program
FYROM	Former Yugoslav Republic of Macedonia
GATT	General Agreement on Tariffs and Trade
GDP	gross domestic product
GEF	Global Environmental Facility
HCR	see UNHCR
HIPCs	heavily indebted poor countries
IAEA	International Atomic Energy Agency
ICAO	International Civil Aviation Organization
ICRG	International Country Risk Guide
ICT	information and communications technology
ICTY	International Criminal Tribune for the Former Yugoslavia
IDA	International Development Association
IGO	intergovernmental organisation
ILO	International Labour Organization
IMF	International Monetary Fund
IMO	International Maritime Organization
IPTF	International Police Task Force (of the United Nations)
IT	information technology
LDC	least developed country
MANPADs	manportable surface-to-air missiles
MDB	multilateral development bank
MINURCA	United Nations Mission in the Central African Republic
MTCR	Missile Technology Control Regime
NACD	nonproliferation, arms control, and disarmament
NATO	North Atlantic Treaty Organization
NEPAD	New Partnership for Africa's Development
NGO	nongovernmental organisation
NPT	Nonproliferation Treaty
OAS	Organization of American States
OAU	Organization of African Unity
ODA	official development assistance
OECD	Organisation for Economic Co-operation and Development
OSCE	Organization for Security and Co-operation in Europe
PCIA	peace and conflict impact assessment
P5	Permanent Five members of the United Nations Security Council (United States, Britain, France, China, and Russia)
POPs	persistant organic pollutants
REACT	Rapid Expert Assistance and Co-operation Teams
RECAMP	Reinforcement of African Peacekeeping Capacities programme

ROSC	report on observance of codes and standards
RRM	Rapid Reaction Mechanism
SALW	small arms and light weapons
SDRM	sovereign debt restructuring mechanism
SFOR	Stabilisation Force in Bosnia and Herzegovina
SG/HR	Secretary General of the Council and High Representative of the Common Foreign and Security Policy of the European Commission
SOLAS	International Convention for the Safety of Life at Sea
SRSG	Special Representative of the Secretary General
TRIPs	Trade-Related Intellectual Property Rights
UNAMA	United Nations Assistance Mission in Afghanistan
UNDCP	United Nations International Drug Control Programme
UNDP	United Nations Development Programme
UNESCO	United Nations Educational, Scientific, and Cultural Organization
UNGA	United Nations General Assembly
UNHCR	United Nations High Commissioner for Refugees
UNIFEM	United Nations Development Fund for Women
UNPREDEP	United Nations Preventive Deployment Force
UNSC	United Nations Security Council
UNSCR	United Nations Security Council Resolution
UNSG	United Nations Secretary General
UNTAET	United Nations Transitional Administration in East Timor
WCO	World Customs Organization
WEU	Western European Union
WFP	World Food Programme
WHO	World Health Organization
WMD	weapons of mass destruction
WSSD	World Summit on Sustainable Development
WTO	World Trade Organization

Chapter 1

Introduction:
The G8's Role in
Global Conflict Prevention

John J. Kirton and Radoslava N. Stefanova

The Challenge of Conflict Prevention

There are few challenges of global governance as compelling, as complex, and as challenging as that of conflict prevention. Since the relatively peaceful end of the cold war, the world has witnessed a proliferation of violent, destructive, and deadly conflict, largely taking place within the once safe confines of the territorial state, and claiming innocent civilians, women, and children as the primary victims (Hampson 2002; Zartman 1995; Gurr 1990, 1993). The global community's failure to prevent deadly conflict has had a horrific cost in human lives. Post-cold war violent conflict has created five million casualties, of whom 95 percent are civilians (Development Assistance Committee [DAC] 2002, 135–151). But the catastrophic legacy extends far beyond. Millions are damaged and scarred and suffer for generations, uprooted from their homes, deprived of their livelihood, social security, community, and families, and left to live in constant fear. The natural as well as the social environments are damaged, often in ways that overwhelm the resources available to cope and the progress already made in sustainable development. Most broadly, the failure of the global community to prevent violent conflict destroys the reality of economic and human development — and any prospects for such development — for countless millions, nowhere more so than among the poorest people of the world. Even before the deadly decade of the 1990s ended with the 1999 Kosovo conflict, the costs to the broader international community, beyond those countries directly at war, were estimated at about US\$200 billion (Brown and Rosecrance 1999). Three quarters of this sum could have been saved and devoted to other essential human purposes had effective preventive measures been mounted in time.

For some countries and regions, the toll has been enormous, assaulting and devastating the most basic of their national interests, common values, and citizens' lives, chances, and hopes. As the war-drenched twentieth century ended, 20 of the 38 poorest countries were in conflict. From 1980 to 1994, 10 of the 24 most war-afflicted countries were in Africa alone. In its 1994 genocide, tiny Rwanda suffered an estimated 800 000 killed, 1.5 million internally displaced, and another 800 000 made international refugees (DAC 2002, 135). The 1999 conflict in Kosovo, the erosion of security in the former Yugoslav Republic of Macedonia in 2000–01, and the ongoing civil war in Chechnya provide haunting reminders that the plague affects not just developing countries, but also affects areas geographically close or adjacent to Western Europe, posing concrete threats to its security.

Although members of the international community have mobilised to alleviate and reverse the devastating effects of violent conflict, the amount and level of violence have far outstripped what committed individuals, civil society organisations, and individual countries have been able to deliver. At the regional level in Europe, in 2001 the European Commission approved a formal communication calling for mainstreaming conflict prevention in its development assistance policies, and for establishing supportive regional integration and links among trade and co-operation (European Commission 2001). At Göteburg in June 2001, the European Council unveiled the European Union's Programme for the Prevention of Violent Conflicts. It contained commitments for giving political priority to preventive action, enhancing early warning and policy coherence, developing instruments for short- and long-term prevention, and creating effective partnerships to this end. In October 2001, a seminar held under EU auspices explored the instruments of co-operation available to the EU for conflict prevention. Elsewhere, the Organization for Security and Co-operation in Europe (OSCE), the Organization for African Unity (OAU) and the African Union (AU), and other regional organisations have also taken up the task.

On a plurilateral plane, the Organisation for Economic Co-operation and Development (OECD) had begun work more than half a decade earlier. Its Development Assistance Committee (DAC) has been concerned since 1995 with development co-operation in conflict situations. In 1997, the DAC's High Level Meeting approved a policy document entitled 'Conflict, Peace, and Development Cooperation on the Threshold of the 21st Century'. Its framework helped raise international awareness about how development co-operation could prevent conflict and support peacebuilding. The DAC shifted its focus to preventing conflict through development co-operation in situations marked by poor co-ordination and bad governance, in part through workshops and commissioned work in 2001. In 2001, the DAC (2001) approved a new policy document, 'Helping Prevent Violent Conflict: Orientations for External Partners'. It also converted its Task Force on Conflict, Peace, and Development Co-operation, created in 1995, into a network encouraging members to mainstream conflict prevention into their policies (DAC 2002).

Within the broadly multilateral United Nations system, serious work at the centre began with the publication of the Brahimi report in 2000 (Panel on United Nations Peace Operations 2000). The Security Council's discussion of the role of the UN in conflict prevention then followed in 2000 and the Secretary General released a comprehensive report on the prevention of armed conflict in 2001 (United Nations 2001). The latter affirmed the need to move from the prevailing 'culture of reaction' to a new 'culture of prevention'. In keeping with the OECD's work, it called for 'structural prevention' aimed at the roots of conflict, addressing the close relationship between sustainable development and conflict prevention, and greater co-operation between international organisations on the one hand and nongovernmental organisations (NGOs), civil society, and private sector firms on the other.

It is hardly surprising that the international community has looked in the first instance to these long-established, well-endowed, 'hard law' organisations, with their formal mandates, massive bureaucracies, and operational programmes to cope with the emerging conflict prevention challenge (Goldstein et al. 2000). But their late start, limited resources and expertise, particular legal mandate, sacrosanct rules and procedures, and organisational culture have rendered their efforts inadequate against a problem that proliferated as the twentieth century came to an ever more violent close. It was in this context that another plurilateral institution, the informal, 'soft law' major market democracies of the G7 and G8 (with Russia) increasingly became involved in the contemporary cause of conflict prevention.

The G8 and Conflict Prevention

In the broadest sense, conflict prevention has been a concern of the G7 since its inaugural 1975 Summit at Rambouillet, France (Kirton 1993). Here the leaders publicly declared in their concluding communiqué that the new institution's central mission was to promote globally the values of open democracy, individual liberty, and social advancement. It further noted that the G7 was actively seeking to manage tensions across the long frozen, East-West, cold war divide. But it was only amid the proliferating disasters of the rapidly globalising, post-cold war world that the G7 and soon the G8 began to focus directly on conflict prevention in its modern sense. This modern conception of conflict prevention goes well beyond earlier efforts at deterrence, compellence, defence, crisis management, and military peacekeeping, truce observation, mediatory diplomacy, and good offices once conflict has erupted, or is on the verge of erupting and spreading (Larus 1965). Rather, it seeks to halt the outbreak of violent conflict at all.

Conflict prevention, in its contemporary sense, can thus be defined as short- and long-term engagement to stop, before it starts, the emergence, outbreak, or spread of any collective violence and the activities that precipitate such violence. It aims not merely to contain conflicts but also to transform those contentious issues in order to eliminate the outbreak of violence and move toward processes that foster co-operation rather than conflict among groups within or across national borders. Clearly, timing is a key component of this working definition, as it distinguishes conflict prevention from other forms of conflict management. It also indicates a particular opportunity when a proactive policy (in the form of intervention or negotiation or other action) is most appropriate to undertake in view of the desired objective (Zartman 1990). Finally, and most importantly, conflict prevention implies a conscious normative commitment, one fundamentally axiological in nature, with an underlying assumption of an *a priori* rejection of violence. In philosophical terms, this approach is the antithesis of Aron's consideration of violence as a legitimate means for regulating political conflict (Aron 1966).

With the collapse of the cold war and of so many closed communist regimes around the world, the need for conflict prevention proliferated. It has become a permanent feature and priority challenge of global governance in the new era. During the early 1990s, the G7 had presciently kept a watching eye on brewing but often overlooked conflicts such as the one in Kosovo; it had warned of the consequences if the disputing parties were to move toward violent efforts to enforce their demands and pointed to the UN's central role in preventive diplomacy. The transition from such efforts to prevent conflict in individual instances through traditional techniques of statecraft to the identification of conflict prevention as a self-contained, general subject in its own right and requiring new instruments and interventions began at the 1993 Tokyo Summit. Inspired in part by UN Secretary General Boutros Boutros-Ghali's 1992 'Agenda for Peace', the G7 leaders first referred directly to conflict prevention and highlighted the importance of strengthening the UN's capacity for preventive diplomacy' (United Nations 1992). Naples 1994 repeated this call and the accompanying consensus on the central role of the UN.

At Halifax in 1995, the G7 leaders assumed the responsibility for conflict prevention themselves. They asked the basic question of whether the existing array of international institutions was adequate to meet the new needs of the approaching twenty-first century. After their broad review and as part of their conclusions, they collectively called on the UN to act more quickly, and on the G7 countries to co-ordinate more closely, in the prevention, management, and resolution of conflicts. To assist them in their new conflict prevention vocation, the G7 leaders affirmed the need for the early warning of crises, the early field entry of international personnel, the role of regional organisations, and improved analysis of conflict-related early warning information with respect to human rights and refugees. They also called for development assistance focussed on those with 'a demonstrated capacity and commitment to use [it] effectively', while taking into account trends in 'military and other unproductive spending' (G7 1995).

From this foundation, the G7 moved ever more expansively during its subsequent seven-year summit hosting cycle to commit to the cause of conflict prevention on a global scale. At Lyon in 1996, G7 leaders concentrated on the process and consequences of globalisation, and included conflict prevention as part of this new *problèmatique*. The chairman's statement that served as the Summit's Political Declaration boldly declared that 'we emphasize the importance of promoting conditions conducive to peace as the surest means to prevent conflict' (G7 1996). It proceeded to single out democracy, human rights and good governance, limits on unproductive and excessive military expenditure, the need for a comprehensive approach that included police training, the importance of action against landmines and conventional weapons harming children, and the use of flexible instruments, including the role of regional organisations. The G7's first-generation agenda for conflict prevention was thus clear. But despite this promising foundation, the constraints on G7 thinking and action were still severe, for the 1996 statement underscored the primary role of the United Nations, the ultimate right of self-defence, action in the post-conflict phase, and instruments such as mediation by the UN and senior diplomats.

The following year, at the Denver 'Summit of the Eight' in 1997, conflict prevention became a priority and acquired an African emphasis. The leaders opened their final communiqué with the words, 'We have agreed to work closely with all willing partners in fostering global partnership for peace, security, and sustainable development that includes strengthening democracy, and human rights, and helping prevent and resolve conflicts' (G8 1997). They noted the need to mobilise a broad assortment of actors to prevent conflict, and recognised the 1997 DAC policy guidelines. Yet they continued to emphasise the key role of the UN in conflict prevention, including through early warning and rapid reaction. They also applauded 'African leadership in developing effective local capacities in conflict prevention, peacekeeping and post-conflict reconciliation and recovery'. Birmingham in 1998 was much the same. The communiqué emphasised the need to 'strengthen Africa's ability to prevent and ease conflict, as highlighted in the UN Secretary General's recent report', and support for Africa-based institutions in this regard (G8 1998).

The following year, 1999, marked a major breakthrough. The Cologne Summit constituted the 'big bang' beginning of the G8's concentrated, comprehensive, coherent work on conflict prevention. In the lead-up to Cologne, inspired by their success in helping bring an end to the conflict in Kosovo, the G8 foreign ministers called for innovation in conflict prevention, especially in regard to long-range democratic institution building (Hampson 2002). Their leaders endorsed the call. G8 foreign ministers held their first ever theme-specific meeting in Berlin in December 1999 on the subject of conflict prevention. Here they asked their political directors — in the new Conflict Prevention Officials Meeting (CPOM) — to translate the general Cologne consensus and agenda on conflict prevention into specific initiatives for approval and action by the leaders at the G8 Okinawa Summit the following year (Kirton, Daniels, and Freytag 2001). At Okinawa, the leaders delivered, both on conflict prevention and on the tightly related but broader cause of promoting human security (Kirton and Takase 2002; Lamy 2002). The Genoa G8 Summit in 2001 again expanded the field of vision and action (Fratianni, Savona, and Kirton 2002). The Canadian-hosted 2002 G8 Summit in Kananaskis, the first held after the 11 September 2001 terrorist attacks on North America, was preoccupied with the need to respond to the new crisis of terrorism. But it also succeeded in advancing the conflict prevention cause in Africa, Afghanistan, and on a broader front (Fratianni, Savona, and Kirton 2003). The 2003 Evian Summit continued the trend.

After several years of increasing activity and concentrated emphasis, it is important to ask how effective the G8's conflict prevention efforts have been. Why have they succeeded and failed? And what can and should the G8 do in the years ahead? Amid the voluminous literature on conflict prevention in the scholarly and policy communities, there is a rich debate about how the global community has acted on conflict prevention, how and why prevention can flourish, and what roles a variety of international organisations can play in this task (Burton 1990; Cross 1998; George and Holl 1997; McRae and Hubert 2001; Rothman 1992; Shiels 1991; Wallensteen 1991). But this literature largely remains confined to assessing how to make the United

Nations work better, perhaps with a little help from regional organisations, *ad hoc* coalitions of the willing, or individual states (International Commission on Intervention and State Sovereignty 2001). Virtually none of it has identified or critically evaluated the G8's actual or potential place in the conflict prevention process, even though this subject has long been a central part of the G7/8's agenda and a core component of its mission since the start. This volume takes up that outstanding task.

The Purpose and Approach

This book has three central purposes. The first is to assess critically how the G8 has dealt with the rapidly globalising post–cold war world's agenda for conflict prevention, during the G8's fourth seven-year cycle from the Lyon Summit in 1996 through to Kananaskis in 2002 and the launch of a new cycle at Evian in 2003. The second is to consider how well the G8 has converged, combined, or competed with other international actors and institutions, above all the UN, to meet this global governance challenge, and how the G8's performance compares with that of its colleagues and competitors in the cause. The third is to identify why the G8 has been effective, and on this basis how it can best serve the global community as it moves through its fifth cycle of summitry, which started in 2003. In short, this book asks what role the G8 plays, what is its relationship with the UN and other international institutions and actors, and how can each work best, alone or together, in the years ahead.

To meet these objectives, this volume combines the contributions of leading experts from most of the G8 countries, and from — or closely associated with — the major international organisations active in the field. It draws heavily from Canadian and European experts, in recognition of the leading role these countries and regions have played in shaping global governance to cope with the challenge of conflict prevention. Most of these contributors have had senior policy experience in critical countries or international organisations, or have served in important advisory or analytical roles in them. Their expertise spans the fields of diplomacy, the military, development, and economics, and brings a wide range of academic disciplines to bear.

The Analyses

Part I begins this exploration by examining 'The Place, Role, and Potential of the G8 in Conflict Prevention'. In Chapter 2, 'Concentrating the Mind: Decision Making in the G7/8 System', Nicholas Bayne confronts the central question of how the G7/8, as an informal, leaders-driven international institution, can contribute meaningfully to conflict prevention in a world full of long-established hard law organisations with formal charters, secretariats, rich experience, and vast resources of their own. He examines how decisions are made, on conflict prevention and other subjects, at the level of the G8 summit and in the larger G7/8 system as a whole. He looks at the contribution of the leaders themselves and of the supporting apparatus. He also considers the role of state and nonstate actors in the G7/8's economic activities, which have become integrally involved with conflict prevention, as well as in the political domain.

Bayne concludes that the leaders have gained new freedom by meeting on their own since 1998, just as the G7/8 began to give priority to conflict prevention. By themselves, the leaders can innovate on agendas and procedures, pursue their political reflexes, and energise their efforts with their peers. At the same time, most co-operation at the summit still comes from the work of the supporting sherpa teams, and from the growing network of ministerial and official level groups, even as non-G8 governments, business, and NGOs become increasingly involved. Although the tension among the new freedom of the leaders, the proliferation of the supporting apparatus, and the increasing involvement of others is not easily resolved, and although each summit finds a different solution, the G7/8 treatment of conflict prevention should follow a predictable course.

In Chapter 3, 'The Intricacies of Summit Preparation and Consensus Building', Robert Fowler considers the institutional framework and mechanisms of the G8, as they relate to conflict prevention, in the context of two central factors: the enormous leadership and activity of the United Nations on the issue in recent years, and the all-consuming nature of G7/8 summitry that causes most subjects to get caught in its net. Thus, even as the summit ensures needed co-ordination between economic and political issues, its increasingly overloaded and cumbersome agenda has made it less agile and more like the repetitious, speech-ridden rituals of the UN. Yet the leaders continue to value the G8 as their own institution, even as they try to get back to basics and focus their efforts on a few central themes.

With regard to conflict prevention, Fowler concludes that the G8's only real role is creating a consensus that can then be taken to other international organisations with the mandate, resources, and legitimacy to put the consensus into effect. Yet this G8 consensus can have an important role in deliberations in the UN Security Council (UNSC) on burgeoning security crises and conflict prevention, if only because four of the G8's members are members of the Permanent Five with veto powers. The G8 thus plays a very large role in determining UNSC and real world outcomes, as the 1999 Kosovo case most dramatically shows. The G8's importance was further evident at the 2002 Kananaskis Summit, where providing peace and security was the most difficult of the many challenges facing G8, African, and UN leaders as they mounted a major effort to reduce poverty in Africa. Yet they persisted in their effort, producing the G8 Africa Action Plan in which providing peace and security, in part by preventing conflict, stood as the essential first step.

In Chapter 4, 'The G8 and Conflict Prevention: From Promise to Practice?' David M. Malone considers the work of the G7/8 in conflict prevention over the past three cycles. He also reviews efforts at operationalising prevention beyond the G8, outlines the UN's conflict prevention activities, explores potential prevention strategies and causes of conflict, and discusses long-term and short-term prevention. He concludes with observations on how the G8 can make a more convincing contribution.

Malone determines, from a review of G7/8 communiqués, that the G8's role has been largely rhetorical, as 'their formal statements have proved evanescent, somewhat faddish, and rarely in any way incisive or influential'. Yet he adds that the G8's focus has practical relevance, as its component countries are influential members of the many multilateral organisations grappling with the complexities of short- and long-term prevention and confronting the barrier of state sovereignty and non-interference in internal affairs that is a core part of their legal framework. While the G8 does not have a large operational role, it has led in spurring norm development and mobilising expertise, especially under the German, Italian, and Canadian chairs. The significance and potential of its work comes from the formidable influence of individual G8 countries within key multilateral organisations such as the International Monetary Fund (IMF), the World Bank, the OECD, regional development banks, and UN economic agencies. It also comes from G8 countries' own initiatives, as in Canada's work on conflict diamonds led by Robert Fowler when he served as ambassador to the UN. As Fowler moved on to serve as host sherpa for the G8 and the G8's African representatives at Kananaskis in 2002, that summit was better able to contribute significantly to conflict prevention. The G7 and G8 have often started or sped up work on the international regulatory framework for economic transactions and crimes (such as drug trafficking and money laundering) in other forums, and the links between such economic activity and violent conflict are now well understood. The time is thus ripe for the G8 to ask if the international regulatory framework adequately addresses economic activity financing conflict, and if an international legal regime is now needed to address conflict-related 'white collar crime'.

In Chapter 5, 'The G8 and Conflict Prevention: Commitment, Compliance, and Systemic Contributions', John J. Kirton, Ella Kokotsis, Gina Stephens, and Diana Juricevic examine the recent record of G8 leaders in generating specific collective commitments on conflict prevention, and in complying with those commitments in the following year. They first examine the overall, political-security, and conflict prevention commitments of the 2000 Okinawa and subsequent summits, and the ambition-significance of these commitments. They then assess the compliance of each G8 member country with them.

The authors find that with 169 overall commitments, including 20 political-security and three conflict prevention commitments, Okinawa was the highest performing decisional summit ever held up to 2000. Okinawa's overall commitments were at the mid-point of the ambition-significance scale. They were slightly higher for G8 political-security commitments than for economically oriented G7 ones. The conflict prevention commitments stood as the most ambitious-significant of those in the political security domain. Moreover, in the ensuing year, G8 members — led by Germany and Britain — kept their priority commitments a historic high 81 percent of the time, with a strong 63 percent performance in the realm of conflict prevention. Subsequent summits have seen a slide in conflict prevention commitments and compliance, even though Canada, France, Germany, Britain, and the U.S. have shown consistent leadership. The pattern suggests that the G8 will realise its full potential as a contributor to conflict prevention only with greater institutionalisation at the official level and among its foreign ministers as well.

Part II, 'Conflict Prevention: The Political-Institutional Framework', expands this close examination of the G8's role and record in conflict prevention to consider the other major international institutions and countries at work in the field, and the progress and problems in the area as a whole . In Chapter 6, 'Conflict Prevention: Performances, Prospects, and Potential', Roberto Toscano first identifies what this fluid field and complex concept of conflict prevention is and is not, and what is known about the causes of conflict. On this basis, he outlines an international agenda for conflict prevention, the role of states and international organisations in delivering it, the actual performance of the international community in conflict prevention over the past decade, and the prospects and potential in the years ahead.

Toscano argues that conflict prevention, as distinct from preventive diplomacy, peace enforcement, conflict management, and peacekeeping, centres on the prevention of violent conflict fuelled by military and economic instruments, through action directed at the political processes related to socioeconomic and other causes of grievance. An appropriate international agenda of conflict prevention includes the role of the major powers, has a comprehensive vision, is aimed at creating a culture of prevention, involves international organisations and private corporations, and employs both global and regional approaches. Against this referent, Toscano finds that the international community's performance in conflict prevention over the past decade has been dismal. Yet although the outstanding challenge is 'awesome', he optimistically concludes that the prospects for conflict prevention are promising.

In Chapter 7, 'U.S. Approaches to International Conflict Prevention and the Role of Allies and International Institutions', Frank E. Loy analyses the many times over the past several decades that the United States and its allies, particularly its allies in the North Atlantic Treaty Organization (NATO), have acted in concert to prevent or bring to an end particular conflicts. As many such instances have been marked by charges and counter-charges between the U.S. and its allies about the effort, it is important to examine the historical attitudes, facts, and political realities in the U.S. that lie behind these strains. Loy thus looks in turn at the still unresolved differences of opinion among U.S. policy makers about the country's appropriate role in conflict prevention in the post–cold war era, the lessons learned from specific conflict prevention experiences, how the great disparity in military capability between the U.S. and its allies shapes U.S. attitudes toward collaboration, specific U.S. concerns about participating in UN peacekeeping operations, and the significant policy shift since the 11 September terrorist attacks.

Loy argues that the cold war reinforced traditional twin pillars of U.S. foreign policy — security from military attack and strengthening the national economy — have been steadily broadened to embrace promoting democracy, the rule of law, environmental protection, and equality between rich and poor. This broadening has led to conflict prevention, to U.S. involvement in international conflicts and to domestic critiques about how difficult it is to create conditions for success when simultaneously engaged in multiple theatres. He then notes that the U.S. will, paradoxically, only rarely and reluctantly engage in longer term actions that fall under the heading of peacekeeping. While this paradox and the lessons of past interventions suggest the value of a permanent UN peacekeeping force, there are several serious obstacles to surmount before a solution along these lines can come. First among these is the focus on U.S. unilateral preventive intervention, if needed, to uphold 'home security'. This focus has only been intensified by the 2003 war in Iraq, and the many terrorist incidents within Iraq and the broader region that have come in its wake.

In Chapter 8, 'Advancing the European Union's Conflict Prevention Policy', Reinhardt Rummel turns the attention across the Atlantic to Europe. He asks if the EU, which was a post-1945 pioneer in conflict prevention on its own long war-torn continent but is a latecomer to the broader effort in the world at large, can reproduce its regional success on a global scale. To find an answer, he considers EU ambitions in its policy on conflict prevention, as well as the key instruments it has employed, its institutional configuration and financial framework for conflict prevention, its partnerships with other international institutions, and the key cases in which the EU has been involved.

Rummel concludes that the EU is still struggling with learning the lessons from its first forays into a more systematic policy on conflict prevention. The process of knowledge building remains marginal to recent efforts to mainstream conflict prevention. The EU's complex institutional structure and low level of expertise in security policy offer obstacles as well. Indeed, the EU must start all over again with conflict prevention, in a more serious and more sophisticated approach, and one in which it finds partners in the UN, the corporate world, the media, and the parties that 'own' the conflicts themselves. The 11 September terrorist attacks may have given an impetus in the right direction, but there remain formidable obstacles to securing the coherence required for this new approach to succeed.

Part III, 'The Socioeconomic Dimension', expands the focus further to include the underlying social and economic causes of conflict and the instruments that can be mobilised in its prevention. In Chapter 9, 'The G8's Role in Promoting Financial Stability', Lorenzo Bini Smaghi examines the G7/8's seminal role in preventing crises in the field of finance, to see if its record and experience there provide grounds or guidelines for developing a promising role for the G8 in the much newer conflict prevention field. He analyses in particular the key issues that are currently being discussed, among the G7 countries and in the other major international institutions, regarding the prevention and resolution of financial crises.

Bini Smaghi concludes that the G7 has focussed on crisis prevention and resolution since the first emerging market crises erupted in the mid 1990s. It has made much progress, notably in making the IMF more accountable and more transparent. Yet much still needs to be done to make financial markets more adept in assessing the risks that are taken by its participants, to create incentives for prompt policy adjustments by debtor countries, and to establish clearer procedures for deciding whether and to what extent to provide financial assistance. Ultimately, the credibility of the G7 and of the IMF depends more on the concrete way in which crises are resolved than on principles and rules. Given these conclusions, the G7's work thus far could suggest several lessons that might be transposable, with care, to the challenge of prevention in the newer, and in many respects quite different, field of violent conflict.

In Chapter 10, 'Foreign Aid: An Effective Medicine, an Addictive Drug, or a Social Placebo?', Mario Sarcinelli considers foreign aid, which G8 foreign ministers have identified as a major instrument of conflict prevention. Using econometric studies that encompass donor and recipient countries, Sarcinelli explores why development assistance has been successful in some cases and useless and even harmful in others, and whether merit or responsibility ought to be attributed to the donor countries, the recipient economies, or both. He provides in turn an overview of foreign aid, the factors that have made it the centrepiece of international development policy, donor motivations in giving aid, the effects of foreign aid on recipient countries, the unpleasant consequences of aid on dependence and corruption, the relationship between aid allocation and the eradication of poverty, and the conditions that would allow for meeting the ambitious targets set by OECD and its DAC. He then considers a tax on foreign exchange transactions (such as a Tobin tax) to finance international public goods and particularly foreign aid.

Sarcinelli concludes that good economic management matters more to developing countries than foreign financial aid does. Yet even in the most difficult cases, where bad management prevails, the international community must maintain a strong direction and dedication to alleviating poverty, perhaps by contributing ideas rather than money, by involving civil society and by working for the long term. Despite efforts to reduce the role of international financial institutions and governments in giving aid, there is no chance that private charitable institutions can succeed on their own, where international agencies and official donors have failed, in convincing poor and poorly run countries to reform their policies and institutions. In this globalising world, those in positions of public authority should thus respond to the principle that no child should be left behind.

In Chapter 11, 'Socioeconomic Vulnerability Analysis and the Culture of Prevention in the Globalisation Era', Umberto Triulzi and Pierluigi Montalbano draw on the insights of vulnerability analysis to move from an *ex-post* to *ex-ante* approach to poverty reduction strategies and, by extension, to conflict prevention. They outline the issue, review the basic principles on the subject, and suggest a shared methodology. They then expand the concept of 'vulnerability in terms of development', highlighting inconsistencies between conflict prevention and development co-operation strategies, and assessing socioeconomic vulnerability analysis as a bridge between conflict prevention and development.

Triulzi and Montalbano argue that the analytically frustrating link missing between conflict prevention and development lies in a new framework of socioeconomic vulnerability analysis in terms of underdevelopment. Introducing a vulnerability lens would allow an identification of the precise kind of causal relationship between economic underdevelopment and relative poverty, on the one hand, and social strife and communal violence, on the other.

Part IV, 'Conclusion', looks ahead to the future challenges in conflict prevention, and the G8's role in meeting them. In Chapter 12, 'From Good Intentions to Good Practice: The G8 and the Future of Conflict Prevention', Gina Stephens and Kristiana Powell analyse the G8's past, present, and possible future role in conflict prevention. They examine the issue of conflict prevention and its surrounding analytical and policy controversies, develop the concept of conflict prevention, and trace the G8's changing involvement and focus in conflict prevention. They identify where its performance could be improved or extended, as a basis for recommendations for future G8 policy within the larger effort.

Stephens and Powell conclude that the G8's efforts to contribute globally to the prevention of armed conflict are laudable indications of the institution's emergence as a centre of global governance. Its treatment of conflict prevention has become more sophisticated and sensitive and moved toward meeting its initial promise of creating a culture of prevention. However, the creation of a permanent G8 working group on conflict prevention would do much to invigorate members' contributions to other multilateral organisations and support advances within domestic bureaucracies. Continued emphasis on the long term and the need to pass all development policies through a conflict prevention filter remain essential. In the face of these challenges, however, the good intentions that prompted G8 action in this area can be transformed into good practice for the future.

The Contribution: New Insights into Conflict Prevention

The conclusions and analyses in this volume seek to make a distinctive contribution to the broader, ongoing debate about what the global community needs for effective conflict prevention and how well and why the existing international institutions and leading governments have met the need. In fact, the mainstream conflict prevention literature has rarely taken into consideration the real policy potential that a high-level informal but influential decision-making forum, such as the G8, can have in helping to stem violence (Lund 1996). The analyses in this volume point to the fact that the G8 is often able to generate consensus on a course of action and then transfer it to international organisations, such as the UN or the OECD, or to interested, willing, and able governments or a coalition of the willing with members that have both the legitimacy and the structural capability to intervene preventively in vulnerable areas. Moreover, the chapters by Bayne, Malone, and Fowler suggest that when the legitimate decision-making mechanisms related to taking preventive action are blocked by indecision or ideological tension, as in the case of Kosovo, the G8 can take the lead in sanctioning a particular course of conduct. As a result, although the G8's role in conflict prevention might be difficult to institutionalise (in fact, it could not be a full substitute for the UNSC), it can nonetheless serve as a valid recourse when the legitimate international bodies are unwilling or unable to intervene. This is all the more true since the very nature of conflict prevention hinges on the generation of enough political will and resulting material resources to intervene pre-emptively, a process that has not yet been streamlined though the decision-making procedures of the competent international organisations, as indicated by Malone, Fowler, Rummel, and Toscano.

Consequently, conflict prevention, as seen through the G8 lens, provides for an approach that some might find controversial (Rocard 1998). But it remains an approach that directly addresses and provides the one major missing link in the concept of preventive strategies — that of the elusive institutionalisation of the political will to intervene in conflicts not directly related to the actors' vital interests. On the one hand, having a clear, legitimate channel for general intervention on the part of a legally grounded and competent organisation would resolve many of the large policy problems faced by preventive interventions in the field, such as common early warning indicators, command and control chains, and rules of engagement. On the other hand, however, such an institutionalised approach, while more legitimate than any alternative, has thus far proven difficult to secure, based on the current level of cohesive decision making generated by the nation-states in the international system (Stedman 1995). Moreover, as Malone, Rummel, and Toscano show, attempts to co-ordinate prevention on the part of the UN or the EU have more often than not produced mediocre, laborious, and sometimes counterproductive policies on the ground. As a result, it is exactly in the lightly institutionalised, leaders-driven context of the G8 where the next best alternative might lie. This is due to its simplified decision-making procedures and ability to generate the needed political will and transpose it at the highest level to the more representative international institutions. Such a conclusion is unprecedented at the conceptual level in conflict prevention analysis. In fact, the practical and the conceptual insights contained in this volume might also be examined in the context of a comparative analysis of decision making and negotiation, rather than in the mainstream, counterfactual conceptualisation of conflict prevention (Tetlock and Belkin 1996). Alternatively, the difficulty in institutionalising conflict prevention can be seen through a classic perspective of *Realpolitik*, which many modern theorists have also found unsatisfactory (Ashley 1986).

Finally, this volume revisits traditional debates on the link between, on the one hand, poverty and macroeconomic mismanagement and, on the other, conflict from the perspective of an institution with a concrete ability to make a difference. The three chapters considering the socioeconomic dimension of conflict prevention address all six economic indicators identified by Theodore H. Morgan (1996) in relation to conflict — trade deficits and unfair trade practices, high-tech (strategic trade) rivalry, national and regional trade discrimination, foreign investment and the acquisition of critical domestic industries by foreigners, outward investment and the 'hollowing out' of the home country, and transborder flows and the distribution of 'good jobs' versus 'bad jobs'. However, many have contested the link between underdevelopment and violent conflict, arguing that poverty alone is not a sufficient trigger for the substantially political grievances that warrant violent conflict (Davies 1962; Moravscik 1999). In fact, although poverty alone is not sufficient cause of violence, the pernicious side effects it produces at a social level — political radicalisation of the afflicted populations, undermined human security through disease and bad sanitary conditions, distorted population growth — are directly associated with the upsurge of conflict. This volume's contribution to the literature on conflict prevention makes this link explicit and proposes concrete socioeconomic strategies to reverse the logic of violence. Bini Smaghi, Sarcinelli, and Triulzi and Montalbano indicate different paths for prevention, based on macroeconomic performance and socioeconomic theory: transparency of the international financial institutions involved, good governance, and a conceptual and policy understanding of state vulnerability. This is an elaboration of the mainstream conflict prevention assumption, which posits that conflict causes and preventive policies are both essentially politically dominated, while economic factors and their social derivatives are conflict triggers or accelerators, rather than root rationales for violence (Lund 1996).

As a result, the particular blend of policy and theory in this volume helps to clarify the conceptual and operational definitions and analyses of conflict prevention, for application both to policy making and to academic work.

New Directions for the G8 in Conflict Prevention

Among the ongoing debates in policy circles about the next steps for the G8 in conflict prevention, this volume offers both a rich menu of specific, practical steps and several clear directions for the G8's work. These are of particular value now that the G8 leaders have launched their fifth cycle of summitry, which now includes Russia, with their summit in Evian-les-Bains, France, in June 2003.

Important policy insights come from some of the conclusions in this book that offer a positive assessment of the few decision-making constraints at the G8's highest levels. These insights can be even more valuable, owing to epistemic idea sharing at lower levels, in fostering more efficient preventive interventions. This conclusion, offered by Bayne, is supported by Fowler's insider view of how the African agenda came to dominate the Kananaskis Summit.

Several other authors highlight the fact that, since 1999, the conflict prevention agenda has come to flourish at the G8 summits. They also point out — as Toscano and Triulzi and Montalbano highlight — that mobilising enough political will for preventive interventions remains a problem. To remedy this, they suggest that the approach should assume a broader normative range, similar to the context in which human rights problems are increasingly addressed in contemporary world politics. Such an approach would not only provide a multiplicity of institutional forums for addressing conflict prevention but would also highlight the links to closely related issues, such as development co-operation, sustainable development, good governance, and the cultivation of civil society. In other words, a change of attitude is at least as important as concrete preventive steps. Based on a quantitative analysis of recent G8 decision making, Kirton, Kokotsis, Stephens, and Juricevic argue that a move in that direction can already be detected. In the same vein, Malone argues that the G8 should seriously consider engaging in strengthening the international regulatory framework in relation to indirect conflict perpetration, through arms sales or other financial transactions that benefit the warlords.

With regard to the ultimate goal of poverty alleviation, the importance of good governance stands out. In particular, Sarcinelli advocates a performance-based approach to countries where an impaired macroeconomic situation is due to structural factors as well as to financial mismanagement and corruption. Such an approach might be difficult to sustain in the background of an increasingly influential 'no-global' consciousness, but it has proven to be the only successful means to improve the predicament of impoverished populations in the medium to long run. Consequently, development aid that has been appropriately channelled should not be dispensed unless coupled with a strict requirement for sound macroeconomic performance. It is in this context that the G8's role in preventing violent conflict should be seen, and it is along this line of reasoning that Powell and Stephens propose the creation of a working group on conflict prevention within the G8. Although institutions such as the UN and, notably, the EU have already created similar formations, as indicated by Malone and Rummel they are often inhibited by a cumbersome, overly bureaucratic, and lengthy decision-making process. By contrast, in the context of the G8, where as Bayne points out leaders' *ad hoc* consultations combined with strong co-operation at the sherpa level can provide an unprecedented flexibility of approach, a concrete institutional decision-making forum might yield significant results.

In conclusion, all authors note a certain normative responsibility on the part of the G8 to institutionalise its recent commitment to conflict prevention. Despite many deficiencies in both the nature of the institution, in its rather *ad hoc* decision-making procedures, and in its overall difficulty in generating effective preventive policies, most contributors to this volume share the view that the G8's potential in the realm of conflict prevention can be significantly reinforced. Given the G8's real ability to influence decisions and generate consensus, in particular at the level of the UN Security Council, the current practice of preventive intervention when the mainstream mechanisms are blocked may be reinforced by a decision to convene regularly in the face of significant crises. In addition, the G8's institutional and political weight specifically at important economic forums, such as the IMF or the World Bank, can do much to foster good governance practices generated as transparent conditionality policies linked to preferential trade agreements, development aid, and loan disbursement. Although it might be difficult to institutionalise this role, G8 mediation and preventive alerts can become a matter of practice.

The G8's decisional agenda has increasingly focussed on conflict prevention since 1999. This volume concludes that the institution can contribute substantively to a global reduction of violence. The G8 possesses institutional and decisional flexibility, which gives it special policy advantages in relation to other institutions. It carries a particularly potent political and economic weight, which make the institution a suitable mediator in complex crises. In addition, the international normative system has evolved to the extent where a leaders-driven forum such as the G8 is not only known to be capable of conflict prevention, but is also expected to engage in it actively. Moreover, the ability of the G8 summit to bring the democratic major powers together — as seen at Evian in 2003, even after the major divisions created in the UN over the 2003 war in Iraq — has shown the resilience of the forum and the major powers' faith in it. It thus stands as a promising institution of global security governance in a world where the conflict prevention task remains acute, as the continuing bloodshed in post-war Iraq and the Congo dramatically show. By placing the emphasis on the concrete development of its potential for conflict prevention, the G8 will respond to a great and growing global need. It will also strengthen its claim to relevance as an institution of global governance as the twenty-first century unfolds.

References

Aron, Raymond (1966). *Peace and War*. Doubleday, New York.
Ashley, Richard (1986). 'The Poverty of Neorealism'. In R. O. Keohane, ed., *Neorealism and Its Critics*, pp. 255–300. Columbia University Press, New York.
Brown, Michael and Richard Rosecrance, eds. (1999). *The Costs of Conflict, Prevention, and Cure in the Global Arena*. Rowman and Littlefield, Lanham, MD.
Burton, John W. (1990). *Conflict: Resolution and Prevention*. St. Martin's Press, New York.
Cross, Peter (1998). *Contributing to Preventive Action*. Nomos, Baden-Baden.
Davies, James (1962). 'Towards a Theory of Revolution'. *American Sociological Review* vol. 27, p. 7.
Development Assistance Committee (2001). 'The DAC Guidelines: Helping Prevent Violent Conflict'. <www.oecd.org/dataoecd/15/54/1886146.pdf> (July 2003).
Development Assistance Committee (2002). 'Countries in Conflict and Poor Performers: What Can Donors Do?' In *The DAC Journal: Development Co-operation Report 2001*, pp. 135–151. Organisation for Economic Co-operation and Development, Paris.
European Commission (2001). 'Communication from the Commission on Conflict Prevention'. COM(2001) 211 final. 11 April. Brussels. <europa.eu.int/comm/external_relations/cfsp/news/com2001_211_en.pdf> (July 2003).
Fratianni, Michele, Paolo Savona, and John J. Kirton, eds. (2002). *Governing Global Finance: New Challenges, G7 and IMF Contributions*. Ashgate, Aldershot.
Fratianni, Michele, Paolo Savona, and John J. Kirton, eds. (2003). *Sustaining Global Growth and Development: G7 and IMF Governance*. Ashgate, Aldershot.
G7 (1995). 'Halifax Summit Communiqué'. 16 June, Halifax. <www.g7.utoronto.ca/summit/1995halifax/communique/index.html> (July 2003).
G7 (1996). 'Chairman's Statement'. Political Declaration, 29 June, Lyon. <www.g7.utoronto.ca/summit/1996lyon/chairman/index.html> (July 2003).
G8 (1997). 'Communiqué'. 22 June, Denver. <www.g7.utoronto.ca/summit/1997denver/g8final.htm> (July 2003).
G8 (1998). 'Communiqué'. 15 May, Birmingham. <www.g7.utoronto.ca/summit/1998birmingham/finalcom.htm> (July 2003).
George, Alexander L. and Jane E. Holl (1997). 'The Warning-Response Problem and Missed Opportunities in Preventive Diplomacy'. Carnegie Commission on Preventing Deadly Conflict. <wwics.si.edu/subsites/ccpdc/pubs/warn/frame.htm> (July 2003).
Goldstein, Judith, Miles Kahler, Robert O. Keohane, et al. (2000). 'Legalization and World Politics'. *International Organization* vol. 54 (Summer).
Gurr, Ted Robert (1990). 'Ethnic Warfare and the Changing Priorities of Global Security'. *Mediterranean Quarterly* vol. 1 (Winter), pp. 82–98.
Gurr, Ted Robert (1993). *Minorities at Risk: A Global View of Ethnopolitical Conflicts*. United States Institute of Peace Press, Washington DC.

Hampson, Fen Osler (2002). *Madness in the Multitude: Human Security and World Disorder.* Oxford University Press, Toronto.

International Commission on Intervention and State Sovereignty (2001). 'The Responsibility to Protect: Report of the International Commission on Intervention and State Sovereignty'. <www.dfait-maeci.gc.ca/iciss-ciise/report-en.asp> (July 2003).

Kirton, John J. (1993). 'The Seven Power Summits as a New Security Institution'. In D. Dewitt, D. Haglund and J. J. Kirton, eds., *Building a New Global Order: Emerging Trends in International Security*, pp. 335–357. Oxford University Press, Toronto.

Kirton, John J., Joseph P. Daniels, and Andreas Freytag, eds. (2001). *Guiding Global Order: G8 Governance in the Twenty-First Century.* Ashgate, Aldershot.

Kirton, John J. and Junichi Takase, eds. (2002). *New Directions in Global Political Governance: The G8 and International Order in the Twenty-First Century.* Ashgate, Aldershot.

Lamy, Steven L. (2002). 'The G8 and the Human Security Agenda'. In J. J. Kirton and J. Takase, eds., *New Directions in Global Political Governance: The G8 and International Order in the Twenty-First Century*, pp. 167–187. Ashgate, Aldershot.

Larus, Joel (1965). *From Collective Security to Preventive Diplomacy: Readings in International Organization and the Maintenance of Peace.* John Wiley and Sons, New York.

Lund, Michael (1996). *Preventing Violent Conflicts: A Strategy for Preventive Diplomacy.* U.S Institute for Peace Press, Washington DC.

McRae, Robert Grant and Don Hubert, eds. (2001). *Human Security and the New Diplomacy: Protecting People, Promoting Peace.* McGill-Queen's University Press, Montreal.

Moravscik, Andrew (1999). 'Taking Preferences Seriously: A Liberal Theory of International Politics'. In C. Lipson and B. Cohen, eds., *Theory and Structure in International Political Economy*, pp. 33–74. MIT Press, Cambridge, MA.

Morgan, Theodore H. (1996). 'Trade and Investment Dimensions of International Conflict'. In C. A. Crocker, F. O. Hampson and P. Aall, eds., *Sources of and Response to International Conflict.* United States Institute of Peace Press, Washington DC.

Panel on United Nations Peace Operations (2000). 'Report of the Panel on United Nations Peace Operations'. The Brahimi Report. <www.un.org/peace/reports/peace_operations> (July 2003).

Rocard, Michel (1998). 'Prévention des conflits: Une synergie d'efforts internationaux'. In P. Cross, ed., *Contributing to Preventive Action*, pp. 7–12. Stiftung Wissenschaft und Politik, Ebenhausen.

Rothman, Jay (1992). *From Confrontation to Cooperation: Resolving Ethnic and Regional Conflict.* Sage Publications, Newbury Park, CA.

Shiels, Frederick L. (1991). *Preventable Disasters: Why Governments Fail.* Rowman and Littlefield, Lanham, MD.

Stedman, Stephen John (1995). 'Alchemy for a New World Order: Overselling "Preventive Diplomacy"'. *Foreign Affairs* vol. 74, no. 3, pp. 14–21.

Tetlock, Philip E. and Aaron Belkin (1996). *Counterfactual Thought Experiments in World Politics: Logical, Methodological, and Psychological Perspectives.* Princeton University Press, Princeton.

United Nations (1992). 'An Agenda for Peace: Preventive Diplomacy, Peacemaking, and Peace-keeping'. A/47/277-S/24111. 17 June. <www.un.org/Docs/SG/agpeace.html> (July 2003).

United Nations (2001). 'Prevention of Armed Conflict: Report of the Secretary General. Executive Summary'. A/55/985-S/2001/574. 7 June. United Nations, New York. <daccess-ods.un.org/TMP/7047019.html> (July 2003).

Wallensteen, Peter (1991). 'The Resolution and Transformation of International Conflicts: A Structural Perspective'. In R. Vayrynen, ed., *New Directions in Conflict Theory: Conflict Resolution and Conflict Transformation.* Sage Publications, London.

Zartman, I. William (1990). 'Negotiations and Prenegotiations in Ethnic Conflict: The Beginning, the Middle, and the Ends'. In J. V. Montville, ed., *Conflict and Peacemaking in Multiethnic Societies*. Lexington Books, Lexington, MA.

Zartman, I. William (1995). *Collapsed States: The Disintegration and Restoration of Legitimate Authority*. Lynn Rienner, Boulder, CO.

PART I
THE PLACE, ROLE, AND
POTENTIAL OF THE G8
IN CONFLICT PREVENTION

Chapter 2

Concentrating the Mind: Decision Making in the G7/8 System

Nicholas Bayne

When a man knows he is to be hanged in a fortnight, it concentrates his mind wonderfully. —Johnson

This chapter is not about conflict prevention as such. It is instead about how decisions are made — on conflict prevention or any other subject — at the G8 summit and in the G7/8 system as a whole. Summit meetings like the G7 and G8, where heads of government meet informally in a small group, are a device to 'concentrate minds' on co-operative decision making, in response to intractable problems where international and domestic pressures interact.[1]

For about 15 years after the G7 summits began, decision making took place on two closely knit levels. One level comprised the heads of government themselves and the foreign and finance ministers, who always accompanied them to the summit. The second was composed of a small team of bureaucrats led by the head's personal representative or 'sherpa'. Follow-up was entrusted to wider institutions. But during the 1990s and early 2000s, the shape of the G7/8 summits changed radically. The heads of government detached their flanking ministers and began meeting by themselves. The supporting apparatus, at both official and ministerial levels, became much more complex and developed a life of its own. Many more outside contributors became involved both in the preparation of the summits and in their follow-up.

This chapter examines the recent development of decision making in the G7/8 system, up to the Evian Summit of 2003.[2] The analysis falls under three headings:

- the contribution of the heads themselves;
- the contribution of the supporting apparatus; and
- the contribution of other actors, both state and nonstate.

Most of the examples will be drawn from economic activities, but there will also be reference to political ones, especially conflict prevention.

The main conclusions of this chapter are as follows:

- The heads of government have gained new freedom by meeting on their own. They contribute independently to decision making by innovation, especially in agenda setting and procedural initiatives, and by following their political reflexes. Meeting their international peers concentrates the minds of the heads most when this also advances their domestic agenda.
- Most co-operation at the summit still emerges from the work of the supporting apparatus, whether by the sherpa team or by the growing network of G7/8 ministerial groups. The preparations enable the heads to add their authority to work in progress, to induce agreement at lower levels, without acting themselves, and at times to go further than is possible at lower levels. Holding the summit concentrates the minds of other ministers and bureaucrats, as well as the heads themselves. But will it still do so if the summits become more detached from their base?
- Other actors — non-G8 governments, business, and nongovernmental organisations (NGOs) — are increasingly involved both in summit preparation and, alongside international institutions, in follow-up. The institutions are treated more persuasively and systematically than before. Such greater dispersion and transparency are necessary, if the summits are to concentrate the increasingly independent minds of other players in the system. But will this involvement lead to a loss of efficiency?
- The tensions among the greater freedom of the heads, the proliferation of the supporting apparatus, and the growing involvement of other actors are not easily resolved and each summit finds a different equilibrium. Thus the treatment of conflict prevention has varied since it became a summit topic in 1999.

Decision Making in the G7/8 Summits: The Contribution of the Heads

The G7 summit was conceived as a personal encounter of the leaders of the world's most powerful economies. The founders believed that bringing the heads of government together would enable them to understand better both the domestic problems of their peers and the international responsibilities that they all shared. This would enable them to solve problems that had baffled their bureaucrats. The bureaucrats themselves ought to be kept out of the process entirely.[3]

Even before the first summit of all, at Rambouillet in 1975, it was clear that this vision was out of reach. The subject matter of international economics was too complex for the heads to reach decisions without some preparation. So they reconciled themselves to playing roles at the summit that had been written for them by others, especially by their personal representatives or sherpas. This was the first stage in institutionalising the summits.[4] But the prospect of informal and spontaneous contacts, at which they could develop their own ideas, continues to exercise a powerful attraction on the heads. This section of the chapter therefore looks at the ways in which the heads make their personal contribution to the summit, without relying on the supporting apparatus.

The Heads and Summit Process

During the 1990s, the heads always professed to want summit procedures made simpler. They complained that the agenda and the documents were too long, giving them no scope to make their own input. As will appear, however, some of their own practices contributed to this expansion.

Size   Once the size of the summit had been settled in the 1970s, at seven powers plus the European Community, the heads resisted any move to add new members. They believed small numbers were essential to informal exchanges. As British prime minister James Callaghan said in 1976:

> The numbers attending are small and compact. Discussions are businesslike and to the point. We do not make speeches at one another. We talk frankly but also as briefly as we can, and a lot of ground is covered (Putnam and Bayne 1987, 44).

In 1991 the heads agreed that British prime minister John Major could invite Soviet president Mikhail Gorbachev as a guest to the London III Summit. But once the Russians came, the G7 had to go on inviting them, as a refusal would be a severe setback to post–cold war reconciliation. By skilful salami tactics, Russian president Boris Yeltsin got invited to more and more of the summit. Eventually, U.S. president Bill Clinton called Denver 1997 'the Summit of the Eight', and British prime minister Tony Blair made Birmingham 1998 the first G8 summit. Russia will host a summit for the first time in 2006.

Despite the political reasons for adding Russia, this enlargement had drawbacks. Yeltsin used to 'make speeches' at his colleagues, although his successor Vladimir Putin picked up the summit's informal mode at once when he arrived at Okinawa in 2000. Russia's comparative economic weakness meant that, until Evian 2003, some issues were kept for the G7 only. So the heads are wary of extending invitations to other powers, such as China (as suggested by Japanese prime minister Keizo Obuchi before Okinawa), because, once invited, they cannot be 'un-invited' without giving offence. There is no agreement among the heads to admit other countries to summit membership.[5]

Agenda and Use of Time   The addition of political issues to the economic summit, from the early 1980s, together with new topics provoked by the end of the cold war, produced severe overloading of the agenda. A campaign led by Major in 1992–93 to shorten both agenda and documentation and to cut down on ceremony, had only short-lived effect. In 1998 Blair tried again, proposing an economic agenda of only three items — employment, crime, and debt relief — for the Birmingham Summit, although new financial architecture was added in response to the Asian crisis. A short agenda at a 'heads-only summit' (see below) allowed the documents issued to be pruned severely.[6] This discipline was observed at most summits thereafter. Both Genoa 2001 and Kananaskis 2002 kept to a rigorous three-item agenda, while at Kananaskis Canadian prime minister Jean Chrétien replaced the standard communiqué by a 'chair's summary' of what the heads had actually discussed. However, French president Jacques Chirac preferred a broad, open-ended agenda, which contributed to overloading the subject matter and inflating the amount of documentation issued at Evian 2003.

Participation   Ever since 1975, the heads had been flanked at the summits by their foreign and finance ministers. This was originally on American insistence, although it also helped those with coalition governments, such as Germany. By the 1990s, however, the heads and their ministers were meeting at the summit in separate groups, with only rare plenaries. In 1998 Blair proposed to separate the flanking ministers in time as well as space. Only the heads came to Birmingham 1998, with foreign and finance ministers meeting a few days earlier. Heads-only summits have now become established and are clearly welcome to the heads themselves.

The establishment of heads-only summits is the fundamental reform of the summit format of the last decade. But its full significance is more complex than it appears. At first sight, meeting alone gives the heads greater freedom to choose their own agenda and develop their own ideas. But this freedom is constrained by other trends in summit decision making, especially the growth of separate ministerial groups and the involvement of nonstate actors in the G7/8 process. These will be analysed later in this chapter.

The Heads and Summit Content

Innovation in Agenda Setting   Each G7 country hosts the summit in turn, in a predictable sequence.[7] Although many topics are carried over from previous summits, the host has the ability to propose as innovative an agenda as the others can accept. This is the point at which the host has most influence over the proceedings and most heads take the opportunity to intervene personally, by writing to, telephoning, or visiting their peers.

Here are some dominant themes for the cycle of summits since France last held the chair:

- For Lyon 1996, Chirac proposed development and invited the heads of the International Monetary Fund (IMF), World Bank, World Trade Organization (WTO), and United Nations to the summit.
- For Denver 1997, Clinton proposed help for Africa.
- For Birmingham 1998, Blair proposed 'employability' — agreeing on the topic bilaterally with Clinton even before Denver.
- For Cologne 1999, German chancellor Gerhard Schroeder proposed debt relief for poor countries, reversing the policy of his predecessor Helmut Kohl. Under the pressure of events in Kosovo he added conflict prevention.
- For Okinawa 2000, Obuchi proposed information technology (IT) and infectious diseases.

- For Genoa 2001, Italian prime minister Giuliano Amato proposed world poverty and conflict prevention again; Silvio Berlusconi, who took office shortly before the Summit, endorsed this choice.
- For Kananaskis 2002, Chrétien gave priority to Africa again (after five years' neglect) and to terrorism (an essential topic after the attacks of 11 September 2001).

Some of the items on the list are recurring summit items, but others, such as Africa, IT, and conflict prevention, are wholly new. This shows how different leaders have added new ideas to the summit agenda — themselves increasing the overload about which they complain. This was particularly evident at Evian 2003, where Chirac sought to add new items — water and famine — to existing priorities such as Africa and disease.

Innovation at the Summit Itself   Innovation by a G8 head at the summit is frequent, but procedural initiatives are more common than substantive ones. Ideas for brand new policies seldom prevail if they have not been filtered through the preparatory process.[8] Thus Clinton made his mark at Tokyo III 1993, his first summit, by suggesting a special meeting of G7 employment ministers. But when at Naples 1994 he proposed without warning a new round of trade negotiations, he was blocked by the Europeans.

The heads launched a striking innovation at Genoa 2001. Over a working dinner, a group of African presidents explained to the G8 their New African Initiative, which later became the New Partnership for Africa's Development (NEPAD). The G8 heads were so impressed that they agreed on their own Genoa Plan for Africa, without any advance preparation. But this was essentially an agenda and did not contain any new substantive commitments. These had to wait until Kananaskis 2002 and were embodied in the Africa Action Plan prepared by the G8 Africa Group. The main innovation coming from the heads themselves at Kananaskis was again procedural — the agreement to let Russia host the summit in 2006, which surprised even the sherpas.

Innovation also includes the personal crusades of certain summit heads, often going beyond the advice of their officials. The most conspicuous of these was Kohl's insistence on getting environmental and nuclear safety issues onto the agenda, in addition to launching, as host, a meeting of G7 environment ministers before Munich 1992.[9]

Political Reflexes   Another personal contribution from the heads comes when their political instincts lead them to pick out certain issues or go against what their officials have prepared. The heads are often moved to react to sudden crises happening just before a summit. For example, a terrorist attack on U.S. servicemen in Saudi Arabia just before Lyon 1996 meant that Clinton persuaded his colleagues to convert material prepared on violent crime into a sharp condemnation of terrorism.

On other occasions the heads' political sense tells them that the conclusions prepared for the summit are not adequate, so that they do not accept them. Halifax 1995 had made detailed preparations on reform of the IMF, rather less on the UN. But the heads themselves decided that the 50th anniversary of the UN that year was an opportunity not to be missed, so that they greatly expanded their conclusions. At Denver 1997, the heads were not satisfied with the progress being made on transborder crime, which worried their electorates. They sought to accelerate G7 work in this area, making crime a major theme for Birmingham the next year. Likewise, the heads were not content with the conclusions on Africa prepared for them at Genoa 2001 and acted to expand them. These interventions by the heads against the grain of the preparations are different from deals struck on the basis of the preparatory work, which are discussed in the next section.

Domestic Motivation   As these examples show, often the leaders make personal use of the summit to respond to domestic pressures or to advance their domestic agenda. Kohl's concern with the environment reflected strong public interest in this subject in Germany. Blair in 1998 and Schroeder in 1999 were newly elected left-of-centre leaders who used the summit to advance their own domestic objectives in employment and social protection. Successive Italian prime ministers promoted conflict prevention because of the domestic disruption caused by the turmoil in the Balkans across the Adriatic, especially by flows of refugees. These political objectives and pressures, of course, do not always have positive effects. At Munich 1992, French president François Mitterrand felt obliged to hold up G7 agreement on concluding the Uruguay Round of the General Agreement on Tariffs and Trade (GATT), for fear that would upset the farming vote before the referendum in France on the Maastricht Treaty. (Chirac in 2003 was sensitive to similar pressures.)

The Heads and Summit Follow-up

Once the summit is over, the leaders rarely intervene to ensure its conclusions are carried out. Late in 1991 and 1992 there was much telephoning between G7 leaders in a vain attempt to conclude the Uruguay Round by the end of the year, as they had promised at the London III and Munich summits. In October 1998, Blair sounded out his colleagues on whether the worsening monetary crisis called for an extraordinary summit — but they were content just to issue a statement encouraging their finance ministers. Likewise, Berlusconi's suggestion of a special summit after the terrorist attacks of 11 September 2001 found no support. But these personal interventions by the leaders are exceptional.[10]

The position is quite different with regard to communicating the summit outcome to the media. All the heads take pains to convey their own views to their national press corps, who have followed them to the summit site. The leaders want to make a good impression back home, which often leads them to stress their personal victories, rather than the agreed-upon results achieved at the summit. Comparing national accounts reveals inconsistencies, which can focus public attention on points of difference rather than agreement.

Summary of the Contribution of the Heads

The main personal contribution of the heads of government to decision making at the G7/8 summit, independent of their officials, can be summarised thus:

- a strong attachment to simplicity of process, recently advanced by the launch of heads-only summit, although some of their other practices conflict with this;
- innovation by the summit host in agenda setting and by all leaders at the summit, although more often in procedure than content;
- political reflexes, triggered by sudden crises or a sense that the preparations are inadequate, and often reflecting domestic pressures or objectives; and
- rare involvement in implementation, but close attention to media treatment of the summit, which can stress differences more than agreement.

The prospect of meeting their peers at the top table thus concentrates the minds of the leaders, especially when this international encounter can also advance their domestic agenda.[11]

The Contribution of the Supporting Apparatus

The preparation of the summit is largely in the hands of the supporting G8 apparatus. Even what happens at the summit itself usually owes more to the preparatory process than to the personal intervention of the heads. This section therefore looks at what supporting G8 bureaucrats and ministers do, both on their own and in combination with the heads of government.

The Supporting Players

The Sherpas   Traditionally, summit preparations have been in the hands of a small team of bureaucrats, led by the sherpas, who are chosen either for their personal closeness to the head or their seniority in their parent department.[12] The sherpas are supported by two sous-sherpas, one each from the finance and foreign ministries, to work on the main summit agenda, and by the political directors from foreign ministries, to prepare foreign policy subjects. Originally the entire group would meet together, but during the 1990s the sherpas, each set of sous-sherpas, and the political directors took to meeting separately, to cover the growing agenda. Plenary meetings of the full team have become rare. In addition, groups of specialist officials have grown up to deal with recurring summit themes, such as terrorism or nonproliferation.

Summit preparations are concentrated in several meetings each spring, to select the agenda and start drafting the necessary documents. In many ways, the dynamics of summit meetings are reproduced at sherpa level. At these small gatherings, discussion is frank, with plenty of personal interaction.[13] The sherpas get to know each other well, they understand each others' domestic background and they develop a sense of solidarity and shared responsibility. The sherpas become adept both at seeing what arguments would prove convincing, against their colleagues' domestic backgrounds, and at picking up ideas from the others that they can use to good effect back home.[14]

The Other Ministers   At the outset, G7 foreign and finance ministers attended the summit as support for the heads. But each group has steadily asserted its independence. During the 1980s, the secretive G5 was absorbed into the public G7 finance ministers, while G7 foreign ministers began meeting on their own on the margin of the UN General Assembly. Since Birmingham 1998, both groups meet just before the summit, but no longer attend it. They also meet at other times: G7 finance ministers on the margins of IMF meetings, G8 foreign ministers as issues require. For example, the foreign ministers held a special meeting on conflict prevention in December 1999, to carry out a remit from the Cologne Summit.

Meanwhile, other ministers have become associated with the summit in the 1990s, largely thanks to personal initiatives by the heads themselves. There are now regular or periodic meetings of environment ministers (promoted by Kohl), employment ministers (backed by Clinton, Chirac, and Blair), energy ministers (started by Yeltsin), education ministers (thanks to Schroeder), interior and justice ministers (focussed on terrorism and crime), and development ministers (new in 2002–03). These ministers meet not only to prepare for summits and carry out instructions from the heads, but also to pursue their own independent agendas. Most of these groups include the Russians, although finance ministers usually meet as G7 only. Each has its own apparatus of supporting officials.[15]

Once the summit began meeting as heads only, these separate ministerial groups no longer felt bound to preserve the strict G7 or G8 format. G8 foreign ministers have invited selected other countries to join them for meetings focussed on specific problems — for example, on Balkan stability in June 1999, in response to the Kosovo crisis. The G7 finance ministers have created a new permanent grouping, the G20, linked to monetary reform in the IMF, which includes major developing countries active in the system.[16]

The proliferation of these ministerial groups counterbalances the effect of the heads meeting alone at the summit and introduces a certain tension. The heads have to decide whether to exercise their own freedom, at the cost of allowing these other groups to operate independently too, or to try to keep control over an ever-expanding pyramid of activity.

Summit Preparations

Agenda Setting   This is the task for the first sherpa meeting of the year. The host head of government, as shown earlier, focusses on new ideas to make that year's summit distinctive. The sherpas, on the other hand, must wrestle with the ongoing summit agenda of items started but not completed in earlier years. This agenda is always under pressure.[17]

The difficult issues that come up to the heads often need recurrent summit treatment, such as with international trade or debt relief for poor countries. While most items can be handed on to other established organisations for follow-up (see below), sometimes the institutions are inadequate, so that the G7/8 remains responsible for them.

The innovative ideas of earlier years, such as employment or information technology, become recurring items later. Even after Blair's reforms of 1998, intended to check this inflation of the agenda, later summits have kept on adding new items — education, conflict prevention, IT, infectious diseases, Africa — without taking old ones off. In general, the hardest part of agenda setting for the sherpas is deciding what to leave out. Choosing an open-ended agenda, as the French did in 2003, makes this especially difficult.

Summit Endorsement — Work in Progress   Endorsement takes up the largest and the easiest part of the summit agenda and documentation. It consists of the heads putting their authority behind work that is going on elsewhere. Often this will be activity that has been generated by earlier summits, so that the heads give their blessing to work in progress. In other cases G8 governments find it useful to have the endorsement of their peers for policies they have decided to adopt already, since this can be useful in overcoming domestic opposition.

This part of the summit agenda, however, is most subject to inflation. There is a strong incentive for G8 governments to expand the area of their policies carrying summit endorsement. But the wider this endorsement is given, the more its value becomes diluted. The move to heads-only summits was intended to allow more issues to be pushed down to other ministers and this is happening, to some extent. The Canadians insisted in 2002 that only issues actually discussed by the heads should appear in the 'chair's summary', but this was already coming under pressure at Evian 2003. Once the heads have lent their authority to a particular subject, they are often reluctant to abandon it, for fear others should conclude that they have ceased to care about it.

Stimulating Agreement at Lower Levels   A more demanding technique is when summit discussion, or even the prospect of it, is used to resolve differences among G7 or G8 members that persist at lower levels and may prevent agreement in wider international contexts. A good example is seen in the international financial architecture agreed upon after the Asian crisis. The essential work on this was done by the G7 finance ministers and their deputies. On some issues, there were deep divisions among them, but the approach of the summits at Birmingham in 1998 and Cologne in 1999 provided an incentive to resolve these differences. The heads gave their authority to what their finance ministers had agreed upon, without adding anything of their own.

The work done since 1999 in conflict prevention also illustrates this well. After the initial impulse from the heads at Cologne, the foreign ministers worked up a detailed programme at their meetings in Berlin in December 1999 and Miyazaki in July 2000. The imminence of the Okinawa Summit, a week after the Miyazaki meeting, concentrated their minds, so that heads only needed to endorse what the foreign ministers had done, without having to discuss it themselves. At Genoa 2001, the heads left the generic subject wholly to their foreign ministers, but identified conflict prevention as a specific element of their African initiative. Accordingly, the section on peace and security contained some of the most precise commitments in the Africa Action Plan agreed upon at Kananaskis 2002. At Evian 2003, the heads followed this up by endorsing the G8/NEPAD Peace Support Plan.

A more controversial example is seen in the summit's involvement in the Uruguay Round negotiations. At three summits — Houston 1990, London III 1991, and Munich 1992 — the heads undertook to complete the round by the end of the year, but because of differences on agriculture they always failed to meet their own deadline. For Tokyo III 1993, however, the preparations called for the G7 trade ministers to meet as the 'Quad' just before the summit itself.[18] The imminence of the summit encouraged the trade ministers to reach agreements that opened the way for the Uruguay Round's final completion in December 1993. Similarly, neglect of trade at the summits leading up the WTO ministerial meeting in Seattle in late 1999 contributed to the disastrous failure to launch a new round of trade negotiations. But in 2001 the approach of the Genoa Summit was used to stimulate and confirm agreement between the trade negotiators of the EU, the U.S., and Japan, which facilitated a much more successful outcome from the WTO meeting at Doha later in the year.

Stimulating Agreement at the Summit Itself   The two techniques described so far cover most of the summit content and often they will produce the most important evidence of G7/8 co-operation. But the heads also play a more direct role. In some cases, they have to engage their own authority to give the necessary impetus to a wide-ranging or innovative programme. The work on IT and the digital divide at Okinawa 2000 is one example of this; the decision to launch the Global Fund to Fight AIDS, Tuberculosis, and Malaria at Genoa 2001 is another. Sometimes agreement can only be reached through the intervention of the heads themselves. This applied to the peace arrangement for Kosovo in 1999. Detailed preparations had been made, but everything hinged on Yeltsin's position, which did not become clear until he reached the Cologne Summit in person. Most of the provisions of the Africa Action Plan had been agreed upon before the 2002 Kananaskis Summit, but the direct intervention of the heads was needed to confirm the figure of US$6 billion per year in extra aid for Africa.

In yet other cases, the heads are able to reach agreements that are not attainable at lower levels. Debt relief for low-income countries provides successive examples of this technique throughout the 1990s. At London III 1991, Naples 1994, Lyon 1996, and Cologne 1999, the heads succeeded in advancing agreement on this subject further than their finance ministers had taken it. Debt relief is thus one area where the summit has become identified as the place where things happen, so that it attracted huge demonstrations to Birmingham and Cologne. Again, at Kananaskis 2002 the heads were able to overcome U.S. reluctance and fix a figure of US$1 billion for replenishing the World Bank trust fund for debt relief, where their finance ministers had failed.

George W. Bush was prepared to accept this US$1 billion figure, because the Europeans, Japan, and Canada had agreed to match the U.S. contribution of US$10 billion over ten years to clean up Russian nuclear and chemical weapons and installations. This agreement could only have been reached among the heads, with the direct involvement of Putin, because at lower levels the Russians had refused the necessary guarantees of access and legal protection. The link between the two agreements illustrates the summit's potential to identify and conclude cross-issue deals.

Such agreements exploit the heads' wish for some achievements of their own. They are not happy when everything at the summit has been 'pre-cooked'. The sherpas try to provide some scope for the heads to go beyond what has been prepared for them. Without this, the heads will be tempted to take their own unprepared initiatives, as described earlier. But this strategy does not always work — and once discord is registered at the summit it may be harder to find agreement elsewhere. This is shown by the summits' treatment of environmental issues before and after the UN Conference on Environment and Development at Rio in 1992. The early summits, from Paris 1989 to London III 1991, were able to stimulate much new thinking on the environment and to feed ideas into the preparations for Rio. However, as discussion moved from broad ideas to specific commitments, it became harder to overcome differences between the United States and Europe. When the summits took up the environment again, at Denver 1997 and Okinawa 2000, in advance of climate change meetings at Kyoto and the Hague, raising the issue to the level of the head of government did not resolve the disagreements.

Domestic Motivation   When the heads are ready to go a bit further at the summit than their officials or ministers, that again usually reflects their judgement of the balance of domestic and international advantage in reaching agreement. Yeltsin knew that the Kosovo settlement was unpopular in Russia, but he did not want to alienate the support of the G7. Schroeder, Blair, and their predecessors were aware of strong public interest in debt relief, mobilised by the Jubilee 2000 campaign. Bush knew that Congress was so keen on the agreement to clean up installations in Russia that they would regard US$1 billion for debt relief as an acceptable price. But these domestic political considerations can also work in the wrong direction. On climate change and biodiversity, the strongest domestic pressures in Europe come mainly from consumer groups and public opinion, while in North America they come from producers and business interests. So agreement on environmental issues may actually be harder to reach at the summit than lower down.

Summit Follow-Up

In contrast to agenda setting and summit preparation, the sherpas play a smaller part in summit follow-up. The G7 and G8 ministerial groups, in contrast, have a growing role in the implementation of summit conclusions. They have much greater flexibility than the summit itself, in the choice of when they meet and whether they involve other countries. But by far the largest responsibility for summit follow-up, however, still rests with wider international institutions. The contribution of these outside bodies is considered in the next section of this chapter.

Summary of the Contribution of the Supporting Apparatus

The contribution of the supporting apparatus to the summit, whether working on its own or together with the heads, can be summarised as follows:

- The traditional sherpa network has been supplemented in the 1990s by the growth of semi-independent G7 or G8 ministerial groups.
- In agenda setting, the hardest task for the sherpas is to decide how to leave things out, so as to keep the agenda under control.
- Summit endorsement of existing policies is valuable in giving the authority of the heads, but this becomes devalued if used too much.
- The prospect of summit discussion can stimulate agreement at lower levels, without a direct contribution from the heads being necessary.
- The sherpas try to take advantage of the heads' desire to achieve something of their own, so as to advance agreement at the summit beyond the preparations — but this does not always work.
- Sherpas take comparatively little part in follow-up; supporting ministers do rather more, but most is done in wider institutions.

The imminence of the summit concentrates the minds of those involved in the preparations, whether these are the sherpa team or the groups of G7 and G8 ministers, and often this is enough to produce agreement. But the question is whether the heads-only summits can still have this concentrating effect in the more dispersed G7/8 system.

The Contribution of Other Actors

During the 1970s and 1980s, summit preparations were held tightly by the sherpas. Summit follow-up was entrusted to other institutions, without much direct involvement by the G7. During the 1990s, however, the self-contained character of summitry began to loosen up and this process has accelerated rapidly since 2000. This phenomenon looks like a direct consequence of the heads meeting on their own. Since the summits have detached themselves from their own ministerial apparatus, they have greater scope to form links with outside bodies, both other governments and nonstate groups. This also reflects a perception by the heads of government of their responsibility to explain policy decisions to their peoples and to reassure them about the impact of globalisation. These changes have gone furthest in preparation and follow-up but now even affect the summit itself.

Contribution to Summit Preparation

For many years, the G7 governments kept summit preparation firmly in their own hands. Other governments had little chance to influence the process directly, except for other member states of the European Community, which were consulted to some degree by the European Commission and presidency. The Organisation for Economic Co-operation and Development (OECD) also held its annual ministerial meeting a few weeks before the summit, so that the non-G7 members could make their views known. As for nongovernment influences, these hardly went beyond visits to the host head of government by business and trade union delegations under OECD auspices. But this hermetic character of the preparations is being eroded rapidly in the 2000s.

Other Governments and International Institutions   The growing involvement of supporting ministers in the preparatory process has enabled other international institutions to be involved. G7 and G8 ministers often invite senior staff members from these institutions to join them. The supporting ministerial groups also allow other governments to become involved, as they are not limited to a strict G7/8 format. A more radical move was made before Okinawa 2000, when most of the G8 leaders met a group of heads of government from developing countries in Tokyo on their way to the summit.[19] A similar meeting took place before Genoa 2001 and, although it remained distinct from the summit itself, it was the direct cause of the G8's initiative on Africa. At Kananaskis 2002, when the G8 heads launched their Africa Action Plan, they invited four African leaders — the Steering Committee of NEPAD — together with the UN Secretary General as participants rather than guests.[20] At Evian 2003, the G8 not only worked with the Africans again but also met a wider group of leaders from developing countries that included, for the first time, major powers such as China, India, Brazil, and Mexico.

Private Business and Nongovernmental Organisations   In 2000, the Japanese prepared the treatment of IT and the digital divide at the summit by involving a range of major multinational companies. They organised a special conference shortly before Okinawa and incorporated most of its findings in the Summit's own report. The involvement of NGOs had taken off at Birmingham 1998, where the Jubilee 2000 campaign organised a march of 50 000 people calling for debt cancellation. Since then, the host government has always met with a delegation of NGOs present at the summit. In 2000, the Japanese provided an NGO centre at Okinawa, and also involved NGO groups in consultations with their sherpa team.[21] These consultations were initially conducted more systematically by the Italians in 2001, involving groups active in conflict prevention such as Saferworld and International Alert.[22] But Italian plans were thrown off course by the violent riots in Genoa during the Summit, in which one demonstrator was killed. To avoid a recurrence of this and to provide greater security after the terrorist attacks of 11 September 2001, Canada held the 2002 Summit in the remote mountain resort of Kananaskis, allowing NGOs no nearer than Calgary, a hundred kilometres away. Likewise, France offered facilities for an 'alternative summit' at Annemasse, 30 kilometres from Evian, but allowed no public demonstrations anywhere near the Summit site.

Contribution to Summit Follow-Up

International Institutions   In contrast to the preparations, summit follow-up has relied on other actors from the outset. The summits of the 1970s and 1980s largely delegated the responsibility for implementing their economic decisions to bodies such as the OECD, the IMF and World Bank, and the GATT. During this time, the summit took a detached attitude to these institutions, handing down its decisions as *faits accomplis* and expecting them to be adopted without further debate. But this approach would no longer work in the 1990s, as more countries became active in the international system and the G7 became less dominant.

When the G7 members conducted their review of international institutions, begun at Naples 1994 and continued until Denver 1997, they realised that they would have to use more tact and persuasion to get their ideas for reform accepted by the wider membership. Meanwhile, the expanding agenda has taken the summit deeper into unfamiliar policy areas. Its links have spread beyond economic bodies to various organs of the United Nations, as well as security institutions such as the Organization for Security and Co-operation in Europe (OSCE). In some subjects, the summit has found the existing institutions to be inadequate, for example in crime and money laundering. This has been a factor behind the creation of G7 and G8 ministerial groups, such as the interior and justice ministers.[23]

Business and Nongovernmental Organisations   Both private business and NGOs started to become involved in summit follow-up during the 1990s. An initial involvement of private business came with the Global Information Society conferences launched at Naples 1994, to promote the wider diffusion of information technology, but these ran out of steam (Hajnal 1999, 38–39). The renewed interest in IT at Okinawa 2000 led to the creation of the Digital Opportunity Task Force, known as the Dot Force, to recommend ways to overcome the digital divide, with strong participation from business and also from NGOs. Business and NGOs were involved in two other programmes launched at Okinawa: the campaign against infectious diseases, leading at Genoa to the Global Fund to Fight AIDS, Tuberculosis, and Malaria, and the G8 Renewable Energy Task Force. Their participation has the merit of tapping additional sources of expertise and financial support, even though these new follow-up structures may be harder to integrate into the existing framework of international institutions. The active involvement of not only business firms but also leading NGOs in these activities has been in striking contrast to the violent public demonstrations on the streets.

Summary of the Contribution of Other Actors

The contribution of other actors to summit decision making can be summarised in the following way.

- The formally hermetic system of summit preparation now gives rather more access to other governments and international institutions, as well as to business and NGOs.
- International institutions have always been entrusted with summit follow-up, but the G8 now treats them more persuasively and systematically.
- There are problems, however, when the institutions are inadequate; involving business and NGOs is increasingly used to compensate for this.

In the early years, it was enough for the summits to make recommendations for these to concentrate the minds of others. But power is now much more widely spread, both among states and among other actors in the system. So other players are increasingly involved and contribute to the results — again at the cost of more dispersed decision making in the G7/8 system.

Conclusion

This chapter has analysed the decision-making methods of the G7/8 system, especially of the summits, as they have developed over the last decade. It remains to establish how the different strands interact with one another.

The G7/8 summit meetings, as noted at the outset, are a device to 'concentrate minds' on finding co-operative solutions to intractable problems where international and domestic pressures interact. Such devices exert a strong attraction not only on the G7/8 leaders, but also on heads of government world-wide. This is shown by the great increase in international summit meetings from the 1990s onward, both in limited groups such as the European Council, the OSCE, and Asia-Pacific Economic Cooperation (APEC), and on a wider scale, such as the Summit of the Americas in 2001 and the World Summit on Sustainable Development in 2002.

The original, tightly knit methods of decision making served the G7 summit well in its early years. But they are no longer an adequate response to the pressures of globalisation, which have brought many new subjects onto the summit agenda and many new actors, both state and nonstate, onto the international stage. After many years when the summit agenda became overloaded, the G7/8 leaders have responded by cutting loose from their governmental apparatus and meeting on their own.

This move gives the heads new freedom of action, which they greatly welcome. But it also confronts them with new and difficult decisions. For example:

- Separating the supporting apparatus from the summit creates new opportunities for the G7/8 ministerial groups, which have developed during the 1990s and 2000s. They can help to prepare for and follow up on each summit, but they can also pursue their own agendas. Will the summits remain detached and allow this process to develop? Or will the heads try to keep control of the G7/8 system, on the grounds that only the link with the summit effectively concentrates the mind?
- Meeting alone also enables the heads to establish links with wider networks, for example of non-G8 governments, private business, and civil society. With the advance of globalisation, these have become essential contributors to decision making, in the preparations and especially in follow-up. Their involvement also helps to make the G7/8 process more transparent. But will this dispersion of activity make it harder to concentrate minds in the intergovernmental institutions, on which the summit still largely relies for implementation?

There are no definitive answers to these questions yet. So far, each summit since Birmingham 1998 has found its own equilibrium. Birmingham sought to give the heads the freedom of a short agenda. Several years on, Genoa and Kananaskis were still faithful to tight agendas and shorter documents, but the French imprudently allowed both to expand again at Evian. Okinawa made major moves toward admitting outside players, aiming to give the summit greater transparency and legitimacy. Genoa continued this trend, especially in its initiative on Africa. The work on Africa for Kananaskis and Evian was done by a special G8 group separate from the sherpas and led to four African leaders (and the UN Secretary General) coming to both summits as participants, not guests. Chirac further expanded this outreach at Evian to include leading developing countries such as China. But so far the G8 heads are not committed to a set pattern of external contacts.

In general, the G8 summit seeks to preserve the sort of flexibility it has shown in treating conflict prevention in the four years since it came on to the summit agenda. In 1999, it was a direct concern of the heads. In 2000, the approach of the summit stimulated agreement among the G8 foreign ministers, so that the heads could simply endorse their work. In 2001, although conflict prevention was a priority topic for the Italian hosts, it did not go beyond the foreign ministers, except where it formed part of the heads' African initiative. In 2002 and again in 2003, the measures prepared on Africa required the authority of the heads, while other conflict prevention issues remained with the foreign ministers. This leaves it open to the G8 in 2004 to determine in the light of events how and at what level to address conflict prevention.

Notes

1 This chapter is adapted from a paper delivered at a workshop held by the European Consortium for Political Research in Grenoble in April 2001 (see Bayne 2003a).
2 Nearly all the examples of decision making at the summits of the 1990s are taken from Bayne (2000, ch. 5, 8, 10). For the 2000 Okinawa Summit, see Bayne (2001b); for the 2001

Genoa Summit, see Bayne (2001a; 2002); for the 2002 Kananaskis Summit, see Bayne (2003c); for the Evian 2003 Summit, see Bayne (2003b).

3 This view was held strongly by French president Valéry Giscard d'Estaing and German chancellor Helmut Schmidt (see Putnam and Bayne 1987, 32–34).

4 For an account of the development of the sherpa process, see Putnam and Bayne (1987, 48–622). A complete list of the summit participants, including the sherpas, from the beginning up to 2000 is in Franchini-Sherifis and Astraldi (2001, 217–253).

5 For an analysis of G8 relations with China, see Kirton (2001a).

6 The communiqué issued after Tokyo III 1993 was down to six pages. At Denver 1997 the heads issued a total of 29 pages of documents. This was cut back by half at Birmingham 1998.

7 The order is France, United States, United Kingdom, Germany, Japan, Italy, and Canada. At the Kananaskis Summit, it was agreed that Russia can host its first summit in 2006.

8 The classic example of a new policy introduced without preparation at the summit is the agreement on hijacking from Bonn I 1978 (see Putnam and Bayne 1987, 87). But even at early summits such initiatives were uncommon.

9 Kohl's crusade goes well back into the 1980s. He tried to hold a G7 environment ministers meeting before Bonn II 1985, but the French declined to come. His political reflexes led him to propose a statement from Tokyo II 1986 on the Chernobyl nuclear accident, which had happened just before the summit (see Putnam and Bayne 1987, 202–203, 213–214).

10 Sometimes the follow-up includes a further summit meeting of the G8 and others, such as the Moscow nuclear safety summit of early 1996 and the Sarajevo summit of July 1999 on Balkan reconstruction.

11 This process has been well analysed by Robert Putnam in his model of 'two-level games', which he developed from his observation of the Bonn I Summit of 1978 (see Putnam 1988; Putnam and Henning 1989).

12 There were some changes in national practice during the 1990s and 2000s. Under presidents Ronald Reagan and George Bush I, the U.S. sherpa had been a senior State Department figure, but Clinton chose his sherpas from his White House staff and so has his successor George W. Bush. Chancellors Schmidt and Kohl had always made the state secretary at the finance ministry the German sherpa, but Schroeder moved the post to his chancellery.

13 As with the summit itself, the arrival of the Russians introduced rather more formality.

14 This again shows Putnam's two-level game model at work (see Putnam 1988; Putnam and Henning 1989).

15 For an analysis of this development, see Hajnal (1999, 35–44).

16 See Kirton (2001b) for an account of the G20 and its role. In 2002, the G20 chair passed to India and, a year later, to Mexico — both non-G8 countries.

17 The growth of 'iteration' at the summits is documented in Bayne (2000, 200–208).

18 The Quadrilateral or 'Quad', composed of the trade ministers of the U.S., Japan, and Canada, plus the responsible European Commissioner, was founded at the Ottawa Summit of 1981, although by 1993 its links with the G7 process had become tenuous (see Putnam and Bayne 1987, 131; see also Cohn 2002).

19 This meeting was arranged without difficulty, in contrast to the resistance by the G7 heads to the proposal from Mitterrand for an encounter with other leaders before the Paris Summit of 1989 (see Bayne 2000, 75, n. 5; Attali 1995).

20 The Africans were Thabo Mbeki (South Africa), Olusegun Obasanjo (Nigeria), Abdoulaye Wade (Senegal) and Abdelaziz Bouteflika (Algeria).

21 For an analysis of the G8's relations with NGOs, see Hajnal (2002b, 38–39; 2002a).

22 NGOs also influence national preparations. Some of the environmental measures agreed upon at Okinawa, such as the Task Force on Renewable Energy and the provisions on illegal logging, were British initiatives worked out in co-operation with NGOs (Budd 2002).

23 One early example of this trend is the Financial Action Task Force against money laundering, founded at the 1989 Paris Summit (Bayne 2000, 66).

References

Attali, Jacques (1995). *Verbatim III*. Fayard, Paris.
Bayne, Nicholas (2000). *Hanging In There: The G7 and G8 Summit in Maturity and Renewal*. Ashgate, Aldershot.
Bayne, Nicholas (2001a). 'G8 Decision-making and the Genoa Summit'. *International Spectator* vol. 36, July-September, pp. 69–75.
Bayne, Nicholas (2001b). 'Managing Globalisation and the New Economy: The Contribution of the G8 Summit'. In J. J. Kirton and G. M. von Furstenberg, eds., *New Directions in Global Economic Governance: Managing Globalisation in the Twenty-First Century*, pp. 171–188. Ashgate, Aldershot.
Bayne, Nicholas (2002). 'Impressions of the Genoa Summit, 20–22 July, 2001'. In M. Fratianni, P. Savona and J. J. Kirton, eds., *Governing Global Finance: New Challenges, G7 and IMF Contributions*, pp. 199–210. Ashgate, Aldershot.
Bayne, Nicholas (2003a). 'Are World Leaders Puppets or Puppeteers? The Sherpas of the G7/G8 System'. In B. Reinalda and B. Verbeek, eds., *Decision Making within International Organizations*. Routledge, London.
Bayne, Nicholas (2003b). 'Impressions of the Evian Summit'. <www.g7.utoronto.ca/evaluations/2003evian/assess_bayne030603.html> (July 2003).
Bayne, Nicholas (2003c). 'Impressions of the Kananaskis Summit'. In M. Fratianni, P. Savona and J. J. Kirton, eds., *Sustaining Global Growth and Development: G7 and IMF Governance*, pp. 229–240. Ashgate, Aldershot.
Budd, Colin (2002). 'G8 Summits and Their Preparation'. In N. Bayne and S. Woolcock, eds., *The New Economic Diplomacy: Decision-Making and Negotiation in International Economic Relations*, pp. 139–146. Ashgate, Aldershot.
Cohn, Theodore H. (2002). *Governing Global Trade: International Institutions in Conflict and Convergence*. Ashgate, Aldershot.
Franchini-Sherifis, Rosella and Valerio Astraldi (2001). *The G7/G8: From Rambouillet to Genoa*. Franco Angelo, Milan.
Hajnal, Peter I. (1999). *The G7/G8 System: Evolution, Role, and Documentation*. Ashgate, Aldershot.
Hajnal, Peter I., ed. (2002a). *Civil Society in the Information Age*. Ashgate, Aldershot.
Hajnal, Peter I. (2002b). 'Partners or Adversaries? The G7/8 Encounters Civil Society'. In J. J. Kirton and J. Takase, eds., *New Directions in Global Political Governance: The G8 and International Order in the Twenty-First Century*, pp. 191–208. Ashgate, Aldershot.
Kirton, John J. (2001a). 'The G7/8 and China: Toward a Closer Association'. In J. J. Kirton, J. P. Daniels and A. Freytag, eds., *Guiding Global Order: G8 Governance in the Twenty-First Century*. Ashgate, Aldershot.
Kirton, John J. (2001b). 'The G20: Representativeness, Effectiveness, and Leadership in Global Governance'. In J. J. Kirton, J. P. Daniels and A. Freytag, eds., *Guiding Global Order: G8 Governance in the Twenty-First Century*, pp. 143–172. Ashgate, Aldershot.
Putnam, Robert (1988). 'Diplomacy and Domestic Politics: The Logic of Two-Level Games'. *International Organisation* vol. 423, pp. 427–460.
Putnam, Robert and Nicholas Bayne (1987). *Hanging Together: Co-operation and Conflict in the Seven-Power Summit*. 2nd ed. Sage Publications, London.
Putnam, Robert and C. Randall Henning (1989). 'The Bonn Summit of 1978: A Case Study in Coordination'. In R. N. Cooper, ed., *Can Nations Agree?* Brookings Institution, Washington DC.

Chapter 3

The Intricacies of Summit Preparation and Consensus Building

Robert Fowler

The Centrality of the G7/8 Summit

In considering the institutional framework and mechanisms of the G8, as they relate to conflict prevention, it is important to recognise two central contextual factors. The first is the enormous activity and leadership of the United Nations in regard to conflict prevention over the past several years. The second is that in the current world, there is very little that any of the G8 governments do that is not somehow caught up in the business of summitry. Indeed, the summit process is all-consuming. From the vantage point of the political staff of leaders, from foreign ministries and even from that of defence departments, the growing impact of summitry on collective decision making in Canada and then on collegial decision making beyond Canada is dramatic.

The summit process is now the process that insures effective co-ordination of macroeconomic policy and broad geo-strategic decision making among the major industrial democracies. Concentration of such authority in a single institution is both positive and makes the instrument a little cumbersome. It does ensure that co-ordination takes place. It further ensures that it takes place in close concert with other similarly placed countries. However, it also means that such policy development is not as agile as it might be.

For decades, summit leaders and their sherpas discussed how elaborate this Christmas tree agenda that was erected in advance of each summit could get, as everyone sought to put their favourite issue and project on the summit agenda and see their preferred solution enshrined in its concluding communiqué. Every year since the early 1980s, the prospective host would always declare: 'Next year we are going to get back to basics. Next year we are going to make it simple. Next year we are going to cut out all the frills. Next year we are really going to get back to the original purpose.' That happened at the Canadian-hosted 2003 Summit at Kananaskis, and the agenda was kept simple, focussed, and relevant (Fowler 2003).

With this proliferation, the summit began to mimic the logic and practice of the United Nations General Assembly. Delegates feel they must repeat every pious platitude, again and again, lest it be construed that they thought it no longer mattered. Yet rather than achieving that purpose, this practice has had, predictably, the opposite effect. It dilutes everything that is actually said, so that the truly important, current, and relevant material that merits being highlighted is missed in that great morass of repetition. This pitfall was avoided at Kananaskis.

The G7/8 Summit and Conflict Prevention

In examining the G7/8 Summit's contribution to conflict prevention, clearly the most effective role it can play is through the act of consensus that the leaders agree to take to other relevant bodies. This is why the French, with good reason, have long held that this summit vehicle is not a *directoire politique*, but rather a very effective *instance d'impulsion*, something more than an agent of influence whereby its agreements on the vital issues of the moment have enormous impact on world management. It works simply because these summit agreements are promoted by this uniquely powerful set of governments in whatever other forums deal with such matters. For years, the G8 had little to say about Africa's plight. Kananaskis changed that. Since that time, when G8 representatives engage on any African issue in any international forum they are informed and guided by the '110 Commandments' of the Africa Action Plan agreed to at Kananaskis, thereby giving thrust and authority to those undertakings throughout the range of international programmes, agencies, and institutions in which the G8 has a not inconsiderable degree of influence.

No one, however, has ever suggested that the summit itself ought somehow to become some kind of conflict manager or conflict preventer. There is the UN Security Council (UNSC) for that purpose. The structure of the G8, the support mechanisms available to it, and, indeed, the kind of deliberations undertaken at summit meetings make such a function utterly impossible, not to say illegitimate. The G8 has no mandate and no authority to take on such a role, and there has been no indication that G8 leaders would be interested in doing so. The composition of the UNSC, however, makes it easy to appreciate the potential impact of summit deliberations — formal and informal — on what does and, above all, what does not happen at the UNSC. Four of the G8 members — the United States, Britain, France, and Russia — sit as permanent members of the UNSC and hold veto power. A similar conclusion can be drawn from the impact of G8 decisions on the North Atlantic Treaty Organization (NATO), or indeed if one assesses the potential impact of G8 decisions on the managing boards or governing councils of most international bodies and institutions.

Thus, on the issue of conflict management, the G8 summit certainly plays a pivotal, if often passive, role with respect to what gets done and does not get done in other forums. In this way, it is indeed an important and powerful institution. It would be surprising if, in an African or, say, Balkan crisis, there were a significant difference of view between what the UNSC decided and what the G8 or G7 had decided or would decide.

Therefore, the G8 plays a very large role in terms of deciding what does and does not happen. But it does so largely indirectly. An example is Kosovo, where the summit leaders encouraged certain things to occur in the operational organisations that had a direct mandate and influence. There are other examples, some with less positive outcomes. Certainly, the willingness of summit participants to engage effectively in Africa in a timely and forceful manner can also be traced back to what has and has not occurred at past summits.

Conflict Prevention and the Kananaskis Summit

Conflict management and prevention in Africa were critical issues at the 2002 Kananaskis Summit. Here, following a decision by G8 leaders at the 2001 Genoa Summit, the centrepiece was to be poverty reduction in Africa. It would be engaged through the G8 Africa Action Plan in response to the New Partnership for Africa's Development (NEPAD), which had been presented by leading African heads of state and government at Genoa. The first of NEPAD's five major issue areas was peace and security. This reflected the fact that one African nation in five was engaged in or affected by conflict. Conflict was destroying the lives of a very large number of Africans. It sapped Africa's confidence and impaired Africa's ability to attract world attention and interest. It was a source of despair for those seeking to come to Africa's assistance.

Indeed, it is estimated that in recent years three million people have been killed in central Africa and the Congo, with close to one million killed and an additional four million displaced in Angola, and another three million killed in Sudan. West Africa has known an equally harsh reality, particularly in Sierra Leone, Guinea, and Liberia. Indeed, the number killed in the ongoing terrorist unrest in Algeria is more than 20 times the number killed in the 11 September 2001 terrorist attacks in the United States. Hence, the issue of peace and security in Africa was, indeed, *sine qua non* to broader efforts to alleviate Africa's plight.

This task of managing and preventing such conflicts directly engaged the second priority issue area of NEPAD: governance. A commitment to a new approach to governance in Africa was based on the African leaders' commitment in NEPAD to engage in a peer review process that would assess governance in Africa and take measures to improve it. It offered partners outside Africa an opportunity to participate. The approach embraced governance in all its parts: political, including the legitimacy of democratic political process, and popular accountability; financial governance and management; and the administrative governance necessary to create a climate that might attract both domestic and foreign investment.

Of the many challenges to overcome in order to reduce poverty in Africa, providing peace and security remains the most difficult. Its importance is undeniable. No one working in Africa can remain blind to the ravages wrought by conflict. This horror has contributed to pessimism and a distressing tendency in western circles to simply write off the African continent. It is also, of course, infinitely expensive. Every cent of the resources that could conceivably be raised to alleviate Africa's suffering could be sucked up in an effort to manage and prevent conflict on that continent, but such an allocation would clearly be indefensible. Thus Kananaskis was necessarily destined to deliver less than what was required to bring peace to Africa. Instead, in approaching conflict prevention at Kananaskis, the Africa Action Plan focussed on the doable and the achievable — that is, on strengthening regional and sub-regional institutions dealing with conflict resolution and peacebuilding training and with disarmament, demobilisation, and reintegration (DDR), on post-conflict management, and on training in negotiations and peacekeeping. It offered South African president Thabo Mbeki assistance with his inter-Congolese dialogue, and supported the process of bringing stability to Burundi. It did not, however, finance the building of an African army, nor did it buy tanks for the Economic Community of West African States (ECOWAS).

Equally difficult was the particular challenge of reducing the proliferation of small arms in Africa. G8 member countries account for a very large proportion of the world arms trade, of which the official part of the arms business in Africa is, in fact, a relatively small part. One of the biggest obstacles was the approach of the African governments themselves. Many African leaders insist that they be able to protect themselves from local bullies. They argue: 'If you make it impossible for us to protect ourselves in the rough neighbourhoods in which we live you will make management of our sovereignty and democratic development impossible.'

Reference

Fowler, Robert (2003). 'Canadian Leadership and the Kananaskis G8 Summit: Toward a Less Self-Centred Policy'. In D. Carment, F. O. Hampson and N. Hillmer, eds., *Canada Among Nations 2003: Coping with the American Colossus*, pp. 219–241. Oxford University Press, Toronto.

Chapter 4

The G8 and Conflict Prevention: From Promise to Practice?

David M. Malone

While the G8 has focussed on conflict prevention over its past several cycles, it has done so at a high level of abstraction as well as thematically. It has not addressed any hard cases, such as Zimbabwe. It has left work at the coal face to the United Nations and to regional organisations, while urging them on (see Hampson and Malone 2002). Does this represent a flight from responsibility or a useful division of labour?

The meetings of G8 foreign ministers and their political directors have been useful over the years. The latter played a critical role in resolving the deadlock between the Russian Federation and North Atlantic Treaty Organization (NATO) countries over Kosovo in 1999, paving the way for UN Security Council Resolution 1244 that set in place interim arrangements for the territory following NATO's bombing campaign. However, if one looks back at political declarations from G8 and earlier G7 meetings — often catalogues of trouble spots and wishful thinking — the nearly inescapable conclusion is that their formal statements have proved evanescent, somewhat faddish, and rarely in any way incisive or influential.[1]

Does this mean that the G8 focus on conflict prevention will have little practical resonance? No. G8 countries are influential members of many of the multilateral institutions that are attempting to come to grips both with short-term prevention of the fire-fighting sort and with longer term prevention, often of a developmental nature, that builds up firewalls. The most prominent among these multilateral institutions is the United Nations, where four of the five permanent members of the Security Council are members of the G8 and where the other four G8 members all play a major role.

At the United Nations, Secretary General Kofi Annan has demonstrated keen interest in operationalising conflict prevention. However, this has proven to be extremely difficult because of the issue of sovereignty and the necessary intrusiveness of both short-term and long-term conflict prevention, or operational prevention and structural prevention, to use expressions introduced to the diplomatic lexicon by the Carnegie Commission on the Prevention of Deadly Conflict (1997). Preventive action is less intrusive than military intervention, but it still feels politically invasive to many of the governments involved. This creates difficulties for the UN and it creates difficulties for G8 governments when they try to act preventively here and there.[2] Nevertheless, the UN Secretariat and several of its agencies have persisted over recent years, working more with nonstate actors, not confining themselves to relations with governments, and dealing with opposition leaders in ways that, for example, the World Bank has great difficulty emulating, given the continued rather conservative prevalent interpretation of its articles of agreement. (On the other hand, the World Bank has been very good at less operational aspects of prevention, including outstanding research on the causes of conflict.[3])

This chapter reviews attempts at operationalising prevention beyond the G8 setting. It outlines conflict prevention efforts by the UN and potential prevention strategies and causes of conflict. It also discusses long-term and short-term prevention, concluding with some thoughts on how the G8 can do a more convincing job of contributing to this effort beyond the rhetoric the world has seen to date.

Conflict Prevention by the United Nations: Opportunities and Constraints

Preventing conflict is the first promise of the UN Charter.[4] And yet it has hardly been observed at all by UN member states, concerned over interference into their own affairs and over preservation of their sovereignty. In an era when the concept of sovereignty itself has been greatly eroded by the Security Council's seriously intrusive body of decisions during the 1990s, this attitude among UN member states is open to question (Malone 1997).

In the 1990s, the failure of international efforts either to forestall armed conflicts or to diminish significantly their destructive effects spurred a range of initiatives to examine more closely and creatively the opportunities for the international system's collective capacity to prevent deadly conflict, as well as the constraints upon such capacity. The UN weighed in at an early stage, making preventive diplomacy one of its four primary instruments in conflict management, along with peacemaking, peacekeeping, and peacebuilding (United Nations 1992). By now, it is generally recognised that diplomacy, *per se*, is one preventive instrument among many that need to be developed and deployed across the full spectrum of international assistance and engagement. However, even on the diplomatic front, there has been comparatively little follow-through.

In 1999–2000, the International Peace Academy launched an analytically crosscutting project on conflict prevention. Its purpose was to identify opportunities for making existing and nascent capacity for conflict prevention more effectively operational within the UN system at large.[5] It aimed to do so by examining recent quantitative and qualitative findings regarding conflict trends and their causes with a view to informing conflict prevention strategy and implementation undertaken by the host of UN departments and agencies active in this area. Although academic insights, however important, can be difficult to translate into policy, a number of important findings and conclusions can be drawn from this early work.[6]

Contrary to conventional wisdom, most research indicates that civil wars decreased in both number and magnitude from 1992 to 1998 (Gurr 2002; Wallensteen 2002).[7] This declining trend could be due to improved efforts by the international community to promote mediation of disputes, deploy force in the face of gross human rights violations, and develop post-conflict peacebuilding initiatives.[8] The trend could also be due primarily to diminishing external support. If so, the reduction in the number of conflicts probably more closely correlates to the reduction of superpower support for proxy wars and the increase in the number of democracies.

Timely response to prevent violent conflict can be difficult because it is hard to identify situations that are appropriate for preventive action. Preconceived typologies and policy responses often skew analysis. Prevention efforts thus require an in-depth understanding of the local context and the perspectives of potential belligerents. Nongovernmental organisations (NGOs) and intergovernmental organisations (IGOs) with a field presence are important partners in reaching out to these groups as well as in information gathering and mediation.

Inequitable access to basic resources and resource scarcity relating to population growth have a high likelihood of contributing to violent conflict. Conversely, a plethora of natural resources can also increase the probability and duration of violent conflict as actors seek to enrich themselves through illicit means (such as mining of conflict-supporting minerals, skimming funds of oil production, and looting of timber). The programmes of some international institutions may also have indirectly contributed to the exacerbation of horizontal inequalities, and hence to the probability of violence. Anticipating and avoiding unintended consequences within an overall context of prevention is a key challenge. This requires better strategic planning and co-ordination among international actors.

Mobilising resources for preventive action is a challenge in the absence of actual violence. Although the United Nations Security Council (UNSC) remains the primary actor for maintaining international peace and security, the Secretary General can help alter the parameters of debate regarding preventive action. That individual needs to be forceful in drawing the attention of the UNSC to specific cases requiring preventive action.

Prevention Strategies

The focus of prevention initiatives has tended to be primarily on crisis management, with a secondary emphasis on development strategies. However, it is the gestation period between these two — often of long duration — that may provide an important window of opportunity for preventive action.

Most current efforts in prevention are also isolated within a particular international organisation or sector of international actors. Yet, because the causes of conflict are interrelated and interact over what can be a protracted timeframe, effective prevention requires an integrated strategy across different sectors (diplomatic, military, political, economic, and social) and periods of engagement. Prevention can be greatly facilitated by incorporating resources and expertise from diverse international, regional, and local policy makers and implementers.

A number of prevention strategies are starting to bridge traditional divisions: complex peacekeeping operations, coercive diplomacy, targeted sanctions, aid conditionality, civil society peacebuilding, and socioeconomic approaches to development. However, attaining policy coherence and strategic co-ordination in implementation also increases in difficulty with the number of actors involved. In particular, the issue of anticipating and managing the unintended consequences of international action is very important.

Diplomatic and Political Strategies

Successful preventive diplomacy is difficult to recognise due to secrecy compounded by the problem of identifying the cause for the absence of violence in a particular situation. Thus 'lessons learned' analyses regarding preventive diplomacy become hard to codify and institutionalise. Late preventive diplomacy — crisis management — tends to be the norm, since earlier efforts by potential mediators are often perceived by states as an unacceptable breach of their sovereignty and since states are reluctant to admit a potential failure in peacefully managing their own affairs.

Membership in regional organisations and strong normative frameworks implemented within and through key international organisations can be important incentives for encouraging nonviolent behaviour by states. Similarly, denial of access or suspension of membership in international and regional organisations can also be used as a disincentive for instigating violent conflict. This has been the case with the Commonwealth, which has proved willing to implement the provisions of its Harare Declaration of 1991 (Commonwealth Secretariat 1991).

Another important diplomatic tool is the strategic authorisation of targeted sanctions. These have been dusted off for increased use since the 1990s by the UNSC. Recent analysis indicates that targeted sanctions can be a powerful disincentive toward violence when properly focussed and enforced.[9] A potential drawback is the unintended negative humanitarian impact of sanctions regimes that are not sufficiently targeted at elites and those responsible for instigating and perpetuating war. Coercive diplomacy is a potential tool for prevention but when it amounts to brinkmanship, there are obvious risks (for example, there may be a need to back up threats with force, thus escalating rather than preventing conflict).

Preventive deployment operations are an important but underutilised tool. Evaluation of successful missions (such as UNPREDEP in Macedonia, MINURCA in the Central African Republic) could provide valuable insight for future operations. The extent to which this success can be replicated depends upon a number of factors, such as the international context and the perceptions held among key member states regarding which situations are strategically important. After the departure of each of these preventive missions, both countries experienced significant violence, raising the question of whether efforts had been made to initiate meaningful peacebuilding during the deployments, without which, obviously, such operations only serve to freeze fighting, not lastingly discourage it.

Humanitarian intervention can also protect civilians and may prevent future armed conflict.[10] However, the international community is far from agreement on a universal doctrine regarding this highly selective practice. Humanitarian intervention must remain a tool of last resort. Its occurrence, in a sense, represents the failure to create and implement a broad-based political culture of prevention (see Chesterman 2001b; Sherman 2000). Nonetheless, such intervention is likely to remain a policy option in the future to forestall imminent mass human rights violations or genocide and perhaps prevent the escalation of conflict.

Development Strategies

Democratisation is a long-term process of political and cultural transformation that can effectively help build lasting peace. Generally, popular consultation and bringing actors together at the local level can help mitigate factors that might otherwise mobilise populations for the recurrence of conflict. However, poorly conducted democratisation can be destabilising, as elites hitherto in charge fight back. The risks during transition require close attention. Elections should be part of a democratisation and peacebuilding process — not just goals in themselves — with timing a delicate issue.[11]

Development assistance plays an important role in conflict prevention by focussing on the structural, root causes. In particular, sustainable development strategies offer an opportunity to attack horizontal inequalities among groups. Yet this can also be a delicate process, because efforts addressing horizontal inequalities and the host of factors that can cause violent conflict necessarily affect local political dynamics and processes. Attendant consequences include possible resistance from those benefiting from the *status quo* or the empowerment of belligerent groups that thrive off gains derived from co-opted aid channels. Systematic analysis of which actors tend to be influenced positively by aid packages and the political consequences thereof needs to be studied further.

Prevention strategies could also benefit from being mainstreamed into the development agenda. For example, the World Bank has launched a study on violent conflict and social capital with case studies of Somalia, Guatemala, Rwanda, and El Salvador in an effort to give further substance to this relatively underused pillar of prevention (Cullen and Colletta 2000). Two projects underway in Rwanda and East Timor deliberately aim to build such capital and foster communal bonds (see, for example, World Bank 1998).

Finally, prevention initiatives need to branch out. It will be important to use the media and transnational advocacy networks more effectively at an early stage to mobilise public opinion (and politicians) in support of prevention efforts.[12] Those involved in prevention need to inform themselves better on the specifics of the cases they seek to address (country- and issue-specific knowledge is often in short supply, even within very large organisations like the UN).[13]

Causes of Conflict: The Example of Zimbabwe

Understanding the causes of conflict is tremendously important. The International Peace Academy, in partnership with a number of other institutions, including the World Bank, has been engaged in extensive research and policy development on this question.[14] Some of the findings are summarised in Figure 4.1, which relates causes of conflict of various sorts, and their phasing, to the types of preventive measures international actors can take.

At the top of the funnel are permissive conditions, and these root causes for conflict are present in many societies. If most or all of them are evident, trouble is on the horizon unless a very good or lucky government is in charge (and this is rare). Bad governments, indeed bad leaders, can be found at the origin of many civil wars. This unfortunate reality needs to be borne in mind, particularly by other governments, which have often tended to lend more legitimacy to these leaders than they should have (and conversely have excessively stigmatised rebellions provoked by the policies of bad leaders). The permissive conditions include both political and economic factors. Poverty itself is not a cause of conflict. Many poor countries and territories manage themselves very well (a remarkable contemporary case is Somaliland, in Northern Somalia, recognised by no other nation in spite of its success in managing itself). Rather, poverty is often a major contributing factor.[15]

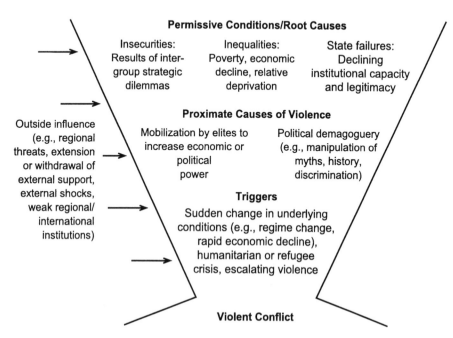

Figure 4.1   Causes of Conflict

There is then a phase of mobilisation, during which proximate causes of conflict are present. Mobilisation of elites, in attempts to increase their political and economic power, is common, as is the instrumental use of myths, history, and narratives of grievance and discrimination. The purpose is group or personal advantage.

Finally, triggers are required for conflict to break out. The two triggers that turn up the most often, in the many convincing academic studies reviewed by the International Peace Academy, are regime change of some sort and rapid economic decline.[16] Generally, by this stage, refugee and humanitarian crises are beginning to break out and violence is escalating.

Because academic approaches can seem theoretical at best, one can invoke the example of Zimbabwe, where, in fact, the permissive conditions were present as long as 15 years ago. Observers saw the proximate causes of current violence five years ago. The country is now unfortunately at the trigger phase. Interestingly, the fact that Zimbabwe is an extremely serious threat to the security of its whole region did not convince the international community, other than the Commonwealth *in extremis* in Abuja on 6 September 2001, to take any particular decisive action. The United Kingdom was left largely to its own devices in addressing the conflict. It was not ideally placed to do this, as the former colonial power. However, to its credit, it took on the problem anyway.[17]

The UK's quandary points to the very important role that neighbouring states can play (but, in the case of Zimbabwe, have not — until recently). Conflict is deeply worrying for them: it can spill into their countries and create serious destabilisation. Equally threatening, it can also suck them in, also with long-term destabilising consequences (as Uganda may have discovered in 2001 due to its adventure in Eastern Congo). Indeed, initially internal conflicts (often stoked by neighbours) have had a tendency to become regional, with alarming results. The conflict in Sierra Leone has involved Liberia almost from its outset and has spilled over into Guinea (Hirsch 2001). The implosion of Zaire sucked in Zimbabwe, Namibia, Angola, Rwanda, and Uganda. The Balkan conflicts have been metastising across the region for ten years now. One tends to think of big powers in conflict prevention, but big powers are often not interested in specific crises that do not seriously affect their interests at all. The interest of Beijing or Moscow in the Zimbabwe conflict is very limited. Even the United States has given it little priority.

The capitals that have mattered most to President Robert Mugabe in assessing strategy relative to his shrinking margin of manoeuvre and the diminishing returns of his land takeover policy have been those of Southern Africa, and one or two other African countries. It has been clear for some time that while many countries of Southern Africa were too weak to take on Mugabe, South Africa could play an important role. Due to the fragility of the sub-region, personal connections stretching back to the anti-apartheid struggle and an as-yet tentative approach to regional leadership, Pretoria was not prepared to take a decisive lead, preferring at best to act with others. Consequently, the role of Nigerian president Olusegun Obasanjo, Africa's elder statesman, became key. It is not coincidental that the possibly conclusive *dénouement* of the crisis occurred in his capital.

Importantly, the parameters of the agreement in Abuja, while concluded under considerable duress for Harare, foresee considerable financial incentives, allowing Mugabe not only to save face (to some extent) but also to achieve some of his objectives by other, more palatable means. During the 1990s, the UNSC excessively invoked punitive measures, notably sanctions, with disappointing results (Malone 2000). While incentives are more expensive for aid-fatigued donors, they are also bound to prove more successful.

Structural Prevention

Long-term structural efforts aimed at economic, political, and social developments, in order to tackle the root causes of conflict, are likely to be the most effective. Ironically, this should occur precisely when the risk of violent conflict may be least apparent, thus making national and international political mobilisation difficult for most structural prevention initiatives.

However, one should not despair. As noted above, conflict is down sharply, both in the number of incidents and in their intensity, since the end of the cold war. Conflict resolution professionals, deeply immersed in the horrors of the individual conflicts they seek to address, tend to generalise excessively on the basis of these vivid experiences. Diplomats are frequently disbelieving when confronted with statistical evidence of a sharp decline in conflicts since 1990. Any nostalgia for cold war stability should be firmly put out of mind when thinking of conflict prevention. The reality is that the world today is a much safer place than it was 15 years ago. This is even though several major inter-state conflicts persist (notably those of the Arab-Israeli theatre, although these have not been particularly murderous overall) and others have arisen, most recently between Ethiopia and Eritrea.

Scholars and research institutions surveying conflict have much to teach policy makers, much of it counterintuitive, on both the spread and the taxonomy of contemporary conflicts. Perhaps more importantly, international institutions such as the UN, the World Bank, and the Organisation for Economic Co-operation and Development (OECD) have been hard at work and productive on conflict and its prevention (United Nations 2001; World Bank 2001; OECD 2001). Even the International Monetary Fund (IMF) has been coming to terms with the relevance of threatened conflict in important client states such as Indonesia.

Donor governments also need to think with modesty, given the means at their disposal, about what aid programmes can do. Aid programmes often represent little more than a drop in the bucket financially (as in India) but they matter to governments, and in some countries they are quite significant. In countries such as Haiti and Guatemala and in territories such as East Timor and the lands controlled by the Palestinian National Authority, aid programmes loom large. In theory at least, they could help to provide inducements for governments to desist from policies that will promote conflict. That they succeed so rarely simply suggests that more thought and better design, bearing conflict prevention in mind, are required. Donor governments — including the United Kingdom, the Netherlands, Germany, Sweden, Canada, and Italy — are not thinking a lot about these issues.

Short-Term Prevention

Short-term prevention, when effective, is usually conducted at a very senior level and quietly behind the scenes. It needs to operate quickly. It generally involves several neighbouring countries, one or two major powers, often the UN Secretary General, and occasionally the head of a regional organisation. Co-ordination can be a problem but by and large, through telephone contacts, a great deal can be achieved.[18] Participants in these prevention efforts are rarely ideological in their contacts with miscreants, be they a government or rebel forces; the participants recognise that parties to a conflict in most respects behave in similar ways during civil wars and are subject to exactly the same pathologies.

Specific cases prove the point. A number of governments and international institutions brought tremendous pressure to bear on Indonesian president B.J. Habibie to allow the deployment of an international force to East Timor. This was done in close consultation with Kofi Annan in order to avert further bloodshed following mass killings in East Timor in September 1999. This pressure came not only from regional governments, including Japan, but also from the World Bank and the leadership of the U.S. armed forces. A united Security Council backed up Annan's own nonstop efforts to secure Habibie's co-operation and a UNSC mission to Jakarta seems to have achieved considerable impact on the Indonesian government. Although the slaughter in East Timor following the referendum on its future status was appalling, much worse could have followed and was averted (Martin 2001).

In Africa, although conflicts continue to rage, there is also reason for some optimism. The Organization of African Unity (OAU), now graduated into the African Union (AU), decided no longer to accommodate in its midst leaders who have come to power through undemocratic means. (The decision is harder to implement than to take, but it is certainly a step in the right direction.) African leaders are also beginning to step down rather than die in office or be forced out of it. In recent years, Abdou Diouf of Senegal withdrew after losing an election, Jerry Rawlings of Ghana did not stand again, and Frederick Chiluba of Zambia, Joaquim Chissano of Mozambique, and Eduardo dos Santos of Angola all stated they will step down at the end of their current terms. The pressure on Charles Taylor, the democratically elected president of Liberia but also an indicted war criminal, to resign in mid 2003 typified an evolution in attitudes toward African leaders by each other and by the broader international community. Julius Nyeyere of Tanzania demonstrated convincingly during the late 1980s and 1990s that there could be life after the presidency, in fact proving much more useful than he had been as a leader. Others now seem willing to follow his lead.[19] Although these developments, extremely positive for future stability in Africa, may be part of the

Zeitgeist, they have not come about without significant international and domestic pressure. Indeed, gestures as small as offering Rawlings a post as a UN goodwill ambassador may have contributed to making life after the presidency more attractive to him. This type of preventive initiative is significant because, although modest, it is doubtless at least moderately effective.

Significant regional successes have also been achieved, largely in Latin America.[20] Latin Americans in the past decade have proven quite good at managing their own affairs. They generally do not want the UN involved in their problems, international or domestic, and they feel much the same way about the Organization of American States (OAS). However, sometimes through informal regional arrangements, when Latin American states face a crisis they are quite good at producing solutions. One example is provided by the Ecuador-Peru conflict that went on for 150 years and ended (by treaty) in the late 1990s thanks to active intermediation by neighbouring countries and the United States.

The OAS took a major step toward entrenching systemic prevention into its culture in 1991 with the Santiago Declaration, its implementing resolution, and a number of applications since.[21] Only months after the declaration's adoption, the OAS took strong measures to attempt to reverse the *coup d'état* that had overthrown Jean-Bertrand Aristide in Haiti.[22] The following year, the OAS condemned undemocratic manoeuvres by Peruvian president Alberto Fujimori, compelling him to appear before an OAS meeting and subsequently to reverse course. In 1983, OAS Secretary General João Clemente Baena Soares worked hard and effectively to reverse a *coup d'état* in Guatemala, almost single-handedly turning the tide. In 1986, OAS Secretary General César Gaviria flew to Paraguay to stand alongside the besieged legitimate president, subjected to a *coup d'état* in slow motion. Even more decisive was the message from Paraguay's economic partners in the sub-regional MERCOSUR trading bloc that they would not deal with a military junta in Asuncion. The new OAS standards, and actions to enforce them, have not always been successful in discouraging less blatant erosions of democratic freedoms in Latin America. But they do stand as a bulwark against gross abuses and serve as an example to other regions, an example the AU has subsequently taken up.[23] Furthermore, OAS member states are co-operating to strengthen their existing normative framework to promote democracy, in part by adopting the new Democracy Charter in 2001 (OAS 2001).

Conclusion

In sum, preventive action is much discussed but little practised. However, a number of recent developments hold some promise that the cynics may yet be confounded. These include determined efforts by Sweden, when holding the presidency of the European Union, to focus attention on the need for prevention (at both its early structural stages and in its late diplomatic phases). These efforts seem to be impressing themselves on the international psyche, and may yet mobilise the EU (among others) to act meaningfully in preventive ways.

Strong advocacy by UN Secretary General Kofi Annan for preventive action is at least embarrassing its opponents. However, efforts by the UN Secretariat to establish an effective unit for the analysis of information have run into heavy weather generated by countries worried that the UN might seek to develop its own intelligence capacity (a far-fetched source of anxiety, given both the UN's limited resources and the reluctance of national intelligence agencies to share much of any real use with the world body).[24] There is also, as already noted, growing interest in the causes of conflict and in their prevention at the World Bank.[25] More generally, but — ominously — more vaguely, a sense exists that military intervention to address conflicts once they have broken out is neither affordable nor feasible in a world where the role and resources of governments (and militaries) are shrinking.

Where does this leave the G8? It clearly does not have a large operational role in conflict prevention.[26] However, it has sought to carve out for itself a leadership role in spurring normative development on this topic. The launch of discussions under German leadership in 1999 was successful, insofar as it was serious, and drew on the best expertise. Japan, when in the G8 chair the following year, alas, seemed as interested in window-dressing as in serious progress on the issue. With Italy's chairmanship, serious work and discussions resumed in 2001.[27] The issue has long been of interest to the Canadian government. This generates optimism that the G8 will continue to pursue serious reflection on conflict prevention.

The significance of G8 interest in addressing the prevention of violent conflict lies, as posited at the outset, in the clout of individual G8 members within other forums. They can influence the key multilateral economic actors — the IMF, the World Bank, the OECD, the regional development banks, and also the UN economic agencies — to be more sensitive to conflict considerations in their planning. They can also spawn initiatives of their own. The ongoing intergovernmental work on conflict diamonds owes much to the role of Robert Fowler, when he was Canada's ambassador to the UN, in tackling diamond trafficking and sanctions busting by UNITA in Angola, within the UNSC. This Canadian initiative spurred other analytical work on the role of economic looting by external actors in the continuing implosion of the Democratic Republic of the Congo. This and other work on sanctions busting in Sierra Leone and Liberia was commissioned by the UNSC. The G8 has also developed an interest in conflict diamonds.

The Kananaskis G8 Summit of 2002 grappled with Africa's multiple security and development crises — for the first time as a G8 priority — as well as with emerging African and other responses thereto, notably the New Partnership for Africa's Development (NEPAD). Fowler's personal involvement, not only as chair of the leaders' Personal Representatives for Africa (APRs), but also as the sherpa of the host country (traditionally a position carrying with it considerable latitude for influencing the G8 agenda as a whole) was tremendously helpful in shaping meaningful discussions among the G8 members and also between them and several NEPAD leaders.

The G7 and G8 have frequently initiated or accelerated work on the international regulatory framework for economic transactions and crimes (such as narco-trafficking and money laundering) in other forums. The relationship between economic activity under cover of violent conflict and the perpetuation of these conflicts is now well understood. During the 1990s, tremendous strides were made in developing an international legal regime to address crimes against humanity, genocide, and massive human rights violations, through the creation of international criminal tribunals (for the former Yugoslavia and Rwanda) and an agreement on the statute for the International Criminal Court. Developing countries, particularly those in Africa, point to the enrichment of brokers and other intermediaries, as well as of large corporations and banks in the industrialised world, on the backs of war-affected African populations. It may now be time for the G8 to consider whether the international regulatory framework sufficiently addresses economic activity financing conflict, and whether an international legal regime may be required to address white collar crime related to conflict. The G8's support for policy work on conflict diamonds and the Kimberley Process was helpful but clearly addresses only a very small part of this disturbing issue. The International Peace Academy intends to advance concrete proposals on these issues in years ahead.

Notes

1   In this, they have been unlike the statements of G7 finance ministers, whose statements, particularly during the mid 1980s — the heyday of attempts to achieve international economic co-ordination — could move markets powerfully.
2   In a mid-2001 address to the General Assembly and to the Security Council, the UN Secretary General released a seminal report on conflict prevention that discusses some of these difficulties (United Nations 2001).
3   See the World Bank's project on the Economics of Civil Wars, Crime and Violence, led by Paul Collier (World Bank 2003).
4   The UN Charter reads at its outset: 'The Purposes of the United Nations are: 1. To maintain international peace and security, and to that end: to take effective collective measures for the prevention and removal of threats to the peace, and for the suppression of acts of aggression or other breaches of the peace, and to bring about by peaceful means, and in conformity with the principles of justice and international law, adjustment or settlement of international disputes or situations which might lead to a breach of the peace' (United Nations 1945, ch. 1, art. 1).
5   This project, 'From Reaction to Prevention: Opportunities for the UN System in the New Millennium', was originally funded by the government of Sweden. The governments of the United Kingdom, Germany, the Netherlands, Portugal, and Italy have since joined Sweden in supporting it financially. See the International Peace Academy at <www.ipacademy.org>.
6   A useful methodology for building bridges between the research community and policy makers could be borrowed from the War-Torn Societies Project. For an assessment of their initial impact, see War-Torn Societies Project (1999). For their current follow-up work, see <www.wsp-international.org>.
7   A slight rise recorded by some researchers since 1998 suggests two questions: Was the mid-1990s decrease an aberration in an overall upward trend recorded since 1945? Or is the post-1998 increase an anomaly in an overall downward trend of the post–cold war era?

8 In the past ten years, 30 percent of conflicts ended with peace agreements — more than during any other decade in the past 50 years.

9 For a sophisticated discussion of various sanctions regimes mandated by the UNSC in the 1990s, see Cortright and Lopez (2000), They found a number of these sanctions regimes to have been effective, at least initially, but argue that sanctions are most useful when seen as an instrument to induce bargaining and compromise. Cortright and Lopez say that without diplomatic give and take, sanctions are unlikely to achieve their stated objectives, and have published a follow-up volume (Cortright and Lopez 2002).

10 On this complex issue, see Chesterman (2001a) and Nabulsi (2000), as well as the reports produced by the People on War project of the International Committee of the Red Cross, available online at <www.icrc.org>.

11 The Institute for Democratic and Electoral Assistance in Stockholm has produced outstanding work in this area. See Harris and Reilly (1998).

12 A useful discussion of the role of international policy networks, as opposed to transnational advocacy networks, can be found in Reinicke and Deng (2000).

13 One such initiative, the creation in November 2000 of the Conflict Prevention and Peace Forum, a small New York–based institution aiming to make available to the UN the best international expertise on impending crises of urgent concern, has been funded by the Department for International Development of the UK government. Key to this initiative's success is whether the UN Secretariat and agencies, and also Security Council members, actually wish to draw on expert knowledge and opinion. The jury will be out for some time.

14 See 'From Promise to Practice: Strengthening UN Capacities for the Prevention of Violent Conflict'.

15 There is much loose talk in the development community about poverty being the principal or only cause of conflict, and this needs to be debunked at every turn.

16 Regime change can come about as a result of peace negotiations and a settlement. Too little understood is the fragility of societies in the wake of peace settlements, when conflict is most likely to break out again (see Stedman, Rothchild, and Cousens 2002; Stedman 2001).

17 The UN did try an initiative based on incentive rather than punishment. The head of the UN Development Programme, Mark Malloch Brown, travelled to Harare early in 2001 and attempted to induce Robert Mugabe to change course, but the crisis may not have yet been ripe for resolution. This potentially important mission also received too little regional and international support. On the concept of ripeness, see Zartman (1975) and Haas (1990).

18 See Sriram (2001), who distils a retreat with Security Council members and some others.

19 The Washington-based NGO Global Coalition for Africa, for example, has launched a programme under which retired African heads of state encourage those in office to follow their example. For more information, see <www.gca-cma.org>.

20 Nevertheless, limited capacity constrains most regional organisations as actors for prevention. Although nearby states have a clear national interest in preventing conflicts within the region, potentially making them important providers of necessary resources for regional action, these resources are often in the hands of actors that are either interested in fuelling conflict or who are ambivalent about resolving it.

21 The OAS's 'Santiago Commitment to Democracy and the Renewal of the Inter-American System' established that representative democracy is an indispensable condition for the stability, peace, and development of the region. It also emphasised the importance of the consolidation of democratic processes and the need to promote disarmament, international peace, and security. This was followed four years later by the Santiago Declaration, which contained 11 measures agreed by the states to build confidence, dialogue, and the exchange of views on hemispheric security matters.

22 The OAS measures, essentially a voluntary trade embargo against Haiti, proved insufficiently robust. Eventually more draconian and universal UN measures were required, including

authorisation of a coalition of countries prepared to use force, before Aristide was restored to power in 1994 (Malone 1998).

23 The OAS was subsequently involved again with Peru, at the time of the unsatisfactory presidential elections of 2000 and in the period that followed, and over an extended period of time in Ecuador, due to extreme turbulence in the democratic processes of that country in 1998–99.

24 See United Nations (2000), specifically the proposal relating the establishment of an ECPS Information and Strategic Analysis Secretariat proposed in paragraphs 65 to 75. Also see Crossette (2000).

25 See World Bank (2001); see also the list of their publications on this topic at <lnweb18.worldbank.org/ESSD/sdvext.nsf/67ByDocName/Publications>.

26 During discussions at a conference held by the University of Toronto's G8 Research Group and the Istituto Affari Internazionali in Rome, 17 July 2001, involving both G8 practitioners and scholars, there was unanimity that the G8 is not well equipped or disposed to address individual situations requiring preventive action.

27 Of the two issues Italy succeeded in getting the G8 foreign ministers to address in their conclusions in Rome in 2001, the role of corporate actors in fuelling (and potentially mitigating) conflict was by far the more convincing. To Italy's credit, this topic was retained in spite of U.S. resistance. The second topic, gender issues in conflict prevention, smacked of political correctness more than of substantive drive. Gender issues can be extremely important in conflict and its prevention, but the G8 did not reach very deeply into the question.

References

Carnegie Commission on Preventing Deadly Conflict (1997). 'Preventing Deadly Conflict: Final Report'. Carnegie Commission on Preventing Deadly Conflict, Washington DC.

Chesterman, Simon, ed. (2001a). *Civilians in War*. Lynne Rienner, Boulder, CO.

Chesterman, Simon (2001b). *Just War or Just Peace? Humanitarian Intervention and International Law*. Oxford University Press, Oxford.

Commonwealth Secretariat (1991). 'The Harare Commonwealth Declaration, 1991'. 20 October. <www.thecommonwealth.org/whoweare/declarations/harare.html> (July 2003).

Cortright, David and George Lopez (2000). *The Sanctions Decade: Assessing UN Sanctions in the 1990s*. Lynne Rienner, Boulder, CO.

Cortright, David and George Lopez (2002). *Sanctions and the Search for Security: Challenges to UN Action*. Lynne Rienner, Boulder, CO.

Crossette, Barbara (2000). 'UN Plan for a New Crisis Unit Opposed by Wary Poor Nations'. *New York Times*, 26 November.

Cullen, Michelle L. and Nat J. Colletta (2000). *Violent Conflict and the Transformation of Social Capital: Lessons from Cambodia, Rwanda, Guatemala, and Somalia*. World Bank, Washington DC.

Gurr, Ted Robert (2002). 'Containing Internal War in the Twenty-First Century'. In F. O. Hampson and D. M. Malone, eds., *From Reaction to Conflict Prevention: Opportunities for the UN System*, pp. 41–62. Lynne Rienner, Boulder, CO.

Haas, Richard (1990). *Conflicts Unending*. Yale University Press, New Haven.

Hampson, Fen Osler and David M. Malone (2002). *From Reaction to Conflict Prevention: Opportunities for the UN System*. Lynne Rienner, Boulder, CO.

Harris, Peter and Ben Reilly, eds. (1998). *Democracy and Deep-Rooted Conflict: Options for Negotiators*. Institute for Democratic and Electoral Assistance, Stockholm.

Hirsch, John (2001). *Sierre Leone: Diamonds and the Struggle for Democracy*. Lynne Reinner, Boulder, CO, and London.

Malone, David M. (1997). 'The UN Security Council in the Post–Cold War World, 1987–97'. *Security Dialogue* vol. 28, no. 4, pp. 393–404.

Malone, David M. (1998). *Decision-Making in the UN Security Council: The Case of Haiti*. Clarendon Press, Oxford.

Malone, David M. (2000). 'The UN Security Council in the 1990s: Inconsistent, Improvisational, Indispensable?' In R. Thakur and E. Newman, eds., *New Millennium, New Perspectives: The United Nations, Security, and Governance*, pp. 21–45. United Nations University Press, Tokyo.

Martin, Ian (2001). *Self-Determination in East Timor: The United Nations, the Ballot, and International Intervention*. Lynne Rienner, Boulder, CO.

Nabulsi, Karma (2000). *Traditions of War*. Oxford University Press, Oxford.

Organisation for Economic Co-operation and Development (2001). 'Helping Prevent Violent Conflict: Orientations for External Partners'. Development Assistance Committee policy statement. <www1.oecd.org/dac/htm/conf.htm> (July 2003).

Organization of American States (2001). 'Promotion of Democracy'. 5 June. AG/RES. 1782 (XXXI-O/01). <www.oas.org/juridico/english/ga01/agres1782.htm> (July 2003).

Reinicke, Wolfgang and Francis Deng (2000). *Critical Choices: The United Nations, Networks, and the Future of Global Governance*. International Development Research Centre, Ottawa.

Sherman, Jake (2000). 'Humanitarian Action: A Symposium Summary'. International Peace Academy, New York.

Sriram, Chandra Lekha (2001). 'From Promise to Practice: Strengthening UN Capacities for the Prevention of Violent Conflict'. Report on a workshop held at West Point, New York, February 2001. International Peace Academy, <www.ipacademy.org/Publications/Reports/Research/PublRepoResePPUNCapacities_body.htm> (July 2003).

Stedman, Stephen John (2001). 'Implementing Peace Agreements in Civil Wars: Lessons and Recommendations for Policymakers'. International Peace Academy, New York.

Stedman, Stephen John, Donald Rothchild, and Elizabeth Cousens, eds. (2002). *Ending Civil Wars: The Implementation of Peace Agreements*. Lynne Rienner, Boulder, CO.

United Nations (1945). 'Charter of the United Nations'. <www.un.org/aboutun/charter> (July 2003).

United Nations (1992). 'An Agenda for Peace: Preventive Diplomacy, Peacemaking, and Peace-keeping'. A/47/277-S/24111. 17 June. <www.un.org/Docs/SG/agpeace.html> (July 2003).

United Nations (2000). 'Report on the Panel on United Nations Peace Operations'. 21 August. A/55/305-S/2000/809. <www.un.org/peace/reports/peace_operations> (July 2003).

United Nations (2001). 'Prevention of Armed Conflict: Report of the Secretary General. Executive Summary'. A/55/985-S/2001/574. 7 June. United Nations, New York. <daccess-ods.un.org/TMP/7047019.html> (July 2003).

Wallensteen, Peter (2002). 'Reassessing Recent Conflicts: Direct vs. Structural Prevention'. In F. O. Hampson and D. M. Malone, eds., *From Reaction to Conflict Prevention: Opportunities for the UN System*, pp. 213–228. Lynne Rienner, Boulder, CO.

War-Torn Societies Project (1999). 'War-Torn Societies Project: The First Four Years'. Geneva.

World Bank (1998). 'Building Trust to Rebuild Rwanda'. News Release No. 99/2003/AFR. <www.worldbank.org/html/extdr/extme/2003.htm> (July 2003).

World Bank (2001). 'Conflict Prevention and Reconstruction'. O.P. 2.30, <lnweb18.worldbank.org/ESSD/sdvext.nsf/67ByDocName/PoliciesandStrategiesDevelopmentCooperationandConflictOP230> (July 2003).

World Bank (2003). 'The Economics of Civil War, Crime, and Violence'. <econ.worldbank.org/programs/conflict> (July 2003).

Zartman, I. William (1975). *Ripe for Resolution*. Oxford University Press, New York.

Chapter 5

The G8 and Conflict Prevention: Commitment, Compliance, and Systemic Contributions

John J. Kirton, Ella Kokotsis, and Gina Stephens, with Diana Juricevic

Since 1999, the G8 has moved rapidly to focus on conflict prevention as a new and substantial component of its agenda, action, and achievements. Starting with the 1999 Cologne Summit and preceding foreign ministers meetings, the G8 maintained the momentum through the December 1999 Berlin foreign ministers meeting, the first ever in G8 history devoted to a single theme, to July 2000, when the foreign ministers at Miyazaki and the leaders at Okinawa moved from agenda setting to action, authorising concrete measures in five core areas. From this firm foundation many looked to Genoa in 2001, to Kananaskis in 2002, to Evian in 2003, and ahead to subsequent summits to build an edifice that would change the international security system as a whole.

Whether the G8 will make this large systemic contribution depends critically on just how potent it has been in advancing conflict prevention in these few short years. There is room for considerable doubt about both its performance and potential (Kühne and Prantl 2000). Many argue that the venerable, established United Nations, replete with a formal charter, big budget, and massive bureaucracy all its own, should be the dominant actor in conflict prevention, as in all other peace and security tasks. Indeed, the powerful Permanent Five (P5) members of the United Nations Security Council (UNSC) may well end any effort to dilute its special status through the construction of a separate, G8-based security institution. Other critics of the G8 charge it with having only an episodic interest in most subjects, implying that the 1999 concern with conflict prevention inspired by Kosovo and Germany will quickly pass as other political priorities and summit hosts exert their pull. Still others see the G7/8 as essentially an economic institution with a limited claim to newer global or transnational issues, and thus a body poorly equipped, intellectually and institutionally, to deal with any security subject. And even those who credit the G7/8 system with considerable ability to arrive at timely, well-tailored commitments across a wide array of issue areas, still call into question how ambitious and significant its collective commitments are, and whether its member countries will comply with them in the months and years after each annual summit ends.

In order to assess the potential of the G8 as a productive forum for advancing the conflict prevention agenda, it is important to examine in detail its recent record in generating commitments and compliance in the specific issue area of conflict prevention, in the political-security domain more generally, and across its agenda as a whole. This chapter thus conducts a systematic evaluation of the commitments made at the leaders level at Okinawa 2000, Genoa 2001, and Kananaskis 2002, and the compliance of its members with them, in comparison with their previous commitment and compliance record. To do so it employs a method for identifying commitments and assessing compliance developed by Ella Kokotsis, a method for assessing the ambition and significance of those commitments created by Diana Juricevic, and data produced by the G8 Research Group under the co-ordination of Gina Stephens. The chapter first examines the number and ambition-significance of the Okinawa, Genoa, Kananaskis, and Evian commitments as a whole, in the political-security domain and in the conflict prevention area. It then assesses how well G8 members complied with their commitments from 2000 to 2003, how this compliance record compares with that of the previous five and twenty-five years, and whether members comply with the particular commitments that count. With this foundation, analysts and policy makers alike can ask why and how the G8 institution works to make and keep meaningful promises, and thus how it can best be used and reformed to promote the cause of conflict prevention in the wider world.

The Commitment Record

Okinawa 2000

The 2000 G7/8 summit held in Okinawa, Japan, was only the second to deal directly and comprehensively with conflict prevention. To what extent did it produce timely, well-tailored, and ambitious collective decisions, or commitments, in this field, as part of its overall work? In addressing this question, it is important to recall that the summits perform many valuable functions, starting with their core deliberative, directional, and decisional roles. Indeed, at the early stages of dealing with new issue areas, such as conflict prevention, their most important function can be the deliberative one of setting the agenda, educating their peers about the subject and its importance, and securing attention for it, and the directional one of establishing and legitimising the issue area, identifying its priority, and establishing the principles that will and should guide its treatment and its relationship with cognate areas. Making actual collective decisions, through the declaration of identifiable, specific, future-oriented, actionable, and measurable commitments in the concluding communiqué, is thus not the only indication of the recent G7/8's contribution to the conflict prevention cause, or even necessarily the most important one. However, in an international political world awash in high-level rhetoric, and badly in need of real action on conflict prevention, the G7/8's decisional record, even at this early stage of its contribution, is of important concern.

In overall terms, the 2000 G7/8 Summit proved to be a most productive meeting, judged by the number and range of decisional commitments made by the leaders in their concluding communiqués.[1] Together, the five documents issued by the leaders at Okinawa offered 169 such commitments (see Table 5.1). Of these, 12 came in the

Table 5.1   G7/8 Commitments by Issue Area, 2000–2002

Issue	Okinawa 2000	Genoa 2001	Kananaskis 2002
World economy	1	1	–
International financial system	6	5	–
Microeconomics			
Globalisation			–
Employment	–	1	–
Education	–	7	–
Ageing	6	–	
Information and communications technology	57	3	–
Trade	4	2	–
Development	15	12	2
Debt relief	9	7	4
Health	15	3	–
Energy	–	–	
Environment	11	9	–
Biotech/Food safety	3	2	–
Nuclear safety/Ukraine	2	–	–
Cultural diversity	2	–	–
Refugees	–	–	–
Human rights	–	–	–
East–West relations	–	–	–
Transition economies	–	–	
Multilateral institutions	–	–	
Crime and drugs	18	2	–
Terrorism	4	–	3
Arms control/Disarmament	7	–	23
Regional issues	–	2	2
Middle East	2	–	–
Africa	2	2	136
Asia Pacific	–	–	–
Europe	2	–	
Conflict prevention	3		
Transport security			19
Total	169	58	189

Note: A dash (–) indicates that the issue was discussed but no commitments appeared in the communiqué.

G7 communiqué, 97 in the G8 communiqué (where Russia joined the original seven), 54 in the G8's separate Okinawa Charter on Global Information Society, and six in the G8 Statement on Regional Issues. The fifth document issued by the leaders, the *G8 Statement on the Korean Peninsula*, contained no actual commitments. In the four documents containing commitments, the commitments were distributed across 18 issue areas, as indicated in the table.

The number of commitments by issue area in the two main G7 and G8 communiqués suggests that the Okinawa Summit had as its main focus and legacy co-operative achievements in the areas of crime and drugs, development, and health, particularly infectious disease. Combining the last two areas, it was thus genuinely a development-oriented summit.

The 54 commitments in the Okinawa Charter on Global Information Society, especially if combined with the three commitments on information and communications technology (ICT) in the G8 communiqué, suggest that Okinawa was also the first G7 digital summit. Yet the heavy emphasis, in this separate charter, on 'Bridging the Digital Divide', led by the 11 commitments specifically under this heading, suggests that development was a primary focus here too.

The 14 commitments in the G8 communiqué that dealt with the political-security subjects of conflict prevention, disarmament, nonproliferation, arms control, and terrorism, together with the six commitments in the Statement on Regional Security, reveal that Okinawa was also a political-security summit. It contained a total of 20 commitments in this realm. Political-security commitments thus took 12 percent of the total. While this may appear to be a small share, it is significant for a G7/8 that developed its formal political-security agenda and supporting process later than others, and that has seen some of its members, notably France, insist that the prerogatives of the G7/8 should not infringe on the UNSC in this domain. Okinawa's commitments on the particular issue areas relating to regional security embraced the three regions of the Middle East, the Balkans, and Africa equally. Perhaps due to the sensitivities of Japan's regional neighbours, no commitments were made on the Korean Peninsula, either in these documents or in the separate statement issued on this subject.

With 169 commitments overall, Okinawa was by far the most decisionally productive summit to that time (Fratianni, Savona, and Kirton 2003, Appendix C). Earlier work by Kokotsis (1999) has shown that the summits from 1989 to 1995 produced a yearly average of 4.8 commitments on climate change, 2.1 on biodiversity, 1.6 on developing country debt (from 1988 to 1995), and 3.5 on assistance to Russia (from 1990 to 1995). A comparison of similar issue areas at Okinawa shows that the G7/8 in 2000 was considerably more productive on developing country debt, much less productive on assistance to Russia (with an economy that was then doing relatively well), and somewhat less productive on climate change and biodiversity. This again confirms the development focus of Okinawa.

Okinawa's political-security agenda offered commitments arranged by issue area as follows: disarmament seven, terrorism four, and conflict prevention three, with nuclear safety/Ukraine, the Middle East peace process, the Balkans, and Africa having two each. Of the non–political-security issue areas dealt with at Okinawa, only five were able to secure higher numbers of commitments, reaffirming Okinawa's status as a genuinely political-security summit in addition to being a development-oriented one.[2]

On conflict prevention more specifically, the foreign ministers at Miyazaki and the leaders at Okinawa authorised action in five core areas: small arms, diamonds, children in conflict, civilian policing, and conflict and development. Recognising that proceeds from the illicit trade in diamonds had contributed to armed conflict and humanitarian crises in Africa, the leaders made their strongest commitment here. They called for an international conference that would consider 'practical approaches to breaking the link between the illicit trade in diamonds and armed conflict, including consideration of an international agreement on certification for rough diamonds' (G8 2000).[3] Their success in fulfilling this important commitment in the post-Okinawa period is addressed below.

Genoa 2001

In keeping with the Okinawa Summit format, the Italian presidency in 2001 strove to limit the agenda at Genoa to three key themes. It chose poverty reduction, the global environment, and conflict prevention. This focus enabled the documents issued by the leaders to be kept relatively short. Genoa generated six documents, including the G8 communiqué, the G7 statement, and four one-page statements — for a total of 15 pages. This marked a notable reduction in the length of leaders-level documentation (Takase 2002). Despite the low volume of documentation, coupled with the distractions of mass civil society protest and the resulting death in Genoa, the leaders made 58 specific, future-oriented measurable commitments in their G7 and G8 communiqués (see Table 5.1). Of these, 10 came in the G7 statement, 43 in the G8 communiqué, two in the G8 Statement on Regional Issues, two in the Genoa Plan for Africa, and one in the Statement by the G8 (Death in Genoa). Although the total of 58 commitments was somewhat below the norm for summits of the fourth seven-year cycle, which began at Lyon in 1996, it exceeded the totals produced by summits in most previous years. The Genoa commitments covered 13 different issue areas, a range slightly smaller than Okinawa 2000 but broader in scope than summits in earlier years.

Moreover, what Genoa lacked in volume it made up for in concentration. Genoa was again a development-oriented summit. Indeed, a full 34 of the 58 commitments (or 59 percent of the total) were contained within the Strategic Approach to Poverty Reduction. Nine more commitments devoted to global environmental issues gave Genoa an overwhelming focus on sustainable development. However, in sharp contrast to the 12 percent at the Okinawa Summit, at Genoa the leaders offered only four commitments, or 7 percent, to political-security issues. They concentrated on crime, drugs, and regional security concerns. Political issues thus had a much lower resonance at this summit, especially as they were dealt with in separate statements on the Middle East and regional issues, rather than within the text of the final G8 communiqué. Commitments that related specifically to conflict prevention fell within the broader context of the Genoa Plan for Africa.

In their meetings, the G8 leaders reaffirmed their foreign ministers' conclusions on political-security issues, reached at the latter's meeting in Rome on 18–19 July. Having defined conflict prevention as a cornerstone of the Genoa Summit, the Italian presidency sought to continue the process begun by the G8 foreign ministers at Berlin in 1999 and continued at Miyazaki in 2000. In Rome, the foreign ministers reaffirmed their commitment to conflict prevention as an 'indispensable element' in their 'international actions and initiatives'. They noted their continued support for action in the five areas identified for Miyazaki — small arms, diamonds, children in conflict, civilian policing, and conflict and development. They added two new initiatives: 'the contribution of women in the prevention of violent conflict and the role of the private sector' (see Appendix D). With respect to women and conflict resolution, the ministers emphasised the importance of the 'systematic involvement of women in the prevention of conflict and resolution of conflicts and in peace-building, as well as women's full and equal participation in all phases of conflict prevention, resolution and peacebuilding'. Given that economic factors frequently serve as instruments of conflict, the ministers argued that the private sector had a tremendous impact in conflict-prone zones and that through 'good citizenship', the private sector could play 'an important and positive role in conflict prevention and post-conflict reconstruction' (see Appendix D, Attachment 1).

Overall, however, the foreign ministers and the leaders at Genoa seemed more interested in specific cases of conflict, particularly within the African context, than in conflict prevention more generally. They did single out their initiative on conflict and development, within which disarmament, demobilisation, and reintegration (DDR) as well as co-operation on water management would receive special attention. As such, the Italians left Genoa rather pleased with the strong conflict prevention component of the Genoa Plan for Africa — a plan that, thanks to the direct contacts of the G8 with African leaders, laid out some very important initiatives. This included a promise from the G8 to assist Africa on a wide range of development activities. On conflict prevention specifically, the leaders noted that although significant progress had been made on this issue in several parts of Africa, 'in many places, conflict remain[ed] a major obstacle to economic and social development'. The leaders thus urged 'continued commitment to conflict prevention, management and resolution by the international community in partnership with African governments, the African Union and sub-regional organizations' (G8 2001). Noting that their partnership would support the key themes of the African initiative — including 'prevention and reduction of conflict' — the strongest commitment from the G8 came on the designation by each member of a high-level personal representative to prepare an 'action plan' for Africa for endorsement at the 2002 Canadian-hosted summit at Kananaskis.

Kananaskis 2002

Despite Kananaskis being the shortest summit in recent G7/8 history, in overall terms it proved to be the most productive summit ever, if judged by the number of commitments produced. The five documents issued at Kananaskis together produced 189 commitments: 12 within the Chair's Statement, 3 within the Enhanced HIPC Initiative, 19 on Transport Security, 23 on the Global Partnership against the Spread of Weapons and Materials of Mass Destruction, and 132 on the Africa Action Plan. Kananaskis, in fact, proved to be a summit of singular focus, for its commitments covered only five broad issue areas in all. Not only did it promise to bring to Africa both enduring development and democratic governance, but it also devoted 70 percent of its commitments to African concerns.[4] A full 25 percent of the 189 commitments were on political-security subjects. The portion rises to 33 percent if the 16 commitments on conflict prevention within the G8 Africa Action Plan (representing 8 percent of the 189 total) are added to the list.

The 11 September 2001 terrorist attacks on North America elevated political-security concerns, in the pre-Summit ministerials and at the Summit itself, to a level not seen at Okinawa and Genoa. Meeting in Whistler, British Columbia, on 12–13 June 2002, the G8 foreign ministers stressed the importance of preventing and combating terrorism by releasing the Progress Report on the Fight against Terrorism, as well as a series of G8 Recommendations on Counter-Terrorism.[5] Recognising the inextricable link between conflict and sustainable development (particularly within the African context), the foreign ministers issued two stand-alone documents on this issue: G8 Conflict Prevention: Disarmament, Demobilisation, and Reintegration and the G8 Initiative on Conflict and Development. The former built on the commitment made at Genoa to focus 'special attention' on DDR in post-conflict situations. Here, the ministers noted that 'the availability of weapons and the resulting insecurity can have an adverse effect (both humanitarian and socio-economic) on the stability and development of a country', and that 'weapons clearly need to be under the strictest of control and where appropriate, destroyed' (see Appendix O). The ministers further pledged to support such programmes by offering 'national expertise to strengthen the planning and implementation of activities as part of a coherent and comprehensive [DDR] plan'.

Building on their pledge at Miyazaki and Rome to consider water management, in the G8 Initiative on Conflict and Development the foreign ministers focussed on promoting co-operative and sustainable management of water resources by linking the potential for conflict with environmental and resource issues. Recognising that sound water management could reduce the potential for water-related conflicts, the G8 committed to the need to reinforce efforts aimed at preventing water shortages through a number of initiatives, including the use of development assistance to 'promote integrated water resource management and good governance in the field of shared water' (see Appendix N).

Along with combating terrorism, at Kananaskis the G8 leaders chose issues of sustaining global growth as well as development in Africa for the cornerstones of their discussions. With only 30 hours to deal with some of the most pressing international issues of the day, the meetings at the leaders' level remained very concentrated. Day one centred on finance issues, trade liberalisation, sustainable development, universal primary education, terrorism, and regional security (primarily in the Middle East and in India and Pakistan). Day two looked almost exclusively at Africa, as African leaders themselves were brought into the discussions for the first time as full partners.[6] This fulfilled the promise made at Genoa to focus on Africa at Kananaskis. In response to the New Plan for Africa's Development (NEPAD) and as a direct follow-up to their commitments made in the Genoa Plan for Africa, the leaders at Kananaskis launched the G8 Africa Action Plan, intended to build on NEPAD's principles of peace, order, and good governance as the basis for strong economic and social development. Noting their optimism about the plan and stating that it marked a historic turning point, African leaders declared the plan an important component in building democracy and development, as it concentrated specifically on those priorities essential to Africa and its people.

Because peace and democratic stability are critical prerequisites for economic growth and sustainable development, the G8 Africa Action Plan devoted an entire section to peace and security. In it, the leaders resolved to make conflict prevention a 'top priority'. They pledged to support African efforts to resolve the principal armed conflicts on the continent. They made 16 commitments to issues related to conflict prevention. By committing to provide technical and financial assistance so that African countries could engage more effectively to prevent and resolve violent conflict, the G8 undertook one of its most ambitious commitments — to 'train African peace support forces, including through the development of regional centres of excellence for military and civilian aspects of conflict prevention and peace support, such as the Kofi Annan International Peace Training Centre' (G8 2002). This commitment, if successfully implemented, would serve as a critical element in the promotion of peace on the African continent. It would enable Africa to deal with its own conflict prevention through the establishment of a future African peacekeeping force.

Evian 2003

Because the 2003 Evian Summit took place in the immediate aftermath of the divisive, U.S.-led coalition invasion of Iraq in the spring of 2003, there was less scope to deal with conflict prevention, either at the G8 foreign ministers meeting in Paris on 23 May or at the Summit itself at Evian on 1–3 June 2003. The Evian Summit generated a new high of 207 commitments, delivered in 13 separate documents embracing a very wide array of issue areas. Of these, 63 commitments (30 percent) were political-security commitments contained in the four documents on weapons of mass destruction, on radiological materials, on manportable surface-to-air missiles (MANPADS), and on terrorism. Here, as elsewhere, very few commitments dealt with conflict prevention as it had been defined at the G8 during the previous four years. Despite the fact that the latest phase of the raging, deadly civil war in the Congo captured headlines in ways that would normally have brought conflict prevention into the heart of a French-hosted G8 summit, the imperative of conflict response, both in the case of Iraq in 2003 and in the broader case of 11 September 2001, crowded the subject out.

The Ambition and Significance of Summit Commitments

In order to attain a more refined understanding of the importance of the summit commitments, it is important to assess their ambition and significance. In the framework developed by Diana Juricevic, an ambitious commitment is one that clearly identifies a goal to be met, measures to attain that goal, and a target date by which that goal is to be completed. A significant commitment is one that is timely and novel, and has appropriate scope (see Appendix 5.1). An application of this framework indicates that the Okinawa Summit, with an average score of 2.8 by equally weighted issue areas and 2.69 by individual commitments, came close to the midpoint of the 0–6 scale for assessing the ambition-significance of a summit's commitments. These scores are consistent with qualitative judgements, issued at the immediate conclusion of the summit, of Okinawa as a summit of 'solid achievement' (Kirton 2000).

It is notable that both the G7 and G8 summits score in this midpoint range. The slightly higher G8 score suggests that the presence of Russia may marginally help and at a minimum does not harm G7/8 performance (although the different set of issue areas dealt with in each forum remains critical factor). This suggestion is reinforced by a direct comparison of the G7 and G8 in similar issue areas (such as the G7's HIPC Initiative versus the G8's debt, and the G7's nuclear safety versus the G8's arms control). By this standard, only the G8's low score on the world economy supports the case for caution in allowing Russia more of a place in the G7's economic and financial domain.

As indicated by Tables 5.2 and 5.3, which combine the G7 and G8 issue areas in a single scale ranked by their ambition-significance score, there is a wide variation by issue area in the performance of the summit. First, issue areas from the G8 rather than the G7 tend to dominate the high ambition-significance list. In fact, no issue area from the G7 ranked above the overall average by equally weighted issue areas. This suggests that the innovative dynamism of the G7/8 system has passed decisively from the G7 to the G8.

Second, the highest scoring issue areas are those that are relatively new to the G7/8 agenda, and, in at least one case (cultural diversity), are entirely new. Leading the list are health, cultural diversity, ageing, ICT, and life science, followed by development, debt, and heavily indebted poor countries (HIPCs). This suggests that while Okinawa was indeed a development summit, in some ways the theme of information technology took precedence in the end (especially if one adds the results of the commitments in the separate Okinawa Charter on Information Technology, which is not included in in this analysis). Even more important, Okinawa was marked by its domestic intrusiveness, through its ambitious and significant commitments in areas long the preserve of domestic politics, and ones where often state/provincial and local governments as well as national ones have significant responsibilities. Above all, Okinawa should be remembered by this calculus as a social policy summit.

This premium on innovation is also evident in the political-security domain. Here conflict prevention ranks first as the most ambitious-significant issue area. More venerable subjects, even those featured at recent summits, such as arms control, crime and drugs, terrorism, and nuclear safety, rank well down on the list. (The regional security commitments issued in a separate declaration are not included in this analysis.) The low ranking of nuclear safety is somewhat of a surprise, given how large the 1999 criticality accident at Tokaimura loomed in Japanese political life (Donnelly 2002).

Table 5.2   2000 Okinawa G8 Commitments Ranked by Average Ambition-Significance

G7 Communiqué

International financial architecture	2.67
Heavily indebted poor countries	2.75
Global financial system	2.67
Nuclear safety	2.00
Average by equally weighted issue area	*2.52*
Average by individual commitments (N=12)	*2.6*

G8 Communiqué

World economy	1.00
Information and communications technology	3.33
Development	3.25
Debt relief	2.80
Health	5.25
Trade	1.50
Cultural diversity	4.50
Crime and drugs	2.21
Ageing	4.00
Life science	3.33
Human genome	2.18
Conflict prevention	2.67
Arms control/Disarmament	2.29
Terrorism	2.00
Average by equally weighted issue area	*2.88*
Average by individual commitments (N=70)	*2.69*
Average of G7 + G8 by Equally Weighted Issue Areas (N=18)	*2.80*
Average of G7 + G8 by Individual Commitments (N=82)	*2.67*

Also noteworthy is the low ranking for those issue areas in which the G7/8 summits, and especially Japanese-hosted G7 summits, have traditionally excelled. Trade stands out, with a very low score that confirms the harsh judgement of informed observers about the Okinawa Summit's performance in this domain (Bayne 2001; Ullrich 2001). Moreover, the low score for world economy, delivered by a G8 that was about to go into sharply slower growth in the coming months, and at a summit hosted in a long stagnant Japan, suggests that complacency rather than prescience and prevention formed the dominant approach.

At first glance, this overall pattern lends support to those who criticise the summit for its episodic focus on an ever-changing array of issues, rather than praise it for its persistent iteration on the most difficult but central issues in the world (Bayne 1999). Yet the solid scores on development, debt and HIPCs, the international financial architecture, and the global financial system belie this criticism. They suggest a good balance between the new and the old. Okinawa was thus at its most productive as an agenda-setting summit for the new century, although it also hung in there to make progress on some persistent problems left over from the old one (Bayne 2000).

Table 5.3   2000 Okinawa G8 Issue Areas Ranked by Ambition-Significance of Commitments

Health	5.25
Cultural diversity	4.50
Ageing	4.00
Information and communications technology	3.33
Life science	3.33
Development	3.25
Debt relief	2.80
Average by equally weighted issue areas	*2.80*
Heavily indebted poor countries (G7)	2.75
Conflict prevention	2.67
International financial architecture (G7)	2.67
Global financial system (G7)	2.67
Average by individual commitments	*2.67*
Arms control/Disarmament	2.29
Crime and drugs	2.21
Human genome	2.18
Terrorism	2.00
Nuclear safety (G7)	2.00
Trade	1.50
World economy	1.00

Promises Kept: Compliance with the Okinawa, Genoa, and Kananaskis Commitments

From Okinawa to Genoa

It makes little sense for the leaders of G7/8 countries to invest their time, reputations, and other resources to generate collective commitments at their annual summits, or for citizens to take these commitments seriously, if the summit's members do not comply with them in the following year. By these standards, the Okinawa Summit of 2000 was the most credible G7/8 summit ever held.[7]

During the ten months that followed the 2000 Summit, G7/8 members complied with the priority commitments made at it 81 percent of the time (see Table 5.4).[8]

As Table 5.5 shows, this 81 percent compliance record compares very favourably with the 39 percent compliance record with the priority commitments of the 1999 Cologne Summit, the 45 percent compliance record of the 1998 Birmingham Summit, the 27 percent of Denver 1997, and the 36 percent of Lyon 1996. Whereas the four summits prior to Okinawa yielded an average compliance score of 37 percent, Okinawa itself soared to 81 percent. Okinawa's exceptional status is confirmed by compliance studies from 1988 to 1995, which yielded a score of 43 percent for the United States and Canada on their commitments to sustainable development and aid to Russia. It is also confirmed by the score of 31 percent (using different methodology) for the compliance of all members with all the economic and energy commitments made at the summits from 1975 to 1988 (von Furstenberg and Daniels 1992) (see Table 5.6).

Compliance with Okinawa's priority commitments was particularly high in the areas of information technology, health, and trade. Here the summit secured a perfect score. The highest complying members were Germany and Britain, the immediately prior hosts, with each scoring perfect. They were followed by France with 92 percent, Italy with 89 percent, Canada with 83 percent, Japan with 82 percent, the United States with 67 percent, and the newest G8 member, Russia, with only 14 percent.

Compliance with Okinawa's core conflict prevention commitment was similarly high. At 63 percent, the priority conflict prevention commitment monitored for compliance called for an international conference that would consider practical approaches to breaking the link between the illicit trade in diamonds and armed conflict. It found considerable support from the G8 in the months following the Okinawa Summit (see Table 5.7). Britain, France, Canada, Germany, and the U.S. all worked toward advancing this commitment in concrete and measurable ways. Italy, Japan, and Russia made less considerable progress. For example, Britain, France, and Germany played seminal roles in all aspects of the Kimberley Process and rallied support for a technical forum on rough diamond certification.[9] They were also vocal proponents of this process at the international diamond ministerial in Pretoria, South Africa, in September 2000. Britain hosted the London Intergovernmental Meeting on Conflict Diamonds in October 2000

Table 5.4   G8 Compliance Scores by Issue Area, 2000–2002

Issue	Okinawa 2000	Genoa 2001	Kananaskis 2002 (interim)
World economy	+0.86		
International financial system		-1.00	+0.14 (Trade)
Microeconomics			
Globalisation			
Employment			
Education		+0.58	
Ageing	+0.86		
Information/communications technology	+1.00	+0.75	
Trade	+1.00	+0.88	0
Development			+0.50
Debt relief		+1.00	−0.80
Health	+1.00	+0.75	+0.25 (Africa)
Energy			
Environment	+0.80	+0.17	+0.25
Biotech/Food safety	+0.75		
Nuclear safety/Ukraine			
Cultural diversity	+0.63		
Refugees			
Human rights			
East–West relations			
Transition economies			
Multilateral institutions			
Crime and drugs	+0.88		+0.25
Terrorism	+0.40	+1.0	+1.00
Arms control/Disarmament			+0.63
Regional issues			
Middle East			
Africa		+0.00	+0.25
Africa peer review			0
Asia Pacific			
Europe			
Conflict prevention	+0.63		+0.60
Total	+0.81	+0.46	+0.25

and provided valuable leadership in crafting and ratifying UN General Assembly Resolution 56 — a resolution strongly supported by France.[10]

Canada was also an active advocate of breaking the link between illicit diamonds and conflict in the post-Okinawa period. In September 2000, Prime Minister Jean Chrétien stated that there was a need to 'deny the agents of violence and conflict their sources of supply', particularly through methods such as 'controlling the illicit trade in diamonds' (G8 Research Group 2001). As a participant in the Kimberley Process, Canada co-sponsored, along with the UK, the concluding international ministerial conference in Pretoria in September 2000. In October of that year, Canada participated in the London meeting, with representatives of 36 other governments involved in the

Table 5.5   G8 Compliance Assessments by Country, 1996–2002[a]

| | 1996–97[b] | 1997–98[c] | 1998–99[d] | 1999–2000[e] | 2000–01[f] | 2001–02[g] |
	Lyon	Denver	Birmingham	Cologne	Okinawa	Genoa
France	+0.26	0	+0.25	+0.34	+0.92	+0.69
U.S.	+0.42	+0.34	+0.6	+0.5	+0.67	+0.35
UK	+0.42	+0.5	+0.75	+0.5	+1.0	+0.69
Germany	+0.58	+0.17	+0.25	+0.17	+1.0	+0.59
Japan	+0.21	+0.50	+0.2	+0.67	+0.82	+0.44
Italy	+0.16	+0.50	+0.67	+0.34	+0.89	+0.57
Canada	+0.47	+0.17	+0.5	+0.67	+0.83	+0.82
Russia	N/A	0	+0.34	+0.17	+0.14	+0.11
EU	N/A	N/A	N/A	+0.17	N/A	N/A
Average	+0.36	+0.27	+0.45	+0.39	+0.80	+0.53

Notes:

a. Scores are an equally weighted average of a country's compliance to commitments made at each summit. At the time of preparation, final scores for the 2002 Kananaskis Summit were not available.

b. Applies to 19 priority issues, embracing the economic, transnational, and political security domains.

c. Applies to 6 priority issues, embracing the economic, transnational, and political security domains.

d. Applies to 7 priority issues, embracing the economic, transnational, and political security domains (illegal trafficking of human beings).

e. Applies to 6 priority issues, embracing economic, transnational, and political security domains (terrorism).

f. Applies to 12 priority issues, embracing economic, transnational, and political security domains (conflict prevention, arms control, and terrorism).

g. Applies to 9 priority issues, embracing economic, transnational, and political security domains (terrorism).

processing, exporting, and importing of rough diamonds. This conference sought to foster greater international support for breaking the link between illicit diamonds and conflict as well as increasing dialogue on a possible certification regime. The international consensus and support forged at London led to UN General Assembly Resolution 56 on 1 December 2000, sponsored by Canada and reaffirming the G8 Okinawa commitment to break the link between rough diamonds, particularly through an international certification process.

The U.S. played a pivotal role on this issue. It had jointly led the initiative to place conflict diamonds on the agenda of the G8 Summit in Okinawa. After the Summit, the U.S. hosted an international conference in Washington on the economics of war. This conference, *inter alia*, opened a direct dialogue with diamond officials from Botswana and Angola. At Kimberley, the U.S. reached an agreement with Belgium and Britain on key aspects of the process. Moreover, the U.S. jointly led an initiative that guided the World Diamond Council in establishing a 'chain of warranties' to hedge against illicit diamonds. In addition, it contributed to the communiqué of the London meeting, ratified UN Resolution 56, and pledged to the General Assembly that it would advance the process of creating certification guidelines for rough diamonds at the international technical conference and workshop to be held in Windhoeke, Namibia, later that year (G8 Research Group 2001).

Although attending most of the post-Okinawa meetings on illicit diamonds, Italy, Japan, and Russia were less active on this issue and made fewer concrete pledges. As the world's second largest diamond producer, Russia was clearly concerned that an international certification scheme might intervene too much in its domestic politics. Russia thus felt reluctant to sign on to any firm decisions. Overall, however, the G8 was collectively able to make important strides on this issue and secure compliance on their commitments to consider practical solutions to de-linking diamonds and armed conflict in the period after Okinawa (G8 Research Group 2001).

From Genoa to Kananaskis

The Okinawa Summit of 2000, with its historic 81 percent compliance record, established an extremely high standard for subsequent summits. The high overall compliance scores, coupled with a similarly strong 63 percent score on the leaders' core commitment on conflict prevention, meant that the bar would be set high for a repeat performance in the post-Genoa period.

That new standard was not met. Compliance scores fell dramatically, as the G8 complied with their priority commitments made at Genoa only 49.5 percent of the time (see Table 5.8). These scores varied widely by issue, with commitments on international terrorism and debt of the poorest securing complete compliance across all summit countries.[11] Compliance scores were also high in the areas of international trade, infectious disease, and the digital divide, followed by universal primary education. A 'work in progress' score came for commitments associated with the Genoa Plan for Africa, while a score in the negative range was awarded for commitments relating to the strengthening of the international financial system.[12] Overall, the highest complying summit member was Canada, the next country in the hosting order, with a score of 82 percent. Canada was followed by France and the UK, both tied at 69 percent, Germany with 59 percent, Italy with 57 percent, Japan with 44 percent, the U.S. with 35 percent, and the newest G8 member, Russia, with only 11 percent. Although notably lower than Okinawa the year before, the overall Genoa compliance average of 49.5 percent compares favourably with summits in previous years (see Table 5.5).

The G8 partnership on Africa established at Genoa was a very significant initiative. It promised help from the G8 on a wide range of development issues, including conflict prevention. The strongest commitment came through the designation by each member

Table 5.6   Compliance Scores by Issue, 1975–2001

Issue Area	1996–2001 Average	1988–1996	1975–1989
Total (per average n)	+39%	43% (C + US)	31%
Economic issues			
World economy	+95%		
Global Information Society/IT	+79%		
Ageing	+60%		
Debt relief	+43%	+73%	
Average of G8 All	*+39%*		
Average of G8 Economy	*+37%*		
Economic issues	+31%		
IFI reform	+29%		
Microeconomics	+29%		
Trade	+26%		+73%
Employment	+19%		
Development	0		+27%
Exchange rate	0		−70%
Demand composition			+23%
Real GNP growth			+40%
Fiscal adjustments			+26%
Interest rate			+22%
Inflation rate			+22%
Energy			+66%
Global/Transnational issues			
Climate change	+100%	+34%	
Health	+100%		
Human genome	+80%		
Biotech/Food safety	+75%		
Cultural diversity	+63%		
Average of G8 on Global/Transnational Issues	*+59%*		

of a high-level personal representative to prepare an action plan for Africa for endorsement at the 2002 Canadian-hosted summit in Kananaskis. Having initiated this process, the G8 leaders had to come through with concrete results. Here the G8 scored exceptionally well: every leader responded promptly to the appointment of high-level officials as their personal representatives for Africa (APRs). This was particularly true for French president Jacques Chirac (long characterised as the champion of African development), who became the first to appoint his APR. As an indication of his strong commitment to this initiative, Chirac designated Michel Camdessus, former managing director of the International Monetary Fund (IMF), and a very prominent and well-respected figure internationally on African development.

In the year following Genoa, the APRs moved swiftly. They met in London in

Table 5.6   Compliance Scores by Issue, 1975–2001, cont'd

Issue Area	1996–2001 Average	1988–1996	1975–1989
Transnational general	+48%		
Average of G8	*+39%*		
Crime	+33%		
Environment	+32%		
Nuclear safety	+29%		
Human trafficking	+25%		
Political/Regional security issues			
Europe	+86%		
East–West relations	+80%		
Landmines	+73%		
Human rights	+71%		
Terrorism	+70%		
Conflict prevention	+63%		
Arms control/Disarmament	+59%		
Average of G8	*+39%*		
Average of G8 on Political/Regional Security	*+33%*		
Security issues	+31%		
Asia	–43%		
Middle East	–43%		
Russia	–86%	+81%	
Governance issues			
Average of G8	*+39%*		
Average of G8 on Governance Issues	*+14%*		
UN reform: Financial	+14%		
UN reform: Development	+14%		

Source: Kokotsis and Daniels (1999).

October 2001, Addis Ababa in December 2001, and Cape Town in February 2002. Each meeting represented critical milestones in the G8's response to NEPAD, as each G8 country pledged development resources in various forms. Italy's Silvio Berlusconi, for example, at a meeting with South African president Thabo Mbeki, affirmed Italy's commitment to the Genoa Plan for Africa by vowing to reach 0.7 percent of gross domestic product for official development assistance (ODA). The U.S. proposed a 50 percent increase in its core U.S. development assistance over the next three years — an overall increase of US$5 billion annually over its current levels. The Canadian government committed CA$500 million as a 'special fund' for NEPAD, while Britain confirmed the cancellation of 100 percent of the debts owed to it by Mozambique. Germany and Japan showed equal resolve as each committed to assisting Africa through the development of enhanced trade relationships (G8 Research Group 2002). Overall, this collective initiative on behalf of the G8 to designate personal representatives led

Table 5.7   2000 Okinawa G8 Summary Compliance Scores

Issue	CDA	FRA	GER	ITA	JAP	U.S.	UK	RUS	Average
Economy	+1	+1	+1	N/A	+1	+1	+1	0	+0.86
ICT	+1	+1	+1	+1	+1	+1	+1	+1	+1.0
Health	+1	+1	+1	+1	+1	+1	+1	N/A	+1.0
Trade	+1	+1	+1	+1	+1	+1	+1	N/A	+1.0
Diversity	+1	+1	+1	+1	+1	−1	+1	0	+0.63
Crime/drugs	+1	+1	+1	+1	+1	+1	+1	0	+0.88
Ageing	0	+1	+1	+1	+1	+1	+1	N/A	+0.86
Biotech	+1	+1	+1	+1	+1	+1	+1	−1	+0.75
Genome	+1	+1	+1	N/A	N/A	0	+1	N/A	+0.80
Conflict prevention	+1	+1	+1	0	0	+1	+1	0	+0.63
Arms control	+1	+1	+1	+1	+1	0	+1	+1	+0.88
Terrorism	0	0	N/A	N/A	0	+1	+1	N/A	+0.40
By country	+0.83	+0.92	+1.0	+0.89	+0.82	+0.67	+1.0	+0.14	+0.808
By issue									+0.784
Overall									+0.814

Notes: The slight variation is due to differential equalisation weightings. The issue average is the average of all countries' compliance scores for that issue. The country average is the average of all issue area compliance scores for a given country. The symbol 'N/A' indicates that no information on a country's compliance score for a given issue area was available; in this case, no compliance score is awarded. Countries were excluded from the averages if N/A appears in the respective column. See G8 Research Group (2002).

to a series of concrete results that the leaders would then use at Kananaskis to set the foundation for the G8 Africa Action Plan.

The detailed and lengthy G8 Africa Action Plan released at Kananaskis also marked an important milestone in the G8's response to NEPAD. It strongly supported its underlying philosophy of allowing Africans to take ownership of their own future instead of relying on the developed North for handouts and policy direction. But to catalyse the process, the G8 had to confirm it was prepared to increase debt relief and ODA. Meeting at Halifax in early June 2002, the G7 finance ministers moved toward agreeing that an additional US$1 billion was needed to move the HIPC Initiative forward. Given that most HIPCs were African, this generous injection of funds was welcomed by those countries for which additional debt relief measures were desperately needed.

At the Kananaskis Summit itself, the leaders produced a historic US$6 billion ODA package for Africa. A key condition of its allocation was concrete measures aimed at ending conflict, which had long since prevented the democratic development of many African states. In fact, NEPAD, through its development of a new relationship with the

Table 5.8   2001 Genoa G8 Summary Compliance Scores

	CDA	FRA	GER	ITA	UK	U.S.	JAP	RUS	Average
Terrorism	+1	+1	+1	+1	+1	+1	+1	+1	+1.0
Digital divide	+1	+1	+1	+1	+1	+1	+1	-1	+0.75
Health	+1	+1	+1	+1	+1	0	0	+1	+0.75
Africa	0	0	0	0	0	0	0	0	0
Education	+1	+1	0	0	+1	0	+1	N/A	+0.58
Growth									
Trade	+1	+1	+1	+1	+1	+1	+1	0	+0.88
Fin. system	+1	0	0	0	0	-1	-1	N/A	-1.0
HIPC	+1	+1	+1	+1	+1	+1	+1	N/A	+1.0
Environment	+0.34	+0.17	+0.34	+0.17	+0.17	+0.17	0	0	+0.17
By country	+0.82	+0.69	+0.59	+0.57	+0.69	+0.35	+0.44	+0.11	+0.53
By issue									+0.46
Overall									+0.495

Notes: The slight variation is due to differential equalisation weightings. The issue average is the average of all countries' compliance scores for that issue. The country average is the average of all issue area compliance scores for a given country. The symbol 'N/A' indicates that no information on a country's compliance score for a given issue area was available; in this case, no compliance score is awarded. Countries were excluded from the averages if N/A appears in the respective column. The full compliance report is available from the G8 Information Centre at <www.g7.utoronto.ca/evaluations/2002compliance/index.html>.

industrialised world, emphasised the importance of material support for conflict prevention and the management of conflict through peacekeeping initiatives, initiatives for which G8 support was critical. Furthermore, the G8 Africa Action Plan committed to providing technical and financial assistance for training African peace support forces through the development of regional centres for military and civilian aspects of conflict prevention, focussing specifically on the Kofi Annan International Peace Training Centre.

From Kananaskis to Evian

The road from Kananaskis to Evian saw a further decline in the G8's compliance performance, both overall and with regard to conflict prevention. The results of an interim compliance study completed six months after Kananaskis show that compliance with the G8's priority commitments came in at 25 percent and the commitment on conflict prevention scored 60 percent (see Table 5.4).[13] After Kananaskis, several G8 member states were involved in a range of activities meant to promote peace, security, and conflict resolution on the African continent, typically in conjunction with UN peacekeeping missions. Interim compliance scores, however, vary by country. France demonstrated the strongest resolve on this initiative, and Canada, Germany, and Britain showed a work in progress.

On 7–8 December 2002, the APRs met in Accra, Ghana, for further implementation negotiations on the G8 Africa Action Plan. This meeting included the Ghanaian president and senior officials from the Kofi Annan International Peace Training Centre. Peace and security in Africa dominated the agenda, with extensive discussions on the issue of a joint plan for the establishment of a future African peacekeeping force (Ministry of Foreign Affairs of the Russian Federation 2002). After that meeting — and having assumed the G8 presidency in January 2003 — France took the lead on fulfilling this Kananaskis commitment, by developing a far-reaching programme for Africa, which it pledged to place at the top of the agenda at the G8 summit it would host in June 2003. Peace and security initiatives, including the training of peace forces, played a prominent role. Furthermore, the French government built co-operative alliances with the RECAMP programme during 2002, including co-operation between the French military and the military in Kenya, Madagascar, and all 14 members of the Southern Africa Development Community for the provision of training, expertise, and equipment for 900 African peacekeepers (Nabakwe 2002).[14] France had also been directly involved in peacebuilding and mediation efforts in a number of regions. The French authorities stressed their contribution to the peace process and conflict resolution in Sudan, Senegal, and Côte d'Ivoire, where France had nominated special envoys, dispatched delegates to oversee the negotiations, and deployed troops to aid and co-operate with the local authorities.

Initiatives by Canada, Britain, and Germany were somewhat less tangible. In 2002, Canada committed CA\$4 million over three years to assist the African Union in conflict prevention and peacekeeping efforts (Prime Minister of Canada 2002). Canada also committed to invest CA\$15 million in the Economic Community of West African

States (ECOWAS) Partnership for Common Security for its initiatives to strengthen policing, border security, civil-military relations, and the region's capacity to support peace and security objectives. To what extent this money would be used for the training of African peacekeeping forces was not yet fully determined as the Evian Summit drew nigh.

Britain and Germany's efforts to comply with their Kananaskis commitments on conflict prevention were limited to reaffirming their support through official statements with minimal translation into actual investment or action. In its 'G8 Africa Action Plan: Towards the 2003 Summit', Britain announced it would 'support the development of a long-term plan to build conflict management capacity in Africa, and specifically, support an effective African peacekeeping force by 2010' (Foreign and Commonwealth Office 2003). And although Germany affirmed its support for the Africa Action Plan and NEPAD, this affirmation was predominantly manifested in statements of Germany's commitment to formulating a concrete plan by 2003 for curtailing conflict in Africa; Germany would provide financial and technical assistance for the planned establishment of an African peacekeeping centre, but the nature and degree of such assistance remained unspecified.

After Kananaskis, the leaders instructed their personal representatives to work for another year on Africa and pledged to review their progress when they met in France in 2003.

By the Evian Summit, compliance with the Kananaskis priority commitments on conflict prevention had fallen to +38 percent (G8 Research Group 2003b). Overall compliance had risen from +25 percent at the start of 2003 to +35 percent. The G8's conflict prevention programme thus seemed less insulated than the overall Summit from the springtime diversions and divisions among the G8 bred by the war in Iraq. As Evian opened, compliance with the Kananaskis commitments on conflict prevention was led by Canada, France, Germany, Britain, and the U.S. with +100 percent. They were followed by Russia with 0, and Italy and Japan with –100 percent each.

The conflict prevention record of the three years from Okinawa to Evian indicates that there is a durable, winning coalition for developing the G8 as an institution for conflict prevention and thus for a new generation of political-security initiatives. The pacific principal powers of Germany and Canada — neither one a member of the P5 — as well as the G8 founders and powers of France, the United States, and Britain have consistently complied with high scores with the G8's commitments on conflict prevention. Italy, Japan, and Germany have usually lagged behind. The pattern suggests that the inhibitions are less ideological, or less grounded in fixed national attachments to the hard law international organisations of over half a century ago, than due to an institutional failing of the G8 architecture itself. As the democratic institutionalist model of G8 compliance performance suggests, the G8's failure to move beyond a conflict prevention officials meeting and the underdeveloped status of the G8 foreign ministers forum (relative to its finance ministers counterpart) are both consistent with the declining level of compliance with conflict prevention observed since the strong start of 2000 and 2001 (Kokotsis 1999). Until such direct G8 political-security institutions can be strengthened, it could well be left to the African-focussed new creations of the APRs and the G8 development ministers forum to take the lead.

Conclusion

Following the precedent-setting 1999 Cologne Summit, where the G8 shifted focus to conflict prevention as a new and substantial component of its agenda, the G8 has shown overall success in generating commitments on conflict prevention at each summit and ultimately complying with them in the post-summit period. A certain degree of momentum, however, was lost on conflict prevention initiatives following Okinawa, when the leaders and their foreign ministers failed to deliver a separate statement on conflict prevention and chose not to transform the Conflict Prevention Officials Meeting from Berlin in 1999 into a more institutionally entrenched G8 conflict prevention working group. Instead, as the leaders' attention shifted at Genoa and Kananaskis to focus more specifically on one thematic area — Africa — the issue of conflict prevention found increased resonance within the broader African context. It is within this context that the G8 has successfully created a synergistic relationship among its economic, political, and social agendas, as it links conflict prevention with a wide range of development activities. From blood diamonds, small arms, and scare resource management to the contribution of women and the private sector in preventing conflict, the G8 has come to recognise both the humanitarian and socioeconomic implications of conflict on the overall stability and development of many African nations. It is precisely this recognition that will likely carry the African agenda — and its conflict prevention components — to new heights after the 2003 French-hosted G8 Summit in Evian-les-Bains, and after the end of the great diversion and division caused by the spring 2003 war in Iraq.

Notes

1 The precise commitments identified and the method and coding instructions for identifying individual commitments are available on the G8 Information Centre at <www.g8.utoronto.ca>.
2 These issue areas include development (15), health (15), crime and drugs (18), human genome/environment (11), and bridging the digital divide (11).
3 The leaders' other two conflict commitments were a commitment to focus on economic development, children in conflict, and international civilian police, and a commitment to exercise restraint in conventional arms exports.
4 Its major rival as a highly focussed summit was Tokyo 1979, with its energy concern.
5 The G8 Recommendations on Counter-Terrorism included a number of preventive components, specifically through the adoption of export controls to govern the manufacturing, trading, transport, and export of small firearms and explosives used in violent conflict.
6 African leaders at the Summit included presidents Olusegun Obasanjo of Nigeria, Abdoulaye Wade of Senegal, Thabo Mbeki of South Africa, and Abdelaziz Bouteflika of Algeria, as well as UN Secretary General Kofi Annan.

7 This section is based on the compliance report published by the University of Toronto's G8 Research Group (2001).

8 This score is on a scale where +100 percent equals perfect compliance and –100 percent shows all members doing nothing to full their commitments or, in fact, doing the opposite of what they had pledged.

9 The Kimberley Process, launched by the government of South Africa, built on UNSC Resolution 1306 and was aimed at considering practical approaches to breaking the link between the illicit trade in diamonds and armed conflict.

10 UN Resolution 56 laid the groundwork for a forum to establish an international diamond certification scheme diminish or eliminate the role of diamonds in fuelling conflicts.

11 Information on debt of the poorest was not available for Russia.

12 'Work in progress' is indicated by an overall average score of 0.

13 These scores for Kananaskis are based on the 2002 Kananaskis Interim Compliance Report produced by the G8 Research Group (2003a).

14 RECAMP is the Reinforcement of African Peacekeeping Capabilities programme, established in 1997 under the auspices of the UN and in conjunction with the Organization for African Unity (now the African Union).

References

Bayne, Nicholas (1999). 'Continuity and Leadership in an Age of Globalisation'. In M. R. Hodges, J. J. Kirton and J. P. Daniels, eds., *The G8's Role in the New Millennium*, pp. 21–44. Ashgate, Aldershot.

Bayne, Nicholas (2000). *Hanging In There: The G7 and G8 Summit in Maturity and Renewal.* Ashgate, Aldershot.

Bayne, Nicholas (2001). 'The G7 and Multilateral Trade Liberalisation: Past Performance, Future Challenges'. In J. J. Kirton and G. M. von Furstenberg, eds., *New Directions in Global Economic Governance: Managing Globalisation in the Twenty-First Century*, pp. 23–38. Ashgate, Aldershot.

Donnelly, Michael (2002). 'Nuclear Safety and Criticality at Tokaimura: A Failure of Governance'. In J. J. Kirton and J. Takase, eds., *New Directions in Global Political Governance: The G8 and International Order in the Twenty-First Century*, pp. 141–166. Ashgate, Aldershot.

Foreign and Commonwealth Office, Government of the United Kingdom, (2003). 'G8 Africa Action Plan: Towards the 2003 Summit'. <www.fco.gov.uk/Files/KFile/G8africaactionplan.pdf> (July 2003).

Fratianni, Michele, Paolo Savona, and John J. Kirton, eds. (2003). *Sustaining Global Growth and Development: G7 and IMF Governance*. Ashgate, Aldershot.

G8 (2000). 'G8 Communiqué Okinawa 2000'. Okinawa, 23 July. <www.g7.utoronto.ca/summit/ 2000okinawa/finalcom.htm> (July 2003).

G8 (2001). 'Genoa Plan for Africa'. Genoa, 21 July. <www.g7.utoronto.ca/summit/2001genoa/ africa.html> (July 2003).

G8 (2002). 'G8's Africa Action Plan'. Kananaskis, 27 June. <www.g7.utoronto.ca/summit/ 2002kananaskis/africaplan.html> (July 2003).

G8 Research Group (2001). 'The 2001 G8 Compliance Report'. <www.g7.utoronto.ca/ evaluations/2001compliance/index.html> (July 2003).

G8 Research Group (2002). 'Keeping Genoa's Commitments: The 2002 G8 Compliance Report'. <www.g7.utoronto.ca/evaluations/2002compliance/index.html> (July 2003).

G8 Research Group (2003a). '2002 Kananaskis Interim Compliance Report'. <www.g7.utoronto.ca/evaluations/2002interimcompliance/index.html> (July 2003).

G8 Research Group (2003b). 'From Kananaskis to Evian: The 2003 Compliance Report'. <www.g7.utoronto.ca/evaluations/2003compliance/index.html> (July 2003).

Kirton, John J. (2000). 'Preliminary Personal Assessment of the Kyushu-Okinawa Summit'. 23 July. <www.g7.utoronto.ca/evaluations/2000okinawa/kirtonassesment.htm> (July 2003).

Kokotsis, Eleanore (1999). *Keeping International Commitments: Compliance, Credibility, and the G7, 1988–1995*. Garland, New York.

Kokotsis, Ella and Joseph P. Daniels (1999). 'G8 Summits and Compliance'. In M. R. Hodges, J. J. Kirton and J. P. Daniels, eds., *The G8's Role in the New Millennium*, pp. 75–91. Ashgate, Aldershot.

Kühne, Winrich and Jochem Prantl, eds. (2000). *The Security Council and the G8 in the New Millennium*. Stiftung Wissenschaft und Politik, Berlin.

Ministry of Foreign Affairs of the Russian Federation (2002). 'Alexander Yakovenko, Official Spokesman of Russia's Ministry of Foreign Affairs, Answers a Russian Media Question about the Outcome of the Meeting of the G8 Personal Representatives for Africa in Accra'. <www.ln.mid.ru/Bl.nsf/arh/74B7F5DD7435E71F43256C90003606 FC?OpenDocument> (December 2002).

Nabakwe, Ruth (2002). 'France Continues Peace Keeping Initiative for Africa'. Pan-African News Agency, Dakar, Senegal, 23 January. <ww.globalpolicy.org/security/peacekpg/region/france.htm> (July 2003).

Prime Minister of Canada (2002). 'Canada Helps Build New Partnerships with Africa'. Ottawa, 27 June. <www.pm.gc.ca/default.asp?Language=E&Page=newsroom&Sub=newsreleases&Doc=africa.20020627_e.htm> (July 2003).

Takase, Junichi (2002). 'The Changing G8 Summit and Japanese Foreign Policy'. In J. J. Kirton and J. Takase, eds., *New Directions in Global Political Governance: The G8 and International Order in the Twenty-First Century*, pp. 105–114. Ashgate, Aldershot.

Ullrich, Heidi K. (2001). 'Stimulating Trade Liberalisation after Seattle: G7/8 Leadership in Global Governance'. In J. J. Kirton and G. M. von Furstenberg, eds., *New Directions in Global Economic Governance: Creating International Order for the Twenty-First Century*, pp. 219–240. Ashgate, Aldershot.

von Furstenberg, George M. and Joseph P. Daniels (1992). 'Economic Summit Declarations, 1975–1989: Examining the Written Record of International Cooperation'. Princeton Studies in International Finance No. 72. Princeton University Press, Princeton.

Appendix 5.1
Ambition-Significance Criteria

The ambition-significance ranking is scored out of a possible six points corresponding to the six criteria. A score of 6 indicates both a high level of ambition and a high level of significance. A score of 3 indicates a high level of ambition but has no level of significance. A score of 0 indicates no level of ambition and no level of significance. The coding manual for assessing the ambition-significance of each individual commitment is presented below.

A. Ambition

1. Does the commitment identify a goal?
    Yes = 1 point
    No = 0 points
2. Does the commitment identify measures to attain the goal?
    Yes = 1 point
    No = 0 points
3. Does the commitment identify a target date by which time the goal is to be completed?
    Yes = 1 point
    No = 0 points

B. Significance

4. Timeliness
    Is the purpose of the commitment to respond to a current crisis?
    Is the purpose of the commitment to prevent/address a future crisis/issue?
    (1 point)
5. Scope
    Is the commitment directed only at G8 countries?
    Is the commitment directed at countries outside G8 membership?
    (1 point)
6. Novelty
    Does the commitment refer to an issue that was addressed in previous Summits?
    Does the commitment refer to an issue that has not been addressed in previous?
    (1 point)

Note that the scoring criteria for (4), (5), and (6) are specific to the particular commitment to be ranked. For example, with regard to scope a particular commitment can be directed only at G8 countries (in this case, a score of 0 would be allocated), while in other cases the commitment may be directed outside G8 membership (in this case, a score of 1 would be allocated). The G8 Research Group has tried to minimise any measurement error associated with this ranking process, including applying a two-stage verification process to ensure that, if any bias exists in the ranking, it is applied consistently across all commitments and across all issue areas.

Taken together, these criteria suggest that each individual commitment, and through normal or weighted averages an entire summit, can be judged as follows:

Ambition-Significance Ranking

0 = No Ambition, No Significance
1 = Low Ambition, No Significance
2 = Moderate Ambition, No Significance
3 = High Ambition, No Significance
4 = High Ambition, Low Significance
5 = High Ambition, Moderate Significance
6 = High Ambition, High Significance

Before applying this framework to the entire set of 169 commitments from the 2000 Okinawa Summit, it must be noted that ranking commitments by ambition-significance is an arduous task involving several methodological challenges. In this exercise, the G8 Research Group is attempting to quantify an essentially qualitative enterprise. Every effort has been made to reduce the level of measurement error and simultaneity bias. Nevertheless, these two problems still exist. As a result, there tends to be a systematic overstatement of the level of ambition-significance for each commitment as well as a systematic overstatement of the level of compliance. Given that the G8 Research Group has been examining this issue in the context of political science rather than economics, no regressions have been employed and the corresponding economic techniques to correct for simultaneity bias have not been used.

With these caveats, the ambition-significance framework has been applied, on a trial basis, to the 12 commitments in Okinawa's G7 Communiqué and to the 97 commitments in the G8 Communiqué. For this exercise, however, the individual sub-commitments have been amalgamated into a single commitment, thus reducing the overall number of commitments from 109 (12+97) to 82 (12+70). (This comes from the consolidation in the G8 Communiqué of commitments in development from 15 to 8, health from 15 to 4, crime and drugs from 18 to 14, and ageing from 6 to 1.)

PART II
CONFLICT PREVENTION:
THE POLITICAL-INSTITUTIONAL
FRAMEWORK

Chapter 6

Conflict Prevention: Performances, Prospects, and Potential

Roberto Toscano

What Conflict Prevention Is Not

Political scientists and practitioners alike traditionally consider conflict prevention an elusive concept, mainly due to its counterfactual nature. The objective difficulty to define it satisfactorily at a theoretical level, coupled with the problem of providing a tangible empirical projection, has induced some mainstream scholars and policy makers to discard conflict prevention *a priori* as a valid theoretical concept, as well as a useful course of action. However, the complexity of the concept is not so overarching as to be unsusceptible to both definition and praxis. A useful initial approach in defining conflict prevention could be to consider what conflict prevention is not.

In the first place, conflict prevention should be distinguished from preventive diplomacy. Preventive diplomacy is one aspect of conflict prevention, but conflict prevention is more than preventive diplomacy. Diplomats have definitely long been familiar with preventive diplomacy. The United Nations Charter spells out the classical panoply of the modes of preventive diplomacy: 'negotiation, enquiry, mediation, conciliation, arbitration, judicial settlement, resort to regional agencies or arrangements, or other peaceful means' (United Nations 1945, ch. 4, art. 33). It seems clear that such instruments can be effective in preventing classical, or inter-state, conflicts. In other words, they constitute the right approach to prevent risks such as the deterioration of relations and possible future conflicts between, for example, Hungary and Slovakia over the Gabcikovo dam, or between Chile and Argentina over the Beagle Channel. They have worked in the recent past.

A totally different story relates to conflicts of an internal nature. These have not totally replaced inter-state conflicts. On the contrary, they are often intertwined, even if today internal conflicts certainly constitute one of the main problems for world peace and stability (see, for example, Brown 1996).

Second, conflict prevention is not peace enforcement. Enforcement action can also have the function of preventing worse evils and wider conflicts. Yet, it would be misleading to believe that once the line is crossed into the use of force, operating in a preventive mode is still possible. For this reason, it is doubtful whether conflict prevention can include sanctions, which the UN Charter identifies as being — together with military action — one of the coercive tools of enforcement (United Nations 1945, ch. 7).

Third, conflict prevention is not conflict management. Once armed conflict has broken out, the attempt to limit or stop it belongs to another sphere of international action, both conceptually and operationally. But even when open conflict has not yet broken out but is already looming, it is unclear whether true preventive actions are possible. In that case, the only possibility is to try 'strategies that the fire department may employ to prevent fire when the match has already been struck' (Permanent Mission of Germany to the United Nations 2000). It is interesting to note — as a sign of growing political awareness of the need for a root-cause approach to conflict prevention — that the foreign policy plank of the Democratic platform for the U.S. presidential election of 2000 was based on the concept of forward engagement. It was defined as follows: 'Forward Engagement means addressing problems early in their development before they become crises, addressing them as close to the source of the problem as possible, and having the forces and resources to deal with these threats as soon after their emergence as possible' (Democratic National Committee 2000). In the different context after the terrorist attacks of 11 September 2001, but essentially following the same logic, the National Security Strategy elaborated by the Bush administration in September 2002 called for a 'forward-reaching, pre-emptive strategy' against hostile states and terrorist groups, while also expanding development assistance and free trade, promoting democracy, fighting disease, and transforming the U.S. military (Lombardi 2002).

Fourth, peacekeeping can be used also with a preventive focus. This was the case in the former Yugoslav Republic of Macedonia, where since 1992 first the UN, then the North Atlantic Treaty Organization (NATO), and now the EU have been responsible for several internationally sanctioned preventive peacekeeping missions.[1] Despite the so-far limited practice of such peacekeeping, based on the rather long-term experiment in Macedonia, it can be considered an area with considerable potential. However, mainstream peacekeeping has traditionally been a *post factum* affair, and it would not be appropriate, at least not until the practice of preventive peacekeeping has been consolidated, to include it in the category of conflict prevention activities.

Fifth, conflict prevention means the prevention of violent conflict, not of disputes and controversies. Indeed, differences of interests and values and controversy are not negative in themselves. They are the very essence of politics, and, indeed, of life in general, whereas the pretence of assuring universal quiet and uniformity is not compatible with freedom and dynamic growth, both economic and social. What has to be prevented is the use of violent means to address differences.

What Conflict Prevention Is

In this light, therefore, conflict prevention can be defined as a range of activities undertaken by third actors in anticipation of violence and with the intention of reversing a cycle of rising tensions believed to culminate inevitably in widespread warfare. In order to illustrate the logic of conflict prevention, it is also necessary to distinguish between the instruments of conflict and the causes of conflict.

The Instruments of Conflict

The disproportionate availability of weapons (disproportionate, that is, compared to what is necessary for reasonably sufficient self-defence) and, especially, the imbalance in such availability have been traditionally identified among the most frequent sources of conflict. There is thus no doubt that arms control and disarmament represent a substantial contribution to conflict prevention. Indeed, in the case of internal conflicts, small arms have therefore recently been identified as a main area for preventive international action. Yet, in a world that has seen the massacre — for the most part with primitive machetes — of probably ten times the number of victims of the Hiroshima bomb, one is forced, if reluctantly, to reconsider the otherwise very dubious and disingenuous slogan of opponents of gun control in the U.S.: 'Guns don't kill people. People kill people.' The control and limitation of the tools of conflict are thus necessary, but are definitely not sufficient.[2]

The same can be said about the way combatants fuel their struggle from the point of view of economic resources. Important cases in point are the conflicts in the Middle East and Central Asia over access to water and oil or the parallel trade in diamonds considered to be one of the main resources behind conflict in places such as Angola and Sierra Leone. It is significant that illicit trade in diamonds has been identified as one of the five initiatives for conflict prevention approved by G8 foreign ministers at their July 2000 meeting in Miyazaki (G8 Foreign Ministers 2000).[3]

The Causes of Conflict

If these are the key instruments of conflict, what are the central causes? In the 2001 report on the prevention of armed conflict, the United Nations spelled out, among the basic premises of the document, the following:

> Preventive action should be initiated at the earliest possible stage of a conflict cycle in order to be most effective. One of the principal aims of preventive action should be to address the deep-rooted socio-economic, cultural, environmental, institutional and other structural causes that often underlie the immediate political symptoms of conflict (United Nations 2001, 2).

After the historic defeat of communism, and the radical weakening of its theoretical foundation, Marxism, one would expect economic determinism to be on the wane. On the contrary, these days conventional wisdom maintains that conflicts, both international and internal, are caused by a struggle for markets, for natural resources, for land, or for a better share of the revenue within a given society (Nye 2001). As a corollary, the only problems really worth addressing for an effective conflict prevention policy would allegedly be of an economic nature. Again, as in the case of arms, a partial truth prevails, one that should be incorporated with a grain of salt into a more complex and more complete picture.

A few things should be clarified. Poverty as such, in absolute terms, is not in itself conducive to conflict. There is no statistically relevant correlation between poverty and conflict. When addressing the correlation between economic factors and conflict, one should instead consider several points.

The first is the trend of economic development, and especially events leading to worsening conditions, as widely elaborated on by Umberto Triulzi and Pierluigi Montalbano in Chapter 11. People do not usually turn to violence because they are undernourished. But they do when the price of bread doubles. So the deterioration of conditions should be monitored, rather than absolute levels.[4]

The second is the increased economic imbalance among social classes or ethnic groups. Many situations throughout the world prove that the combination of ethnic diversity and growing economic disparity is a sure recipe for violent conflict. 'It does not seem to be poverty itself that is the causing agent [of conflict]; the majority of poor countries are experiencing peace most of the time. It is the disparate development, along regional, ethnic or religious dividing lines, of poverty and need alongside privileged groups that leads to tension' (Permanent Mission of Germany to the United Nations 2000). It is amazing how clearly this fact becomes apparent just by scanning the news relating to so-called ethnic conflicts the world over.[5]

The third is external imbalance, that is, increasing growth differentials among neighbouring countries. In a globalised world, the problem is that of proximity combined with diverging economic conditions. Such consideration, for instance, is evidently one of the main elements of the Mediterranean strategy of the European Union, which includes a strong focus on conflict prevention (Aliboni, Guazzone, and Pioppi 2001).

Fourth, the focus should be on socioeconomic roots of conflict, rather than on economic roots. People are affected not by production levels or aggregate figures, but by concrete conditions, by a quality of life in which factors such as education or the state of the environment play a very significant role.

And last, economic factors do not directly produce conflict. They must always go through a stage of explicit formulation of grievances and organised political action. Groups do not confront each other because they are poor or disadvantaged, but because they feel deprived of their rights, sometimes threatened in their very survival, by some other group.[6]

Attention should thus shift from economics to politics. In all conflict, and especially in inter-ethnic conflict, material root causes of a socioeconomic nature constitute a potential that does not translate into actual group confrontation by some natural mechanism. It does so because, usually thanks to successful political and ideological action on the part of leaders, groups come to believe that the only way to guarantee their rights (from the right to speak their own language to the right to have a fair share of national wealth; from the right to have their political weight recognised sometimes to the very right of survival) is to use force, and preferably to constitute their own political entity. So-called ethnic conflicts are usually about the nation-state: which state, whose state (Burton 1990; Horowitz 1985).

Conflict prevention, therefore, can be attained mainly by proving that rights can be protected without violence. It can also be attained by proving that political losers (even when regular elections do take place) do not lose their life or their livelihood, and at a minimum must share power. For example, the August 2001 Ohrid agreements in Macedonia, which were mediated by the EU and the U.S. and accepted by both ethnic communities, were a serious attempt at conflict prevention intended in this sense (Ackermann 2002). This attempt should prompt a reflection on democracy and on the way it is actually applied beyond the respect of its formal rules and procedures. Africa is an especially relevant area of concern, given an often harsh, zero-sum nature of political competition.

Nor should one forget what has been defined as 'the incendiary role of corruption'.[7] Indeed, good governance and the rule of law are the most effective tools in conflict prevention. Without the accountability of leaders and without recognised and effective channels of grievance formulation and redress, violence on the part of desperate losers and insecure winners is always looming.

An International Agenda for Prevention

On the basis of the preceding analysis, it is possible to draw some basic conclusions on a possible preventive international agenda. First, power entails responsibility. Therefore those countries with more economic and political clout should take upon themselves the commitment to submit their international action to a conflict impact assessment, similar to what is already accepted for the preservation of the environment (despite controversies over the U.S. acceptance of the international environmental regime). They cannot pretend not to know that what they do, or fail do to, has profound consequences on the possibility of conflict. One of the most significant cases is development assistance. It should be clear that development, although always positive in strictly economic terms, can become a destabilising and conflict-generating factor insofar as it disrupts the old equilibrium and, as it is often the case, favours one sector of the population (often one ethnic group) to the detriment of another (Morrow 1990). Conversely, development assistance should be explicitly and consistently tailored to pursue not only development, but specifically development without conflict.[8]

Second, preventive action must be as comprehensive as possible. Although the politics of conflict is central, the causes of conflict are always manifold and complex.[9] Thus it would be useless to address the problem with a single-factor approach, be it weapons, economic aspects, political leadership, ideology, or human rights (Grant 1993). It follows logically that conflict prevention especially demands from international actors (starting with the most influential) that they should show coherence — that is, consistency in policies and actions. However, frequent deadlocks at the level of the most legitimate international forums, such as the UN Security Council (UNSC), indicate that rather narrow political considerations still determine the larger policy choices for the most influential international actors.

Third, it is indeed true, as the G8 stressed at Miyazaki in 2000, that the world needs a culture of prevention, in the sense of developing a constant and alert awareness of the need for a preventive approach to international relations. At the same time, it also needs a culture *for* prevention. That is, it needs to be able to articulate, and to assist from the outside, cultural expressions of nations and groups that stress dialogue instead of the clash of cultures (or civilisations), that value difference as an asset rather than as a disharmony to be overcome or at most tolerated, and that do not build (in the first place in classrooms, mainly through the teaching of history) stereotyped, hostile images of other nations and groups.[10] The 2001 World Conference on Racism should have been seen in this light, making the most of its conflict prevention potential.

Fourth, both states and international organisations are using a regional approach to a preventive action or a post-conflict strategy. An important case in point is the Stability Pact for South-Eastern Europe. The regional dimension, however, is much more than a modality for outside assistance in the prevention of conflict. It is instead a specific strategy that can be pursued by concerned countries (or entities, in the case of the intricate territorial and constitutional formulas applied in the area of former Yugoslavia) and assisted from the outside.[11]

At the July 2000 Assembly of the Organization of African Unity (OAU), UN Secretary General Kofi Annan said: 'The European Union, which is probably the most successful example of conflict prevention in the last half-century, began as an economic community — specifically, a coal and steel community. After the devastation of World War II, France and Germany decided to make another war impossible by jointly administering resources which were then the "sinews of war". Is it unthinkable that Africans could work together on similar lines? Why not create an "African Oil and Diamond Community"?' (United Nations 2000).

Preventive action is a responsibility that does not belong exclusively to governments and international organisations. It also belongs to private corporations, especially large ones. Indeed, given the impact that, in the world of globalised business, the operations of private firms have on the socioeconomic situations in many countries (most dramatically in those that are both economically and politically weak), it is apparent that leaving this aspect outside the discourse of conflict prevention would result in a fatal gap. Similarly to what is being done in the field of the environment, multinational corporations should be both summoned to respect existing rules and encouraged to develop and respect self-regulated codes of conduct with a view to contributing to the prevention of conflict.

In 1999, Annan promoted a global compact of world business leaders aimed at obtaining their commitment to policies that favour world governance by action in specific areas concerning human rights, labour, and environment. Nine principles were identified, in those three categories.

- Human Rights:
  1. Support and respect the protection of human rights;
  2. Make sure their own corporations are not complicit in human rights abuses.
- Labour Standards:
  3. Uphold freedom of association and right to collective bargaining;
  4. Eliminate forced labour;
  5. Abolish child labour;
  6. Eliminate discrimination.
- Environment:
  7. Support a precautionary approach to environmental challenges;
  8. Promote greater environmental responsibility;
  9. Encourage the development of environmentally friendly technologies (United Nations 1999).

It is true that addressing human rights, labour conditions, and environmental issues means addressing the root causes of conflict. But why should one not make conflict prevention not only an indirect consequence, but also an explicit goal of positive corporate action? It would be useful to introduce a tenth principle: World business will strive to submit its own policies and programmes to a conflict impact assessment.

Performance

The above guidelines make it possible, now, to assess the actual performance of the international community, as compared to the actions that ideally should be carried out in the pursuit of an effective agenda for conflict prevention.

A cursory look at the history of the past ten years shows that performance in conflict prevention has been dismal. One can evade the problem by saying that the world will never know how many conflicts were prevented by wise and incisive policy. Yet there a succession of announced disasters (from Rwanda to Kosovo) should induce some strong self-criticism.

Has it been so because of the reluctance of the international community to act, to engage, and, especially, to pay the political and financial price for its action? Yes, in that the reluctance is evidently there. But no, in that if one considers events *ex post,* the international community — in particular, its more robust members — ultimately end up doing and paying quite a lot. So, while all were reluctant to decide and to act before the genocide in Rwanda (by now they should be willing to accept a sort of collective guilt for that terrible omission), in the aftermath of the horrendous slaughter they did, went, and spent.

To understand this phenomenon, Figure 6.1 applies the tools that can be put to work for conflict prevention to a timeframe, since the panoply of instruments is gradually reduced as violent conflict approaches: in the face of imminent confrontation, only military tools can effectively exert a preventive role. It is worth emphasising that the best prevention is early prevention, and that early prevention addresses root causes. Early prevention means wide prevention; late prevention means narrow prevention. When peace reigns, there is no concern, no fear, no need to do anything in a conflict-prevention mode. And yet, when troubles start looming on the horizon (through mounting tensions and evident risks), there also arises the possibility to act with a full range and combination of options. One goes from culture (from inter-ethnic education and dialogue to the role, often perverse, of history and the way it is taught) to economics and on to politics.

Conflict prevention is unequivocally not — and should not be — an additional aspect of international relations. It should not entail specific mandates and *ad hoc* organisations. It is a special attention, a special focus, a special concern that should be systematically mainstreamed into every aspect of international activities. Given the multi-causal roots of conflict, everything, in a way, can have an impact. Thus, no all-encompassing mandate for a hypothetical 'conflict prevention organisation' is feasible. Moreover, such an organisation already exists — the United Nations. This is immediately clear if one examines its charter.

However, in the aftermath of the 2003 war in Iraq, the UN and its core institutions need to regain legitimacy, if their significant potential for conflict prevention is to be credible in the future. In the meantime, single-actor pre-emptive doctrines, such as the U.S. National Security Strategy, while technically more effective due to the

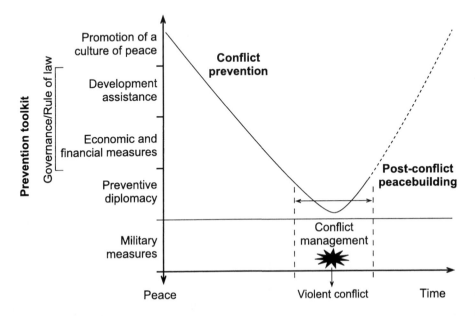

Figure 6.1   Conflict Prevention Curve

possibility of circumventing complex consensus-building mechanisms at a multilateral level, lack the international legitimacy vital for successful preventive activities. Furthermore, it makes a lot of difference, for the very results achieved, if one acts with a conscious purpose in mind or not, especially because action throughout this wide array of goals and tools tends to be plagued by contradictions and inconsistencies. Development assistance is a case in point. It is significant that one of the guiding principles recalled by Development Assistance Committee (DAC) of the Organisation for Economic Co-operation and Development (OECD) in its guidelines on conflict and development is to 'do no harm' (Development Assistance Committee 2001). Indeed, there can be cases in which a development programme is 100 percent successful if it is assessed in terms of growth of GROSS NATIONAL PRODUCT, export results, and employment, and yet it nonetheless increases the risk of conflict. This is because it develops one area and not the next; because it includes a social (and often also ethnic) group and excludes the next; because it disrupts the previous equilibrium in situations that leave the losers and the excluded with no other way of redressing the balance than the use of organised, armed violence.

Mainstreaming, coherence, and comprehensiveness are therefore the basic rules of conflict prevention. These are hard and complex tasks, but not impossible to accomplish. Indeed, the world already knows enough to determine what risks contribute to conflict and what, on the contrary, helps prevent it.

The difficulty of a root-cause approach to conflict prevention, however, does not stem only from inconsistencies and from the compartmentalised way in which foreign policy tends to be conceived and implemented. Another very significant limitation derives from what could be called the beneficiaries of preventive action.

Because the roots of conflict (whatever the economic precursors) are eminently political, countries at risk perceive every outside attempt to address them as an infringement of sovereignty. Sovereignty is in many cases the last refuge of *génocidaires* and ethnic cleansers. But one cannot underestimate the strength and the legitimacy of this concern, voiced also by leaders and governments that are decent and credible members of the international community. This latter group includes countries such as India, one of the most articulate and consistent champions of sovereignty in international forums. Thus, inevitably, outside action is easier *post factum*, after conflict has broken the back of countries (and regimes) and even more so when the international community has established *de facto* protectorates and is able to carry out post-conflict peacebuilding with minimal local interference. Such peacebuilding, of course, has preventive effects (indeed, at preventing a relapse into conflict), but takes place in a totally different context.

Prospects and Potential

The task is awesome. Political will is apparently even more scarce than financial resources. And yet the prospects for conflict prevention, for its stable and substantial insertion as a component of the international discourse, are promising.

June 2001 saw the release of two interesting documents: the report entitled 'Prevention of Armed Conflict' (United Nations 2001) and — at the European Council in Göteburg — the EU Programme for the Prevention of Violent Conflict (European Commission 2001).

In April of the same year, the High Level Meeting of DAC had approved the supplement to the 1997 Guidelines on Conflict, Peace, and Development Co-operation (see Development Assistance Committee 2001). Conflict prevention is also being studied and addressed in many other multilateral forums, from the Organization for Security and Co-operation in Europe (OSCE) to the United Nations Development Programme (UNDP), as well as in a number of nongovernmental institutions and organisations.

Sceptics may say that the fact that there seems to be a growth industry in conflict prevention is no guarantee that the result will be more actual conflict prevention. They may also add that this growing visibility of the issue is but one more manifestation of ineffective, if not counterproductive, moralism in foreign policy (Stedman 1995). This is an example of what Italians call *buonismo* ('good-ism').

This view is incorrect. In the first place, norms and principles are legitimate (and effective) components of international relations. Although values do indeed lend themselves to both controversy and instrumental utilisation, not taking them seriously implies missing important trends in public opinion that have weighty political repercussions. In a way, what has been said about human rights can also be said about conflict prevention, an aspect of international relations that today not even the most sceptical of sceptics would dismiss as irrelevant.

But the promising prospects for the preventive discourse do not derive only from the mere fact of the explicit attention that the issue is drawing in a multiplicity of forums. The way in which it is addressed is also extremely important.

If one reviews the basic premises spelled out at the beginning of the UN report on conflict prevention (United Nations 2001), the results are as follows. The first is the clear indication that 'conflict prevention is ... an activity best undertaken under Chapter VI of the Charter' — it is important to distinguish it from Chapter VII enforcement. The second is the statement that 'the primary responsibility for conflict prevention rests with national governments'. At the same time, there is reference to the important role played by civil society. The third is the focus on 'the deep-rooted socio-economic, cultural, environmental, institutional and other structural causes that often underlie the immediate political symptoms of conflicts'. The fourth is the need for 'a comprehensive approach that encompasses both short-term and long-term political, diplomatic, humanitarian, human rights, developmental, institutional and other measures'. The fifth is the strong, mutually reinforcing link between conflict prevention and 'sustainable and equitable development'. The sixth is the need for co-operation of 'many UN actors' as well as 'member states, international, regional and sub-regional organisations, the private sector [nongovernmental organisations] and other civil society actors'.

In the European Union, conflict prevention (defined as an important element of all aspects of the external relations of the EU) has been introduced as a permanent dimension of both the Common Foreign and Security Policy and the European Security and Defence Policy, in view of the drafting and implementation of a coherent and comprehensive preventive strategy. It is important to quote the Göteburg document: 'all relevant institutions of the Union will mainstream conflict prevention within their areas of competence' (European Commission 2001).

Furthermore, the G8 itself has been very active. The Italian presidency of the G8 in 2001 felt that the issue (which it inherited from the Japanese presidency after its introduction by Germany in 1999) had a special interest in conflict prevention. This is because it allows the G8 to give a coherent and comprehensive signal of a common concern for world governance, and also for openness to dialogue and co-operation with both governmental and nongovernmental actors.

In fact, conflict prevention, in its root-cause, non-enforcement, co-operative interpretation (the same interpretation that constitutes the premise of Annan's report), lends itself in a very special way to dialogue with developing countries. It addresses the prevention of conflict in relation with development, and not — as developing countries fear — as a zero-sum alternative between resources for security and resources for development. It is clearly an alternative to the use of force that, if prevention is not carried out or is ineffective, may become necessary to manage or stop conflict once it has broken out. At the same time, conflict prevention is also a privileged ground for dialogue and co-operation with nongovernmental organisations (NGOs) and civil society in general. This is both because it addresses the themes at the centre of their concern and activities (human rights, small arms, development, children in war, and so on) and also because the G8, in dealing with this issue, is giving a growing space to civil society and recognising its significant responsibility and positive contribution. In 2001, the G8 included two new items within the conflict prevention agenda: the role of private business and the role of women (and especially their organisations) in prevention. This is a significant addition that goes against the caricature of the G8 as an oligarchic, closed club of rich countries deaf to the demands and the role of civil society.

Finally, the 2002 G8 Summit in Kananaskis must be examined from the point of view of the issue of conflict prevention. It is significant that under the Canadian presidency conflict prevention has been thoroughly mainstreamed. Indeed, it would be a mistake to infer a lower status for conflict prevention from the fact that the subject has received fewer explicit mentions and less explicit space — compared to previous documents — in the texts approved at Kananaskis. Of course, the main focus of the Summit was (inevitably) terrorism. Yet conflict prevention was an important dimension of the political approach dominating the discussions. In addition to two items that needed finishing touches, having already been addressed under previous chairs (water as a main aspect of conflict and development, and disarmament, demobilisation, and reintegration, or DDR), a conflict prevention approach was very much evident in the way that Kananaskis addressed the situation in post-conflict

Afghanistan. It is important to note, in this respect, that the Conflict Prevention Officials Meeting (CPOM), the working group operating under the G8 political directors, focussed totally on Afghanistan, in particular addressing two specific aspects of conflict prevention on which it had previously developed guidelines and principles: security sector reform and DDR.

But perhaps the most meaningful and incisive demonstration of how to mainstream conflict prevention was given, under the Canadians, by the G8 Africa Action Plan, the initiative of support to that New Partnership for Africa's Development (NEPAD) that originated from the 2001 G8 Genoa Summit. There is no doubt, in fact, that the whole initiative is inspired by the same premise that the G8 has repeatedly endorsed: development is impossible in the presence of conflict and, conversely, conflict is made less recurrent by development. NEPAD makes this link very explicit, as does the G8 Africa Action Plan. It is enough to run through the text in order to find several of the priorities identified by the G8 in its conflict prevention exercise starting under the Germans in 1999: DDR, small arms, natural resources fuelling conflict (in particular diamonds), and child soldiers. Moreover, the 2002 Kananaskis Summit gave a lot of attention to the closely related subject of preventive diplomacy, in particular in the case of the tensions between India and Pakistan. Furthermore, the 2003 Evian Summit confirmed the trends laid out the year before: mainstreaming conflict prevention and its specific focus on Africa.

One could therefore venture to say that the conflict prevention exercise within the G8 graduated from priority setting and standard setting to the area of policy, moving from theory to practice, from the general to the specific. Thus, since 1992, as a general category of analysis and of mainstreamed political action, prevention has become one of the main areas for the G8, and perhaps one of the most promising.

Clearly, the promotion of conflict prevention on the agendas of the G8, the UN, the EU, the OSCE, and the OECD, among others, has been fundamentally important in developing a modern approach to international conflict. Yet much remains to be done on a practical level. First, the most important mechanisms for international action, prime among them being the UNSC, need to be re-legitimised in the wake of the 2003 war in Iraq. If the process is to succeed, some reform of current international decision-making mechanisms might also be necessary.[12] However, because the core concept of conflict prevention entails encroachment on national sovereignty — generally taboo in current international law — it is crucial that the intervention be sanctioned by an institution that can credibly claim to represent the majority of states.

Second, when addressing the root causes of conflict, a reappraisal of traditional development strategies is required. The alleviation of poverty should be paired with a more comprehensive assessment of basic local needs in the target areas — political and sociocultural, as well as economic needs. Particular attention is needed in transition regimes and in ethnically diverse societies with recent histories of conflict. Adhering to fundamental democratic principles, while taking account of local leadership in decision making, is absolutely required. Such an approach is increasingly more political and cultural and less purely economic. Given the political nature of violent conflicts, it would be more appropriate to shift the focus of current development assistance accordingly.

The third and final point to be made is that involving NGOs as well as powerful international corporations in the effort would be essential. Co-ordinating intelligence gathering and channelling information into early warning systems and risk analyses databases might be mutually beneficial to both governmental and nongovernmental actors. Comprehensive and multilateral efforts are clearly needed in order to embed a conflict prevention culture into the international normative establishment. The scope of such endeavours clearly transcends individual administrations. It is in this context that the G8's latest efforts over the past two years should be seen — in helping to consolidate an axiological framework essential for conflict prevention activities.

Notes

1 For details, see Ackermann (2002) and Stefanova (1997).
2 See, for example, the report of the International Action Network on Small Arms (2003) assessing the implementation of the UN Programme of Action on Small Arms.
3 It is also interesting to note that of the other four initiatives, three can be classified as instruments (both as instruments for conflict and instruments against conflict): small arms, children in armed conflict, and international civilian police. Only one — conflict and development — addresses root causes.
4 The case of Zimbabwe — similar to what has happened in several conflict-plagued African countries — gives evident support to this proposition: 'In the last decade, the percentage of people living in poverty has surged from 40 percent to more than 65 percent. Wages have fallen to pre-independence levels. The government can no longer pay creditors, buy adequate fuel or supply medicines to hospitals' (Swarns 2000).
5 For example, from a report on inter-ethnic violence in the Moluccas: 'Muslim and Christian villagers, who have lived peacefully side by side for generations, have been attacking one another with home-made guns and bombs packed with nails. ... During the colonial era, the Dutch favoured the Christians, giving them choice government positions. But after Indonesia achieved independence, things swung the other way. In the 1960s and 1970s, the government encouraged thousands of Muslims from other parts of Indonesia to settle in the Moluccas under a policy aimed at diluting the overwhelming Christian majority. Over the years and with incentive from Jakarta, many of the Muslims became prosperous merchants while Christians were relegated to farming and fishing. ... [According to a local observer], during the Suharto years, the military put all the problems under the carpet. Nothing was solved in an open or transparent manner. So when he fell, all of those old problems that were never fixed, mixed with economic deprivation and political struggles, started to erupt' (Chandrasekaran 2000).
   The same can be said for tribal conflict in Africa, where the ethnic factor is not *per se* conflictive, if not combined with socioeconomic diversification. This is, of course, the case for the Hutu and Tutsi in Rwanda, but also for less genocidal and less well-known conflicts, such as the one between the Lendu and Hema tribes in the Congo: 'The Lendu, like the Hutu, are Bantu farmers who have lived in the region for many centuries. The Hema, like the Tutsi, apparently migrated from areas around the Nile more recently, though still hundreds of years ago. Like the Tutsi, the Hema tend to be richer, in this case farming plantations of cattle and coffee once owned by Belgian colonialists. The Lendu outnumber the Hema,

though it is unclear by how much. ... Local authorities and aid groups say the recent violence began when a few Hema sought to extend the reach of their plantations onto land occupied by Lendu' (Fisher 2000).

The same combination of ethnicity and economic differentiation has proven explosive in the Fiji Islands, with autochthonous inhabitants pitted against the Indian community (dominant in business and also in politics) and in the Solomon Islands.

6 For example, from Côte d'Ivoire: 'As world commodity prices have foundered and the economy has stagnated over the last two years, some political leaders have blamed foreigners. Lootings have increased in immigrant neighborhoods, often while the police stand by and do nothing. As a result, tens of thousands of foreigners, many of whom have lived here for generations, are fleeing' ('Immigrant Workers Fleeing Ivory Coast' 2001).

7 In a candid report published in 2001 by a group under the Chinese Communist Party's Central Committee, corruption is cited as 'the main fuse exacerbating conflicts between officials and the masses', adding 'if there are no channels for letting off steam, the repressed discontent of individuals could well up into large-scale social instability' (quoted in Manning 2001). On the same issue, see also Pomfret (2000). The following day in the same newspaper, Waldron (2000) commented on the riots: 'The protesting miners were as angry about corruption as about poverty.'

8 For example: 'Ethnic violence broke out on the main island of Guadalcanal in 1999 between locals and settlers originally from the neighbouring island of Malaita. Many Malaitans, whose ascendants often had arrived in Guadalcanal during the Second World War, had found wage employment or risen to become a part of the business and political elite. Resentment among locals progressively grew until an outbreak of village burning, kidnapping and murder against Malaitans occurred.' From the same report: 'Managing ethnic tensions is closely related to strategic development issues, including unsolved problems of access to land for vital infrastructure and commercial use, as well as for housing' (Development Assistance Committee 2000).

9 The following article deserves to be quoted extensively, since it is almost a textbook case on the multi-causal nature of conflict: 'Vietnam's central highlands have been transformed over the past decade by an influx of migrants from the densely populated coastal plains and the rapid expansion of coffee cultivation over huge tracts of previously virgin jungle. ... But the rapid changes have led to simmering tensions between the highlands' traditional inhabitants and the new arrivals. "It's got to stem from land", one Vietnam-based coffee trader said of the demonstrations. "The minorities are feeling squeezed by the ethnic Vietnamese migrants." ... Grievances over land encroachment have been exacerbated by mounting religious tensions. According to the U.S. State Department's annual report on religious freedom, an increasing number of minority people in the central highlands have converted to Protestantism, partly influenced by evangelical radio broadcasts. Protestant worshippers are often subjected to arbitrary detention by local officials, the report said' (Kazmin 2001).

10 The way history is taught can be a serious conflict-generating issue. Both China and South Korea have reacted in very strong terms to textbooks, introduced in Japanese schools, containing a so-called revisionist view on the misdeeds of Japanese imperialism before and during World War II (Struck 2001). Seoul went so far as to interrupt co-operation with Tokyo in the cultural and military fields.

11 For example, on NATO's approach to security through regional co-operation, see Stefanova (2000).

12 For a comprehensive discussion, see Glennon (2003).

References

Ackermann, Alice (2002). 'Macedonia in a Post-Peace Agreement Environment: A Role for Conflict Prevention and Reconciliation'. *International Spectator* vol. 37, no. 1, pp. 71–82.

Aliboni, Roberto, Laura Guazzone, and Daniela Pioppi (2001). 'Early Warning and Conflict Prevention in the Euro-Med Area'. Istituto Affari Internazionali Occasional Papers No. 2.

Brown, Michael, ed. (1996). *The International Dimensions of Internal Conflict.* MIT Press, Cambridge, MA.

Burton, John W. (1990). *Conflict: Human Needs Theory.* St. Martin's Press, New York.

Chandrasekaran, Rajiv (2000). 'Christian-Muslim Conflict Rages in Indonesia's East'. *International Herald Tribune*, 20 June.

Democratic National Committee (2000). '2000 Democratic Party Platform'. 15 August. <www.democrats.org/about/2000platform.html> (July 2003).

Development Assistance Committee (2000). 'New Zealand's Aid Programme to the Solomon Islands: Note by the Secretariat'. DCD/DAC/AR(2000)2/24/ADD2. 13 April. Organisation for Economic Co-operation and Development, Paris.

Development Assistance Committee (2001). 'The DAC Guidelines: Helping Prevent Violent Conflict'. <www.oecd.org/dataoecd/15/54/1886146.pdf> (July 2003).

European Commission (2001). 'EU Programme for the Prevention of Violent Conflicts'. Göteburg, 15–16 June. <www.utrikes.regeringen.se/prefak/files/EUprogramme.pdf> (July 2003).

Fisher, Ian (2000). 'For Central Africa, More War and Horrors: Congo's Tribal Strife Spins Out of Control'. *International Herald Tribune*, 14 February.

G8 Foreign Ministers (2000). 'G8 Miyazaki Initiatives for Conflict Prevention'. Miyazaki, 13 July. <www.g7.utoronto.ca/foreign/fm000713-in.htm> (July 2003).

Glennon, Michael J. (2003). 'Why the Security Council Failed'. *Foreign Affairs* vol. 74, no. 3, pp. 16–35.

Grant, James P. (1993). 'Jumpstarting Development'. *Foreign Policy* Summer, pp. 124–136.

Horowitz, Donald L. (1985). *Ethnic Groups in Conflict.* University of California Press, Berkeley, CA.

'Immigrant Workers Fleeing Ivory Coast'. (2001). *International Herald Tribune*, 2 February.

International Action Network on Small Arms (2003). 'IANSA Report Implementing the Programme of Action 2003'. London. <www.iansa.org/documents/03poareport/index.htm> (July 2003).

Kazmin, Amy (2001). 'Vietnam Bars Foreigners from Riot-Hit Areas'. *Financial Times*, 9 February.

Lombardi, Ben (2002). 'The "Bush Doctrine": Anticipatory Self-Defence and the New U.S. National Security Strategy'. *International Spectator* vol. 37, no. 4, pp. 91–105.

Manning, Robert A. (2001). 'Beware of Chinese Weaknesses before the 2008 Olympics'. *International Herald Tribune*, 18 July.

Morrow, James D. (1990). 'When Do Power Transitions Lead to War?' Working Paper in International Studies No. I-90-15. Hoover Institution.

Nye, Joseph S. (2001). 'Globalization and Discontent'. *The World Today* vol. 57, no. 8/9, pp. 39–40.

Permanent Mission of Germany to the United Nations (2000). 'Speech by the Federal Minister for Economic Co-operation and Development, Heidemarie Wieczorek-Zeul, at the Workshop on Crisis Prevention and Development Co-operation'. New York, 19 April. <www.germany-info.org/UN/stsp_04_19_00.htm> (June 2001).

Pomfret, John (2000). 'Miners' Riots Reveal the Pain of Change in China'. *International Herald Tribune*, 6 April.

Stedman, Stephen John (1995). 'Alchemy for a New World Order: Overselling "Preventive Diplomacy"'. *Foreign Affairs* vol. 74, no. 3, pp. 14–21.

Stefanova, Radoslava (1997). 'Preventing Violent Conflict in Macedonia: A Success Story?' *International Spectator* vol. 32, no. 3/4, pp. 99–120.

Stefanova, Radoslava (2000). 'Fostering Security through Regional Cooperation in South-East Europe: A Role for the EAPC'. *International Spectator* vol. 35, no. 4, pp. 97–107.

Struck, Doug (2001). 'History Rift Strains Japan's Relations with Its Neighbors'. *International Herald Tribune*, 25–26 August.

Swarns, Rachel L. (2000). 'Mugabe Talks Defiance, But Is Zimbabwe Listening?' *International Herald Tribune*, 10 April.

United Nations (1945). 'Charter of the United Nations'. <www.un.org/aboutun/charter> (July 2003).

United Nations (1999). 'The Nine Principles [of the Global Compact]'. <www.unglobalcompact.org> (July 2003).

United Nations (2000). 'Secretary General Says United Nations Stands "Ready to Help Africa, Wherever and However It Can"'. Press Release SG/SM/7485/Rev.1. 10 July. <www.un.org/News/Press/docs/2000/20000710.sgsm7485r1.doc.html> (July 2003).

United Nations (2001). 'Prevention of Armed Conflict: Report of the Secretary General. Executive Summary'. A/55/985-S/2001/574. 7 June. United Nations, New York. <daccess-ods.un.org/TMP/7047019.html> (July 2003).

Waldron, Arthur (2000). 'The Rumblings of an Avalanche Threaten China'. *International Herald Tribune*, 7 April.

Chapter 7

U.S. Approaches to International Conflict Prevention and the Role of Allies and International Institutions

Frank E. Loy

Over the last several decades, the United States and its allies — particularly its allies in the North Atlantic Treaty Organization (NATO) — have acted in concert a number of times to prevent or bring to an end certain kinds of conflicts. These conflicts have begun with attacks and counterattacks among ethnic groups, with ethnic cleansing, with mass violations of human rights, or with the collapse into chaos of countries with inept or criminal leadership. What all had in common is that they brought misery and death to a large number of ordinary, noncombatant citizens and threatened to spread the turmoil to neighbouring countries — and triggered strains and schisms among the coalitions that responded to them. These remain a threat to future efforts at conflict resolution or prevention. The responses to the 11 September 2001 terrorist attacks only masked those strains momentarily, coming in the wake of the immediate sympathy for the victims and the rather impulsive solidarity with the United States that followed. When, a little more than a year after the Al Qaeda strike, the possibility of a preventive war in the Persian Gulf arose, the conceptual and moral schism between the U.S. and many of its traditional allies in what concerns the conduct of a preventive war was ever more evident (Applebaum 2003).

The charges and counter-charges among coalition partners take various forms — charges of failure to consult, of unilateral decision making, of allies too weak to lend their weight to the task at hand, of phoney alliances. The differences on the best way to respond to the threat from Iraq in 2003 illuminated two developments with long-term significance: first, the inherent weakness of European decision making on foreign policy and, second, a rupture with traditional supporters of the U.S., such as Germany, among others, largely based on differing moral perspectives. It marked one of the deepest Euro-Atlantic divides since the creation of NATO.

The administration of President George W. Bush is increasingly seen in Europe as having an ideological affinity for militarism and as being primarily driven by oil politics. However, having made the preventive intervention doctrine the major pillar of its foreign policy, the U.S. sees European reluctance to accept it as an inherent strategic weakness that is combined with operational inability (Kagan 2003).

Bush's National Security Strategy 'essentially abandons concepts of deterrence — which dominated defense policies during the Cold War years — for a forward-reaching, pre-emptive strategy against hostile states and terrorist groups, while also expanding development assistance and free trade, promoting democracy, fighting disease, and transforming the U.S. military' (United States Department of State 2002).

Because of the unprecedented gravity and nature of the current divide between Europe and the U.S., it is important to explore how the relevant attitudes in the U.S. came about. Specifically, four key issues need to be considered. The first examines the still unresolved differences of view among U.S. policy makers about just what the U.S. role should be in the field of conflict prevention in the post–cold war era. Second are the lessons that seem to have been learned from some specific conflict prevention experiences. The third issue is the way in which the great disparity in military capability between the U.S. and its allies shapes U.S. attitudes toward collaboration. The fourth issue raises some specific U.S. concerns about participating in United Nations peacekeeping operations.

The Origin and Evolution of U.S. Policy Making on Conflict Prevention

The concept of conflict prevention has changed markedly in recent decades. The early part of the twentieth century was characterised by colonial hegemonies that rather successfully — and often brutally — suppressed opposition, ethnic conflict, and regional wars. Later, in a strange and even perverted way, the cold war held in check disorderly societies and the regional or civil conflicts that they could spawn. The Soviet empire exerted both the will and the force to repress local or regional conflicts. Concurrently, the western world's response to the threat of Soviet expansion or aggression, led by the U.S., provided additional glue that held often disparate nations or groups together.

With the end of the cold war, it became more difficult for major powers to impose their discipline on potentially belligerent societies. Not only was the glue gone, but changes were also taking place in many developing countries, or in areas that had been recently freed from communist rule, that almost assured turmoil: the move from autocratic toward democratic systems of governance, rapid population growth, and the shift from a centralised economy to a market economy, a process during which formerly closed economies were promptly set adrift in a world of global markets.

At the same time, the nations of the industrialised world underwent a different change: a change in mindset about what was appropriate practice. After centuries of imperial rule, imposing one's practices and institutions on disorderly societies seemed out of favour.

As the century drew to a close, the predictable conflict and chaos did indeed grow. By one count, in 1998 alone there were 27 significant conflicts in the world, including 25 that involved violence within states. Of the latter, nine were in sub-Saharan Africa.

The conflicts became not only more numerous, but also became bloodier and involved more combatant countries. And, as a study by the World Bank shows, they lasted longer (Collier, Hoeffler, and Söderbom 2001). The study examined conflicts since 1960 and suggests that wars started after 1980 lasted three times longer than those that began in the preceding two decades.

Although these developments represented a threat and a worry to all the G8 countries (and indeed all of Europe and most of the rest of the members of the Organisation for Economic Co-operation and Development), in the U.S. they triggered a different, more fundamental re-evaluation of foreign policy goals. Historically, U.S. foreign policy had been based on two pillars: assuring security from military attack and strengthening the U.S. national economy. The pursuit of the latter goal took various turns. Sometimes it led to tariffs and other forms of protection, and at other times it led to promoting the economy through liberalised trade. But in both cases the motivation was the same.

Then, rather suddenly, these goals no longer appeared to reflect true U.S. interests adequately in this new and disorderly world. There is no precise point to mark the beginning of this re-evaluation. But one key moment was the administration of Jimmy Carter. By putting human rights objectives near the top of his foreign policy agenda, he forced the U.S. to rethink just what really constituted its national interest.

Subsequently, this agenda of what might be called nontraditional interests was broadened further. The U.S. talked of its interest in promoting democracy more widely, in encouraging the concept of government under a rule of law, and in addressing international environmental problems. Some suggested that, at the base of U.S. foreign policy concerns, the country needed an even more ambitious objective: reducing the chasm between the rich and the poor countries of the world.

This rethinking of goals was not entirely limited to periods of Democratic administrations. For example, Ronald Reagan, drawing on his own personal popularity and strength, launched the National Endowment of Democracy and its four institutes to help — overtly and at a substantial level of effort — nations that sought to achieve a more democratic system of governance. More recently, certain traditionally conservative and often Republican elements in the U.S. Congress have taken the lead in promoting certain categories of human rights, sometimes somewhat selectively. They have been particularly vigilant about violations of human rights in current or former communist countries, and in assuring the right to worship without interference or pressure from the state. Some of the rhetoric of the Bush administration urging regime change in Iraq, while having multiple motivations, may reflect that trend.

The fact that the U.S. moved so far and so fast in putting these new goals close to the centre of its foreign policy goals put great strain on the political consensus within the U.S. Profound differences emerged — not always along party lines — between the 'realists', with a more traditional outlook focussed on traditional national security concerns, and those who embraced the new, broader agenda. The former tended to view the latter as a bit fuzzy, as the promoters of a 'romantic' foreign policy, as Bush's foreign policy advisor once described Bill Clinton's administration.

This schism deepened when the implications of the change became clearer. Failure to realise these broadened foreign policy goals looked to be more serious than first thought — for example, continued failure to uphold human rights in a developing country could well lead to bloody conflicts. And realising these goals was also more complex and costly. Securing these broader U.S. goals would require more than technical assistance, more than money, or even more than providing military weapons or training. When long dormant differences with neighbours or differing ethnic groups were reopened with actual military conflicts or with ethnic cleansing, or when a state simply ceased to function as a working entity because of corruption, criminal behaviour, or ineptitude, these traditional tools were not enough. More was required, and the 'more' was first active diplomacy to prevent conflicts that, it soon became clear, would often only succeed if it was backed by the input of military force.

This realisation produced the charge from realists that this broadening of U.S. foreign policy goals was really the product of a noble, if fuzzy, idea in search of a strategy. How could the U.S. pursue conflict resolution without getting involved in innumerable conflicts around the world — a process without borders or without an end? Was there a rational divide between the cases where the U.S. should intervene and the rest?

The realists' argument was anchored by two propositions. The first was that many of these wars had their roots in ancient enmities and deeply entrenched conflicting senses of identity — whether ethnic, tribal, or religious — the origin of which was centuries old. The cold war had masked these conflicts for a time, but with its end the old hatreds again took on the character of historical inevitability, and that made intervention a hopeless task.

The second argument was that, even if there were a substantial chance of success, the costs of intervention were too high and the U.S. interest too low. This view may have been best encapsulated by a former U.S. ambassador to Somalia who noted that some countries are 'not a critical piece of real estate for anybody in the post-Cold War world' (Richburg 1994).

The U.S. Military Capabilities and Its Role as a Global Police Officer

In one form or another, this sort of calculation — whether or not to take military action as part of conflict prevention efforts — must be made, and is made, by any country willing to intervene (Jentleson 2000). But in the U.S. it has a considerably sharper edge, and it is therefore a more politically charged decision. Behind that lies the history of U.S. ambivalence toward international engagements, but also, much more important, three very real facts. First, the U.S. is the only superpower today. Second, the disparity in the level of military capability between it and the rest of the world, including its allies, is huge, and not narrowing. Third, the 11 September terrorist attacks changed the U.S. concept of permissible behaviour and seemed to support a new doctrine hinged on preventive military intervention to uphold the vital national interests of the U.S., even, if necessary, in defiance of allies and international law (Farer 2002).

The budgetary disparity in military spending is huge. The U.S. defence budget, counting the US$48 billion increase proposed by Bush for the 2003 fiscal year, is about double the budget of all other NATO countries combined. The U.S. will spend about 3.5 percent of its gross domestic product on defence, compared to 2.2 percent for its European NATO allies. On a per capita basis, even before that increase, the annual U.S. expenditures were three times those of the rest of NATO (O'Hanlon 2002).

Furthermore, with the exception of the British, European military forces are antique. Europe lacks smart bombs, stealth aircraft, or the kind of drones and aircraft that successfully spotted targets in Afghanistan. And although Europe has pledged to modernise, it never seems to happen. The European rapid reaction force was declared operational in May 2002, but subsequent simulation exercises revealed congenital command-and-control flaws, a fact that cast doubt over whether the force could succeed in a real combat situation. The 1999 European Defence Capabilities Initiative remains largely a diplomatic and industrial forum for discussion, despite ambitious commitments pledged. The multi-country military cargo plane is having a hard time getting off the ground. As a result, the Euro-Atlantic disparities grow wider. As Lord Robertson (2002), NATO's secretary general, said, 'mighty Europe remains a military pygmy'.

The U.S. military and defence capability has clearly placed the U.S. in a somewhat singular position. It has permitted the U.S. to pursue its interests with a clout that others may envy, and do not have. And it has permitted — or so it has seemed to some — the U.S. to do so without needing the aid of others. The strong sense of strategic self-sufficiency explained why, in 2003, the U.S. seemed ready to conduct a war in the Persian Gulf outside the framework of NATO, the UN, or, indeed, without key European allies.

This very capability, however, has also meant that the U.S. is called upon to put out more fires than others. Why else would it establish a strategy of maintaining the capability to fight two regional conflicts at once? The U.S. military commitment is to be found virtually everywhere: from the Balkans to the Mediterranean, to Southeast Asia, to the Korean Peninsula. Thus, there is a real-world context to the question the U.S. must often ask itself: Is fire fighting any of its business? Does it really want to become a fire fighter (or a police officer) in this particular instance?

The vision of the U.S. service men and women engaged in strife in numerous places around the world certainly played a key role in the decision of the Clinton administration not to sign the convention to ban landmines or the Rome Statute of the International Criminal Court. While it had sought ways to reformulate these accords to make them ratifiable by the U.S. Senate, the Bush administration rather gleefully turned its back on them and declared them of no interest to the U.S., exasperating its European allies.

Without deciding for the moment whether these decisions were wise, one must acknowledge that the calculus is different for a country that has some 37 000 troops stationed in hotspots such as the border between North and South Korea, and that led both the first Gulf War and the effort to dislodge Slobodan Milosevic in Serbia.

This belief — that the U.S. will be called upon to bring military action in numerous other theatres — has also contributed to the nonsensical U.S. policy that holds that, while the U.S. might bring arms and troops to a conflict, it will only rarely and reluctantly engage in longer term actions that fall under the heading of UN peacekeeping.

After the 11 September attacks, however, it became clear that despite its military capability, the U.S. was vulnerable to large-scale terrorist attacks. As a result, an unprecedented policy inaugurated by the Bush administration to intervene both militarily and politically in countries known to harbour terrorist networks became central to U.S. foreign policy. Military build-up, consequently, increased further, thus widening ever more the Euro-Atlantic capabilities gap. But the tension between the U.S. and its European allies with regard to the limits of conflict prevention reached a new peak in 2003, with the new U.S. strategic doctrine centred on the premise of preventive military intervention, with or without allies, inside or outside the UN framework, anywhere where the U.S. perceived a terrorist threat. The U.S. no longer appeared to be only operational, but also ideological. This engendered some ideological responses. Some European countries, such as Germany, rejected on normative grounds the idea of an all-out war outside the internationally recognised structures. Others, such as France, were traditionally resentful of what they saw as U.S. unilateralism in world affairs. Virtually all, with the exception of Britain, were reluctant to discard the UN and contribute to what they saw as the de-legitimisation of the UN Security Council. Clearly, however, the preventive intervention doctrine had taken U.S. foreign policy making to a different level: one where it was increasingly alone in undertaking action, but also one where it had an unprecedented decision-making and operational flexibility (Dockrill 2002).

Determinants of U.S. Preventive Intervention

The consideration of finding an institutional framework for any U.S. preventive action, however, remains a matter of discussion in U.S. academic and policy-making circles. There are four important dimensions in the process.

First is the question of whether the anticipated effort is a short-term humanitarian affair, designed to relieve immediate suffering, or whether the objective is a much more ambitious one: the building of a viable state.

Second is whether neutrality on the part of the U.S. is really an option. And if an honest assessment makes it clear that the answer is no, then the question is whether the U.S. is willing to take sides. Once this line has been crossed, involvement will surely last a very long time, including some form of post-conflict military presence. The events of 11 September 2001 have considerably tilted this calendar (Gedmin 2002), as have the subsequent events in Afghanistan and Iraq.

Third, the question of whether the U.S. can count on meaningful help from neighbours of the conflicted area has taken a more important dimension. In a situation where allied help at the level of NATO, or the European Union, can no longer be taken for granted, a traditional alliance building within the surrounding strategic environment is very important. That is also a fundamental part of Bush's 'coalition of the willing' intervention doctrine.

Fourth, is there a realistic assessment of how the anticipated intervention upholds America's vital interests? In the aftermath of 11 September, interventions that are not strictly related to what is perceived within the administration as U.S. 'homeland security' and domestic integrity will clearly not be given the consideration they previously had.

It is worth reconsidering, in the light of the analysis above, that the U.S. experience in Somalia was a turning point in America's pre–11 September experience with intervention to resolve a conflict. Three of the above questions were in play. The common view is that what the U.S. learned in Somalia was that the U.S. resists incurring casualties. However, the lessons learned from Somalia are somewhat more subtle.

The civil war began when President Ali Mahdi refused to yield his position to a challenger warlord, Mohammed Aidid. The conflict that resulted brought a famine and enormous suffering. The international community, slow in recognising the severity of the situation, did not intervene for some time. Several African leaders sought to mediate between the warring factions, particularly at the Djibouti Conference of 1991. At that time no western government supported these mediations with resources, and the UN was not in a position to do so. Italy offered to help resolve the conflict and worked seriously toward that end. But its efforts were rejected by Aidid, who did not believe in Italy's neutrality.

The UN became involved in January 1992, and produced a UNSC-mediated cease-fire that did not last. Violence ensued again, and compromised the already difficult humanitarian effort to provide food to the populace.

The media coverage that followed made it politically difficult for the United States to do nothing. In response, the U.S. sent troops, with the announced humanitarian mission to ensure that the food got through.

All this was done in the absence of a cease-fire and, contrary to what is commonly believed in Europe, it was generally understood just how difficult and dangerous the mission would be. In fact, the worst that might have been anticipated did happen. That is, the local clans, many of which supported Aidid, interpreted the U.S. effort (and that of some others) to assure a secure food supply as interference on the side of Mahdi. That led to a UNSC resolution that sought to disarm the population and capture Aidid. In one of the ensuing skirmishes, a small number of U.S. and some Pakistani lives were lost. Within a year, all troops had been withdrawn. Chaos reigned again.

What are the lessons to be drawn from Somalia? First, the U.S. erred by not distinguishing between a humanitarian effort — which might be doable through the efforts of nongovernmental organisations (NGOs), the International Committee of the Red Cross, the World Food Programme, or the like — and the need to build a state in Somalia, which required levels of military commitment and resources that, it became clear, no one was willing to provide.

Second, although there were promises of intervention by neighbouring states, they lacked credibility, principally because they were not backed by resources. Third, the mediation efforts — first by Italy and then the UN — were not considered neutral enough. The latter, in the end, looked very much like taking sides. Fourth, if a regime change was the real objective, the level of military deployment needed to be much more substantive, both in terms of ground troops and equipment.

The U.S. Attitude toward a United Nations Umbrella for Preventive Intervention

One substitute for a series of stitched-together *ad hoc* alliances in every peacekeeping situation would be to rely on a permanent UN peacekeeping force. Is there a chance that the UN can fashion such force? The U.S., again, is viewed as a stumbling block, because it is correctly thought that the likelihood of U.S. participation in such an exercise is remote.

Some of the fullest and most thoughtful discussion of what issues are raised in trying to fashion such a force can be found in the August 2000 UN Report on Peacekeeping Operations (Panel on United Nations Peace Operations 2000). An analysis of it reveals some of the tough problems related to U.S. involvement.

If endorsed, the proposal would significantly expand both the scope and the frequency of UN military operations. There would be more robust rules of engagement for UN forces (although it is not quite clear what that really means), and the traditional canons of impartiality would be reinterpreted to permit these forces to take sides in conflicts.

These are two realistic suggestions, in light of the difficulty encountered in past efforts. But they present problems. For example, at present the consent of the parties is necessary before UN troops are engaged. Lakhdar Brahimi, chair of the panel, would do away with the need for that consent. He suggests, in effect, a force that could be used not only for peacekeeping but also for much more aggressive peacemaking.

Of course, Article 43 of the UN Charter does contemplate something of this sort. Secretary General Trygvie Lie, soon after the launch of the UN, suggested the establishment of a force of some magnitude. But the cold war scuttled those plans, and today the UN has neither such a force nor an agreement that it should have one.

The suggestion to use such a force to prevent or resolve conflicts raises at least two other problems of concern to the U.S. The first is if the intervention is considered within the UN framework, the question looms as to whether Security Council approval would be needed to deploy it. For most Americans today the answer has to be an unqualified yes. Such deployment would be the most delicate step the UN can take. It ought not to be undertaken without the assent of the organisation's principal body charged with assuring security. It is unlikely that a number of countries, including the U.S., would be politically able to approve such a force without this requirement.

The requirement of UNSC approval raises the spectre of Security Council vetoes. At one time, there was the hope of some that vetoes would disappear from the scene with the end of the cold war. But that will not happen. Thus there is a legitimate fear that if the Security Council is unable to act by reason of a veto or a threatened veto, the UN will actually be weakened, not strengthened, by the creation of such a force.

A second issue concerns the kind of force that the UN might be able to assemble. The experience in Sierra Leone and the Congo should sound a note of caution. In both instances, western nations have refused to supply troops to the UN command. That raises the question of whether a force drawn purely from developing countries would be effective. It is a delicate issue. It is very likely that such forces would be less trained and less professional than troops from developed countries. There is a risk that they would, in fact, be something like mercenaries. In Sierra Leone and the Congo, there have been constant charges of incompetence, of corruption and bribery, and of infighting among the UN forces. Fear of a repeat of this state of affairs makes it politically difficult for the U.S. to assign forces to UN units.

These fears, plus fears, valid or not, of a slow and inefficient decision-making process created by an overly bureaucratic and porous mechanism under a UN umbrella, make U.S. participation in such a military operation highly unlikely. Instead, there will be a strong argument that making use of the NATO institutional framework, which is already in place — and where the U.S. can address both its command-and-control concerns and operate within a structure where the professionalism of the force employed cannot be disputed — might be a valid alternative, if a UNSC mandate is in place.

Toward a New U.S. Preventive Intervention Doctrine

After the terrorist attacks of 11 September, there undoubtedly is a growing interest within the US to engage in preventive military action. However, the policy conceptions behind that interest are fundamentally different from the policy trend to be found in U.S. foreign policy making through the 1990s. The emphasis is now on upholding homeland security, rather than engaging in alleviating humanitarian disasters or intervening in cases of grave human rights abuses abroad. This change has deepened American differences with European allies and sharpened distrust in UN institutions. As a result, in the near term, the UN institutional framework as an umbrella even for *ad hoc* preventive interventions is even less likely to be upheld by U.S. policy makers. While this policy is, in fact, harmful to U.S. long-term policy interests, it will remain U.S. policy for some time — at least as long as the current administration remains in office.

References

Applebaum, Anne (2003). 'Here Comes the New Europe'. *Washington Post*, 29 January.

Collier, Paul, Anke Hoeffler, and Mans Söderbom (2001). 'On the Duration of Civil War'. Policy Research Working Paper WPS 2681. World Bank, Washington DC.

Dockrill, Saki (2002). 'Does a Superpower Need an Alliance?' *Internationale Politik* vol. 3 (Fall), pp. 9–12.

Farer, Tom (2002). 'The Bush Doctrine and the UN Charter Frame', *International Spectator* vol. 37, no. 3, pp. 91–100.

Gedmin, Jeffrey (2002). 'Transatlantic Ties after 9/11: An American View', *Internationale Politik* vol. 3 (Fall), pp. 13–18.

Jentleson, Bruce W., ed. (2000). *Opportunities Missed, Opportunities Seized: Preventive Diplomacy in the Post–Cold War World*. Rowman and Littlefield, Lanham, MD.

Kagan, Robert (2002). 'Power and Weakness', *Policy Review* June/July, pp. 3–28.

O'Hanlon, Michael (2002). 'Restraining the Growth of the U.S. Defense Budget'. Congressional Testimony, 28 February, U.S. Senate Budget Committee. <www.brook.edu/dybdocroot/views/testimony/ohanlon/20020228.htm> (July 2003).

Panel on United Nations Peace Operations (2000). 'Report of the Panel on United Nations Peace Operations'. The Brahimi Report. <www.un.org/peace/reports/peace_operations> (July 2003).

Richburg, Keith B. (1994). 'Africa in Agony: Somalia Slips Back to Bloodshed'. *Washington Post*, 4 September.

Robertson, Lord (2002). 'Speech at the First Magazine Dinner'. 24 January, London. <www.nato.int/docu/speech/2002/s020124a.htm> (July 2003).

United States Department of State (2002). 'Bush Sends New National Security Strategy to Congress'. 20 September. <usinfo.state.gov/regional/nea/sasia/text/0920bush.htm> (July 2003).

Chapter 8

Advancing the European Union's Conflict Prevention Policy

Reinhardt Rummel[1]

The European Union is both a pioneer in conflict prevention and a latecomer to it. It is a pioneer in regard to advancing the idea of conflict prevention within Europe and among the European nation-states. In fact, the main purpose of the 50-year-old unification process was to bind together France and Germany as well as other European states to make sure they would not go to war again, as they had for centuries. By tying their sovereignty to a supranational core, the member states of the EU decided to entangle their future in commonly agreed rules and institutions and to invite other states to join. The union has now grown to 15 and is likely to see the accession of ten more members in 2004, taking the population of the EU to almost half a billion.[2] Thus European states have turned from a tradition of belligerence and repeated fighting to a culture of co-operation and peaceful conflict resolution. As a side effect, the establishment and development of the EU have been intimately associated with a high degree of prosperity and stability within its borders.

Can the European states reproduce such a success story outside the EU? This goal must be much harder to achieve because whether other regions of crisis quit the habit of war and engage in peaceful approaches to conflict will not only — not even primarily — depend on the Europeans. Given its positive experience at home and its influence in the world, however, the EU holds many decisive keys to advancing the culture of prevention world-wide. Conflict prevention policy is a major component of modern security policy. At present, the EU continues to be principally a common market and an economic entity, with trade and development relations in the foreground and foreign and security policy in embryonic stages. Conflict prevention and crisis management have lately been added to the agenda and the EU seems to be determined to use the new challenges to emerge as a more forceful actor in the arena of international politics.

Such assertive behaviour will inevitably lead the EU into more intra-European and, in fact, transatlantic disputes over strategic goals and the most appropriate ways to achieve them, as the Iraq war in 2003 demonstrated impressively. Most EU members lean toward avoiding war and reject pre-emptive intervention (Ackermann 2003). Unlike the United States, a superpower in all respects, the EU needs to make careful choices when it identifies its assets for conflict prevention. That selection process regularly includes the political ambition to assist others with reducing violence, the build-up of specific tools and devices within the EU, the creation of an institutional framework, and the preparation of the financial basis for European conflict prevention policy. This chapter describes and assesses the EU's potential for conflict prevention, therefore, focussing on the output rather than the outcome of its activities.[3]

European Union Ambitions in Conflict Prevention Policy

Today, the EU's approach to conflict prevention links to two main sources. One is connected with developments in the mid 1990s, when the EU saw mass killings in regions such as the western Balkans and sub-Saharan Africa. These conflicts had been considered critical before, but the international community — including the EU and its member states — did not intervene early enough to avoid genocide and massive destruction. The other source of the EU's current approach is more recent and stems from its experience in the Kosovo war as well as the response to the 11 September 2001 terrorist attacks, when Washington dominated international crisis management to an extent that the Europeans had no choice but to follow the U.S. lead. In the case of Iraq in 2003, Washington did not manage to get all the Europeans on board, but, here too, the U.S. created a situation within which — this time after the war — the Europeans seemed to have no option but to join the U.S. in rebuilding law and order in the country.

In the mid 1990s, the EU and its member states believed they could have made a difference by acting early to reduce large-scale human suffering (including outright genocide as happened in Srebrenica or Rwanda). Likewise, they could have tried to avoid having their investments in foreign aid and development over the years wiped out by civil war and transborder fighting within days or weeks. The human and the material costs of doing 'too little too late', however, required a switch in the EU's approach to the developing world as well as to the states in transition in the Balkans, Eastern Europe, and the former Soviet Union. In its relations with Africa, the EU via the European Commission advanced a new concept of conflict prevention (see European Commission 1996), while the Organization for Security and Co-operation in Europe (OSCE) was supported in promoting the activities of its High Commissioner for National Minorities and Vienna-based Conflict Prevention Centre.

The opportunities missed in Kosovo to stop the escalation of the conflict between the Serbs and the Albanians and the subsequent military intervention, including the heavy bombing of Serbia, made the Europeans think twice. It is hard to see how a European civilian approach could have changed Slobodan Milosevic's mind, just as it is inconceivable how an EU policy could have neutralised Bin Laden–driven terrorism or pushed Saddam Hussein from his authoritarian throne with anything other than military means. Yet European capitals and publics were deeply concerned by these three elements, which all led to a massive military response carried out by the U.S. and supported by some Europeans. Given the EU's ambition to refrain from the use of military force in international relations and to conduct an independent foreign policy, consequences for the further process of EU building seemed to be inevitable.

There was something of an outcry of 'never again'. The EU leaders in Brussels would not have necessarily favoured a response different to that of the American leadership, but it was brought home to them that, once violence started to dominate, the EU had few options left. Hence the logical consequence was to act earlier, in more forceful and better targeted ways. Brussels had been encouraged in these conclusions by the wider debate on the international stage, particularly at the level of the G8 countries and within the United Nations (Panel on United Nations Peace Operations 2000). They all urged a shift in emphasis from crisis management and post-war reconstruction to early action and the prevention of violent conflict.

This strategic shift has come about within a couple of years and can be traced back to a few key decisions and declarations made by the 15 heads of state and government since 1999, who subsequently asked the presidency of the EU, the Secretary General of the Council and High Representative of the Common Foreign and Security Policy (SG/HR), and the European Commission to develop and implement the full range of an EU conflict prevention policy. Of particular significance in this regard were three documents:

- the joint report by the SG/HR and the Commissioner for External Relations of the European Commission (November 2000) (European Commission 2000b),
- the Communication from the European Commission on Conflict Prevention (April 2001) (European Commission 2001b), and
- the EU Programme for the Prevention of Violent Conflicts issued by the European Council in Göteburg under the Swedish presidency (June 2001) (European Commission 2001f).

Prepared at the request of the heads of state and government, the joint report demonstrated the determination of the European institutions to work together to design and implement a more proactive foreign and security policy for the EU. Many conflicts, in particular the war in Kosovo, had shown the lack of sophistication of the existing early warning systems and proved the need for a stronger political will to improve the EU's capacities of early action. This was confirmed in the joint report: 'The Council has repeatedly emphasised the importance of effective early action to prevent violent conflict. Our experience of the consequences of conflict has been instrumental in the development of civilian and military crisis management capabilities, and is a driving factor in the development of a more effective and responsive Common Foreign and Security Policy (CFSP). A key challenge now facing the Union is to ensure the most effective use of the full range of tools which have become available in order to prevent conflict from occurring in the first place' (European Commission 2000b).

The discrepancy between ambitious goals and available instruments, on the one hand, and the lack of common and coherent action, on the other, remained a demanding challenge. During the presentation of the communication on conflict prevention on 11 April 2001, Commissioner Chris Patten remarked that 'the EU can make a real contribution towards the construction of peace and stability in the world. Not only because it is a major actor on the international scene and the world's largest aid donor, but even more due to the fact that the EU was itself born from a war, and was designed so as to prevent conflicts. The search for peace is one of the founding reasons for the EU's existence. The impact of our policies in this area is however crucially dependent upon a clear political will and a capacity for coherent and well co-ordinated action' (European Commission 2001c). Patten expressed the widespread assessment that, in principle, EU member states were not short of assets to intervene appropriately, but they were lacking the clout to unite for action.

While the joint report and the communication are largely characterised by stocktaking and listing what has been done in the EU that can be called conflict prevention, the EU Programme looks ahead and lists the areas in which the EU intends to take initiatives in the future. The heads of state and government promise to set clear political priorities for preventive action, to improve early warning, action, and policy coherence, to enhance its instruments for long- and short-term prevention, and to build effective partnerships for prevention. This list did not reach the status of a 'common strategy' as the Swedish presidency had originally aimed for. But it represents the most explicit and the highest ranking commitment made by the EU on conflict prevention. Presenting the EU Programme the Swedish foreign minister Anna Lindh was convinced that it 'will not only make the EU the international actor it has the potential to be. It will also contribute to a global partnership for prevention' (European Commission 2001f, 4).

Poul Nielson (2001), EU commissioner for development and humanitarian assistance, has been less optimistic in this regard:

> If EU member states are serious about conflict prevention they have to be more disciplined in taking stands on foreign policy positions vis-à-vis developing countries. We cannot have a High Representative on the basis of a low common denominator. The 'C' in CFSP stands for 'Common' not 'Convenient'. A main obstacle to a credible European contribution to conflict prevention are the barely co-ordinated views expressed by member states. I would not be honest with you if I did not point to this obvious lack of sufficient political will in member states to accommodate the unity in messages which is absolutely crucial to the credibility of Europe's common foreign policy.

Nielson seemed to be confident, however, that a simple procedural change would help to make the full EU potential available: 'There is only one recipe for this: a Community method. Allow me to repeat the message of President [Romano] Prodi last year to the European Parliament that the task currently confided to the office of the High Representative should become community competence'.

This statement proves that the EU continues to be split in its attention between the foreign policy problem on the ground and the goal of European integration in the foreign policy field. EU leaders know that successful conflict prevention requires dealing with immediate threats as well as with gradually escalating disputes. They must address trigger factors such as violent protests or the assassination of a public figure, as well as the root causes of conflict such as poverty, lack of good governance and respect for human rights, and competition for scarce resources. To organise a meaningful answer to the complex range of these challenges requires a rich arsenal of instruments.

Key Instruments: Moving Beyond Relabelling

In the early stages of its conflict prevention policy, the EU was tempted to regroup under the title of 'prevention' some of its existing programmes on development and democracy building or projects on media, human rights, and strengthening of civil society. While this was not altogether wrong, it did not represent an actual shift in focus and priority. That shift only came about after the EU's conceptual documents had been elaborated at the end of the 1990s.

The Capacities of the EU: Mobilising Comprehensive Assets

The EU can choose from an extensive set of economic, financial, political, and military means for either direct preventive action or for more long-term structural approaches. The long-term instruments comprise trade, development co-operation, human rights, and environmental policies as well as political dialogue and arms control. The short-term instruments include a wide range of diplomatic tools as well as confidence-building measures and humanitarian assistance. Many of these traditional means of the EU's relations with third countries are now adapted to the new challenges of conflict prevention.[4] Likewise, those capabilities that have been recently developed within the framework of the European Security and Defence Policy (ESDP), and consist of civilian as well as military means, can also contribute to the EU's capabilities to prevent conflicts.

Following their June 2001 programme, the EU heads of state and government decided first of all to strengthen the expertise within the EU's foreign policy on human rights and democracy and to engage more in disarmament, demobilisation, and reintegration (DDR), as well as de-mining, with a view to reducing further violence outside the EU. The European Council agreed to examine how instruments for disarmament, arms control, and nonproliferation, including confidence- and security-building measures, can be used systematically for preventive goals. These instruments are being applied in all stages of a conflict cycle, during times of still stable peace, for early warning purposes, as a means of containing outright war, and for the period of post-conflict stabilisation.

The EU decided to invest in both the reduction of the factors that cause or promote violence as well as the extension of inhibiting factors that help to pre-empt and avoid violence. Thus it would support the ratification and implementation of agreements to tackle the problem posed by the unregulated spread of small arms and light weapons in all its aspects, including the proposed UN Programme of Action. The EU member states and the European Commission would also tackle the illicit trade in high-value commodities, including by tackling work to identify ways of breaking the link between rough diamonds and violent conflicts and through support for the Kimberley Process. In terms of inhibiting factors, the EU would invest in programmes for good governance and an active civil society. This means, among many other things, more action targeted at supporting democracy and particular attention paid to support the electoral process, including electoral observers, administration of justice, improved police services, and human rights training for the whole security sector.

The EU thus moved beyond the narrow concept of preventive diplomacy and would also make other sectors such as trade, security, and development serve the purpose of prevention. 'I consider development co-operation as the most important contribution Europe can make to preventing conflicts in developing countries', claimed Nielson (2001) while pointing to a lesson of the multi-sector approach that he had learned as the commissioner for development: 'We should resist the temptation of trying to devise a one-size-fits-all policy on conflict prevention. Europe does not need to adopt a nicely packaged collection of instruments.' At the same time, it was obvious to European leaders that at least the Europeans had learned the lesson that violence cannot simply be encountered with violence. As Finnish president Maarti Ahtisaari (2001) put it: 'Experience in Kosovo and elsewhere has demonstrated that military forces are not suited to all crisis management tasks'. In fact, the prevention package needs to include civil and military instruments, just as it needs to encompass incentives and sanctions as well as structural and immediate means.

The Rapid Reaction Mechanism: Addressing Preventive Timeliness

Following a critical revision of its instruments for conflict prevention, the EU discovered that its response capacities were far too slow to deal with those cases of conflict prevention that required immediate action. In the words of Patten (2001c): 'The important thing about conflict prevention is that it should be quick and effective, and I repeat the word "quick".' Already the Helsinki European Council had called on the commission in December 1999 to set up a rapid reaction facility that would allow for a pragmatic and instant response in situations of escalating armed conflict. The facility should be designed to accelerate the provision of finance to support EU activities world-wide, to contribute to operations run by international organisations and to fund the activities of nongovernmental organisations (NGOs). It took some time until the regulation that established the Rapid Reaction Mechanism (RRM) was adopted by the General Affairs Council in February 2001. Since then the RRM has been used both to conduct one-off actions arising out of a crisis situation, such as the one in Macedonia in late 2001, and to kick-start projects or programmes that require long-term follow-up through other assistance instruments, such as those in Afghanistan in early 2002.

In general, the RRM measures are aimed at restoring the conditions of stability under which the main co-operation programmes of the EU can achieve their objectives. These can include measures to restore the rule of law, to promote democracy, human rights, peacebuilding, and mediation initiatives, to demobilise and reintegrate combatants, to reconstruct the infrastructure, and to conduct strategic planning for the economic, administrative, and social rebuilding of countries affected by crisis.[5] The basis of the RRM remains existing EU instruments capable of providing a large spectrum of actions and reactions. EU measures, in turn, remain the key to any possible follow-up initiative that might be required after the first emergency operation has elapsed.

The added value of the RRM, as opposed to previously existing EU instruments, is its speed and flexibility in situations of high tension immediately prior, during, and after crises. Patten praised the particular features of the mechanism: 'In times of urgent needs we cannot anymore afford the luxury to be bogged down by bureaucratic constraints and deliver Community instruments with unnecessary delays' (European Commission 2001d). The RRM has world-wide coverage and can mix a number of measures under one short-term intervention, according to the needs of the crisis. The EU, and particularly the European Commission, which administers the funds, is now in a better position to organise and support the mobilisation of member states' civilian experts (in areas such as mine clearance, customs, mediation, training of police or judges) in crisis situations.

At present, the RRM has quite limited funds. The total endowment in the 2001 budget amounted to 20 million euros (of which some 18 million have been used); for 2002, it was 25 million euros in the financial perspective.[6] The funds are intended primarily to enable rapid stabilising actions as precursors for eventual longer term assistance. A dividing line is also drawn between the scope of the RRM and the regulation concerning the EU's humanitarian aid. Interventions on the basis of the RRM are aimed at preserving or re-establishing the civic structures necessary for political, social, and economic stability. Although the European Community Humanitarian Organisation (ECHO) is politically neutral, the RRM interventions operate in the context of crisis management and drive a political agenda. Thus, the EU is not only continuing its well-established role as a donor, but becomes a 'player', too.

It is therefore with some justification that criticism has emerged concerning the transparency of the RRM decision-making process as a written procedure. Without any doubt there are also downsides to such a rapid reaction mechanism (Backhurst 2001). However, those who drafted the council regulation have been well aware of this problem: 'There is a need for maximum transparency in all matters concerning the implementation of the Community's financial assistance as well as proper control of the use of appropriations' (European Commission 2001e).

Civilian Crisis Management: Dispatching the Right Instruments

One of the lessons learned in the conflict prevention cases of the 1990s was that the main problem is not with early warning but with early action. Having addressed this problem with the newly created mechanism, at the 2000 European Council meeting in Santa Maria de Feira, Portugal, the EU moved to determine the best mix of instruments and develop those that would be needed in critical cases but were either scattered across the EU or did not exist in any of the member states. Four crucial fields that needed development were identified: police, rule of law, civilian administration, and civil protection.

Concerning the police, the EU member states committed themselves to creating a force of 5000 policemen to be made available for civilian crisis management, including 1413 officers who would be deployable within 30 days. The ministers in charge of police have met several times since 1999 to pledge these police capabilities. They did not reach a formal agreement but made good progress on the composition, the command, and the interoperability of the police forces. The main problems lie in the political decision making, the legal framework of the operation, and its financing, but these had to be solved when the EU Police Mission (EUPM) began functioning in Bosnia in January 2003.[7]

The Council of Ministers had already allocated the assignments for the EUPM in March 2002. The preparation period extended to December 2002 in order to avoid a power vacuum when the UN's International Police Task Force (IPTF) took over. Compared to the IPTF, the EUPM has a slightly different mandate and significantly fewer personnel: 500 police officers and a good 300 international and local staff. Of the 30 states to have previously dispatched police personnel to the IPTF, 18 are still involved. In addition to the EU member states and candidate states, Russia, Canada and Switzerland are also participating. From the point of view of its size and composition, the mission is manageable and, in this respect, a suitable test for the EU's leadership qualities.

EUPM personnel are answerable to the UN's High Commissioner in Bosnia-Herzegovina, Paddy Ashdown from the UK, in his second function as the EU's Special Envoy. The operational management of the mission is delegated to Danish police inspector Sven Christian Frederiksen, whose reports are sent to the EU foreign ministers via Ashdown and the High Representative for CFSP, Javier Solana. The EU Council of Ministers' Political and Security Committee retains political control of the mission. The sum of 38 million euros per year, divided between the EU budget and the contributions from the member states, has been set aside for the period from 2003 to 2005 — an arrangement that took a great effort to achieve.

In contrast to the IPTF, the EU mission hardly deals with any executive responsibilities, but is instead intended to contribute to setting up a professional police force in Bosnia-Herzegovina through monitoring, consultancy, and inspection. The police force is to be prepared to deal effectively with organised crime, human trafficking, drug trading, and corruption, with the objective of conforming to EU norms. Overall, the task in a still tense post-war region remains as demanding as it is dangerous. For this reason, special importance is given to the co-operation between EUPM and the Stabilisation Force in Bosnia and Herzegovina (SFOR).

The EU police capacity will engage in training, advisory, monitoring, and executive missions. The European Commission's contribution is substantial, as it focusses on local capacity building in countries dealing with crisis or emerging from crisis. The commission has also adopted a number of programmes to support police training and infrastructure in various countries such as Guatemala, El Salvador, South Africa,

Algeria, and, more recently, Macedonia. More generally, the EU plans to support operations led by the UN and the OSCE as well as conduct autonomous operations led by the EU and combine them with other components of preventive intervention, such as the rule of law and the establishment of public administration (Rummel 2003b).

In the field of rule of law and civil administration, a major problem faced by the EU is the lack of suitably qualified and available personnel ready for deployment in international missions. This also poses a problem for the UN, the OSCE, and other institutions engaged in international peace missions. In the commission's view, the best way to build up the EU's capacity in this field is by developing common training programmes and mechanisms to make staff rapidly available (European Commission 2001b). The goal has been set to identify 200 experts to be called upon to contribute to crisis management and prevention. EU co-operation programmes already provide for strengthening the administration of justice in many partner countries. In this area, as in that of civilian administration, the difficulty of building up an EU response capacity in crisis situations often relates to the lack of readily available personnel in the member states.[8]

With regard to civilian administration and civil protection, the EU is less specific with its goals. It has been identifying various key fields relevant for countries in a conflict prevention situation. As an example, EU institutions and member states have started redirecting crucial contributions toward re-establishing viable local administrations, be it for the sake of tax collection or the functioning of customs regimes. The council has adopted a new co-ordinating mechanism that provides for the co-ordination of national civil protection bodies, early warning and information exchange, co-operation for training civil protection personnel, and the establishment of a database. These capacities have been designed for and used as the response to international organised crime and its regional and local variations.

Military Instruments: The European Union as a Newcomer

Already in 1999 European leaders agreed on the perspective of a common security and defence policy. The 15 EU member states formally decided to create a rapid reaction force of 60 000 at the Nice European Council in December 2000. Subsequently, some progress has been made in creating a military structure within the Council of Ministers (see below), in identifying the various national components of the force, and in launching a process for the establishment of the respective military infrastructure. The rapid reaction force should be operational from 2003 onward and should concentrate on humanitarian relief, peacekeeping, and crisis management independently of NATO. In the end, it should allow for autonomous European interventions based on a combination of military and nonmilitary instruments of crisis management as well as conflict prevention.

Assembling the common force has progressed less quickly than promised by the heads of state and government. The delay does not leave individual European countries paralysed in cases such as Afghanistan or Iraq, however, because they can always participate in coalitions of the willing with the U.S. But for the time being the common security and defence policy has only a limited range of action. Missions at the lower end of the so-called Petersberg Tasks, such as Operation Concordia in Macedonia since March 2003, can be taken over by EU-led forces, while more demanding contingencies remain out of range for a collective European approach.[9] One crucial reason is that access to NATO capabilities in terms of logistics as well as command and communication will continue to be a hurdle for swift action or indeed for any action. The long pending agreements between the EU and NATO have finally made more reliable support by NATO for EU-led missions possible. But it will still take some time to see how co-operation between the two organisations will work out in practice.

In the context of developing the ESDP, it is argued that military capability gives credibility to the CFSP and other EU external interventions. The argument needs to be more differentiated depending on the country in question. As an example, Serbia and Zimbabwe are two different situations and the decision-making parameters of Slobodan Milosevic and Robert Mugabe are not the same, nor is the credibility of any European threat of military intervention. As Nielson (2001) points out, 'in Africa, Europe's credibility comes from our development co-operation. And our ability to prevent conflict stems from development instruments'.

Despite Nielson's preferences, the potential of the ESDP might still be increasingly useful for developing countries when questions about security sector reform, arms control regimes, mine sweeping, proliferation, and surveillance tasks arise with a preventive concept in mind. Likewise, peacekeeping operations as well as preventive deployments are important tasks to be addressed by the ESDP, especially when they are accompanied by nonmilitary measures; this, of course, requires a much higher degree of orchestration of the various preventive instruments of the EU. A first test case is the EU peacekeeping mission Artemis in the Democratic Republic of Congo, which started in June 2003.

It can be stated that the civilian tasks are generally no less important than the military component of the ESDP. Rather, they are part of a civilian-military continuum to be developed as a particular quality of the EU's security policy. Despite the pioneering nature of the EUPM and Operation Concordia, by no means can the ESDP be considered sufficiently advanced. This applies both to the civilian and the military components, which are not discussed in great detail here. Compared to the military component, there has been cautious progress in the civilian area. Furthermore, the developments cannot be described as balanced, because the civilian component is significantly smaller from the point of view of personnel and material than is the military one. In the end, the two components are not yet sufficiently prepared for a combined deployment (Rummel 2002).

Institutional Set-Up: Mainstreaming Conflict Prevention

During the 1990s, the EU had to complete its external relations sector by including foreign policy and security and defence policy on the European level. That new EU sector then underwent major conceptual and institutional reform driven by events such as the end of the cold war, increasing globalisation, and the need as well as the opportunity for the prevention of armed conflict. This required significant shifts in the structure and function of the traditional set of EU institutions, which led to the creation of a number of new bodies and initiated a wide range of mainstreaming activities. Mainstreaming conflict prevention is defined as 'the process of establishing an in-house "culture of prevention" and providing appropriate means and procedures to effectively follow a mainstreamed policy objective, i.e. conflict prevention' (Conflict Prevention Network 2001b, 7; see also European Commission 2001b, 10). The reforms of the EU's institutional structures were reflected in the draft constitution hammered out by the European Commission during its deliberations from February 2002 to July 2003.

The High Representative and the Policy Unit

The single most visible position in the EU that deals with conflict prevention on a continuing basis is the Secretary General of the Council/High Representative of CFSP. This office is mandated by either the heads of state and government or the foreign ministers of the EU but can also propose initiatives of its own. The SG/HR can make suggestions within the council and is dispatched to almost all the hot spots that figure on the EU's foreign policy agenda. The office is supported by the Policy Planning and Early Warning Unit (Policy Unit), which has the task of monitoring and analysing developments in areas relevant to the CFSP. It also draws on the information sources of member states, is in close contact with the EU delegations in third countries and with international organisations, and co-ordinates the special envoys on missions to critical regions of conflict such as Central Africa, the Middle East, the western Balkans, and Afghanistan.

    The SG/HR's most intensive contact within the institutional organisation of the EU is, however, the relationship with the commissioner for external relations, given that both offices share the same agenda but complement one other in doing policy. External relations commissioner Chris Patten (2002) describes their joint tasks in the following way: 'We work to develop common policies which enable us to combine our diplomatic, economic and other strengths to achieve shared objectives. Javier Solana is the representative of Europe's foreign ministers in articulating and implementing the shared policies which they have agreed, and my job is to ensure that all the instruments that Member States have agreed to use at a European level for example in fields like development assistance, political cooperation and trade are brought together effectively in support of the agreed policies.' This sounds like a plausible and smooth division of labour, but the interinstitutional isolationism and redundancy of the two positions are open to criticism. Therefore, the draft constitution proposes combining the two positions under the roof of one European foreign minister who would then be able to pull the strings together: short-term and long-term measures as well as political and military instruments.

Decision-Making Machinery: The Challenge of Coherence

In addition to the existing institutional set-up consisting of the Committee of Permanent Representatives, the network of European correspondents, the group of Relex Counsellors, and the CFSP working groups, a new series of committees was established for the professional treatment of the tasks of crisis management and conflict prevention that, so far, had been taken care of outside of the EU in either NATO, the Western European Union (WEU), or in multilateral *ad hoc* groups.

The new Political and Security Committee has become the lynchpin of both the CFSP and the ESDP. It has a central role to play in the EU's definition of a crisis and its follow-up. The committee is composed of national representatives at senior and ambassador levels, within the framework of member states' permanent representations. The European Commission is fully associated with the committee's work, through its own representative. The committee makes recommendations on the future functioning of the CFSP, including the ESDP, and deals with the daily management of foreign policy issues, such as the preparation of the deliberations of these subjects in council sessions. In the event of a crisis, the committee analyses the situation and examines the options that might be considered as the EU's response.

The Political and Security Committee is provided with the necessary military advice and recommendations on all military matters within the EU by the newly established European Union Military Committee. The EU Military Committee directs all military activities within the EU framework, including the European Union Military Staff, which provides military expertise and support to the ESDP, including the conduct of EU-led military crisis management operations. The EU Military Staff performs early warning, situation assessment, and strategic planning for the Petersberg Tasks, such as in the cases of Concordia and Artemis. It identifies national and multinational forces and implements policies and decisions as directed by the EU Military Committee. The Military Committee's chair attends meetings of the Council when decisions with defence implications are to be taken.

The Politico-Military Group examines the respective aspects of all proposals within the framework of CFSP. The Committee for Civilian Aspects of Crisis Management advises on the political aspects of nonmilitary crisis management and conflict prevention. So far it has given priority to the implementation of specific targets for policing and has been instrumental in setting up and monitoring the EUPM in Bosnia. It has also dealt with strengthening the rule of law and other nonmilitary instruments as already discussed (Piana 2002).

Reorganising the European Commission

In the summer of 2000, the incoming European Commission presidency reorganised its external relations. Four commissioners now represented different dossiers: external relations, development and humanitarian assistance, trade, and the enlargement of the EU. The commissioner for external relations (at present Chris Patten) holds a co-ordinating function within this group. Conflict prevention has mainly been dealt with by Patten and his administration. Within the general directorate for external relations, conflict prevention used to be co-ordinated by the Policy Planning Unit, which convened the planning units of the respective other general directorates and reported to the Director General.

In 2001, a new unit was created for conflict prevention, crisis management, and political issues relating to the African, Caribbean, and Pacific group of states (ACP). It is charged with mainstreaming conflict prevention, developing tools and inputs for civilian crisis management, and dealing with the academic and NGO communities including the Conflict Prevention Network (CPN), which provides expertise to EU institutions in complex emergencies and critical regions of the world.[10] The unit publishes significant documents on conflict prevention, such as the Communication of April 2001, introduces conflict prevention in the country strategy papers, and trains officials both in Brussels and in the delegations in conflict prevention skills.[11] It also hosts the Cell for Civilian Crisis Management, which is still in the making, and, more important, the financial RRM.

Taken together, these institutional innovations in EU foreign policy represent a remarkable extension of the intergovernmental bodies of the EU. The communitarian institutions such as the European Parliament and the European Commission missed the opportunity to promote their role within the new sector of EU conflict prevention and crisis management. Even the SG/HR function, which could have been interpreted as a communitarian position, leaned more toward the council's committees, the foreign ministers, and the presidency than toward the European Commission and Parliament. This shift of balance has also implications for the political acceptance and democratic interplay regarding at times costly and controversial interventions of the EU.[12]

Another set of problems comes with the lack of a single structure for decision making and implementation of prevention policies. Too often, information is not shared among the EU institutions, and they work against each other. In Renata Dwan's (2001) assessment, the 'complex structure and multiple components provide serious obstacles to either swift or effective action on a cross-cutting issue like prevention. Successful implementation depends on political leadership from the Council and follow-up from successive EU presidencies as well as the development of active information and co-ordination frameworks between member states, the Commission and the Council to develop real policy coherence.' It also demands a commitment of financial resources, an issue that was noted by the European Parliament in its review of the Communication, which called for an increase in the budget for external actions ('ESR News in Brief' 2002; Dwan 2003). Although it is true (at least in many cases) that conflict prevention is less costly than uncontrolled escalation, preventive interventions still require reliable funding.

Financial Framework: Is Conflict Prevention Expensive?

Contrary to common wisdom, conflict prevention is expensive, at least in all those cases where structural prevention is required, and certainly in those cases where one wants to be sure that conflict prevention is successful. Is the EU prepared to accept that a conflict prevention policy requires double funding — first for the accumulation of those preventive capacities it still lacks, and second for running the daily agenda of prevention? Given the huge cobweb of financial relations built up by the EU over the last decades, it seems that both the money and the procedures are now in place to support extensive policies of EU conflict prevention.

As the 2001 Report of the European Commission (2001i) points out, financial assistance to third countries is one of the central components of the EU's external action, alongside with trade policy and political dialogue.[13] It is thus an important tool for promoting the fundamental values of the EU and for meeting the global challenges such as conflict prevention and peacebuilding in the twenty-first century. Brussels is one of the major actors in international co-operation and development assistance; in total, the European Community and the member states provide some 55 percent of the total international official development assistance (ODA). This assistance was originally concentrated on ACP countries but had been extended, and today finances projects in more than 140 countries, many of them affected by armed conflict.

As with other international donors, the EU faces the challenge of increasing the quality, focus, and impact of its financial assistance. This challenge is particularly great for the European Commission because the overall volume of its commitments has increased rapidly from 3.3 billion euros in 1990 to 9.3 billion euros in 2000 — some 10 percent of the entire world-wide ODA. This fact and the new focus are the main reasons why the European Commission launched a fundamental reform of its external assistance programmes, which included concentrating ODA to a limited number of priority areas with the overriding objectives of poverty reduction in developing countries and better integration of the partner countries into the global economy. It also embarked on an ambitious parallel programme of measures to improve the quality and the timely delivery of projects significantly while ensuring robust financial management. These reforms must go further to include political goals in EU programmes (as with the country strategy papers mentioned above).

The main feature of the 2001 budget was the discussion on the financing of the stabilisation programme for the western Balkans. The allocations under the external action heading totalled 4 928 672 million euros for commitments and 3 920 997 million euros for payments (see Table 8.1). The increase for commitments over the 2000 budget was only 2.1 percent, compared with an increase of 7.6 percent for payments. The budget also provided for the flexibility instrument to be used to release 200 million euros for Serbia, so that the real margin was only 6.3 million euros. Serbia can receive 240 million euros out of the total allocation of 839 million euros for the western Balkans. This amount takes into account the restoration of democracy in Serbia and the 75 million euros in advance financing for Kosovo, which had been made possible in 2000 by redeployment within the heading. The CFSP appropriations are far smaller than in 2000, because administrative expenditure for special envoys has been transferred to the Council section.

Late in 2001, the European Commission adopted a communication that proposed improving the procedures for funding civilian crisis management under the CFSP. It aimed to get around the financial constraints and procedural obstacles to CFSP operations by establishing a new flexibility instrument for funding civilian crisis interventions and facilitating recourse to the current emergency reserve. An interinstitutional agreement was also concluded regarding three categories of crisis management operations that can be financed by the EU:

• operations carried out in the framework of a European Community instrument under the first pillar (mine-sweeping, emergency civilian aid, civil protection aid, human rights, institution strengthening, election observation missions, food aid, infrastructure rebuilding, and economic aid);

Table 8.1   European Commission Budget 2001

External Action	Amount (million euros)	%
Action Defined by Geographical Area		
Pre-accession aid (applicant countries) (B7-0)	3 240 000	39.67%
Pre-accession aid (Mediterranean countries) (B7-0)	19 000	0.23%
Co-operation with Mediterranean third countries and the Middle East (B7-4)	896 320	10.97%
Co-operation with the new independent states and Mongolia (B7-5 2)	469 280	5.74%
Co-operation with Asia (B7-3 0)	446 000	5.46%
Co-operation with Latin America (B7-3 1)	336 250	4.12%
Co-operation with southern Africa and South Africa (B7-3 2)	122 000	1.49%
Co-operation with the Balkans (B7-5 4)	839 000	10.27%
Food Aid and Humanitarian Aid Operations		
Food aid and support operations (B7-2 0)	455 000	5.57%
Humanitarian aid (B7-2 1)	473 000	5.79%
General Co-operation Measures		
Other co-operation measures (B7-6, B7-5 1, B7-5 3)	389 540	4.77%
International fisheries agreements (B7-8 0)	273 440	3.35%
External aspects of certain European Community policies (B7-8 1 to B7-8 7)	71 842	0.88%
European initiative for democracy and human rights (B7-7)	102 000	1.25%
CFSP (Common Foreign and Security Policy) (B8-0)	36 000	0.44%
	8 168 672	100.0%

Source: European Commission (2001h).

- CFSP operations without any military or defence implications that are funded from the CFSP budget line (the council decides on common action and the budget, while the European Commission makes commitments, signs contracts, and releases funds); and
- CFSP operations with military or defence implications that do not come under the EU budget (such as the deployment of the Rapid Reaction Force).

The Commission concluded that the budgetary procedures applying to CFSP operations were too cumbersome and that the CFSP budget would be insufficient if the EU were, for example, to extend the surveillance mission in the Balkans or launch a huge police operation. The European Commission suggested the use of a new crisis flexibility instrument that would make it possible to mobilise funds even when there was no budget latitude left and, more importantly, without having to change the financial perspectives in the framework of the usual budget. Thus, it tried to counter the option under consideration by the council (which had the support of several member states) of funding civilian CFSP operations in a crisis situation through a new *ad hoc* fund, with funding from the member states.

Funding via member states may appear attractive, but it exposes a number of issues:

- the Maastricht Treaty does not cover how such a fund would be managed and controlled (unless it were managed by the European Commission, like the European Development Fund);
- it would increase the gap between the first and second pillars and could therefore damage the coherence of the EU's external actions;
- the lack of parliamentary control would raise serious doubts concerning the obligation of accountability for the breakdown of responsibility between the two branches of the Budgetary Authority; and
- an *ad hoc* fund outside the regular budget might be seen as a way of getting around the normal budget procedures.

The European Commission demonstrated that even if funding such operations from the existing budget procedure has been over-bureaucratic in the past, the budget remains the most appropriate way to fund operations because it is the best way of ensuring good governance and transparency and the coherence of the EU's actions under both the CFSP and the European Community itself (Missiroli 2002).

Building Partnerships: The European Union as a Co-operative Power in Conflict Prevention

In the EU Programme, the heads of state and government stated that the 'EU must build and sustain mutually reinforcing and effective partnerships for prevention with the UN, the OSCE and other international and regional organisations as well as civil society. Increased co-operation is needed at all levels, from early warning and analysis to action and evaluation. Field co-ordination is of particular importance. EU action should be guided by principles of value added and comparative advantage' (European Commission 2001f, 10). Making full use of recent work on intensified EU-UN and EU-OSCE co-operation in conflict prevention and crisis management, the EU has expanded its exchange of information and, to a limited extent, its practical co-operation with the UN system, the OSCE, the Council of Europe, other sub-regional organisations, and the international financial institutions. In accordance with the principles agreed at the Feira and Nice summits, the EU and NATO have increasingly contributed to conflict prevention by co-operating in crisis management in critical regions such as the western Balkans.

Additional fields of partnership and mutual learning have been tapped. Joint training programmes for field and headquarter personnel of the EU, the UN, and the OSCE have been developed, benefiting from the European Commission's preparedness to fund some of these multilateral courses (Hopmann 2003). Likewise, the EU contributed to the strengthening of preventive capacities of regional and sub-regional organisations outside Europe, such as through the European Commission's recommendation to support regional integration efforts, in particular organisations with a meaningful conflict prevention mandate. Beyond the governmental level, the EU has been keen to catch up with other international pioneering actors such as the UN and Canada in intensifying information, dialogue, and co-operation with prevention-focussed humanitarian actors, including the International Committee of the Red Cross, relevant nongovernmental and academic organisations, and the private sector (Carey 2003).

The EU has used the G8 as a platform to promote the subject of conflict prevention in general, and with particular emphasis on certain aspects, starting with the German-hosted Cologne Summit in 1999. The subsequent Japanese- and Italian-hosted summits also pushed the subject forward. At Cologne in 1999, the G8 foreign ministers agreed, for the first time, on the need to improve their policies on conflict prevention, focussing on more marked respect of the UN Charter, and on strengthening democratic institutions, human rights, and the rule of law. The leaders' final communiqué also called for greater attention to this issue (G8 1999), which led to an *ad hoc* G8 session on conflict prevention later that year in Berlin. During Japan's year as G8 host, the G8 Conflict Prevention Officials Meeting (CPOM) was created. In Miyazaki, on 13 July 2000, the G8 foreign ministers approved the Miyazaki Initiatives for Conflict Prevention, which reflected a comprehensive approach, analysing the various roles played by each factor at every stage of the development of crises and taking into account the diversity and complexity of causes of conflicts (G8 Foreign Ministers 2000). The document focusses on five areas: small arms and light weapons, conflict and development, illicit trade in diamonds, children in armed conflict, and international civil police. Under the Italian chair, on 18–19 July 2001 the G8 foreign ministers' adopted the G8 Roma Initiatives on Conflict Prevention, which addressed the topics of women in conflict prevention and corporate responsibility (see Appendix D).

The focal point of the G8 Genoa Summit was, in fact, poverty reduction strategies. The European Commission identified measures to support the economies of the weakest countries with an integrated strategy. On the issue of trade, the European Commission suggested that the G8 follow the EU's example of its 'Everything But Arms' initiative, by providing duty-free and quota-free access for all products originating from the least developed countries. In the area of social investments, particularly the sectors of education and health, European Commission president Romano Prodi referred to the EU action plan on fighting communicable diseases, which had been adopted by the European Council earlier that year.

As a product of the Genoa Summit, a joint expert group on conflict prevention was established in order to prepare consultations within the G8 framework for the Kananaskis Summit in 2002. Such bilateral initiatives, which are intended to catch synergies and advance agenda items at the working level, form part of the specific co-operative diplomacy that characterises the G8. Likewise, the G8 members try to enhance their external reach by teaming up with other agenda-setting international groupings (Penttilä 2003). This is the case when the G8 summits included meetings with the representatives of the New Partnership for Africa's Development (NEPAD) and the African Union (AU), as well as with the Secretary General of the UN. The imperative of conflict prevention as advanced by the UN and included in the NEPAD documents supports the G8's declarations and commitments. A certain division of labour has developed within the G8 with regard to conflict prevention, with the U.S., France, and the UK concentrating on programmes that support training in military peacekeeping, and Germany, Canada, and the EU focussing on regional and civil-military co-operation as well as post-conflict rehabilitation. Despite the fact that the G8 regularly assesses the agenda of regional crises, however, at the 2003 Evian Summit, the participating EU member states and the European Commission did not intend to extend an operational role for conflict prevention to the G8 (G8 Africa Personal Representatives 2003).

A Selection of EU Cases of Prevention

Since its implementation in 2000, EU conflict prevention policy has included on its agenda a long list of cases where Brussels has offered support. The monthly bulletin listed case after case, from East Timor to Colombia, from Montenegro to the Fergana Valley, from Palestine to Zimbabwe. Beyond the geographical cases, the EU was dealing with a larger number of functional issues of conflict prevention, such as water and conflict, drug trafficking, illicit trade, money laundering, and conflict diamonds. A few of these cases, most of which remain on the EU's agenda, illustrate the variety of the EU's approaches, although they do not provide a complete picture or even give a full assessment of the impact of EU preventive action.[14]

Macedonia

In 1999, the EU proposed the new Stabilisation and Association Process for five countries of southeastern Europe. On 16 June 1999, a feasibility study on opening negotiations with the former Yugoslav Republic of Macedonia came to a positive conclusion. Subsequently, the council adopted negotiating directives for a Stabilisation and Association Agreement. In March 2000, the EU representation in Skopje was upgraded to a permanent delegation of the European Commission, which also marked the start of negotiations between the EU and the former Yugoslav Republic of Macedonia to conclude the agreement. In June 2000, the European Council at Santa Maria de Feira confirmed that its objective remained the fullest possible integration of the region's countries into the political and economic mainstream of Europe and affirmed that 'all the countries concerned are potential candidates for EU membership' (European Commission 2000c). Following the successful conclusion of the negotiations at the Zagreb Summit of 24 November 2000, the Stabilisation and Association Agreement and the Interim Agreement were signed in Luxembourg on 9 April 2001. With the Interim Agreement, the parties allowed the trade and trade-related matters of the Stabilisation and Association Agreement to enter into force on 1 June 2001.

On 3 October 2001, the European Commission adopted a decision to finance a confidence-building programme for the former Yugoslav Republic of Macedonia under its RRM. The main objective of this programme, for which the budget was 10.3 million euros, was to provide rapid support for implementing the Ohrid Framework Agreement of 13 August 2001, which had been signed by the main political leaders of the government coalition. It was very important to support this agreement in order to reduce inter-ethnic tensions and avoid escalation of the conflict or even spillover to neighbouring countries. The package was conditional upon full ratification of all constitutional amendments and a new law on local government (European Commission 2001g).

Taken together with the military mission Amber Fox (supported by NATO), the political and financial EU measures can be regarded as one of the most successful recent cases of prevention. But it has also become obvious that the careful orchestration of various actors is indispensable in complex emergencies: 'The Macedonian crisis ... showed that the EU has to act in concert with other actors, most notably with NATO, the OSCE and the U.S. Without these combined efforts which significantly increased the external pressure upon the local parties, the settlement and the implementation of the agreement would not have been possible. Here again, the course of the crisis highlighted the serious dangers if these actors are not willing to co-operate, to share information and resources as well as to develop a common platform for action' (Schneckener 2002, 37).

Small Arms

Reducing trade in small arms and in diamonds is addressed as a key, long-term priority in the joint report of the SG/HR and the Commissioner for External Relations (European Commission 2000b, p. 19). A European Parliament resolution (March 2001) also addressed uncontrolled trade in light weapons. The EU took the lead *en bloc* in the fight against the destructive effects of small arms trading, having already established in 1998 a code of conduct governing exports to third countries, and a Council Joint Action pledging to combat the destabilising spread and accumulation of small arms. The EU thus entered the UN Conference on the Illicit Trade in Small Arms and Light Weapons as one of its most enthusiastic participants, and had a co-ordinated and clear position thanks to the Joint Action. The EU would like to see legally binding measures covering criteria for export control, marking and tracing of weapons, brokering, surpluses, and information exchange. The EU is also pushing for a thorough follow-up process with biannual meetings and a second conference.

In countries with potential conflict, the customs sector — due to its role in preventing trafficking of various kinds, including of small arms — deserves particular attention. The EU has targeted many countries, particularly in the ACP region. In Bosnia, one of the most effective programmes has been the Customs and Fiscal Administration Office.

International Terrorism

The EU addressed the challenge created by the terrorist attacks of 11 September 2001 both at home, with tightened control, and internationally, with broad co-operation on civilian issues. At the time of the attacks, the military arm of the EU, the Rapid Reaction Force, was still in the making. Only individual member states joined in with the U.S. in this regard. The EU's response to international terrorism was nevertheless efficient. Within days of the attacks, a series of policy proposals were proposed, which led to a plan of action adopted by a special European Council held in Brussels on 21 September 2001. This plan comprised measures in a range of areas where the EU has been contributing effectively to an immediate response to the threat of international terrorism and has addressed some of its structural sources of support. Among the key areas were police and judicial co-operation, the diplomatic front, humanitarian aid, air transport security, economic and financial measures, and emergency preparedness. Patten (2001d) set the tone for the EU's response: 'The investment we make in sustainable development is as much part of our global security as the investment we make in our armed forces. The aftermath of 11 September ... provides an opportunity to make that investment ... Sustainable development is about winning a peace, not a war, but for that victory to be won, actions will have to follow words — and that is always the hard part.'

On 30 November 2001, the European Commission adopted an amended proposal on freezing the assets of persons and entities with a view to combating terrorism. The purpose was to create an EU-wide tool to prevent and suppress the financing of terrorist acts. This proposal amended an earlier one made in October 2001, to take account of amendments proposed by the European Parliament and at the council, as well as to adapt it to UN Security Council Resolution 1373 on the fight against terrorism. The council then made a decision on the basis of this amended proposal and, in parallel, prepared the political declarations and decisions concerning the military and civilian intervention in Afghanistan (Bredel 2003).[15]

Patten's statement on the situation in Afghanistan was significant: 'We can and should aim to facilitate a political settlement and having facilitated it we then walk away. We have to make sure that a better government which will emerge from that sad embittered country will be able to count on the long-term support of the international community to rebuild in the ruin of the medieval ferocity which has been unleashed on Afghanistan for the last few years (Patten 2001a). On 13 December 2001, the European Commission decided to finance a 4.9 million euro programme to start the political, economic, and social reconstruction of Afghanistan and the neighbouring countries in the post-Taliban era, using the RRM.[16] By spring 2002, the EU representative in Kabul had a total of 200 million euros, assembled from various EU programmes. These funds were intended to assist with rehabilitation projects and with building up societal infrastructure in order to prevent any new fighting in Afghanistan and to help with drying out the bases of international terrorism.

The EU recognised that to be more effective in the fight against terrorism and on the world stage, it must make its ESDP fully operational. On 19 November 2001, the General Affairs Council included joint sessions with defence and interior ministers, who discussed the creation of the EU Rapid Reaction Force, both in the military and the police fields. The EU asked its high representative for foreign and security policy to study the possibility of extending the EU's competence on defence in the face of increased insecurity in the international environment after the 11 September terrorist attacks.

Conclusions

The EU is still struggling with the lessons it learned from the first years of its more systematic conflict prevention policy. The process of knowledge building remains at the margin of the recent efforts of mainstreaming conflict prevention. The complex institutional structure is no advantage, nor is the relatively low level of expertise in security policy within the traditional bodies of the EU. Many of those in the European Commission and the delegations who are charged with security-related missions simply lack the factual as well as methodological understanding of peacebuilding, conflict prevention, and crisis management. On-the-job training is certainly one way of trying to reduce the deficits; another would be to draw more on external expertise. Paradoxically, both of these options are not given significant attention: new tasks are added but institutional learning is not promoted in parallel.

With the new Unit for Conflict Prevention, Crisis Management, and ACP Political Issues, a certain 'professionalism' was introduced into the European Commission's activities. If one looks closer, however, one is less sure. The mainstreaming process has been on the sidelines. The European Commission is no longer at the forefront of conflict prevention. Most of the promises of the 2001 Communication have not been realised; there is little conceptual innovation, and almost no inspiration for the commissioner in charge of conflict prevention, let alone for the SG/HR and the Policy Unit. As was written in the *2000/2001 CPN Yearbook*, 'on balance, one must assume that, notwithstanding its commitment to conflict prevention and improvement in this field, the EU and most of its member states remain predominantly involved in conflict management. In practice, it proves difficult to balance long-term considerations on conflict prevention with shorter-term concerns' (van de Goor and Huber 2002, 22). This raises questions: Is it clear what the requirements and implications of a 'culture of prevention' are for the everyday work of the EU institutions, pillars, cabinets, and directorates? Are the appropriate resources available and can they be implemented in a timely manner? Who is assuring the initiative in each specific case and who can be held accountable for lack of action? Which agency controls cost-effectiveness?[17]

In a sense, the EU must start all over again with conflict prevention and, this time around, dig deeper and be more serious and more sophisticated. The UN is certainly a partner and a source of knowledge and inspiration for such a second round of mainstreaming EU conflict prevention on a higher level (Sriram and Wermester 2002). More partners should be considered among the corporate world and the media.[18] And the activities must be geared toward the parties that own those conflicts that have a dangerous tendency to escalate (Mekenkamp, van Tongeren, and Veen 1999). The concept of addressing the root causes of armed conflict is not very prominent in the European Commission's Communication. It remains difficult to operationalise. A focus on problem areas may be more functional (conflict oriented) and more rewarding.

Including the concept of conflict prevention in the country strategy papers (promoted both by Patten and Nielson) has proven very difficult to implement. Solana's 2000 report stressed the need to enhance coherence by bringing together all means and resources available to the EU (European Commission 2000b). The first section, entitled 'Coherent Action: The Central Challenge of Conflict Prevention', makes this crystal clear: 'The central issue for the Union is one of coherence in deploying the right combination and sequence of instruments in a timely and integrated manner. This demands greater coherence and complementarity at several levels: between the instruments and capabilities available within each pillar, between the pillars themselves, between Member State and Community activities, and between the Union and its international partners in conflict prevention' (7).

On 23 June 2000, the European Union signed a new partnership agreement with 77 ACP countries in Cotonou. Lasting 20 years, the Cotonou Agreement replaces all former Lomé Convention agreements and sets out a framework of co-operation, trade, and political dialogue between the EU and the ACP states. The principles of Article 11 of the Cotonou agreement and the political dialogue of its Article 8 offer scope for addressing conflict prevention in ACP countries. The implementation of Article 11, however, is limited by the difficulty to find relevant expertise on a case-by-case basis. The integration of conflict prevention initiatives within the country strategy papers is particularly difficult. This action is still in process. It should be linked to the efforts of NEPAD and the suggestions from the 2003 Evian Summit (G8 Africa Personal Representatives 2003).[19]

Overall, the EU has a better developed approach to incentives to prevent conflict, compared to sanctions as instruments of foreign policy ('Reconstructing Post-Conflict

Societies and the German Involvement' 2003). Most of the EU's measures and traditions are part of an international donor's strategy and a trade and development interest rather than an expression of a forceful intervention policy. Certainly, the art of preventive intervention would require the skills of a sophisticated diplomatic management as well as the political will to take on potentially risky and costly responsibilities. Brussels could make conflict prevention the trademark of its foreign policy, but, for the time being, the political acceptance and the support inside the EU for such a strategic ambition is still too weak. The coalition of a few member states (the Scandinavian states, the Netherlands, and the UK), the Policy Unit in the Council, and parts of the European Commission are not strong enough to achieve more than a start in such a strategic direction. Even within the European Parliament, only a few of the members are committed to prioritising conflict prevention. Those in the EU system who concentrate on crisis management, rehabilitation, and post-conflict reconstruction continue to dominate the scene.

Notes

1   The author is grateful for the research assistance of Arzu Hatakoy at the Stiftung Wissenschaft und Politik in Berlin.
2   The announcement and the expectation of enlargement of the EU are already regarded as producing a moderating effect that reduces the inclination toward the use of force (see Rummel 1996; on the next enlargement round, see Missiroli 2003).
3   See Ginsberg (2001) for an explanation of the most important distinction between the output of the EU's external policy and the outcome of its interventions.
4   Patten (2001b) described this process of adapting traditional means to the new task of prevention: 'Let me turn now to civilian crisis management more generally. Here too we are trying to learn from experience in the Balkans and elsewhere. Whether in sending fuel to Serbia over the Winter, or converting financial credits into budgetary support for the Palestinian authority, we are adapting our existing instruments so as to respond in a helpful and effective way in unstable and potentially explosive situations.'
5   The scope of potential intervention includes the alleviation of financial crises, human rights work, election monitoring, institution building, media support, border management, humanitarian missions, de-mining operations, police training and the provision of police equipment, civil emergency assistance, rehabilitation, reconstruction, pacification, resettlement, and mediation.
6   The original ideas on the financial scope had been somewhat more optimistic. See the separate budget line B7-671 (5 to 12 million euros for each intervention, 40 million euros per year after 2001) (European Commission 2000a).
7   For more information, see European Union Police Mission (2003).
8   According to the European Commission's own judgement, 'experience has shown, for example in the area of *human rights monitoring*, that the development of common training modules is one of the best means of building up capacity at EU level. The Commission has therefore launched a project for the setting up of a network of training institutions in the Member States for the development of training modules for personnel to be deployed in peace keeping missions. Such modules will be developed *together* with Member States and should be *compatible* with UN and OSCE modules, for example the new OSCE *REACT*

[Rapid Expert Assistance and Co-operation Teams] system. This need not necessarily imply the establishment of new structures at the level of the Union, but should be built on *strengthened co-operation* between Member States and especially through *synergies* between *existing* training programmes and institutes' (European Commission 2001a).

9   See for more information on Operation Concordia, see the European Union Operation in the Former Yugoslav Republic of Macedonia (2003).

10 The CPN was run as a series of projects from 1997 to 2001 by Stiftung Wissenschaft und Politik in Berlin, and financed by the European Commission. Its advisory board included members of the European parliaments as well as representatives from the council. Over five years, the CPN built up a network of some 100 institutional members (think tanks and NGOs) and 600 individual members (researchers, practitioners, and so on) on whom the EU institutions could draw for expertise in all cases of conflict prevention. On the basis of its consultative experience, the CPN developed tools and handbooks for EU conflict prevention policy. It also participated in the G8's preparatory meetings. In 2002, the CPN project was up for renewal but the tender procedure was aborted and the network was finally cancelled because of a new financial regulation that came into force on 1 January 2003. For a report on the CPN's creation and activities, see Rummel (2003a). A follow-on organisation was created by the CPN staff (see <www.conflict-prevention-associates.org>).

11 For this purpose, the unit has developed a comprehensive handbook (Conflict Prevention Network 2001a).

12 'The shifting of key responsibilities to the CFSP sector suffers from the serious drawback that these areas of policy are largely outside of the control of Europe's citizens: the European Parliament has effective mechanisms of control available for dealing with the EU Commission, but in the CFSP domain it has only consultative rights and no say in decision-making. Up to now, the degree of accountability and control, which security and military policy have been subject to, has been minimal — restricted, in fact, to the domain of budget proposals. The democratic deficit must be made good' (Debiel and Fischer 2000).

13 European Commission's Report on the Implementation of the European Commission's External Assistance (2001i) brings together, for the first time, all the actions taken in the framework of the different external aid programmes in 2000, except pre-accession instruments, macro-financial aid, CFSP, and the Rapid Response Mechanism.

14 Impact assessment is among the most demanding tasks of conflict prevention. Neither the academics nor the practitioners have, as yet, come up with satisfactory approaches. For an overview from an EU perspective, see Lund and Rasamoelina (2000).

15 For more information on the EU's response to the 11 September attacks, see European Commission (2002).

16 When he announced the decision, Patten said: 'The challenges we face in providing quick support to the peace deal in Afghanistan are tailor-made for the new Rapid Reaction Mechanism'.

17 With regard to the demand for both accountability and cost-effectiveness, see Rummel (2000, 28–31).

18 For a much wider catalogue of inspiring examples of successful conflict prevention, see the European Centre for Conflict Prevention (1999).

19 The G8 Africa Personal Representatives' implementation report includes the Joint Africa/ G8 Plan to enhance African capabilities to undertake peace support operations.

References

Ackermann, Alice (2003). 'The Idea and Practice of Conflict Prevention'. *Peace Research* vol. 40, no. 3, pp. 339–347.

Ahtisaari, Martti (2001). 'EU's Civilian Crisis Management Capability: How to Make It Credible?' 4 April, Studia Generalia Fennica, Brussels. <www.ahtisaari.fi/?content=speech&id=5> (July 2003).

Backhurst, Jane (2001). 'The Rapid Reaction Facility: Good News for Those in Crisis?' 18 January, Voluntary Organisations in Cooperation in Emergencies. <www.reliefweb.int/ w/rwb.nsf/0/dcfc869a75eb8314c12569dc005b2128?OpenDocument> (July 2003).

Bredel, Ralf (2003). 'The UN's Long-Term Conflict Prevention Strategies and the Impact of Counter-Terrorism'. *International Peacekeeping* vol. 10, no. 2, pp. 51–75.

Carey, Henry F., ed. (2003). 'Mitigating Conflict: The Role of NGOs'. Special Issue. *International Peacekeeping* vol. 10, no. 1.

Conflict Prevention Network (2001a). 'The Practical Guide of Conflict Prevention'. CD-ROM. Berlin/Brussels.

Conflict Prevention Network (2001b). *Record of Preventive Capacities: Mainstreaming Conflict Prevention. A Survey by the Conflict Prevention Network.* Stifftung Wissenschaft und Politik, Berlin.

Debiel, Tobias and Martina Fischer (2000). 'A Conflict Prevention Service for the European Union'. Berghof Research Centre for Constructive Conflict Management, Berlin.

Dwan, Renata (2001). 'Conflict Prevention and CFSP Coherence'. In A. Missiroli, ed., *Coherence for European Security Policy: Debates — Cases — Assessments.* Institute for Security Studies of WEU, Paris.

Dwan, Renata (2003). 'Conflict Prevention'. In Stockholm International Peace Research Institute, *Armaments, Disarmament, and International Security: SIPRI Yearbook 2003*, p. 107. Oxford University Press, London.

'ESR News in Brief' (2002). *European Security Review* no. 10 (January), p. 5.

European Centre for Conflict Prevention (1999). *People Building Peace: 35 Inspiring Stories from Around the World.* European Centre for Conflict Prevention, Utrecht.

European Commission (1996). 'The EU and the Issue of Conflicts in Africa: Peace-Building, Conflict Prevention, and Beyond'. SEC(96) 332. Brussels. <europa.eu.int/comm/ development/prevention/communication-1996.htm> (July 2003).

European Commission (2000a). 'General Report 2000: Annexes'. Table II: Legislation under the Consultation Procedures (19/26). <europa.eu.int/abc/doc/off/rg/en/2000/com0601.htm#pt0745.0> (July 2003).

European Commission (2000b). 'Improving the Effectiveness of European Action in the Field of Conflict Prevention'. Report presented to the Nice European Council by the Secretary General/High Representative and the Commission, Document No. 14088/00. <register.consilium.eu.int/pdf/en/00/st14/14088en0.pdf> (July 2003).

European Commission (2000c). 'Santa Maria da Feira European Council: Presidency Conclusions'. 19–20 June. <europa.eu.int/european_council/conclusions/index_en.htm> (July 2003).

European Commission (2001a). 'Civilian Crisis Management'. November. <europa.eu.int/ comm/external_relations/cpcm/cm.htm> (July 2003).

European Commission (2001b). 'Communication from the Commission on Conflict Prevention'. COM(2001) 211 final. 11 April. Brussels. <europa.eu.int/comm/external_relations/cfsp/news/ com2001_211_en.pdf> (July 2003).

European Commission (2001c). 'Conflict Prevention: Commission Initiative to Improve EU's Civilian Intervention Capacities'. 11 April, Brussels. <europa.eu.int/comm/external_relations/cfsp/news/ip_01_560_en.htm> (July 2003).
European Commission (2001d). 'Council Adopts Rapid Reaction Mechanism Commission Now in Position to Intervene Fast in Civilian Crisis Management'. 26 February, Brussels. <europa.eu.int/comm/external_relations/cfsp/news/ip_01_255.htm> (July 2003).
European Commission (2001e). 'Council Regulation (EC) No 381/2001 of 26 February 2001 Creating a Rapid-Reaction Mechanism'. Brussels. *Official Journal of the European Communities* vol. 44 (27 February), pp. 5–9.
European Commission (2001f). 'EU Programme for the Prevention of Violent Conflicts'. Göteburg, 15–16 June. <www.utrikes.regeringen.se/prefak/files/EUprogramme.pdf> (July 2003).
European Commission (2001g). 'EU Support for Building Confidence in fYROM'. 4 October, Brussels. <europa.eu.int/comm/external_relations/see/news/ip01_1368.htm> (July 2003).
European Commission (2001h). 'General Budget of the European Union for the Financial Year 2001'. The 2001 Budget in Figures. <europa.eu.int/comm/budget/pdf/budget/syntchif2001/en.pdf> (July 2003).
European Commission (2001i). 'Report on the Implementation of the European Commission's External Assistance'. D(2001) 32947. <europa.eu.int/comm/europeaid/reports/status_report_2001_en.pdf> (July 2003).
European Commission (2002). 'EU Action in Response to 11th September 2001: One Year After'. 9 September. <europa.eu.int/comm/110901> (July 2003).
European Union Operation in the Former Yugoslav Republic of Macedonia (2003). 'Operation "Concordia"'. <ue.eu.int/arym> (July 2003).
European Union Police Mission (2003). 'Bosnia and Herzegovina: EU Police Mission (EUPM)'. <ue.eu.int/eupm/homePage/index.asp> (July 2003).
G8 (1999). 'G8 Communiqué Köln 1999'. 20 June, Cologne. <www.g7.utoronto.ca/summit/1999koln/finalcom.htm> (July 2003).
G8 Africa Personal Representatives (2003). 'Implementation Report by Africa Personal Representatives to Leaders on the G8 Africa Action Plan'. 1 June, Evian. <www.g7.utoronto.ca/summit/2003evian/apr030601.html> (July 2003).
G8 Foreign Ministers (2000). 'G8 Miyazaki Initiatives for Conflict Prevention'. Miyazaki, 13 July. <www.g7.utoronto.ca/foreign/fm000713-in.htm> (July 2003).
Ginsberg, Roy H. (2001). *The European Union in International Politics: Baptism by Fire*. Rowman and Littlefield, Lanham, MD.
Hopmann, Terrence P. (2003). 'Managing Conflict in Post–Cold War Eurasia: The Role of the OSCE in Europe's Security "Architecture"'. *International Affairs* vol. 40, no. 1, pp. 75–100.
Lund, Michael S. and Guenola Rasamoelina, eds. (2000). *The Impact of Conflict Prevention Policy: Cases, Measures, Assessments*. Nomos, Baden-Baden.
Mekenkamp, Monique, Paul van Tongeren, and Hans van de Veen, eds. (1999). *Searching for Peace in Africa: An Overview of Conflict Prevention and Management Activities*. European Platform for Conflict Prevention and Transformation, Utrecht.
Missiroli, Antonio (2002). 'Euros for ESDP: Financing EU Operations'. Occasional Papers No. 45. Institute for Security Studies. <www.iss-eu.org/occasion/occ45.pdf> (July 2003).
Missiroli, Antonio (2003). 'EU Enlargement and CFSP/ESDP'. *European Integration* vol. 25, no. 1, pp. 1–16.
Nielson, Poul (2001). 'Building Credibility: The Role of European Development Policy in Preventing Conflicts'. Speech delivered at the Foreign Policy Centre, 8 February, London. <europa.eu.int/comm/commissioners/nielson/speeches/index_arch_en.htm> (July 2003).

Panel on United Nations Peace Operations (2000). 'Report of the Panel on United Nations Peace Operations'. The Brahimi Report. <www.un.org/peace/reports/peace_operations> (July 2003).

Patten, Chris (2001a). 'Commission Statement on the Situation in Afghanistan'. 2 October, Strasbourg. <europa.eu.int/comm/external_relations/news/patten/sp01_429.htm> (July 2003).

Patten, Chris (2001b). 'Debate on Conflict Prevention/Crisis Management'. Includes Commission statement on the situation on the border between the FRY/Kosovo and Fyrom, 14 March, Strasbourg. <europa.eu.int/comm/external_relations/news/patten/ip_01_123.htm> (July 2003).

Patten, Chris (2001c). 'Rapid Reaction Force'. Remarks in the European Parliament, 17 January. <europa.eu.int/comm/external_relations/news/patten/rrf_17_01_01.htm> (July 2003).

Patten, Chris (2001d). 'Sustainable Development "From Sound-Bite to Sound Policy"'. 29 November, London, Forum for the Future. <europa.eu.int/comm/external_relations/news/patten/sp01_600.htm> (July 2003).

Patten, Chris (2002). 'Developing Europe's External Policy in the Age of Globalisation'. 4 April, Central Party School, Beijing. <europa.eu.int/comm/external_relations/news/patten/sp02_134.htm> (July 2003).

Penttilä, Risto E.J. (2003). *The Role of the G8 in International Peace and Security*. Oxford University Press, Oxford.

Piana, Claire (2002). 'The EU's Decision-Making Process in the Common Foreign and Security Policy: The Case of the Former Yugoslav Republic of Macedonia'. *European Foreign Affairs Review* vol. 7, no. 2, pp. 209–226.

'Reconstructing Post-Conflict Societies and the German Involvement' (2003). *German Foreign Policy Dialogue* vol. 4, no. 10 (24 April), pp. 1–24.

Rummel, Reinhardt (1996). 'Conflict Prevention in Central and Eastern Europe: Concepts and Policies of the European Union'. In S. Melnik and W. Heinz, eds., *Human Rights, Conflict Prevention, and Conflict Resolution: An Introductory Reader*. Freidrich Naumann Stiftung, Brussels.

Rummel, Reinhardt (2000). 'EU Conflict Prevention Network'. In A. Björkdahl and G. Sjösedt, eds., *Future Challenges to Conflict Prevention: How Can the EU Contribute?* Swedish Institute of International Affairs, Stockholm.

Rummel, Reinhardt (2002). 'From Weakness to Power with ESDP.' *European Foreign Affairs Review* vol. 7, no. 4, pp. 453–471.

Rummel, Reinhardt (2003a). 'EU-Friedenspolitik durch Konfliktprävention: Erfahrungen mit dem Conflict Prevention Network (CPN)'. In P. Schlotter, ed., *Europa-Macht-Frieden*, pp. 240–277. AFK-Friedensschriften, Hamburg.

Rummel, Reinhardt (2003b). 'How Civilian Is the ESDP?' *SWP Comments* vol. 6. <www.swp-berlin.org/english/pdf/comment/swpcomment2003_06.pdf> (July 2003).

Schneckener, Ullrich (2002). 'Developing and Applying EU Crisis Management: Test Case Macedonia'. European Centre for Minority Issues. <www.ecmi.de/doc/download/working_paper_14.pdf> (July 2003).

Sriram, Chandra Lekha and Karin Wermester (2002). 'Preventive Action at the United Nations: From Promise to Practice?' In F. O. Hampson and D. M. Malone, eds., *From Reaction to Conflict Prevention: Opportunities for the UN System*, pp. 381–398. Lynne Rienner, Boulder, CO.

van de Goor, Luc and Martina Huber, eds. (2002). *Mainstreaming Conflict Prevention — Concept and Practice: CPN Yearbook 2000/2001*. Nomos, Baden-Baden.

PART III
THE SOCIOECONOMIC DIMENSION

Chapter 9

The G8's Role
in Promoting Financial Stability

Lorenzo Bini Smaghi

The Issue of Legitimacy

The heads of state and government of the six most powerful nations met for the first time in 1975, in Rambouillet, France, with the objective of restoring economic and financial stability after the turbulence created by the breakdown of the Bretton Woods system. The leaders of France, the United States, the United Kingdom, Germany, and Japan continued to meet annually since then, along with the leaders of Italy and Canada, although the main themes of their deliberations changed through time. More recently, the focus of G7 and lately G8 summits (after Russia was added in 1998) has been on issues linked to the fight against global poverty, environmental and food safety, and international security. The economic dimension has been sharply reduced.

This change of focus has led many to question the legitimacy of G7/8 governance. On all these broader issues, the G7/8, while representing a large proportion of the world economy, reflects the interests of only a minority of the world's population and nations. How is it possible to discuss the fight against poverty without the world's poorest countries sitting at the table? How can the G7/8 discuss the environment without taking into account the needs of the emerging economies whose primary objective is economic development? The broadening of the issues discussed at summits to a highly comprehensive agenda has led to a serious questioning of the legitimacy of the world's richest nations meeting to discuss them in isolation. Since the 2001 Genoa Summit, the leaders cannot escape this question.

However, the question of legitimacy is less critical for economic issues. These are now largely tackled by finance ministers and central bank governors, who meet more often and have the technical instruments to address the critical issues affecting the world economy. The legitimacy of the G7/8 — on economic and financial issues (Russia has been part of this economic club since 2003) — derives mainly from the ability to solve problems, as will be seen.

In the mid 1970s, the main concern of the largest economies flolwed from the exchange rate fluctuations that emerged as a result of the different economic policies that followed the first oil shock. However, attempts to stabilise exchange rates produced mixed results. There is a vast literature analysing the experience with exchange rate intervention, and the conditions under which these have been successful in counteracting excessive market fluctuations (see, for example, Bergsten and Henning

1996). Co-ordinated foreign exchange intervention by the largest economies has become increasingly rare. The latest major intervention took place in 2000, to counter an excessive depreciation of the euro against the dollar.

Several factors have led to a reduced emphasis on G7 policy co-ordination of exchange rates. First, the attempts in the late 1970s to co-ordinate policies around exchange rate targets led to fiscal and monetary policies that were not entirely consistent with the domestic objectives of the respective countries, in particular in regard to inflation and economic growth goals. Second, the deepening of financial markets progressively reduced the effectiveness of official intervention. Third, experience showed that policy authorities were not necessarily better equipped than market participants to assess whether market exchange rates were misaligned, against the referent of the underlying economic fundamentals. In such circumstances, it was preferable for the former to abstain from any intervention.

In the early 1980s, concern for the international community thus shifted from exchange rates to financial stability. The main threat became debt crises in emerging markets, which arose repeatedly and spread at an accelerating pace. In the 1990s, the main shocks came from the Mexican crisis in 1995, the Asian crisis in 1997, the Russian default in August 1998, the Brazilian crisis in 1999, and the Turkish and Argentinean crises in 2000–01.

The size of these economies and their external exposure transformed these crises from local to international ones. Even the International Monetary Fund (IMF), in some cases, was unable to deal with these cases on its own, and thus requested the assistance of its largest shareholders. The G7 came to play an increasingly important role in tackling international financial instability, for several reasons.

First, over the years the G7 developed a strong and efficient co-ordination mechanism, initially aimed at exchange rate intervention but easily extendable to address other problems that required prompt action. When quick decisions have to be taken, the G7 has shown its ability to deliver and to lead international institutions in acting speedily. This derives from a joint commitment of the G7 countries to achieve common positions when a crisis erupts.

Second, the G7 countries largely share a view on the appropriate way to tackle financial crises. This facilitates their ability to reach a common understanding and thus enhances their ability to act quickly. Undeniably, on some general issues — most notably the way and extent in which the private sector should contribute to solving crises — differences of views have emerged, as will be discussed below. However, these differences have not hampered the G7 from taking cohesive action when a crisis comes.

Third, the G7 countries hold nearly 50 percent of the votes in the IMF. They thus represent an important reference and interlocutor for IMF management and for the debtor country in the course of crisis management and resolution.

Fourth, the G7 countries have been able to supplement IMF financial support with bilateral aid, when required. They have thus been instrumental in helping affected countries to overcome their crises. This position gives the G7 countries considerable leverage when requesting that IMF financing take place on the terms and under the conditions that they consider appropriate.

Last, most of the creditors of the emerging market countries are members of the G7. This gives more weight to the G7 countries in ensuring that the solutions designed by the international financial institutions safeguard their citizens' interests, but also respect their responsibility to involve the creditors in the resolution of the crisis.

These factors have provided legitimacy to G7 countries in guiding the international institutions in addressing crises situations. The G7 has repeatedly addressed the issue of financial stability, particularly with a view to reforming the way in which the IMF operates. Following the Mexican crisis, the G7 in Halifax (1995) and in Lyon (1996) made several recommendations aimed at reducing the risks of future crises and at strengthening the role of the IMF in order to promote financial stability (G7 1995a, 1995b, 1996; G7 Finance Ministers 1996). After the Asian crisis, at the 1999 Cologne Summit the G7 finance ministers (1999) produced a report on Reforming the Architecture of the International Financial System. The word 'financial', instead of the term 'monetary' used previously when referring to the international system, marked the evolution in the role of the IMF from only promoting monetary stability, through appropriate macroeconomic and exchange rate policies, to also promoting sound domestic and international financial markets. The Asian crisis indeed showed that sound macroeconomic policies are not enough if financial markets are not sufficiently strong to support highly variable capital flows, following shocks inside and outside the country. Weak financial markets can multiply the impact of a balance-of-payment crisis on domestic income and employment, thus making the adjustment even harsher for the country.

The next two sections of this chapter examine the main issues discussed among the G7 countries and within the international institutions on the prevention and resolution of financial crises. The aim is not to be exhaustive, as an overview of the main issues is available from IMF documents, and a widespread academic literature burgeoned after the Asian crisis. Rather, the objective is to focus on some key issues, going forward, on which the G7/8 countries are currently reflecting.

Crisis Prevention

Everyone would agree that crisis prevention is essential for the effective functioning of financial markets and the world economy. Everyone would also agree that it is very difficult to prevent crises, largely because no two crises are alike. Crisis prevention was revived as a main issue for discussion among G7 countries after the 1997 Asian crisis, because the regular surveillance of Asian countries before the crisis appeared to have missed some important elements. The 1999 G7 Report on G7 Finance Ministers to the Köln Economic Summit gives prominence to this issue (G7 Finance Ministers 1999). Much progress has been made since then, but much remains to be done, as shown by the Argentinean crisis of 2001–02.

International Monetary Fund Surveillance

One of the main tasks of the IMF is to monitor economic and financial developments in the member countries, with a view to ensuring that appropriate policies are implemented and to promote the stability of the international financial system. However, in no way can IMF surveillance replace effective surveillance by market participants themselves, since they can base their investment decisions only on their own assessment of the situation. Public authorities should not create moral hazard, by acting as rating agencies or giving assurances to markets that their investments are somehow safe or protected.

Surveillance is one of the IMF's main responsibilities. It is instrumental for promptly identifying difficulties and inducing counteracting measures aimed at preventing crises. Effective IMF surveillance is thus crucial for crisis prevention. Indeed, it has been under intense scrutiny since the 1997 Asian crisis, and remains the subject of debate, particularly over the main issues of coverage, independence, and publicity.

The Asian crisis showed that IMF surveillance did not cover some relevant aspects of countries' economies, related in particular to the structure of domestic financial markets. Article IV surveillance documents have recently been enriched with such analysis. Vulnerability indicators have been developed, and included in the reports.

Much of the work that followed the Asian crisis was devoted to the development of internationally agreed-upon codes and standards, in particular concerning capital markets, including prudential supervision, accounting, and money laundering. The exercise was initially criticised by emerging markets and developing countries, as these standards had been established on the basis of industrial countries' practices. For instance, standards on supervisory aspects are directly inspired by the work of the Basle Committee on Banking Supervision, in which mainly representatives of the G10 countries participate. The emerging and developing countries found it not only politically incorrect but also very costly to adopt standards developed by advanced economies. The implementation of these standards thus remains voluntary. But there is increasing pressure for a broad participation. The G20 countries, in particular, have nearly all indicated that they will lead in this project.[1]

IMF surveillance has also been extended to the financial sector through specific monitoring procedures, such as the Financial Sector Assessment Program (FSAP) or reports on the observance of standards and codes (ROSCs). The result of this surveillance is made public. However, it appears from several market surveys that market participants are not yet devoting enough attention to these reports. This hampers the great effort put by the IMF, the World Bank, and the countries themselves into increasing the transparency of their financial systems. The Financial Stability Forum (2002) has made concrete suggestions to improve the visibility of countries' adherence to codes and standards.

The increased focus on structural financial issues should not deflect attention from other more traditional areas of a country's economic performance, in particular its fiscal and monetary policies and its exchange rate regime. The case of Argentina has shown that crises can emerge even in countries with highly sophisticated capital markets, simply as a result of bad policies or an incorrect exchange rate regime. The currency board adopted by Argentina in the early 1990s required a degree of flexibility in the labour market and in fiscal policy that was not available. Recent IMF surveillance reports on Argentina suggest that there was insufficient emphasis on the analysis of the consistency among the various policies and in particular the sustainability of the currency board.

In fact, the whole issue of the sustainability of exchange rate regimes was largely set aside after the Asian crisis. A consensus emerged, even among G7 countries, that intermediate exchange rate regimes were more difficult to sustain and more demanding in terms of policy consistency. Only corner solutions, either flexible exchange rates or currency boards, could be viable. This thesis was confirmed by the Brazilian experience in 1998–99 and by Turkey in 2000–01. The Argentinean experience, however, showed that even one of the two corners is not so easy to sustain after all.

More work is therefore needed in the field of exchange rate regimes. In the fall of 2001, the Argentine authorities and the IMF were considering two options for Argentina after a possible devaluation: a pure float or a dollarization. The delay in devaluing the peso made the second option unviable, given the lack of a sufficient amount of dollars left at the central bank after the withdrawal of bank reserves. However, before the crisis peaked, the IMF had not come out with a clear analysis of the two alternatives.

The recent experience has also shown the need for a more independent IMF assessment of the various countries' economies. One issue of concern is the degree of candour in evaluating the economic situation in a country. There is indeed some evidence that IMF staff tend to be more candid in assessing countries that do not have IMF programmes than those that do. Criticism of economic policies is at times inclined to be more open for industrial countries — the pension system is a usual target of strong IMF recommendations — than is the case for emerging markets. Here, the IMF language tends to be much more cautious, maybe for fear that this could exacerbate market tensions.

There may be two main reasons for such asymmetric behaviour. The first is that for countries that have IMF programmes, special attention might be given to avoiding scaring market participants away from investing in the country. Countries with IMF programmes are likely to be more subject than others to changes in market sentiment. It is only natural that the IMF would be biased on the side of caution. The second reason is that surveillance may lead to a questioning of the adequacy of an IMF programme, not only in regard to the implementation, but possibly also in regard to its design. There is thus a natural tendency for IMF surveillance staff to avoid criticising their colleagues who designed the programme. Indeed, the team in charge of surveillance often includes the same personnel who designed the programme. There is thus an apparent conflict of interest within the IMF staff itself that needs to be resolved. This issue has been under consideration by the IMF management and the shareholders.

One way to resolve the conflict is to increase the publicity of the documents produced by the IMF, so as to make clear the various responsibilities in the staff. However, this is not necessarily the right solution, since publicity may in fact reduce the candour of some statements, again for fear that this could excite market participants. It would not be appropriate if the IMF played the role of whistle blower for the markets, as this would reduce the responsibility of the latter in taking risks.

Expectations of Crisis Resolution

One way to prevent a crisis is to make the crisis, when and if it occurs, easier to resolve. This can reassure market participants of the country's ability to overcome a crisis, and thus make them less prone to disinvest rapidly at the first sign of tension. There are several ways to influence market expectations.

A first is to adopt collective action clauses (CACs) that facilitate debt restructuring in case of default in bond contracts. Without CACs, restructuring bond contracts requires the consensus of all bondholders. This may be very difficult to achieve because of the incentive for marginal bondholders not to agree to the restructuring and to maximise the value of their assets by asking for the reimbursement of the face value and threatening litigation. The ability of vulture funds to bring countries in default to court, with a view to obtaining the full value of their assets, has made debt restructuring very difficult and disorderly. If debt restructuring only requires the consent of a qualified majority of bondholders, as is the case if CACs are attached to the bond contract, the relative power of vulture funds would be reduced and the whole process of debt restructuring would be facilitated.

This would also facilitate crisis prevention because it would make market participants more aware of the risks of default. Furthermore, it would reduce the need for official assistance in case of crisis, and would thus reduce the moral hazard that investors may face when they expect that some countries will, in any event, be bailed out by the IMF and the international community.

Another way to influence market expectations is to build up strong means of defence for use in case of crisis. One instrument is the contingent credit line (CCL), a special IMF financing facility that provides access to huge financing at penalty rates and under certain conditions to be satisfied for eligibility. These conditions refer in particular to the soundness of the financial system and the appropriateness of the underlying macroeconomic policies. The CCL has been established mainly as a way to help countries face liquidity crises, particularly in the case of contagion, where the underlying debt position is considered to be sustainable. The availability of such an instrument, which strengthens the means of defence, should in principle discourage market participants from conducting speculative attacks against the country.

CACs and the CCL have not yet been significantly employed by emerging market countries. The main reason is the fear that the adoption of such instruments can be interpreted as a sign of weakness by the markets. Indeed, an application to the CCL or the adoption of CACs should be started in good times, when there are no tensions in financial markets, so that the latter do not get suspicious. Moreover, in good times there is little incentive to adopt instruments that help prevent crises that are not seen as imminent.

A number of emerging countries, instead of applying for a CCL, prefer to use ordinary IMF financing in a precautionary way, accepting IMF conditionality and regular programme reviews in order to obtain an ongoing endorsement of their policies from the IMF.

On the other hand, CACs are seen as implying additional costs in the borrowing rate, because they would differentiate the debt instrument from those generally available in the markets. This is at the origin of the request by emerging market countries that CACs be adopted not only by themselves but also by industrialised countries, both for their domestic and foreign debt. Industrial countries have until now shown little interest in changing the clauses of their bond contracts and to lead by example.

Market Surveillance

The Asian crisis has shown that one of the main problems is that market participants do not adequately assess the risk of their investments. The crisis is thus an unavoidable consequence of a mistaken assessment. This may occur even in highly developed and sophisticated markets. However, the latter generally have a much stronger structure and greater ability to resist sudden shocks. Wealth losses can thus be experienced without major market disruption. In emerging market economies, however, financial market structures are not robust enough to resist a major reversal of capital flows. In addition, debt is often denominated in foreign currency. Capital flow reversals thus translate into major pressure in the foreign exchange markets.

Part of the fragility of these countries' financial markets is unavoidable, although the IMF and the World Bank have launched important assistance programmes aimed at strengthening financial structures. As already noted, since Cologne in 1999 the G7 has insisted on the need to adhere to internationally agreed codes and standards related to financial markets, in the field of accounting practices, statistical reporting, supervisory rules, and so on. The assessment and monitoring of these standards and codes should serve as incentives for countries to implement them as quickly as possible and as information for market participants to enable them to assess the risks of their investment decisions better.

One area of responsibility for public authorities is facilitating the ability of market participants conducting their own surveillance and assessment of market prospects. This entails promoting maximum transparency on all data needed by participants to conduct their own assessments. The Asian crisis has shown that market participants largely based their assessments on inappropriately reported data, such as on the amount of international reserves available to the central bank. The G7 has put a lot of pressure on the IMF and other members to improve the quality and transparency of statistical data, particularly with regard to government and central bank transactions.

Crisis Management

The G7 traditionally plays an important role in the resolution of financial crises, for the reasons already explained. This means that the G7 countries are closely associated with all the main steps of the negotiation between the debtor country and the IMF. A financing package can hardly be approved without the consent of the G7. On these issues, the G7 countries systematically try to achieve a joint position, and to ensure that it is reflected in the IMF board through their respective executive directors.

The frequency with which crisis have occurred in the second half of the 1990s has induced the G7 to reflect on the ways to resolve them. Several problems have been and are still being addressed.

Moral Hazard

The first problem is how to avoid the impression in financial markets that whatever the crisis, the IMF and the international community will always intervene to help a country overcome the crisis with financial assistance. Such an expectation might have developed in the markets after the huge financing packages delivered to Mexico in 1995 and Southeast Asian countries in 1997. Indeed, the speed at which interest rate spreads on emerging market bonds converged after the crisis seemed to confirm that market participants expected a quick return to normality after the IMF intervention.

The Russian crisis of 1998 helped dispel the doubts that some countries were too big to fail and that the IMF and the G7 would always help countries obtain the financing required to overcome a crisis. The sharpness of the financial markets' adjustment to the Russian default indicated that markets were indeed experiencing some form of moral hazard. The fact that the prospect of a default could no longer be dismissed, following the Russian experience, induced a broad reallocation of portfolio composition toward less risky assets.

The Argentinean default at the end of 2001 entailed less dramatic effects on other markets because investors' portfolios had diversified and asset allocation was more clearly differentiated. Thus in practice contagion did not occur. The Argentinean crisis made it clear in the markets that the possibility of default cannot be excluded and that the IMF is not the lender of last resort in all circumstances. Ultimately, the best way to avoid moral hazard is to let default occur, as in the cases of Russia and Argentina.

It is, of course, very difficult to judge when a country has reached such an unsustainable position that there are no alternatives to default. In the cases of Brazil in 1998–99 and Turkey in 2000–01, the G7 decided that the country, although experiencing a sharp crisis, could still recover with the help of the international community. The experience proved, *ex post*, that these decisions were the right ones.

However, for Russia and Argentina default came after a long series of IMF financing packages that were used to gain time but also mislead market participants to believe that the country would in the end be bailed out. This hypothesis is probably correct in the case of Russia, as shown by the strong financial impact of a default that most did not expect. But in the case of Argentina, the financing package approved by the IMF in 2001, just a few months after the announcement of the default, might have helped market participants differentiate better between Argentinean debt and other emerging market debt, and thus avoid contagion at the time the default was declared. Despite a lack of empirical evidence on this point, there is no support for the hypothesis that the 2001 Argentinean package created moral hazard.

Access Limits

The second problem is how to implement an approach to crisis resolution that can be more predictable to market participants. After the Asian crisis, several have called for reducing the amount of discretion in the management of financial crises and for establishing a system of rules or presumptions. Rules should encompass various aspects.

The first is access to official financing by debtor countries. The huge financing packages made available to Asian countries and to Brazil, Argentina, and Turkey have all represented exceptions to the normal access limits to IMF financing. Establishing more rigid access limits reduces the pressure on the IMF to act as a lender of last resort, while increasing pressure on the debtor country to implement a stronger adjustment package and on private creditors to remain involved in filling part of the financing gap. While this argument may be true in theory, practice may show that there is not always much to be gained by establishing rigid access limits. In particular, there are limits to the sharpness of the macroeconomic adjustment that a country can impose on itself and on its citizens. If the crisis is largely one of liquidity, excessive domestic adjustment may not be desirable. Furthermore, in cases of high market turbulence, there may be little hope of the country immediately recovering market access. There thus remains little alternative to providing most of the financing needs through official financing. The main condition is that the country's debt profile is sustainable over time and thus that the country is financially sound. The second condition is that there should be a reasonable presumption that market access conditions will be restored rather quickly.

Recent experience suggests that IMF financing has been consistent with these principles, except perhaps in the case of the 2001 package for Argentina. At that time, there were serious doubts about the sustainability of Argentina's external position, even within the IMF and among G7 countries. The package was ultimately decided upon, although disbursed only in a small part, because of three main factors: first, the strong commitment of the Argentinean authorities to implement all that was needed to eliminate the financing gap, in particular through an additional budgetary adjustment; second, the fear that, without a clear-cut case that Argentina's situation was unsustainable, the restructuring would have taken place in a very disorderly manner and the IMF would have been blamed for it; and third, the financing package was expected to gain some time for market participants to differentiate between Argentinean risk and other sovereign risks in the region, thereby reducing contagion.

The experience showed that the few months gained after 11 September indeed allowed an avoidance of market contagion. When the Argentinean authorities declared a default, it was clear, even in the minds of most Argentineans, that the responsibility for such a situation was Argentina's and not that of the international community.

Private Sector Involvement

The involvement of the private sector is another aspect related to the resolution of financial crises that some would want to subject to more rules. Most experience has shown that officially financed rescue packages tend to replace private capital, instead of playing a catalytic role. This may be true, especially in the short term, as the combination of the domestic adjustment programme and official financing may not be immediately sufficient to restore the country's credibility in the markets. In addition, the involvement of the private sector requires some form of co-ordination of market expectations. This is not always very easy to implement. In the Asian crisis, with a few banks as the main creditors, authorities were able to engineer an efficient form of moral suasion, inducing banks to roll over their positions. This co-ordination was more difficult in the case of Brazil. It did not work at all in the case of Turkey in 2000–01, as the monetary authorities of the G7 countries did not agree on the need to pressure their respective financial institutions to remain engaged in the country.

In fact, although most would agree that in principle the private sector should contribute to financing a country's external deficit, this is much more difficult to implement, especially on a voluntary basis. Some form of policy intervention may be ultimately required, to reassure market participants that all the others will behave consistently with their commitments.

If voluntary solutions do not work, more constraining forms of private sector involvement may have to be implemented. Such a constraint would be a standstill, whereby payments are temporarily suspended, to allow some time to enact measures for an orderly resolution of the crisis. Alternatively, the country might resort to restructuring its external debt. This latter solution is particularly costly for the country, as it is likely to interrupt market access for a long time. Furthermore, restructuring is costly, not only for residents but also for the local banking system and for foreign investors. It is difficult to ensure a fair burden sharing, while maintaining the economy in a condition to recover promptly. Finally, the risk of litigation is high, making it difficult for a country to agree with its creditors on a fair haircut.

A Sovereign Debt Restructuring Mechanism

Argentina's attempts toward the end of 2001 to restructure its domestically held debt show the difficulty of conducting such an exercise in a piecemeal approach. What is lacking at the international level is a bankruptcy law, which would enable a country to negotiate fair terms of restructuring with all its creditors, protecting the debtor against vulture creditors and the creditors themselves against unfair treatment by the debtor.

In the fall of 2001, the IMF proposed working on a sovereign debt restructuring mechanism (SDRM) at the international level. The mechanism entailed major changes in international financial relations. Two basic approaches can be identified.

The first approach would empower the IMF, or some other international institution, to establish, at the request of the debtor country, the terms of restructuring, conditional on which the IMF itself would start again lending to the country. This solution gives substantial power to the IMF, which creates no small problem, given that the IMF itself is a creditor of the country activating the SDRM. It would thus involve a conflict of interest. In addition, this solution would require a change in the Articles of Agreement regulating the statutes of the IMF, something the U.S. authorities have been reluctant to do in the past.

An alternative is to adopt an international treaty changing the way national financial market regulations deal with bankruptcy. This would allow debtor countries to restructure their debt with the consent of a majority of the creditors, rather than the totality, debt contract by debt contract, as is the case today. This solution would also be very difficult to implement because it requires ratification by all countries and the modification of all respective market regulations.

In the absence of a structured solution, the availability of CACs in debt contracts would allow individual contracts to be restructured through an agreement with only a majority of holders of such contracts, rather than all. Unlike the SDRM, no international treaty would be required. But the restructuring would be more burdensome for the debtor country, because it would require that each debt contract is restructured one by one.

Overall, there is no doubt that the international community needs some form of SDRM. But its adoption would represent a major step forward in transferring sovereignty on the regulation of financial markets to a supranational authority. This is unlikely to be accepted by the major countries. Even emerging market economies are sceptical about such a mechanism, as they fear that its adoption would further reduce the inflow of capital to their countries and increase the cost of debt. This has been one of the main reasons why CACs have had little success thus far.

Work on the SDRM is likely to continue. But it should not derail the effort undertaken by the IMF, pressured by the G7, to improve the framework for crises resolution that was agreed at the 2000 Prague annual meetings.[2]

The Prague Framework

The Prague framework tries to strike a balance between rules and discretion, by establishing a set of presumptions and procedures to implement these presumptions.

The first element of the crisis resolution framework is that the official community, in particular the IMF, should provide financing only if the country's external debt position is considered to be sustainable. The main responsibility for assessing sustainability lies with the IMF board, based on the input provided by IMF staff. Making such an assessment is not an easy task. But it is ultimately the only way to rationalise a decision and justify its accountability. The assessment must be made on the basis of a rigorous analysis and input from the staff, and be as transparent as possible. The G7 countries have committed not to press the IMF to provide financing, or to provide the financing themselves, to countries that the IMF judges as having unsustainable positions.

The decision to grant financing to Argentina in September 2001 was based on a positive assessment, although with high risks, of the possibility of the country getting into a sustainable position. That judgement changed two months later, as the inability of the Argentinean government to deliver on its commitments led the IMF to suspend payments.

The second pillar of the Prague framework is access limits. Some would want to make these limits more rigid, but ultimately exceptions have to be allowed. It is thus a matter of establishing a clear presumption that exceptions must be true exceptions and, as such, justified on the basis of adequate analysis. The decision to make an exception should be reached through a transparent *ad hoc* procedure.

The third pillar of the Prague framework is that the private sector should be involved in the resolution of the financial crisis. Ideally, involvement should take place on a voluntary basis, within a short period of time, and under conditions consistent with the sustainability of the country's external position. If the involvement of the private sector entails, as in the case of the early 2001 Argentinean swap, a worsening of the debt profile, it should be avoided. If the private sector cannot be involved on a voluntary basis, other means have to be studied, as noted above.

Ultimately, some form of coercion, for instance in the form of standstill, cannot be excluded, if this is required to gain time and to design some more appropriate voluntary solution. Work on these instruments is going on at the IMF, especially on the link between standstills and lending into arrears.

There seems to be consensus, especially among Europeans, that the work on the SDRM, which has a long-term horizon, should not take resources away from efforts to strengthen and refine the Prague framework, which in the short term is the appropriate reference in addressing crises.

In April 2002, the G7 agreed on a two-track action plan aimed at facilitating crisis resolution. The first track consists of encouraging the adoption of CACs in major financial centres by emerging market economies. The leading-by-example of advanced economies, especially some European ones, could help encourage others to adopt such market conventions. The second track is to pursue the development of an SDRM framework, assessing its effectiveness and legal practicability. The IMF has engaged in intense dialogue with the private sector and emerging market economies to clarify issues and make the mechanism more palatable. Work on the second track is expected to continue for some time.

Conclusion

The G7 has put crisis prevention and resolution at the centre of its agenda since the first crises erupted in the mid 1990s. Since then there has been much progress, especially in making the IMF, the institution in charge of this task, more accountable and more transparent. However, much remains to be done, to make financial markets more able to assess the risks taken by its participants, to create incentives for prompt policy adjustments by debtor countries, and to establish clearer procedures for deciding whether and to what extent to provide financial assistance to a country. Ultimately, the credibility of the G7 and the IMF depends more on the concrete way in which crises are resolved than on principles and rules. In this respect, how the Argentinean crisis unfolds will be crucial. If the process of debt restructuring is managed efficiently by the new government in the course of 2003, the need for elaborated mechanisms might be reconsidered by the international community. If instead the restructuring is delayed and leads to unfair results for creditors, the case for an SDRM will be further strengthened. The sceptics might be convinced.

Notes

1   Much information is available from the IMF's website at <www.imf.org>. Information on the G20 is available from the G8 Information Centre at <www.g8.utoronto.ca>. Documentation and useful web links on financial crises and the reform of the international financial architecture are available at Nouriel Roubini's Global Macroeconomic and Financial Policy Site at <www.stern.nyu.edu/globalmacro>.
2   The Prague framework draws from the 'framework for private sector involvement in crisis resolution' included in the report of the G7 finance ministers (1997) for the Cologne Summit.

References

Bergsten, C. Fred and C. Randall Henning (1996). *Global Economic Leadership and the Group of Seven*. Institute for International Economics, Washington DC.
Financial Stability Forum (2002). 'Compendium of Standards'. <www.fsforum.org/compendium/about.html> (July 2003).
G7 (1995a). 'Halifax Summit Communiqué'. 16 June, Halifax. <www.g7.utoronto.ca/summit/1995halifax/communique/index.html> (July 2003).
G7 (1995b). 'The Halifax Summit Review of International Financial Institutions: Background Document'. 16 June, Halifax. <www.g7.utoronto.ca/summit/1995halifax/financial/index.html> (July 2003).
G7 (1996). 'Economic Communiqué: Making a Success of Globalization for the Benefit of All'. 28 June, Lyon. <www.g7.utoronto.ca/summit/1996lyon/communique/index.html> (July 2003).
G7 Finance Ministers (1996). 'Finance Ministers' Report to the Heads of State and Government on International Monetary Stability'. 28 June, Lyon. <www.g7.utoronto.ca/summit/1996lyon/finance.html> (July 2003).
G7 Finance Ministers (1999). 'Report of the G7 Finance Ministers to the Köln Economic Summit'. 18 June, Cologne. <www.g7.utoronto.ca/finance/fm061999.htm> (July 2003).

Chapter 10

Foreign Aid:
An Effective Medicine, an Addictive
Drug, or a Social Placebo?

Mario Sarcinelli

After the Second World War, at least for many years, foreign aid became the main instrument to achieve stability in global governance, in reaction to the economic and financial disintegration of the 1930s, the moral and political obligation to help countries ravaged by war or emerging from colonial status, and the strategic need to contain the contagion of communism as well as the expansionist policy of the USSR. The amount of resources mobilised through this instrument has been huge: around US$1 trillion in finance, contributed multilaterally by international agencies, such as the World Bank, the International Development Association (IDA), and a score of multilateral development banks (MDBs), and bilaterally by dozens of the wealthiest economies, was poured into one hundred countries or so and into tens of thousands of projects and activities.

What are the results of such a huge and protracted effort at international co-operation? As often happens they have been mixed. According to the World Bank (1998, 1),

> Foreign aid has at times been a spectacular success. Botswana and the Republic of Korea in the 1960s, Indonesia in the 1970s, Bolivia and Ghana in the late 1980s, and Uganda and Vietnam are all examples of countries that have gone from crisis to rapid development. Foreign aid played a significant role in each transformation, contributing ideas about development policy, training for public policymakers, and finance to support reform and an expansion of public services. ... On the flip side, foreign aid has also been an unmitigated failure. While the former Zaire's Mobutu Sese Seko was reportedly amassing one of the world's largest personal fortunes (invested, naturally, outside his own country), decades of large-scale foreign assistance left not a trace of progress. Zaire (now the Democratic Republic of Congo) is just one of several examples where a steady flow of aid ignored, if not encouraged, incompetence, corruption, and misguided policies. Consider Tanzania, where donors poured a colossal $2 billion into building roads over 20 years. Did the road network improve? No. For lack of maintenance, roads often deteriorated faster than they could be built.

This extensive quotation is intended to give full credit to the World Bank, the main agency set up at Bretton Woods to cope with reconstruction and development, for its candid assessment of foreign aid.

The aim of this chapter is neither to break new ground nor to uphold a particular thesis either in favour of or against foreign aid to help less developed countries. It is to try to understand why it has been successful in some cases and useless and even harmful in others — whether merit or responsibility has to be attributed to the donor countries, the recipient economies, or both. Instead of relying on country studies providing detailed knowledge of the conditions and causes that made for success or failure, but also producing results that can hardly be generalised, this chapter refers to a number of econometric studies that span the donor and the recipient countries. This strand of research has not escaped criticism for the inadequacies of the theoretical framework and statistical techniques, as well as the inability to prove beyond any doubt causally clear, robust relations when trying to explain growth (Kenny and Williams 2001; Temple 1999). While these caveats must be borne in mind when interpreting econometric results, they do not justify rejection *a priori* of any empirical studies in the field of growth or aid.

The next section of this chapter contains an overview of foreign aid and of the reasons that made it the centrepiece of international development policy. The donors' motivations in giving aid as they emerge from econometric testing are reported in the following section. Next comes a discussion of the effects of foreign aid on recipient countries, followed by a consideration of the unpleasant consequences of aid on dependence and corruption. The chapter goes on to examine the relationship between aid allocation and the eradication of poverty, together with the chances and the conditions that would make for the fulfilment, in a geographically balanced way, of the ambitious targets set by Development Assistance Committee (DAC) of the Organisation for Economic Co-operation and Development (OECD). The issue of the proceeds of a tax on foreign exchange transactions (Tobin tax) to finance international public goods and particularly foreign aid is then tackled, as well as the a-tax proposed by Giulio Tremonti. As conflict prevention has become prominent in the political agenda of G8 foreign ministers, unless there is direct intervention, aid is the main tool to reach it, as shown later in the chapter.

An Overview of Foreign Aid

The wastage of foreign aid resources did not materialise abruptly in this or that country. Disillusion with the effectiveness of foreign aid has been growing for a long time among donor countries, and the mismanagement of recipient economies has been highlighted by the press, the economic profession, and some political and social circles. Indeed, one might ask why the foreign aid mechanism has been allowed to go unchallenged for such a long time.

The first and foremost reason was the bipolar world that emerged from the Second World War and came to an end with the crumbling down of the Berlin Wall, the end of communist rule in Central and Eastern Europe, and the dissolution of the USSR. The West's strategic need to retain the allegiance of marginal countries disappeared and with it the propensity to finance their governments, whatever their performance in terms of economic governance, democratic institutions, and respect for human rights. The second determinant was a reassessment of the role of the state in organised society as a result of the rediscovery of liberal and sometimes libertarian principles and, at least in Europe, as a consequence of the foundering of the communist model. Economic freedom, self-reliance, and market allocation have become the main tenets of a society in which aid, including that directed to poorer countries, is more and more part of the realm of philanthropy, rather than a paramount responsibility of the government. The third element worth mentioning in regard to foreign aid is the changed focus: initially, it was supposed to jump-start or to increase growth like the Marshall Plan in post-war Europe did, but as of late it has been aiming to eradicate poverty.[1]

While it is hardly possible to fight poverty unless the economy grows, in many cases and for many years the flows of foreign aid as well as any ensuing benefits of growth were appropriated by the ruling classes, with little left to improve the condition of the poor, often huddled in slums in big cities, exposed to famine and illnesses, deprived of any education. As distribution became a crucial element, the morphology of foreign aid changed. The emphasis on big projects in physical infrastructure (dams, roads, power generation and transmission, and so on) has diminished and more foreign attention and money have gone into social infrastructure (for example, education, sanitation, health care).

As a share of donors' gross domestic product (GDP), official development assistance (ODA) — foreign aid defined by the OECD by adding together grants and loans with a grant component of at least 25 percent — declined in the 1990s to a level not different from the 1950s: less than 0.25 percent. The aim of the 1980s was to boost foreign aid up to 0.7 percent of donors' GDP, although the most sanguine supporters of resource transfer to poor countries were dreaming of pushing it to the round figure of 1 percent. Such a relative decline cannot be attributed entirely to a fall in the strategic interest or the altruistic concern of donor countries, or to the poor performance of many aid-receiving economies, although all these factors have been at work. To explain the negative trend of foreign aid, it is important first to consider the model that, for a few decades since the 1950s, guided development economists and policy makers. In the early days, there was a widespread conviction that poor countries could not emerge from their dire situation because of a lack of physical and human capital, which could be remedied neither by compressing consumption already at or near subsistence level, nor by tapping international capital markets, unwilling to incur high risks.

Therefore, a market approach to development was *de facto* impossible. The only solution was the government, which became the privileged channel for foreign official funds, both in the form of aid and loans (or development finance) to accumulate capital. International financial markets were allowed to expand in the 1960s and showed their efficiency by making the eurodollar and eurobond segments materialise, while international banks in the 1970s were willing to incur huge country risks by recycling the surplus of oil-producing countries. Consequently, the old development model appeared not only inefficient, but also outdated. As often happens, the economic sentiment turned against the government, seen as the source of all failures and incapable of performing a demiurgic role for development. The market was then regarded as the overwhelming allocator of resources not only for developed but also for developing countries.

The debt crisis that erupted in Mexico and spread to all developing countries in the 1980s showed that the markets could neither be relied upon to avoid over-indebtedness, nor to assure a minimal and smooth financing of countries in financial distress. The sentiment turned again, favouring a more balanced role for the government and the markets. Joseph Stiglitz wrote in 1989 that 'market failures are particularly pervasive in [least developed countries]. Good policy requires identifying them, asking which can be directly attacked by making markets work more effectively ... and which cannot. We need to identify which market failures can be ameliorated through nonmarket institutions.... We need to recognize both the limits and strengths of markets, as well as the strengths, and limits, of government interventions aimed at correcting market failures' (202). This requires a division of labour that cannot be very rigid, as the strengths and limits of markets and government differ from country to country and for the same country over the long haul. However, a criterion or a rule of thumb is needed to assign development responsibilities to the two players. The current trade-off favours the markets, particularly where they can be strengthened through liberalisation, privatisation, and globalisation, thus leaving to the government mainly the areas in which intervention and coercion are required, that is the production of public goods. There is no easy substitution between market and government — policies have to be pursued that strengthen the former, and make the latter efficient in the delivery of public services. If policies are able to trigger a virtuous cycle, economic, legal, and political institutions will strengthen, thus reinforcing the development process.

Whether the current balance between markets and government, certainly appropriate for developed countries that are still busy downsizing the public sector in the economic and social fields, is fit for developing countries remains to be seen: where local institutions are weak, markets do not necessarily work better than government. What can be said at this moment is that currency and banking crises have become more frequent and have affected developing and transition countries. The last victim of this epidemic is Argentina, where the banking crisis mechanics worked differently from South-East Asia. In the meantime, the simple development goal of the past synthesised by the increase in per capita income has been replaced by a spectrum of economic and social targets: growth, poverty eradication, health and literacy improvements, women's advancement, and environmentally sustainable development.

Goals and Motivations of Aid Donors

Back in 1996, the DAC produced a strategic report in which donors, in consultation with foreign aid recipients, not only set out long-term goals but also delineated the type of partnership likely to foster development. While developing countries should commit themselves to building an effective policy environment and should set out key priorities that make growth benefit the poor, the donors should provide increased financial support for such policies and place particular emphasis on participation, capacity building, and knowledge transfer.

As to the goals, the following should be achieved by 2015:

1. the proportion of people living in extreme poverty to be cut by half;
2. universal primary education to be achieved in all countries;
3. progress toward equality of sexes and empowerment of women to be achieved through eliminating discrimination in primary and secondary education by 2005;
4. mortality rates for infants and children under age five to be reduced by two thirds and that for mothers by three quarters;
5. access to gynaecological services through the primary health system for all women and girls of child-bearing age to be provided as soon as possible and anyway by 2015;
6. sustainable development strategies to be implemented in all countries by 2005 so that losses of environmental resources can be reversed by 2015.

Although, as discussed later, there is a fair chance that the slashing of poverty by half will be fulfilled by the envisaged date, an extraordinary and protracted effort is required on the part both of developing and donor countries to achieve even some of those goals. Development is no longer seen as the more or less mechanical result of increased investments in physical and human capital, but has to be regarded as a co-operative game between the donor and the recipient country; consequently, the analysis of past experiences may help to understand what made for success in some cases and what went wrong in some others, what pitfalls can be avoided and what risks can be minimised. The DAC defined the role of the donors in a coherent and targeted way as if, instead of a multitude of different aid-giving entities, there were some kind of benevolent dictator able to allocate the scarce resources in order to maximise the return — that is, the lifting of the highest number of people out of extreme poverty together with the other five goals that would improve the quality of life (DAC 1996). Foreign aid is given both on a multilateral and a bilateral basis. The two forms are fundamentally different in their rationale and in their effects (see, for example, Burnside and Dollar 2000, 863–864). As bilateral aid makes up about two thirds of the international income transfers, it is worth exploring whether it is the 'moral vision' (Lumsdaine 1993) that makes wealthy nations mindful of the dire straits that poor countries find themselves in, or whether there are other, more powerful and strategic considerations that explain foreign aid.

Focussing on bilateral aid, Alberto Alesina and Beatrice Weder (1999, 35) set out the objective 'to create better measures of strategic interests and to estimate a full model of donor behaviour, so that we can see the relative importance of political-strategic interests versus poverty, institutions and policy in the developing world'.[2] *Ceteris paribus*, a country relatively open to trade gets 20 percent more aid, one that is relatively democratic 39 percent more, one with a relatively long colonial past 87 percent more, one with a relatively Japan-consistent voting pattern at the United Nations 172 percent more, while Egypt receives aid to an extent much higher than countries with similar characteristics and Israel incommensurably more than Egypt. According to the report, 'these results suggest that, in explaining aid flows, political and strategic considerations are at least as important, and arguably more important, than recipient's policy or political institutions' (Alesina and Dollar 2000, 40). Besides democracy, no other institutional variable, such as civil liberties or rule of law, seems to have a bearing on donors. On the contrary, foreign direct investment (FDI), which tends to flow heavily to richer countries, responds to trade openness and the rule of law, but is insensitive to democracy and strategic variables.

A further elaboration confirms that colonial past has a greater weight than democracy or trade openness as foreign aid determinant. More democratic countries get more aid than undemocratic ones, and open economies receive more aid than closed ones. But the real difference is between countries with and without a colonial past: a nondemocratic former colony receives about US$25 per capita and a democratic noncolony about US$14; a closed former colony gets around US$23, while an open noncolony takes in just US$14.[3]

An analysis by individual donors sheds more light on aspects already highlighted, but also shows interesting peculiarities. The voting at the UN on the part of aid-receiving countries is significant for all the major players in international relations, that is the U.S., Japan, France, Germany, and the UK. However, the analysis does not indicate whether aid is used by major players to secure political support at the UN General Assembly, or whether UN votes are simply the expression of political ties, alliances, or geopolitical interests that in turn contribute to determine aid flows. This second interpretation seems by far the most likely, yet even accepting the first one would lead to the same conclusion — namely that foreign aid is an instrument to achieve strategic objectives.

A key variable in all these exercises is the recipient's income per capita. All things being equal, poorer countries get more from most donors, but there is a great variation in the elasticity of aid to poverty. The Nordic countries show the highest value, followed by the U.S. and the Netherlands, while France and Japan among the major donors have the lowest. As regards trade openness, the U.S., the UK, France, Japan, Australia, Austria, and the Nordics get good marks from the regressions, because they give more aid to countries that enact good economic policy, but the political variables (former colony status, voting at the UN) are so strong as to dwarf the role of the economic one. Furthermore, democracy in the recipient country is highly rewarded through aid by the U.S., the Netherlands, the UK, the Nordics, and Canada. At the other end, France seems to be hardly motivated by democratic institutions when granting aid, while Germany and Japan are in between.

Alberto Alesina and David Dollar (2000) also investigate whether a country that decides to democratise its institutions or liberalise its foreign trade can expect to be rewarded by an increase in the inflow of aid.[4] In the move toward greater democracy, aid per capita was on average US$27 in the three-year period preceding the episode, US$41 during it, and US$35 in the following three years; in three quarters of the episodes, aid increased. In the episodes in which there was a move toward an authoritarian regime, aid decreased but to a lesser extent than in the opposite case of democratisation. When the same test is carried out to see the reactions of bilateral donors to episodes of trade liberalisation or restriction, the willingness to reward democratisation does not extend to liberalisation. These asymmetric results are confirmed by other methodologies. Political values, such as democracy, seem to be a better driver of aid than economic ones, such as liberalisation. Therefore, the allocation of bilateral aid among recipient countries responds more to strategic and historical variables (Middle East, voting pattern at the UN, colonial past) than to the economic policy and political institutions of recipient countries.

Craig Burnside and David Dollar (2000) have, to some extent, investigated the allocation of foreign aid among low-income countries. The main results for total aid are that, besides donor's strategic interests, recipient's initial income and population are the most important variables, with small countries getting more. After controlling for these variables, an index of good policies does not show any tendency for total aid to reward countries that implement them. When distinguishing between bilateral and multilateral aid, the former is heavily influenced by strategic variables, thus confirming the findings of Alesina and Dollar, while the latter are quite sensitive to good policies.

According to Shantayanan Devarajan, David Dollar, and Torgny Holmgren (2001, 6), who have conducted a case study of ten African countries, if 'donors thought that they had no effect on policy at all, the rational way to allocate aid would be based on how poor countries are and the observed quality of their policies. [The] study shows that this approach is also the best way to ensure that aid has a positive effect on policy. It avoids disbursing large-scale finance into bad policy environments … It puts resources into the good policy environments in which financial assistance has a positive effect.'

Effects of Aid on Recipients

An increasing strand of literature on development studies the effects of foreign aid on receiving countries, particularly after a number of emblematic, negative cases, such as Zaire or Zambia, have been highly publicised in the press and have contributed to the spread of aid fatigue in donor countries' public opinion. In the mid 1990s, research carried out on a large sample of developing countries concluded that foreign aid was not producing the expected effects on investment and growth (Boone 1996). More recently, a number of studies have been conducted by researchers associated with the World Bank. The interactions among foreign aid, macroeconomic policies, and economic growth in recipient countries have been investigated by Craig Burnside and David Dollar (2000) on the hypothesis that aid responds to the same policies that are conducive to growth. Therefore, countries pursuing sound economic policies are on a growth path that can be accelerated by the injection of foreign aid funds. Where major distortions prevail, there is no growth, and aid is wasted in public consumption, both legal and illegal. To the extent that international capital markets are imperfect and discriminate against well-run, poor countries, foreign aid increases resources at the disposal of the receiving country. The outcome will depend on whether it is invested or not and on the productivity of capital: both are affected by policy distortions. In general, the growth rates of developing countries can be explained in terms of initial income, institutional and policy distortions, aid, and the interaction of aid with distortions.[5]

When the aid variable is introduced into the model, it has a positive effect on growth where there is a 'good' policy environment. According to Burnside and Dollar, this result is confirmed with outliers included or excluded, middle-income countries present or absent. Is it possible that aid is instrumental in bringing about good policies? In their published paper, Burnside and Dollar say that policy was treated as a dependent variable in an earlier draft of their study to see whether it was sensitive to exogenous changes in aid. As it did not show any systematic effect on the policy index, there is no evidence that over the estimation period foreign aid made for the adoption of good macroeconomic policies.

Another thorny question that researchers have often struggled with is the strong positive relationship between aid and public consumption, given the total or, more likely, partial fungibility of aid (Feyzioglu, Swaroop, and Zhu 1998). Burnside and Dollar, using a lower income sub-sample, also find that government consumption is a strong and positive function of bilateral aid, while this is not true for that granted by multilateral organisations. Since government consumption was never significant in growth equations, the relationship between aid and government consumption explains why aid is generally not effective. Their final conclusion is that 'on average aid has had little impact on growth, although a robust finding was that aid has had a more positive impact on growth in good policy environments. This effect goes beyond the direct impact that the policies themselves have on growth.... Making aid more systematically conditional on the qualities of the policies would likely increase its impact on developing country growth. This would be true as long as conditional aid of this type had plausible incentive effects' (864).

Burnside and Dollar's estimates have been challenged by others. Henrik Hansen and Finn Tarp (2001), for example, maintain that the inclusion of cases omitted as outliers weakens their robustness. Patrick Guillaumont and Lisa Chauvet (2001) argue that not only do negative terms-of-trade shocks affect growth, but their omission may also overstate the effect of policy. Indeed, terms-of-trade shocks often plague small developing countries, with sizeable negative effects on growth in the long term, as demonstrated by large-sample econometric analysis (Dehn 2001). Paul Collier and Jan Dehn (2001) maintain that if shocks have consequences on growth, their omission in evaluating aid effectiveness may cause problems at the level of interpretation as well as at the level of policy prescription.[6] Introducing shocks into the analysis by Burnside and Dollar shows that negative ones, as expected, reduce growth and at the same time make results robust to choice of sample: outliers do not have to be discarded any longer.

Moreover, increased aid can be directed to offset effects on growth from negative shocks, and if targeted to counteract the latter instead of rewarding good policies, its effectiveness is claimed to be higher. Finally, introducing terms-of-trade shocks into the analysis of Alesina and Dollar does not show that donors have taken them into consideration when allocating aid. However, the Stabex mechanism devised by the European Economic Community (now the European Union) to compensate for the shortfalls in export earnings of some developing countries was so slow as to be procyclical. Unless something better can be devised, shock-compensating aid is unworkable, whatever its merits.

Aid Dependence and Good Governance

Following Burnside and Dollar (2000), good policies are conducive to higher growth, and aid in such a framework can certainly accelerate it, but aid has been a blunt instrument in promoting the adoption of good policies. If this finding can be generalised, aid should not have an impact on good governance to be understood as a set of institutions that establish and consistently enforce predictable rules. However, good governance can be seriously undermined by encouraging rent-seeking, heightening distributional conflict to the detriment of productive efforts, and sometimes feeding corruption windfalls in the form of aid, but also of natural resources. In Africa the control of diamond-mining areas has been at the origin of armed conflicts, such as in Sierra Leone. In some poor countries, such a deterioration is due to 'Zairean disease', so named after the country that squandered both aid and natural resources. In developed countries, when gas or oil is found, a similar syndrome goes under the name of 'Dutch disease', but it produces mainly a weakening of manufacturing and agricultural sectors.

Theory does not provide a clear answer to the question of the impact of aid on governance. There are reasons to believe that aid could be positively related to good governance, for instance, either because it loosens budgetary constraints that do not allow hiring and training of civil servants entrusted with delicate and fundamental responsibilities (for example judges, police officers, tax collectors) or because it finances programmes to strengthen the legal, budgetary, or accounting systems. However, external resources can make the life of recipient governments easier, whether they are committed to reform and improving the condition of the poor or whether they just carry on doing nothing (Rodrik 1996). In the case of the latter, aid is counterproductive and so interrupting it would possibly spur the beneficiary country to bite the bullet, as happened in Korea and Taiwan when the United States put an end to its generous aid.

Political scientists have indeed pointed out that foreign aid, if sufficiently large, creates a greater allegiance of the governing class to the providers of foreign aid than to the taxpayers or the local civil society. As aid replaces tax revenue, the fight to control its flows becomes fierce and may generate armed conflict. It has been maintained that it was large-scale aid that undermined Somalia's social contract in the 1980s and made for the disappearance of any central authority (Maren 1997).

Therefore, foreign aid provides rent seekers in the political arena with plenty of opportunities, to the detriment of quality in the public arena and entrepreneurship in the productive sectors.

When theory is unable to provide a clear-cut answer, all the hopes are pinned on statistical and econometric research, but its limitations have to be borne in mind. Jakob Svensson (1998) has produced some empirical evidence that windfalls and foreign aid in countries with a divided policy process are on average more liable to extensive corruption. To test the effects of aid on governance in a cross-country analysis, Stephen Knack (2000) uses the subjective indexes, prepared by the International Country Risk Guide (ICRG).[7] If aid dependence affects the quality of governance negatively, those countries that enjoy higher levels of aid should see their position on the ICRG scale deteriorate over time. The basic regressions show that changes in population have no significant effect on the quality of governance, while increases in GDP are significant and positive, thus moving together with improvements in the ICRG index. Aid with negative and highly significant coefficients explains a large part of the change in the dependent variable. Alternative estimating procedures not only confirm the result, but also strengthen it, and the basic regressions appear robust to reasonable changes in the sample.

According to Knack, the more a country relies on foreign aid as a source of public revenue, the lower is the quality of its governance. A related legitimate question is whether higher flows of aid go to poor countries with efficient institutions. A synthetic measure of their functioning is certainly corruption. Therefore, one would expect that corrupt governments receive less foreign aid. Alesina and Weder (1999) followed upon on earlier work (see Alesina and Dollar 2000), and found that their investigation intended to provide an answer to four questions: Do corrupt governments receive more or less aid, both multilateral and bilateral, after controlling for other determinants of aid? Do international organisations pay more attention to corruption or do individual donors behave in a significantly different way, or both? Do private capital flows behave differently from official aid? Does foreign aid increase or decrease corruption?[8]

To test whether aid goes to less corrupt countries, total foreign aid, scaled in turn by GDP, population, and government expenditure, is regressed against the corruption variable, after controlling for other determinants of foreign aid, following by and large Alesina and Dollar (2000). For degrees-of-freedom problems, two specifications are used: a minimalist specification with very basic variables and a full one. The definitions of aid and the specifications produce six regressions, which in turn produce the message that more corrupt governments are not discriminated against by foreign donors. Moreover, when aid is scaled by the size of public expenditure, there is some evidence that the more corrupt the government, the higher the flow of foreign aid. Recourse to the other indicators of corruption shows these results to be robust.

When only bilateral aid is targeted, the different behaviour of individual donors is highlighted. Scandinavian countries, together with Australia, seem to be more generous toward less corrupt governments. The U.S. finds itself at the other extreme: the higher the level of corruption, the greater the inflow of American aid. While this result can be explained by the strategic interests of a superpower, it is reassuring to note that the variable of political rights indicates that more aid is channelled by the U.S. to more democratic countries. When contrasting multilateral organisations and bilateral donors, no systematic and statistically significant differences emerge, as neither seem to have an anticorruption target. As to private capital flows, FDI that, as a rule, is expected to be sensitive to bribery seems to react negatively to a higher level of corruption, but the relationship is not very strong in most specifications. Finally, in order to measure the effects of aid on corruption, a link is established between aid received in a previous period and the amount of corruption reported in a country. Two exercises that experiment with different time lengths provide no evidence that aid received in a previous period goes to a country that is less corrupt later on, but do show many cases in which the reverse is true, although the data are not statistically significant.

Aid and the Eradication of Poverty

Researchers have not only been assessing the role of a good policy and institutional environment for putting aid to good use, but have also been trying to estimate the allocation of aid that would produce the maximum reduction in poverty, thus allowing a comparison with the allocation that actually prevails. Collier and Dollar (2001), building on the earlier work by Burnside and Dollar (2000), estimate the effect of aid upon income and reconfirm that the former acts on the latter to the extent that the policy environment provides the right incentives.[9] The drastic reduction in the sample size when compared to that used by Burnside and Dollar seems to be responsible for the insignificance of the variables making for diminishing returns to aid. Since their presence is *a priori* justified and critical for a poverty-efficient allocation of aid, Burnside and Dollar's estimate of diminishing returns to aid is assumed. The marginal efficiency of aid with reference to income increases is thus established. To arrive at the optimal allocation of aid for poverty reduction, both the policy environment and the mapping from changes in income to changes in poverty are relevant for each country. This combination produces a function in which aid reduces poverty, but is subject to diminishing returns.

To arrive at a poverty-efficient allocation of aid, the marginal cost of poverty reduction must be equalised across beneficiary countries. Such an allocation depends, of course, on the given size of the overall aid available. For each global aid budget, there is a poverty-efficient allocation. Using alternative poverty measures or poverty lines, the poverty-efficient allocation of aid turns out to be very similar. According to Collier and Dollar (2001, 34), 'if the present global flow of aid were efficiently allocated, the marginal cost of lifting a person permanently above the $2 per day threshold would be $665. Because of diminishing returns to aid, this marginal cost exceeds the average cost. The total annual reduction in poverty achieved by an efficiently allocated aid program of $36bn would be 82 million people, so that the average cost of taking a person permanently out of poverty would be only $445.'

To what extent does the actual allocation diverge from the poverty-efficient one? First, aid seems to have a wrong relationship with policy, after controlling for poverty: when the policy environment is favourable to poverty reduction, aid tapers off, while the opposite should be the case. The actual average cost of reducing poverty of US$1.205 is about three times higher than the poverty-efficient cost, which means that, in addition to the 30 million people being lifted out of poverty by the current distribution of aid, another 51 million could move beyond the poverty line through a change in allocation that makes the eradication of poverty the real lodestar of aid giving. Unfortunately, it is easier to state a goal than to change the habits and the underlying interests to achieve it.

Instead of considering the volume of aid and assessing how it could be made more efficient in reducing poverty, Collier and Dollar (2001) take as given the DAC poverty reduction objective set out by the donor countries, in consultation with the beneficiaries — that is, among other things, the reduction by half of the proportion of people living in extreme poverty by 2015. This produces a third tool, the volume of aid, in addition to the reform of policies and institutions in a way that makes possible the growth of income and the reduction of poverty, and the reallocation of aid among recipient countries so as to equalise the marginal cost of reducing poverty.

There are now three problems to be solved. The first concerns the beneficiary countries with policies and institutional environments that are not very poverty efficient, as they do not minimise the cost of lifting people out of poverty permanently. Therefore, the international goal of halving poverty depends heavily on their reform. The second has to do with the overall allocation of aid for which a radical change is hypothesised, although some movement has already been noticed: by 1998, a clearer relationship between the allocation of aid and better policies seems to have emerged (Dollar 2000). Donors are supposed, therefore, to allocate aid efficiently, taking into account the population bias that makes aid per capita smaller the larger the recipient country. This constraint is accepted as a fact of life, which can hardly be removed without concentrating and channelling aid flows to a very large extent toward populous countries, such as China and India. The third problem equates the marginal benefits of aid expenditure to the western electorates with the marginal cost of poverty reduction. By assuming that the western taxpayers' marginal evaluation of poverty reduction does not change with respect to the relatively small changes in poverty owing to variations in aid budgets, all the adjustment due to an increase in the poverty efficiency of aid is brought about by the diminishing returns to aid in poverty reduction. This endogenises aid flows.

In a baseline scenario, countries' growth rates are calculated on the basis of recent experience, initial conditions, and current economic policies. By using the average relationship between income growth and poverty reduction resulting from a number of empirical studies, poverty rates to 2015 can be obtained. Even with current growth trends and policies, there is a good chance the DAC target will be met. However, the distribution of the poverty reduction is unsatisfactory, as most of it takes place in East and South Asia and rather little in Africa, while a worsening of poverty affects Eastern Europe and Central Asia. By adding to the baseline projections the estimated impact of both policy change and aid that is poverty efficient but for the population bias, the stage is set to build a number of counterfactual scenarios with particular reference to the laggard regions, Africa and Eastern Europe–Central Asia. If donors allocate aid to maximise poverty efficiency, those regions would see a doubling of the projected poverty reduction. But if current policies and institutions are not changed there is little room for putting additional aid to good use.

A Tobin Tax to Finance Foreign Aid?

Since just before the 2001 Genoa Summit, transnational nongovernmental organisations (NGOs) have become more vocal in their request for a levy on foreign exchange transactions in the tax systems of the great developed countries and the main financial centres. The revenue would finance transfers, investments, and technical assistance to the benefit of developing countries. Advocacy NGOs are politically active in many countries. International access, greatly facilitated by the internet, gives them visibility and a sort of legitimacy as defenders of the environment, the poor, and underrepresented groups in the global community. Their aim is to influence decision making at national and, above all, international levels by trying to influence policy making of international institutions, such as those established at Bretton Woods, or of country groups, such as the Organization of American States (OAS) or the G7/8.

Their demands usually acquire momentum on the eve of major gatherings. Unfortunately, as of late the meetings of international financial institutions, as happened at the World Bank/International Monetary Fund meetings in Prague in 2000, and or of special groups, such as the Summit of the Americas in Quebec City and the Genoa Summit in 2001, are often marked by disorder, notwithstanding the peaceful aims and attitudes of the NGO community. A tax on foreign exchange transactions is not new: it was proposed back in 1972 by James Tobin (1974) to increase the efficacy of macroeconomic policy. Five years later, in making the presidential address at the Eastern Economic Association, he reiterated the proposal (Tobin 1978). However, it did not make much headway with either the political milieu or the academic community. Genuine interest was shown in 1994 at the World Summit for Social Development and on the margins of the 1995 G7 Halifax Summit. At the 1996 meeting of the American Economic Association, some academics also aired their worries about the excess volatility of exchange rates. The Tobin tax started to be seen as a useful device, provided implementation problems were soluble.

Three points are worth restating about the Tobin tax: its original objectives were reducing short-term, 'round-trip' transactions on foreign exchange markets and increasing the autonomy of macroeconomic national policies; any transaction tax can be avoided to the extent that there is competition among jurisdictions, that is when the tax is not applied uniformly and universally market operators have an incentive to domicile their transactions in off-shore centres, or it engenders asset substitutions within the jurisdiction, such as when a tax induces to substitute other assets for foreign exchange to pursue the same objective; and tax revenue becomes minimal when the tax is either successful because it wipes out short-term round-tripping or is avoided through transaction migration or asset substitution. In efficient markets, therefore, countries that tax foreign exchange transactions are doomed to lose business to the advantage of tax shelters or to distort their own financial market.

However, when Tobin revisited the subject in 1996, he wrote that a universal foreign exchange transaction tax would produce a huge revenue to be devoted to the financing of international activities, such as augmenting the resources at the disposal of the World Bank (Tobin 1996). On the basis of the three-year survey conducted by the Bank for International Settlements in 2001, a 0.1 percent rate on the volume of foreign exchange transactions would produce between US$250 and US$300 billion yearly. Of course, the precise definition of the tax base, the possible deflation of the foreign exchange market, and the other possibilities of circumventing the tax obligation would make for a much lower revenue, but it is nonetheless a huge amount. This revenue would be collected by individual governments that would retain a share for their general budget (for instance, 50 percent by large countries, 100 percent by small ones) and then devote the rest to the fulfilment of international goals. NGOs are attracted by the potentially huge revenue of a Tobin tax, by the automatic or quasi-automatic financing of developing countries' needs, and by a possible role in the allocation and management of these funds.

In the lead-up to the Genoa Summit, there was considerable political pressure in favour of a Tobin tax. This pressure is reflected in the report submitted by the G7 finance ministers, to the leaders, which restates the practical difficulties that prevent such a proposal from being a valid instrument to stabilise international markets. The subject was also included in the agenda of a subsequent meeting of EU finance ministers. On that occasion, Giulio Tremonti (2001), Italy's Minister for Economy and Finances, elaborated on a proposal he had already announced to the international press. As a counterproposal to the request of a Tobin tax by the 'no global' movement, he advocated an a-tax or de-tax, where 'a-' or 'de-' stands for 'without'. The scheme would give all the buyers in any transaction the chance to direct, for instance, 1 percent of the price paid in favour of a worthy cause pre-selected by the seller, including aid to development, whereas the tax authorities would make the donation exempt from tax. The proposed mechanism extends provisions that are rather common in the field of income tax. Such an ingenious scheme, however, is just the opposite of what a Tobin tax is supposed to achieve: the latter would base resource transfer to the least developed countries on a possibly global macro decision; the former would make it depend on innumerable micro decisions by consumers, as intermediated by sellers. Private charity would replace international public solidarity. Moreover, it is unlikely such a change would make foreign aid more poverty efficient.

Whatever the theoretical merits and the practical difficulties of a Tobin tax, is financing development countries' needs through an *ad hoc* tax instrument worth pursuing? In the light of the empirical research reviewed above and even taking into account all the methodological caveats, the answer must be no. The allocation of bilateral aid might be less biased toward the strategic interests of the donors, but there is no assurance, because it is unlikely that governments would completely allocate a share of their tax proceeds to third parties. Moreover, as aid seems to favour distribution conflicts and even corruption, more aid is likely to increase dependence: any drug destroys the body, human or social, that absorbs it. Finally, the availability of more aid does not lift people out of poverty to the extent possible, unless the policy and institutional environment are such as to promote growth. A more or fully automatic income transfer in favour of poor countries would not provide the right incentive for them to grow out of their indigence. Aid remains fundamental in any endeavour to help developing countries, but it requires a spirit of partnership with clear roles and responsibilities for donors and recipients.

Aid and Conflict Prevention

When the G8 foreign ministers met at Miyazaki before the 2000 Okinawa Summit, they identified five subjects on which they thought the G8 had a comparative advantage: small arms and light weapons, conflict and development, illicit trade in diamonds, children in armed conflict, and international civil police (G8 Foreign Ministers 2000). It is not clear why the G8 would have more competence or power to deal with these tragic aspects or a new institution (namely, international civil police), but these issues certainly deserve such a high level of international attention. Whether they can be tackled in an operational way or simply form the subject of diplomatic efforts to enshrine rights and duties in international protocols is something left to political expediency and the strategic importance of a particular area.

The subject of conflict and development, however, is one on which foreign relations experts and economists can co-operate in order to avoid the former and to strengthen the latter. Steady and sustainable development depends on political stability and, one hopes, democratic rule. Yet even if stability prevails in a nonhomogeneous country for some time, sooner or later international aid, *inter alia*, will cause distributional conflict within the ruling classes, the (rudimentary) public administration, and a society based on clanship, unless economic and social development sets in and makes the benefits of growth available in a relatively fair way. Therefore, donors cannot merely provide funds or aid in kind but must be conscious of the allocative as well as the distributional consequences of their transfers. Nonetheless, finding ways to avoid making the situation worse through international aid, as in Somalia, must remain high on the agenda.

Where instability prevails, the paramount objective moves from the economic realm to the political. But unless there is some form of military intervention — even if it was successful in Kosovo and disastrous in Somalia — international aid remains the main instrument during an emergency and afterward in order to buttress any political or diplomatic initiative.[10] Even if pursuing economic and political targets simultaneously is deemed possible in situations of mild instability, development assistance strategies are inevitably modified to take conflict prevention into account, to ensure quick action to avoid conflict, or to engineer a smooth transition from emergency to post-conflict development assistance; with regard to the last aspect, the G8 foreign ministers in Rome promised to pay special attention to disarmament, demobilisation, and reintegration (DDR) (see Appendix D). Unless there is a sufficient increase in the total amount of foreign aid, the original goals of poverty eradication and economic development will suffer whenever a serious risk of conflict arises. Of the three aims mentioned above, the most interesting and challenging is the first, which, according to the Miyazaki declaration, is based upon the two pillars of institution building and the apportionment and management of natural resources (G8 Foreign Ministers 2000).

Institution building, a wide-ranging subject that encompasses the public, social, and economic domains, depends on the recipient country's level of development in the particular field, and requires full ownership of the process by the beneficiary. Unless the beneficiary is convinced of the necessity to acquire the institutional capacity to run and maintain schools, hospitals, roads, and so on, no lasting contribution to the welfare of a developing country will be made by aid-financed facilities in any of the three sectors. The lack of maintenance by local residents is often another proof of aid dependence.[11] Institution building in the field, for instance, of nondiscrimination *vis-à-vis* a minority, if anything, is more delicate and depends even more on internalisation of the need to avoid conflict and on consistency of behaviour.

With reference to apportioning and managing natural resources, water is and will increasingly remain a contentious subject, as world population increases, cities and industries expand, and deforestation and air pollution grow. At Rome, the G8 foreign ministers committed themselves to devoting special attention to co-operation in water management (see Appendix D). In the case of Israel and Palestine — a hot situation indeed — there are economists who believe that if water is not allowed to turn into a political dispute that calls upon sovereignty, heritage, and national security to buttress national positions, the problem can be solved through a holistic approach (see, for example, Askari and Brown 2001). Regional water management can be accomplished using an optimisation model that allocates water so as to maximise net benefits and give rise to shadow prices. Therefore, through better domestic water management and open recognition of the needs of neighbouring countries, a crisis can be avoided — or perhaps only postponed. Even to secure a deferment, two prerequisites are absolutely necessary: a co-operative attitude among the countries concerned, which is incidentally utterly lacking in the whole Middle East, and an honest, impartial broker who can foster the holistic approach, adjudicate possible disputes, and help to manage the system in a context, both economic and financial (that is, by allowing water rights to be traded). The World Bank has been indicated as the *deus ex machina* able to perform such a function. That it is the best suited among the existing international institutions there is no doubt, but there is little assurance that it will be successful over time. Just in terms of the different birth rates of Israel and Palestine, for example, such success is unlikely. The more populated water-lacking country will ask for water rights to be redistributed, and the other will resist because it sees no reason to accept a deterioration in its well-being. The same can be said if the two economies choose different productive specialisations that require divergent water input per GDP unit. Unless water can be made more plentiful at the prevailing cost per unit or the two communities develop a sense of common destiny that makes them feel as though they were one, conflicts will recur.

Conclusion

According to the World Bank (1998, 103), 'good economic management matters more to developing countries than foreign financial aid does. Policy and institutional gaps hold back economies that lag behind, not financing gaps. Aid money has a big impact only after countries have made substantial progress in reforming their policies and institutions'. It is difficult to disagree. However, from an ethical and political point of view, the question remains of what can — or should — be done for those countries that not only are poor but also have political leaders insensitive to the needs of their population and to the suggestions coming from the international community. The devastating effect of aid addiction, caused by throwing even more money at the problem, must be avoided absolutely. Making money available on condition that relevant reforms are introduced has little chance to succeed. Unless there is a strong movement within the poor country in favour of such reforms, these are felt as a sort of foreign imposition that hinders the process of ownership. A way out of the quandary might appear to be the selection of certain projects in strategic sectors, but the fungibility of aid on one side and the need for a minimum of decent governance on the other make the alternative rather shaky. The World Bank recommends contributing more ideas in addition to money, involving civil society, and working for the long term. Even in the most difficult cases, the international community must maintain a strong sense of direction and dedication, if not to eradicate poverty, at least to alleviate it. Sharp criticism has been levelled at the World Bank and its fellow MDBs by the Meltzer Commission (Meltzer 2000), appointed by the U.S. Congress to recommend future U.S. policy on major international institutions. While the commission agreed with the World Bank's approach, the majority of its members found fault with its implementation and recommended the following. 'To function more effectively, the development banks must be transformed from capital-intensive lenders to sources of technical assistance, providers of regional and global public goods, and facilitators of an increased flow of private sector resources to the emerging countries. The common goal should be to reduce poverty; their individual responsibilities should be distinct. Their common effort should be to encourage countries to attract productive investment; their individual responsibility should be to remain accountable for their performance. Their common aim should be to increase incentives that assure effectiveness' (86). The issue in dispute is lending by international financial institutions accused of impinging on the role of capital markets, not their mission as providers of grants, to be funded openly by the industrialised nations, as direct subsidies. However, these grants must finance only part of the cost of supplying services (such as vaccinations and primary education) and must be based on performance and audited independently. And if the poor country government is unable or unwilling to meet its cost share for services provided to the population? Alas, no grants.[12]

Were this approach to prevail across the board, only private charities, religious as well as secular, would take care of these difficult cases. To some extent, there is already such a tendency: Tremonti has been granted authority by the Italian parliament to enact an a-tax or de-tax. Were private, voluntary sources to substitute for ODA to a substantial extent, as Tremonti openly maintains, philanthropy will be reinstated in the role of social appeaser, thus providing a placebo to the uneasy conscience of individual donors, but no solution to the predicament of the recipients. In fact, there is no better chance for private charitable institutions to succeed where international agencies and official donors have failed — in convincing poor and poorly run countries to reform their policies and institutions.

As President George W. Bush says, no child is to be left behind. In this globalised world, can we afford to leave behind a score of poor countries in Africa and, maybe, in Eastern Europe and Central Asia?[13]

Notes

1   The U.S.'s generous aid was very successful in triggering the European revival because it was made conditional on the co-operation among highly developed beneficiary countries.
2   The main independent variables used in the econometric exercises to explain foreign aid to beneficiary countries are trade openness, democracy, civil liberties, former colonial status, foreign direct investment, initial income, and population, to which a measure of donor strategic interests proxied by the recipient's United Nations voting pattern is added. Several regressions are run to explain aggregate bilateral aid flows. Referring just to the base specification, the coefficients obtained through panel regressions using five-year averages over the period from 1970 to 1994 are revealing.
3   With regard to the colonial past of a receiving country, this seems to be a characteristic that attracts more aid both from the former coloniser as well as from other donors. Since there is no discriminating attitude on the part of the latter against other country's former colonies, this explains why the status of former colonial has turned out to be particularly important.
4   By using time series and isolating the episodes when there is a change in the democracy index of at least one standard deviation over a three-year period, the data set produces 59 observations in which democracy becomes higher and 42 in which it goes down.
5   The empirical test of the hypothesis uses a refined definition of foreign aid (grants plus the grant element of each concessional loan, highly correlated anyway with ODA), a range of policy and institutional distortions, a policy index incorporating the budget surplus, the inflation rate, and the openness dummy developed by Jeffrey Sachs and Andrew Warner (1995). The data are relative to a panel of 56 countries and six four-year time periods between 1970–1973 and 1990–1993.

6   To obviate this difficulty, a variable has to be constructed that is clearly exogenous to policy and aid; following Angus Deaton (1995), shocks are measured by an index of export prices. After suitable manipulation, 179 positive and 99 negative shock episodes are identified for the sample of 113 countries.

7   Data are available since 1982 for a large number of countries, on corruption in government, bureaucratic quality, and rule of law. As each has six degrees, adding them together produces an 18-point scale. At the time of the estimate, aid data were available until 1995. Besides aid, defined as ODA scaled by GDP or by government expenditures, other main independent variables are the increase in population and that in GDP, as both may justify improvements in the quality of governance.

8   Corruption indicators are available from various sources and seven from six of the latter are used throughout the Alesina and Weder's paper. Fortunately, they are highly correlated. The indicator most widely used in academic research, as well as in their paper, is that supplied by the ICRG.

9   This result has been reached by amplifying the range of policies through recourse to a new World Bank measure that refers to 20 aspects of the policy environment, restricting the estimation period for the relationship between aid and policy to 1990–1996, because after the 1970s it may have changed, and enlarging the coverage to 86 countries.

10 According to Paul Collier and Anke Hoeffler (2002), countries emerging from civil war retain a normal absorptive capacity for aid in the first three post-conflict years and double it in the next seven.

11 According to Robert Klitgaard (1990, 98), an Equatorial Guinea resident once said in respect of his compatriots' lack of infrastructure maintenance: 'Everything is given to them, they don't take care of anything and don't have to.'

12 Although the language used in the Genoa communiqué is highly diplomatic, there is an indication of the U.S. Republican administration's position on the set of goals to be pursued and advocated by the G8 (Appendix G). At the meetings, discussions centred on pursuing the current policies to relieve the debt of heavily indebted poor countries (HIPCs), to enhance the participation of less developed countries in the global trading system, to open them up to higher private investment, and to promote initiatives in the fields of health, education, and food security. With regard to meeting the OECD's international development goals for aid, there is only a commitment to untie aid to less developed countries, to support a meaningful replenishment of the IDA, to use more of its resources for grants for education and health, and to launch an under-funded facility to fight HIV/AIDS and other diseases.

13 At the Kananaskis Summit in 2002, the G7 leaders addressed the factors likely to prevent the HIPC Initiative from delivering the promised debt reduction and made recommendations to secure the participation of all creditors, to complete the financing of the scheme, and to assure debt sustainability at completion point. In support of the New Partnership for Africa's Development (NEPAD), the G8 adopted the Africa Action Plan to establish enhanced partnerships with performing African countries. The name of the game now is partnership, based on mutual accountability and responsibility between developing countries and donors. It was repeated in Monterrey, Rome, Kananaskis, and Johannesburg, and at Windsor, where the G8 development co-operation ministers met to stress the role of development co-operation encompassing aid, trade, and investment policies. The hope of better days should never diminish, but relatively low growth in donor countries and the long-term war against terrorism are dimming the prospects for a quantum leap in the fight against want, disease, and illiteracy in poor countries. The 2003 Evian Summit provided some reassurance and held out the prospect for a new international finance facility.

References

Alesina, Alberto and David Dollar (2000). 'Who Gives Foreign Aid to Whom and Why?' *Journal of Economic Growth* vol. 5, no. 1, pp. 33–63.

Alesina, Alberto and Beatrice Weder (1999). 'Do Corrupt Governments Receive Less Foreign Aid?' NBER Working Paper No. 7108. <papers.nber.org/papers/w7108> (July 2003).

Askari, Hossein and Catherine Brown (2001). 'Water Management, Middle East Peace, and a Role for the World Bank'. *Banca Nazionale del Lavoro Quarterly Review* vol. 54, no. 216, pp. 3–36.

Boone, Peter (1996). 'Politics and the Effectiveness of Foreign Aid'. *European Economic Review* vol. 40, no. 2, pp. 289–329.

Burnside, Craig and David Dollar (2000). 'Aid, Policies, and Growth'. *American Economic Review* vol. 90, no. 4, pp. 847–868.

Collier, Paul and Jan Dehn (2001). 'Aid, Shocks, and Growth'. Working Paper No. 2688. World Bank, Washington DC.

Collier, Paul and David Dollar (2001). *Globalization, Growth, and Poverty: Building an Inclusive World Economy*. World Bank and Oxford University Press, Washington DC and New York.

Collier, Paul and Anke Hoeffler (2002). 'Aid, Policy, and Growth in Post-Conflict Societies'. Working Paper No. 2902. World Bank, Washington DC. <econ.worldbank.org/files/19228_wps2902.pdf> (July 2003).

Deaton, Angus (1995). 'International Commodity Prices, Macroeconomic Performance, and Politics in Sub-Saharan Africa'. Princeton Studies in International Finance No. 29. Princeton University Press.

Dehn, Jan (2001). 'Commodity Price Uncertainty and Shocks: Implications for Economic Growth'. Paper presented at the Royal Economic Society Annual Conference. April, University of Durham.

Devarajan, Shantayanan, David Dollar, and Torgny Holmgren (2001). 'Aid and Reform in Africa: Lessons from Ten Case Studies'. World Bank, Washington DC.

Development Assistance Committee (1996). 'Shaping the 21st Century: The Role of Development Co-operation'. Organisation for Economic Co-operation and Development, Paris.

Dollar, David (2000). 'Has Aid Efficiency Improved in the 1990s?' Mimeo. World Bank, Washington DC.

Feyzioglu, Tarhan, Vinaya Swaroop, and Min Zhu (1998). 'A Panel Data Analysis of the Fungibility of Foreign Aid'. *World Bank Economic Review* vol. 12, no. 1. <www.worldbank.org/research/journals/wber/revjan98/panel.htm> (July 2003).

G7 Finance Ministers (2001). 'Strengthening the International Financial System and the Multilateral Development Banks: Report of the G7 Finance Ministers and Central Bank Governors'. 7 July, Rome. <www.g8.utoronto.ca/finance/fm010707.htm> (July 2003).

G8 Foreign Ministers (2000). 'G8 Miyazaki Initiatives for Conflict Prevention'. Miyazaki, 13 July. <www.g7.utoronto.ca/foreign/fm000713-in.htm> (July 2003).

Guillaumont, Patrick and Lisa Chauvet (2001). 'Aid and Performance: A Reassessment'. *Journal of Development Studies* vol. 37, no. 6, pp. 66–92.

Hansen, Henrik and Finn Tarp (2001). 'Aid and Growth Regressions'. *Journal of Development Economics* vol. 64, no. 2, pp. 547–570.

Kenny, Charles and David Williams (2001). 'What Do We Know about Economic Growth? Or, Why Don't We Know Very Much'. *World Development* vol. 29, no. 1, pp. 1–22.

Klitgaard, Robert E. (1990). *Tropical Gangsters*. Basic Books, New York.

Knack, Stephen (2000). 'Aid Dependence and the Quality of Governance: A Cross-Country Empirical Analysis'. Working Paper No. 2396. World Bank, Washington DC. <econ.worldbank.org/docs/1151.pdf> (July 2003).

Lumsdaine, David H. (1993). *Moral Vision in International Politics: The Foreign Aid Regime, 1949–1989*. Princeton University Press, Princeton.

Maren, Michael (1997). *The Road to Hell: The Ravaging Effects of Foreign Aid and International Charity*. Free Press, New York.

Meltzer, Allan H. (2000). *Report of the International Financial Institutions Advisory Commission*. United States Congress, Washington DC.

Rodrik, Dani (1996). 'Understanding Economic Policy Reform'. *Journal of Economic Literature* vol. 34, no. 1, pp. 9–41.

Sachs, Jeffrey and Andrew Warner (1995). 'Economic Reform and the Process of Global Integration'. Brookings Papers on Economic Activity, No. 1.

Stiglitz, Joseph (1989). 'Markets, Market Failures, and Development'. *American Economic Review* vol. 79, no. 2, pp. 197–203.

Svensson, Jakob (1998). 'Foreign Aid and Rent-Seeking'. Working Paper No. 1880. World Bank, Washington DC. <econ.worldbank.org/files/11578_wps1880.pdf> (July 2003).

Temple, Jonathan (1999). 'The New Growth Evidence'. *Journal of Economic Literature* vol. 37, no. 1, pp. 112–156.

Tobin, James (1974). 'The New Economics One Decade Older'. Eliot Janeway Lectures on Historical Economics in Honour of Joseph Schumpeter, 1972. Princeton University Press, Princeton.

Tobin, James (1978). 'A Proposal for International Monetary Reform'. *Eastern Economic Journal* vol. 4, no. 3-4 (July/October).

Tobin, James (1996). 'Prologue'. In M. ul Haq, I. Kaul and I. Grunberg, eds., *The Tobin Tax: Coping with Financial Volatility*. Oxford University Press, New York.

Tremonti, Giulio (2001). 'Pour une anti-taxe Tobin'. *Le Monde*, 12 September.

World Bank (1998). 'Assessing Aid: What Works, What Doesn't, and Why'. Policy Research Report, World Bank. <www.worldbank.org/research/aid/aidtoc.htm> (July 2003).

Chapter 11

Socioeconomic Vulnerability Analysis and the Culture of Prevention in the Globalisation Era

Umberto Triulzi and Pierluigi Montalbano

It is widely accepted that trade openness, the international movement of factors of production, and the international circulation of information have stimulated the economic and political progress of nations. At the same time, some experts believe this increased economic interrelation has also led to wider marginalisation and inequality (Triulzi and Montalbano 1997). This chapter argues that these phenomena have not only increased global inequalities but have also caused greater risk exposure and, in general, increased feelings of vulnerability. These consequences have occurred at different levels: workers in industrialised countries complain about competition from lower cost labourers from developing countries; likewise, workers in poorer nations are threatened by multinational companies that act without concern for long-term development objectives; financial markets, as well, fear the increase in costs and risk margins tied to international financial crises (Yusuf 2001).

This world-wide feeling of vulnerability to various risks is neither unprecedented nor unfounded. According to the World Bank (2001), economic crises, along with natural disasters and conflicts, are one of the main reasons for aggregated shocks and increases in the incidence of poverty at the international level. Integrated economies, as a result, seem to be more susceptible to further negative externalities, especially if markets are not working well (Dercon 2001). Not surprisingly, then, developing countries, transition economies, and small states, in the midst of increased integration with the global economy but without adequate markets and infrastructure to support it, have been particularly affected by international crises (Easterley and Kraay 1999). As a result, between 1990 and 1997, more than 80 percent of developing countries experienced at least one year of negative per capita output growth owing to an economic crisis, natural disaster, or conflict (World Bank 2001, ch. 9). A crucial question that emerges is whether it is globalisation *per se* that determines vulnerability or whether it is weak institutional development that is the root cause. Assuming it is the latter, one can argue that developing countries are among the most vulnerable.

In addition, it is generally agreed that these macroeconomic crises have resulted in world-wide financial instability, but at the local level the impact of such crises on the poor has been largely overlooked. Even if we agree that crises affect the poor and the rich indifferently, it must be conceded that the negative impacts are much more devastating for those who are poor or are near the poverty line, even in situations in which the crisis does not affect the local population disproportionately (Lustig 2000). This is because the poorest experience a reduced ability to save and lack full access to general public or private safety net systems (World Bank 2001, ch. 8).

Although empirical analyses have until now been unable to show a clear correlation between international crises and poverty, this inability is the result of the fact that traditional indicators of inequality and poverty do not accurately capture the full impact of economic crises on the standards of living of local populations. Crises often result in a noticeable movement of populations along the poverty line and, consequently, those who risk falling into poverty following crisis situations do not generally figure in standard poverty indicators. Generally speaking, only a minority of the population could be considered chronically poor (consistently below the poverty line), while a much larger portion of the population can be considered, more generally, to be vulnerable to poverty. Comparing 13 panel studies in developing countries in Latin America, Africa, Asia, and Russia, Bob Baulch and John Hoddinott (2000) confirm a surprisingly large percentage of temporarily poor households (from a low of 20 percent to a high of 66 percent) in relation to the percentage of chronically poor (on average 10 percent, but never more than 25 percent) for each region.[1] This means that traditional poverty analyses, which consider only those who are below the poverty line at the time of the analysis, fail to take into account a large percentage of the population that nevertheless has an increased chance of falling below the same line in the near future.

It is to the latter that policies and *ad hoc* interventions need to be directed, in order to reduce the probability that a mere situation of increased risk exposure will negatively affect well-being simply due to a lack of tools or particular socioeconomic characteristics. Hence, vulnerability analysis, with its forward-looking approach, is necessary to identify the vulnerable and design more appropriate risk management tools for them. Only through an analysis of socioeconomic vulnerability, which shifts the focus of strategies for poverty reduction from *ex post* to *ex ante*, can we definitively change the objectives and potential beneficiaries of poverty reduction policies and social protection programmes (Holzmann 2001).

A Review of Basic Principals

The concept of vulnerability as a method of analysis does not override traditional studies; instead, it offers a different angle from which to examine the dynamics of development and poverty and understand their various manifestations.

The term 'vulnerability' has its origins in the most recent evolution of development analysis. It grew out of the awareness that the evaluation of simply disposable assets, at the micro and macro levels, is not enough to obtain a complete understanding of the degree of sustainability of the poor's behaviour; rather, it is necessary to analyse the dynamics and characteristics of the strategies and reactions of different social groups in different political and socioeconomic contexts.

Currently, however, there is no unanimous or consistent definition of the phenomenon of vulnerability, nor is there a complete and systematic theoretical analysis of it. As a result, there are several possible measurements, depending on the context in which vulnerability is analysed. The biggest impediment to measuring the determinants of vulnerability, however, is that vulnerability analysis must make statements about future poverty. What really matters, consequently, is not precisely the current values of the analysed variables, but rather the ability to understand their future dynamics and make interventions when needed (Dercon 2001).

The Economic Perspective of Vulnerability Analysis

The economic literature considers vulnerability a possible loss of well-being due to a combination of the level of risks (characterised by different magnitudes, frequencies, and lags) and the types of risk management tools (distinguishing among reducing, mitigating, and coping strategies). The method used to measure vulnerability is largely monetary, using indicators such as income and per capita consumption in relation to a standard poverty line.[2] In order to evaluate the dynamics of poverty in the short term, the economic approach primarily uses panel studies and focusses on households (Alwang, Siegel, and Jorgensen 2001). There is, nevertheless, a growing literature dedicated to the macroeconomic analysis of vulnerability (Triulzi et al. 2003; Thomas 2003).

In general, it is agreed that vulnerability represents the combination of the probabilities that negative effects will occur, along with a measurement of their severity based on a certain function of well-being (Glewwe and Hall 1998). Apart from a few theories, however — for example, the likely relationship between temporary shocks and long-term vulnerability (Pritchett, Suryahadi, and Sumarto 2000) — there is still much debate over the meaning and reasons underlying the dynamics of vulnerability and shifts in poverty levels.

According to some experts, the probability that unpredictable or negative events will occur depends on the availability of risk management tools, as well as on the characteristics of the units of analysis. In this context, socioeconomic vulnerability can be defined as an expected loss of well-being, above a socially accepted norm, which is caused by the occurrence of uncertain risks or events and the lack of appropriate risk management instruments (Holzmann 2001). The negative occurrence, namely hazard, depends on the interaction of risk exposure and the actual availability of appropriate risk management tools, both related also to the specific characteristics of the unit of analysis. The optimal solution to a situation of vulnerability, then, requires the explicit consideration of a time dimension in order to assess the instruments available and the specific characteristics of the units of analysis at every point in time.

Even from an economic point of view, consensus on a common definition, methodology, and vision of vulnerability analysis has yet to be reached. This has made it difficult to shed light on the particular economic aspects of vulnerability. In addition, current economic studies have largely ignored a number of relevant issues, such as those related to a lack of policy credibility, or the inconsistency between short-term strategies and long-term commitments (Triulzi and Montalbano 2001b), or even those derived from exclusion from vulnerability reduction policies (Dercon 2001).

The Analysis of Vulnerability: Beyond the Economic Approach

Beyond the economic approach, a wider definition of vulnerability has recently been developed, informed by the so-called 'asset-based approach', which considers poverty to be the result of an inadequate access to a range of assets, tangible and intangible, at a certain moment. In this context, the negative manifestation of a risk is defined as a situation in which, in addition to a current loss of well-being, there is an expected future reduction in income, consumption, and investment. The defining element of the so-called asset-based literature is precisely its focus on the methods with which individuals and households can modify the portfolio of resources to obtain a more opportune management of risks (Reardon and Vosti 1995).

Another vast field of research on vulnerability is linked to the sustainable livelihoods literature, inspired by the works of Amartya Sen, that introduced ethical considerations relative to an individual's liberty to pursue objectives and obtain entitlements (Triulzi 1998). Likewise, this approach is concerned with identifying livelihoods that are capable of maintaining and increasing the productivity of resources, ensuring access to different types of assets and income-generating activities, and guaranteeing adequate stocks and flows of food and capital to satisfy basic needs. Introduced at the World Summit on Environment and Development in 1992, the sustainable livelihood approach considers four complementary objectives together: economic development, sustainable management of resources, poverty eradication, and food security. These are pursued by means of evaluating four different aspects of sustainability: economic efficiency, environmental integrity, social justice, and the ability to react to diverse types of shock. Together with the recognition of the concept of human security, this approach represents the most evident example of the desire to arrive at a multi-period and dynamic analysis that can verify the actual abilities of individuals and move away from the static analysis of current assets (Gnisci 2000). In this context, vulnerability is viewed as the likelihood that people's livelihoods can deteriorate over time (referred to as livelihood vulnerability).

The livelihood vulnerability approach can be considered an extension of the literature on food security, which considers food production and consumption as the most important components of the livelihood of a population, social group, or economic system (Maxwell et al. 2000). It follows, then, that this approach views vulnerability merely as a state of food insecurity. The Food and Agiculture Organization (FAO) and the World Food Programme (WFP) have logically been the most active in this aspect of vulnerability analysis. Their main objective is the creation of a food early warning system (FEWS) able to assist policy makers in the identification of the most vulnerable areas and social groups. The WFP, for instance, defines vulnerability as the likelihood of a consistent decline in levels of access to food consumption beyond a determined minimum threshold. The literature on food security draws specific poverty maps and aggregates indexes of vulnerability — that is, signals capable of indicating the degree of vulnerability that individuals, social groups, and the overall socioeconomic system experience in relation to the risk of inadequate food consumption. According to the FAO's Food Insecurity and Vulnerability Information and Mapping Systems (FIVIMS), vulnerability to food insecurity is related to a wide range of factors, not only those specifically linked to climate and agricultural aspects (FAO 1998). A particular vein of the literature on food security vulnerability also analyses the strictly health and nutritional aspects of the problem (Mason 1984).

Recently, an attempt was also made to combine the sustainable livelihoods approach with environmental vulnerability, defining vulnerability as the exposure of individuals or social groups to a slight reduction in livelihood as a result of an environmental change (Ahmed and Lipton 1997). In the context of this approach, a model was constructed that could provide adequate projections on the expected negative impacts of global warming and climate and ecological change linked to indicators such as annual rainfall, floods, and so on (Dinar et al. 1998).

Towards a Shared Methodology

It is evident even from this brief review of the various approaches in the current literature on socioeconomic vulnerability that no unequivocal conceptualisation of the phenomenon or a proper empirical analysis is on the horizon. The different approaches presented above tend to be alternatively theoretically strong or empirically weak (Alwang, Siegel, and Jorgensen 2001), without a solid, unique method of analysis.

Reaching a shared methodology to analyse socioeconomic vulnerability is, however, not an easy task. The notion itself of vulnerability further hinders the possibility of agreeing on a universal conceptualisation and requires the creation of new tools and *ad hoc* methodologies. From a theoretical point of view, the phenomenon can be compared to a newspaper picture that, viewed from a distance, appears clear and sharp but, viewed up close, becomes blurred and grainy. Likewise, the analysis of vulnerability at the broader level appears to be a distinct and objective phenomenon; as soon as it is analysed on a deeper level, however, the concept tends to dissolve in a haze of the multifarious situations of vulnerability, resulting in context-specific interpretations that impede a full and complete understanding of its overall significance. In sum, each vein of research on vulnerability demonstrates clearly and in detail a specific aspect of the problem.

An exhaustive analysis, nonetheless, requires a holistic approach capable of uniting the diverse elements of the phenomenon. The goal of socioeconomic vulnerability analysis, then, must be to seek to identify the criteria and methodologies that can adequately indicate objective situations of vulnerability, as well as specific thresholds below which certain levels of well-being are no longer acceptable in socioeconomic terms.

Experts in the area of vulnerability are gradually converging on a schema that considers vulnerability to be the result of the aggregation of three distinct components: risk factor, or the probability that the distribution of events can cause a reduction in well-being; risk management, or the group of actions that are undertaken *ex ante* or *ex post* in reply to the negative manifestations of risks; and the negative manifestation of the phenomenon that derives from the combination of the risk factor with the management strategies of its negative component (Heitzmann, Canagarajah, and Siegel 2002).

A proper measurement of vulnerability must concentrate, above all, on the analysis of the nature of shocks, as well as people's reaction strategies, in order to be able to study the concrete manifestations of the phenomenon in different socioeconomic contexts.

In addition, a more profound analysis of the specific characteristics of risks is required. Given the numerous types and unpredictable impacts of risks, a better system for classifying risks is clearly needed: by source (for example, natural risks or those tied to human activity), by degree of correlation (idiosyncratic or covariant risks; micro-, meso-, or macro-level risks; and so on), by frequency (repeated or once-only risks), and by intensity (catastrophic or non-catastrophic risks, and so on). Only through a greater understanding of the decomposition of risks that affect units of analysis can policies be harmonised appropriately. All risks must be considered — from the simplest, which are statistically, independently, and identically distributed, to the most difficult but unfortunately most common, cases of co-variate and auto-correlated risks. Conflicts, for instance, typically set off a chain reaction, meaning that the occurrence of a crisis directly increases the probability that another will strike again. The same could be said about the likelihood of a series of bad macroeconomic events, which could affect the functioning of markets, economic policies, or asset distribution (including social capital).

Risks, however, are only one side of the coin. Although risks are exogenous, vulnerability is endogenous, as it is the result of strategies employed by individuals and communities to face risks (Dercon 2001). These strategies are, in turn, the result of people's socioeconomic characteristics and the availability of risk management tools. In addition to analysing risks, therefore, individual and community strategies, instruments, and risk management activities must also be assessed, together with the nature of the various instruments and the various socioeconomic characteristics of the unit of the analysis. Moreover, as with risks, risk management activities must also be differentiated: by their degree of formality (informal, market-based, and public arrangements) and by the levels of the actors involved (micro, meso, and macro). There are, of course, no general rules that can determine *a priori* which risk management strategies are preferable over others. Similarly, there are no rules that determine which level of formality is more desirable over another. The optimal choice depends on the characteristics of the risks, together with the characteristics of the instruments, actors, and various social and economic contexts. At the same time, while risk mitigation strategies (such as taking children out of school) often prevent vulnerable people from falling into poverty in a given period, they could also increase people's vulnerability in the future. As the World Bank (2001) has emphasised, in the long run, households should be encouraged to take risks, rather than prevent them.

Taking risks and indeed benefiting from high returns are necessary preconditions for growth and poverty reduction. In addition, the concept of adaptability must be considered as a valid reaction strategy to risks.

Vulnerability, viewed in this light, could be seen as an evolutionary process generated by cumulative factors (Davies 1996), meaning that it can both worsen or improve in relation to various changes in its surrounding environment and endogenous factors.

Moving Forward: New Lines of Research

The Need for a New Approach to Vulnerability

A primary focus of socioeconomic vulnerability, from a macroeconomic perspective, should be to assess the dynamics of certain variables that could signal countries heading toward a reduction of well-being according to different types of risk and different socioeconomic characteristics and management tools.

More specifically, the goal is to improve understanding of the dynamics of developing countries in a globalised world; the type, magnitude, and frequency of shocks they have to face; their ability to cope with these shocks as well as the relationship among those shocks, their socioeconomic characteristics, and the likelihood of them leading to underdevelopment. In a globalised world, the ability of people and communities to cope with risks needs to change rapidly; traditional mechanisms are under pressure, natural endogenous shocks are becoming less important than human-made external shocks, and people risk being affected in unprecedented ways (Dercon 2001).

In this context, it is even more important to reach a better understanding of risks and the interactions between them (including co-variances), using contextual as well as noncontextual survey techniques and quantitative as well as qualitative data. The role of the magnitude and frequency of macroeconomic shocks must be separated from the role of the socioeconomic characteristics of nations and the robustness of their macroeconomic strategies and institutions. In sum, a more systematic way is needed to integrate this plethora of information into an objective and more widely accepted framework.

Reaching this goal, however, is a formidable challenge that involves a number of different aspects.

First of all, the general problem of empirically measuring vulnerability must be taken into due consideration. Most scholars analyse different forms of vulnerability, adopting a common monetary unit of measure. Others, recognising the intrinsic incompatibility of the various manifestations of vulnerability, measure it using different yardsticks, and in this way contribute to deviating from an objective vision of the phenomenon. Basic questions — such as the aggregation of the various dimensions of vulnerability into specific indicators, the objective analysis of the phenomenon in relation to its numerous subjective dimensions, the comparability of results over time and in space — must be defined. Even if it is assumed that an optimal methodology and measurement technique do not exist, the need to work toward a conceptualisation of vulnerability, at both the theoretical and the empirical level, and toward a definition of a more shared methodology, is nevertheless necessary.

There is also a need to evaluate the phenomenon in relation to a specific benchmark (Alwang, Siegel, and Jorgensen 2001). Implicit in the notion of vulnerability itself, in fact, is the persistence of a situation of proximity to a certain benchmark, together with a high probability of going over that limit even at minimum levels of risk. The vulnerable are precisely those who have a greater likelihood — *ceteris paribus* — of falling below that benchmark, if the manifestation of a risk occurs.

At the same time, some common misunderstandings of vulnerability must be avoided, especially when discussing the notion of vulnerability to poverty. This inevitably requires rehashing the longstanding debate over the traditional distinction between poverty and vulnerability. Both these concepts possess a time dimension and can be analysed *ex ante* as well as *ex post*, just as their processes and adjustment mechanisms can be studied at different points in time. Nevertheless, while poverty analysis gives us context-specific situations, vulnerability analysis is tied to the likelihood that a certain situation will happen in a future circumstance. This makes vulnerability an intrinsically dynamic and forward-looking concept, in contrast to the traditional evaluation of poverty and underdevelopment. Vulnerability is, more precisely, the continuous forward-looking state of expected outcomes (Alwang, Siegel, and Jorgensen 2001).

In addition, the literature frequently uses the empirical evidence on the variability and volatility of incomes and consumption as a proxy for the degree of vulnerability (see, for example, Glewwe and Hall 1998). The concept of vulnerability, however, is something more than the simple variability of consumption insofar as it also requires that this variability cause a decline in consumption beyond the minimum level considered acceptable by a socioeconomic norm (the benchmark). Consequently, vulnerability analysis must concentrate exclusively on downturn shocks, namely the range of the volatility function that includes the movements that go below the benchmark. This tightening of the field of study forces vulnerability analysis to ignore the negative consequences of risk management that translate into a permanent reduction in income or improvements in economic well-being over the long term — that is, all phenomena that are included in the area of variability analysis (Alwang, Siegel, and Jorgensen 2001).

Going into detail regarding the methodologies and techniques that could be employed in this new framework is beyond the scope of this chapter. Nevertheless, even if only at the conceptual level, this new approach to vulnerability could shed light on a relevant area of socioeconomic analysis that has up to now not been fully explored: the relationship between conflict prevention and development.

Vulnerability, Conflict Prevention, and Development

Because the socioeconomic vulnerability approach carefully considers the notion of vulnerability in terms of well-being, it could provide the missing link between conflict prevention strategies and development co-operation policies.

The need for a new approach to conflict prevention and development co-operation schemes is evident in light of the recent failures of policies in each area respectively. A chronic lack of information, excessive use of *ad hoc* strategies, mismanagement, and badly planned interventions in the area of conflict prevention policy have negated all efforts made in this direction and spoiled the credibility of the international actors involved, as evidenced by the most recent tragic events. In addition, the current shift in the nature of conflict poses an immense challenge for the international community (Development Assistance Committee 2001a). Along with the failure of conflict prevention and resolution, there has also been a failure of development co-operation policies and the structural inability of international organisations to solve problems linked to poverty and underdevelopment (Triulzi and Montalbano 2001b). This double deficiency has resulted in increased interest on the part of the major international organisations in creating more appropriate analytical methodologies and exploring new areas of study.

One of the first actors to enter onto this new stage was the Development Assistance Committee (DAC), which created the Network on Conflict, Peace, and Development Co-operation (CPDC) in 1997 for the express purpose of linking policies on conflict prevention strategies with those on international development co-operation. The CPDC looks at how to work conflict analysis, risk assessment, and prevention lenses into established development co-operation mechanisms. One of its main objectives is to integrate conflict prevention and peacebuilding efforts within international development co-operation policies. As highlighted by the DAC, a new culture of prevention must be fostered in which peace and conflict impact analysis and risk and vulnerability assessments are mainstreamed to become as common as cost-benefit analysis (DAC 2001b).

The DAC's CPDC represents an important and necessary first step toward achieving this goal and increasing the understanding of the links between conflict prevention and development co-operation. Nevertheless, a significant gap between conflict prevention strategies and development policies still remains.

The first step in bridging this gap is understanding it. Differences in the culture and background of experts in these two distinct fields, for instance, have rendered it difficult for conflict prevention analysts and development co-operation policy makers to find common ground. This is not surprising if one considers that, prior to the creation of the CPDC, conflict prevention had always been considered a distinct and separate discipline from development co-operation. The CPDC, in fact, represents the first ever international forum where conflict and peacebuilding experts from bilateral and multilateral development co-operation agencies meet to define common approaches in support of peace. Although necessary, this union of distinct cultures makes achieving consensus on policies and strategies more difficult. On the one hand, authorities on conflict prevention rarely understand socioeconomic vulnerability, as their focus is on the political shocks that cause conflict rather than on dynamic and long-term economic risk factors; on the other hand, development co-operation policy makers are overly concerned with the physical realisation and outcome of individual development co-operation projects, without enough consideration of their effects in a broader context. Not surprisingly, these differences in background reflect differences in analytical methodologies. While conflict prevention analysis employs the early warning system methodology to assess the impact of risk factors on political crises, development co-operation policy relies almost exclusively on traditional long-term economic analysis. Although both are integral to the understanding of conflict and development, respectively, neither is sufficient to understand the link between the two.

This methodological incongruence between conflict prevention and development strategies has not been singularly observed. According to the UN's Economic and Social Council, economic factors have played a large part in conflicts in Europe; it is undeniable that economic inequalities, economic decline, social marginalisation and exclusion, as well as conflict over access to employment, credit, land, and natural resources all fuelled conflict in Europe during the 1990s (United Nations 2001). There is a growing consensus that the root causes of conflict tend to be economic in nature. However, multilateral bodies addressing economic issues, such as the economic dimension of the Organisation for Economic Co-operation and Development (OECD), do not have activities that, strictly speaking, prevent conflict. Similarly, conflict prevention bodies need to reinforce the economic dimension of their analyses and policies. Although they recognise that the absence of violent conflict is a necessary condition for economic and social development (DAC 2001a), the opposite — that economic and social development is necessary for the prevention of conflict — has been overlooked. Instead, international security bodies tend to focus their attention on rapid military, diplomatic, and political solutions. The result is a lack of effective policies and programmes that address the real social and economic roots of both conflict and development issues.

This has been compounded by the fact that, generally speaking, there are insufficient institutional mechanisms that promote reciprocal consultation between experts and ensure project efficacy and efficiency, resulting in technical problems of co-ordination. Although the CPDC has made considerable efforts in remedying these problems, it has still been unable to resolve its difficulties in co-ordinating conflict prevention interventions with development co-operation policies. A plausible explanation points to the difficulty in determining the most appropriate tools to carry out the stated objectives. In most cases, conflict prevention and development objectives are overly ambitious and unrealistic in proportion to the expected time period in which they are to be achieved, resulting in a limited choice of tools to use. This, in turn, reduces the possibility of obtaining the desired results. Development co-operation, in particular, seems to be subject to a certain type of time inconsistency, in which its long-term objectives (such as economic growth and equality, poverty reduction, or supply of basic needs) do not correspond to the instruments employed in development programmes, which tend to privilege primarily short- to medium-term tools and be used to resolve emergency situations (Triulzi and Montalbano 2001a). The result is that international security and development bodies, under pressure to supply quick and immediate responses to conflicts, are unable to implement solid policies consistent with long-term objectives. This inconsistency between long-term objectives and short-term tools makes co-ordinating joint interventions difficult, and poses a considerable challenge to the CPDC.

Establishing a real culture of prevention means, however, relying on a specific culture of monitoring and evaluation. At present, conflict prevention strategies and development co-operation policies are both based on a limited number of variables and rely on an elementary notion of evaluation. Consequently, this has led to ineffective and inconsistent monitoring and evaluation mechanisms, which has heavily influenced the efficiency and efficacy of policies and programmes. Only establishing a proper system — in which projects provide significant statistical data (monitoring) and undergo *ex ante* (before), *in itinere* (during), and *ex post* (after) analyses (evaluations) — can ensure adequate levels of continuity and efficacy as well as identify beforehand any potential glitches and possible measures to avoid them. A monitoring and evaluation system in the particular area of conflict and development would have to be able to measure and interpret the dynamics of changes correctly over time. Furthermore, this system would have to be able to select the most accurate socioeconomic and political indicators that could provide the necessary data to understand dynamic phenomena and obtain more coherent policies.

Conclusion

Today's reality is a far cry from where it ought to be. The current means of measuring and evaluating conflict and development phenomena are still based primarily on static, *ex post* criteria. Violent struggle and poverty, however, are not static or constant states of being. Moreover, there are varying degrees of conflict and different levels of economic well-being. Crisis, for instance, results in a significant amount of movement within close margins along the poverty line. An *ex post* analysis, in this case, would not be able to differentiate between those who are chronically poor and those for whom the crisis is the cause of their poverty. Consequently, it would be unable to determine those risks that are more or less likely to cause a decline in well-being (or an outbreak of conflict, or famine). Furthermore, *ex post* analyses would not be able to provide the necessary information to intervene in advance and prevent the negative effects of downturn risks. To be able to determine and prevent such risks, a monitoring and evaluation system is needed to look not only at current conditions of poverty and conflict but also at the potential economic, social, and political changes and risks that could lead to improvements or declines in well-being.

A socioeconomic vulnerability analysis, one that assesses vulnerability in terms of well-being, could improve co-ordination of these two distinct worlds, because it addresses the long-term objectives of development co-operation and, at the same time, promotes a forward-looking and preventive outlook consistent with conflict prevention strategies. It could provide a common and shared methodological platform for development co-operation policy makers and link directly to conflict prevention strategies. At the same time, it could strengthen monitoring and evaluation mechanisms as it promotes *ex ante* analyses, more preventive measures, and a continuous process of assessment to measure dynamic changes in development.

For these reasons, a new framework based on socioeconomic vulnerability approach could be considered the missing link between conflict prevention and development co-operation. It could remedy current incongruencies and bridge, once and for all, the gap between conflict prevention and development. Instituting a vulnerability lens, in sum, would allow for the potential identification of the precise kind of causal relationship between economic underdevelopment and relative poverty, on the one hand, and social strife and communal violence, on the other.

Notes

1   Although the measurement error can substantially alter the estimates, later studies that attempted to reduce this error have nevertheless shown significant percentages of temporary poverty.
2   Economists generally analyse the standard deviation of the change of the variables over time.

References

Ahmed, Ismail and Michael Lipton (1997). 'Impact of Structural Adjustment on Sustainable Rural Livelihoods: A Review of the Literature'. IDS Working Papers No. 62. Institute of Development Studies, Sussex. <www.ids.ac.uk/ids/bookshop/wp/wp62.pdf> (July 2003).

Alwang, Jeffrey, Paul B. Siegel, and Steen L. Jorgensen (2001). 'Vulnerability: A View from Different Disciplines'. Social Protection Working Paper No. 23304. World Bank, Washington DC.

Baulch, Bob and John Hoddinott (2000). 'Economic Mobility and Poverty Dynamics in Developing Countries'. *Journal of Development Studies* vol. 36, no. 5, pp. 1–24.

Davies, Susanna (1996). *Adaptable Livelihoods: Coping with Food Insecurity in the Malian Sahel*. St. Martin's Press, New York.

Dercon, Stefan (2001). 'Assessing Vulnerability to Poverty'. Paper prepared for the UK Department for International Development. <www.economics.ox.ac.uk/members/stefan.dercon/assessing%20vulnerability.pdf> (July 2003).

Development Assistance Committee (2001a). 'The DAC Guidelines: Helping Prevent Violent Conflict'. <www.oecd.org/dataoecd/15/54/1886146.pdf> (July 2003).

Development Assistance Committee (2001b). 'DAC Network on Conflict, Peace, and Development: Draft Programme of Work and Budget, 2001–2002'. Organisation for Economic Co-operation and Development, Paris.

Dinar, Ariel, Robert Mendelsohn, Robert Evaenson, et al. (1998). 'Measuring the Impact of Climate Change on Indian Agriculture'. World Bank Technical Paper No. WTP402. World Bank, Washington DC.

Easterley, William and Aart Kraay (1999). 'Small States, Small Problems?' Working Paper No. 2139. World Bank. <econ.worldbank.org/docs/800.pdf> (July 2003).

Food and Agriculture Organization (1998). 'Report on the Development of Food Insecurity and Vulnerability Information and Mapping Systems'. Rome, 2–5 June. <www.fao.org/docrep/meeting/W8497e.htm> (July 2003).

Glewwe, Paul and Gillette Hall (1998). 'Are Some Groups More Vulnerable to Macroeconomic Shocks than Others? Hypothesis Tests Based on Panel Data from Peru'. *Journal of Development Economics* vol. 56 (June), pp. 181–206.

Gnisci, D (2000). *La vulnerabilité: Proposition d'un instrument novateur pour l'analyse des phénomènes socio-économiques*. IPALMO, Cesia, Rome.

Heitzmann, Karin, R. Sudharshan Canagarajah, and Paul B. Siegel (2002). 'Guidelines for Assessing the Sources of Risk and Vulnerability'. Social Protection Discussion Paper No. 0208. World Bank, Washington DC.

Holzmann, Robert (2001). 'Risk and Vulnerability: The Forward Looking Role of Social Protection in a Globalizing World'. Social Protection Working Paper No. 23161. World Bank, Washington DC.

Lustig, Nora (2000). 'Crises and the Poor: Socially Responsible Macroeconomics'. Inter-American Development Bank, Washington DC. <www.iadb.org/sds/pov/publication/publication_21_1566_e.htm> (July 2003).

Mason, John B. (1984). *Nutritional Surveillance*. World Health Organization, Geneva.

Maxwell, Daniel, Carol Levin, Margaret Armar-Klemesu, et al. (2000). 'Urban Livelihoods, Food and Nutritional Security in Greater Accra'. IFPRI Research Report No. 112. International Food Policy Research Institute, Washington DC.

Pritchett, Lant, Asep Suryahadi, and Sudarno Sumarto (2000). 'Quantifying Vulnerability to Poverty: A Proposed Measure, Applied to Indonesia'. Policy Research Working Paper No. WPS2437. World Bank, Washington DC.

Reardon, Thomas and Stephen Vosti (1995). 'Links between Rural Poverty and the Environment in Development Countries: Asset Categories and Investment Poverty'. *World Development* vol. 23, no. 9, pp. 1495–1506.

Thomas, Timothy S. (2003). 'A Macro-Level Methodology for Measuring Vulnerability to Poverty, with a Focus on MENA Countries'. Paper presented at the 4th Annual Global Development Conference 'Globalization and Equity', 19–21 January. Cairo.

Triulzi, Umberto (1998). 'Amartya Sen: A Different Kind of Economist'. *Politica Internazionale* vol. 5.

Triulzi, Umberto and Pierluigi Montalbano (1997). 'Mondalizzazione degli scambi'. [Globalisation of Trade]. *Politica Internazionale* no. 3 (May–June).

Triulzi, Umberto and Pierluigi Montalbano (2001a). 'Development Co-operation Policy: A Time Inconsistency Approach'. Research Report No. 2/2001. Roskilde University, Roskilde, Denmark.

Triulzi, Umberto and Pierluigi Montalbano (2001b). 'Vulnerability Analysis and the Globalization Process'. *Politica Internazionale* no. 3–4.

Triulzi, Umberto, Carlo Pietrobelli, Luca De Benedictis, et al. (2003). 'Trade Shocks and Socioeconomic Vulnerability with an Application to CEECs'. Paper presented at the 4th Annual Global Development Conference 'Globalization and Equity', 19–21 January. Cairo.

United Nations (2001). 'The Role of Economic Factors in Conflicts in Europe: How Can the Multilateral Security Bodies Addressing Economic Issues Be More Effective in Conflict Prevention?' Discussion paper, 19–20 November. Villars, Switzerland.

United Nations (2001). 'The Role of Economic Factors in Conflicts in Europe: How Can the Multilateral Security Bodies Addressing Economic Issues Be More Effective in Conflict Prevention?' Discussion paper, 19–20 November. Villars, Switzerland.

World Bank (2001). *World Development Report 2000/2001: Attacking Poverty.* Oxford University Press, New York.

Yusuf, Shahid (2001). 'Globalization and the Challenge for Developing Countries'. DECRG. World Bank, Washington DC. <www1.worldbank.org/economicpolicy/globalization/documents/wps2168.pdf> (July 2003).

PART IV
CONCLUSION

Chapter 12

From Good Intentions to Good Practice: The G8 and the Future of Conflict Prevention

Gina Stephens and Kristiana Powell

As an institution, the G8 has consistently sought new and increasingly useful ways to contribute to a stable international order in the post–cold war era. Traditionally, it has contributed by acting as a catalyst for the peace and security agendas of other international forums (such as the United Nations, World Bank, and the International Monetary Fund, to name a few). In recent years, however, the G8 has directed its security focus toward the development of an international conflict prevention regime that incorporates the participation and utilisation of all relevant international and regional actors. Although this new focus on conflict prevention is characterised by what David Malone calls 'a high level of abstraction' in Chapter 4, its sustained emphasis within the summit process has done much to highlight the unique and beneficial ability of the G8 to provide impetus to a variety of conflict prevention processes within other, more diffuse organisations.

This chapter examines the past, present, and possible future roles of the G8 in the area of conflict prevention. First, it will consider the issue of conflict prevention itself and the controversies that exist, both within and outside the academic community. Scholarly literature in the field will be analysed in order to define the concept of conflict prevention and the issues relating to its implementation. The chapter then traces the G8's involvement in conflict prevention to date, as well as the evolution of that involvement and how the focus has shifted over time. This discussion is guided by the understanding offered by John Kirton and Radoslava Stefanova in the introduction that mainstream approaches to conflict prevention tend not to take into account the role played by an informal and lightly institutionalised forum like the G8 in preventing violent conflict. This chapter then analyses, based on this record, areas where the G8's participation in this multilateral concern could be improved or extended. It concludes with a number of recommendations for future G8 policy on conflict prevention, identifying areas where its unique configuration as an institution allow it to contribute most effectively to this larger effort. Indeed, the effectiveness of G8 action on conflict prevention could be boosted by a greater comprehension of the need for a holistic approach to this problem. By applying a conflict prevention lens to development policies, the G8 — and the entire international community — will be better placed to prevent the very causes of conflict long before violent, armed clashes occur. Only by addressing the deeper roots of conflict can the G8, and other institutions, truly move beyond good intentions in this area.

Conflict Prevention: Striving for Conceptual Clarity

The end of the cold war brought a multitude of complex changes in the international system and in the dynamics of conflict. Today, increasingly violent and unresolved ethnic conflicts and civil wars, a growing gap between industrialised states and economically underdeveloped countries, world-wide environmental degradation, and the spread of transnational crime contribute to a turbulent political and social climate. The nature of warfare in the new international system has created a need to supplement traditional concerns of state security with a broader consideration of intra-state violence and domestic civil war as well as nonmilitary threats such as overpopulation, the spread of infectious disease, mass migration, social inequity, and a lack of economic opportunity. In 2002, Project Ploughshares estimated that there were 37 armed conflicts occurring in 30 countries around the world, with 38 percent of them occurring in Africa.[1]

These conflicts have devastating and far-reaching effects, effects that often spill over the conflict's original state boundary. In addition to the tragic loss of lives and widespread human rights violations that are products of civil wars, these conflicts destroy badly needed infrastructure, and impede or reverse development and discourage investment (Geingob 2000). Violent civil conflict can also have a profound impact on the environment, causing the wide-scale destruction of forests and mountains and the unchecked exploitation of natural resources (Vayrynen 1998; Foster 2001). In addition, these conflicts contribute to food insecurity and its counterpart, the spread of disease, which in itself may indirectly contribute to conflict in the long run. Furthermore, longstanding violent conflict or civil war often creates a 'culture of violence', characterised by the tendency to solve disputes through violent means rather than peaceful ones (Breines, Connell, and Eide 2000), and a 'militarized society' in which families and individuals arm themselves in self-defence or to prey on others (Geingob 2000).

These developments contribute to a cycle of violence. The causes of these civil wars are difficult to isolate, and vary extensively from case to case. Literature on the inter-related causes of civil wars in Africa points to, for example, widespread inequality among different groups, a history of division based on ethnic or racial lines, resource scarcity, pervasive poverty, insecurity and fear among populations, poor governance, greed and the desire to profit from war, and grievance with the state of affairs in a country. Within the academic community, the literature tends to consider the multi-causal nature of conflict and present integrated recommendations in response to a number of potential causes and effects of conflict. The value of preventing the occurrence, escalation, or recurrence of conflict is usually considered in terms of a cost-benefit analysis, weighing the costs of early action against the risks of escalation without earlier involvement. Michael Brown and Richard Rosecrance (1999) test the popular adage that an ounce of prevention is worth a pound of cure. Their work focusses on whether conflict prevention is cost-effective from the perspective of outside parties, including neighbouring countries, regional powers, and, more generally, the international community. In nine case studies of both failed and effective prevention, including Rwanda and Somalia, the costs of conflict escalation far outweighed the costs of early action (Brown and Rosecrance 1999). That analysis considers the costs of intervention to third parties. But studies completed by the World Bank and United Nations University/World Institute for Development Economics Research stress the internal costs of conflict in terms of loss of lives, damaged facilities, and foregone production (Carment and Schnabel 2001).

As Martin Landgraf (2000) argues, these findings have been largely internalised by international actors involved in conflict prevention and a consensus has been reached on the notion that the prevention of violent conflicts needs to be considered a long-term, proactive activity rather than a short-term and reactive one. Indeed, international institutions such as the United Nations and the World Bank are gradually moving from a policy focus on intervention and crisis management to an emphasis on conflict prevention. Moreover, institutions such as the Organisation for Economic Co-operation and Development (OECD) have come to recognise that conflict prevention should not be considered an isolated branch of policy but rather needs to be incorporated into current policies. Given that conflict prevention has found a permanent position on the international agenda, academics, nongovernmental organisations (NGOs), and practitioners are compelled to consider effective approaches to conflict prevention.

Before considering the work of academics, NGOs, and governments, however, it is first necessary to develop the conceptual and theoretical foundations of conflict prevention with an eye to the G8's comparative advantage in the field. As an organisation with concentrated power and influence that allow it to play a key role in international agenda setting, the G8 is uniquely suited to serve as the global nexus for action in preventing conflict. Sharing an overlapping membership in many of the most influential, multilateral organisations in the areas of development, finance, and security, the G8 members are well placed to provide leadership and an impetus toward a truly holistic approach to conflict prevention — particularly in Africa. Yet conflict prevention (treated as an issue bundle) is a relatively new focus for the G8 and, to a lesser extent, its multilateral partner institutions. As Malone observes, both the G8 and the international organisations that share its conflict prevention agenda are still 'attempting to come to grips both with short-term prevention of the fire-fighting sort and with longer term prevention, often of a developmental nature, that builds up firewalls'.

Thus, with the constantly evolving approach to this issue, the first step in this examination is to establish a clear understanding of the notion of conflict itself. What is it exactly that the international community should be aiming to prevent? According to David Carment and Albrecht Schnabel (2001, 14), 'conflict properly channelled can be constructive and transformative. It can be a positive constructive process under certain conditions'. Indeed, conflict often serves as a catalyst for positive change; moreover, the pursuit of justice may sometimes lead to conflict. Efforts that seek to blindly prevent conflict may serve the perpetuation of injustice (Daudelin 2002). The goal of conflict prevention then, as Roberto Toscano observes in Chapter 6, is the prevention of violent conflict. He reminds us that conflicts are 'the very essence of politics, and, indeed, of life in general, whereas the pretence of assuring universal quiet and uniformity is not compatible with freedom and dynamic growth, both economic and social'. Drawing a similar conclusion, Carment and Schnabel (2001, 16) note that conflict prevention, therefore, requires some form of 'social engineering'.[2] Consistent with these perspectives, Michael Lund provides a useful working definition of conflict prevention as

> governmental and nongovernmental actions, policies, and institutions that are taken deliberately to keep particular states or organized groups within them from threatening or using organized violence, armed force, or related forms of coercion such as repression as the means to settle interstate or national political disputes, especially in situations where the existing means cannot peacefully manage the destabilizing effects of economic, social, political, and international change (Quoted in Carment and Schnabel 2001, 15).

Conceptual clarity also requires a consideration of various forms of conflict prevention. A central conceptual muddle confuses the thinking and action of third parties: NGOs, governments, and the media often obscure the distinction between reactive humanitarian and peacekeeping interventions, on the one hand, and, on the other, more proactive efforts aimed at alleviating the problems and tensions that lead to conflict in the first place (Lund 2000). This reactive-proactive confusion is reflected in the thinking on the phases of conflict that attract third-party concern and involvement. As Lund notes, 'many recent publications on the subject of how third parties should deal with conflicts still automatically focus, without explanation, only on the conflicts' advanced stages, as if conflicts are presented to the international community suddenly as full-blown humanitarian crises and wars' (12).[3] Conflicts start without violence. Although reactive involvement to prevent the escalation of conflict once violence has broken out is in itself an important objective of the international community, responding proactively to the root causes of conflict is equally important — it prevents the human, political, social, and economic costs of violent conflict.

It can be useful to distinguish between 'light' and 'deep' prevention (Miall 2000). Light prevention refers to actions intended to avert the outbreak of large-scale violence once the conflict has reached a potential breaking point. Deep prevention, however, addresses the root tensions in society, often, but not exclusively, focussing on the latent, pre-violence or post-violence stages of conflict.[4] These categories reflect understandings of the causes of conflict. Joseph Nye differentiates between immediate triggers of conflict and deeper underlying structural sources of tensions that may lead to the eruption of conflict over time (quoted in Miall 2000, 24). The International Peace Academy fleshes out these concepts by identifying a trigger as 'a catalyst which spurs violent conflict' under various combinations of structural sources of tension, including insecurity, inequality, private incentives, and perceptions (Cater and Wermester 2000, 3).

Light prevention responds to triggers; deep prevention addresses structural conditions. Although light and deep prevention address different causes of conflict, there is a useful distinction between these two forms in terms of the duration of preventive initiatives. Light intervention involves short-term involvement at critical stages of a conflict. Deep intervention, however, addresses longer term issues and initiatives. Since this chapter is concerned primarily with the G8's role in deep intervention, it is helpful to consider the parameters of this form of prevention. Long-term prevention seeks to provide long-term stability and includes 'any activity that advances human security, alleviates poverty and threats to the environment, increases respect for human rights, or fosters good and stable governance' (Carment and Schnabel 2001, 13).

With the increase in civil, regional, and ethnic conflict in the 1990s, and the resulting large-scale humanitarian interventions undertaken by the UN, with the participation of G8 members, the cost of a reactive policy on conflict has become all too clear to the international community, and especially to the G8 countries that often fund and participate in intervention and post-conflict reconstruction efforts. The first-hand experience of the very real emotional (human) and financial toll of violent conflict has led to the G8 adopting deep intervention approaches to their own conflict prevention initiatives and to those that they spur within the broader global community. The next section of this chapter examines the progress of the G8's conflict prevention agenda, and demonstrates the evolution of an approach that is informed by the benefit of longer term developmental policy initiatives.

Conflict Prevention and the G8

The G8 was originally formed as an institution designed to deal mainly with co-ordinating macroeconomic policy, but the depth and breadth of the policy issues it deals with has grown exponentially since the end of the cold war. This expansion has been particularly notable in those issues that are politically global in nature, which has brought it into tighter co-operation both internally and externally with other international organisations, such as the International Monetary Fund (IMF), World Bank, and the UN. One issue where the G8's agenda is particularly intertwined with that of other international organisations is the area of conflict prevention. The substance and results of the first large-scale conflict prevention initiatives (at the foreign ministers meeting in Miyazaki in 2000, and, to a lesser extent, with the leaders at Genoa in 2001) will be examined, as well as the newest conflict prevention initiatives that form an integral part of the G8 Africa Action Plan unveiled at the 2002 Kananaskis Summit.

The Origins of Conflict Prevention as a G8 Issue

While agenda items dealing with areas of conflict prevention have been dealt with by the G7/8 since the early 1990s, as an institution its interest in the issue has been particularly notable in the later half of that decade. Conflict prevention was first mentioned in the political communiqué issued at the Tokyo 1993 Summit, which specifically highlighted the need to strengthen the UN's capacity for 'preventive diplomacy, peacemaking, peacekeeping, and postconflict peacebuilding' (G7 1993). Substantive treatment of conflict prevention issues by the G7/8 itself, however, was initially introduced under the larger rubric of transnational organised crime. At the 1995 Halifax Summit, the issue of firearms trafficking was added to the summit's agenda and a special working group (the G7/P8 Experts on Transnational Organized Crime) was formed to deal with this issue among a host of others (G7 1995). G8 focus on illicit arms trafficking increased in the years following Halifax. This intense scrutiny yielded many policy benefits, not only in domestic policy among the G8, but also in other organisations such as the UN, catalysing the progress toward the Firearms Protocol of the UN's Economic and Social Council (ECOSOC) and encouraging the work of the UN's Panel of Governmental Experts on Small Arms (Hampson 2002, 112). This early attention to conflict prevention highlights the many advantages to be gained by sustained G8 involvement.

While the G8 is in many ways a deliberative body rather than a decisional one, its restricted membership (confined to the most powerful democratic nations of the world) makes it one of the more flexible institutions and one that can provide leadership to those organisations that have more diffuse and slow-moving mechanisms for policy implementation.

The Conflict Prevention Focus: Cologne 1999

In realising that the increased occurrences of intra-state, regional, and ethnic conflicts are highly destabilising on an international scale, the G8 began to seek solutions for the underpinnings of conflict itself. Thus, the G8's approach to conflict turned to prevention. Indeed, awareness of the more holistic nature of conflict prevention (as a bundle of issues with inter-related elements) was apparent when, in the lead-up to the 1999 Cologne Summit, the G8 foreign ministers openly stated that there was a need for policy improvement and innovation in the area of conflict prevention — especially in the more general, long-range areas of building democratic institutions (G8 Foreign Ministers 1999b). The leaders' final communiqué also called for further attention to this area, leading to an *ad hoc* ministerial session on conflict prevention in Berlin in December 1999 (G8 1999).

Berlin 1999

It was in Berlin that the foreign ministers marked the beginning of a comprehensive approach to conflict prevention by the G8. With the understanding that the primary responsibility for maintaining international peace is conferred on the United Nations Security Council (UNSC) by the UN Charter, the G8 foreign ministers explored how the G8 might approach conflict prevention. Most importantly, they indicated that a holistic approach that identifies the underlying causes of conflict was necessary:

> The causes of armed conflict are multiple and complex. Its prevention requires an integrated comprehensive approach encompassing political, security, economic, financial, environmental, social and development policies, based on the principles of the UN Charter, the rule of law, democracy, social justice, the respect for human rights, a free press and good governance (G8 Foreign Ministers 1999a).

The foreign ministers asked their political directors to meet regularly to shape specific conflict prevention initiatives for the 2000 Okinawa Summit, which became the G8 Miyazaki Initiatives for Conflict Prevention. Although this particular group was not institutionalised as an official working group, each of their *ad hoc* sessions was referred to as the Conflict Prevention Officials Meeting (CPOM). The CPOM was dedicated exclusively to examining the 'various roles played by each factor at every stage of the development of crises, ... taking into account the diversity and complexity of causes of conflict' (G8 2001).

Miyazaki 2000

The G8 Miyazaki Initiatives for Conflict Prevention, released on 13 July 2000, were created in accordance with a conceptual framework guided by what the G8 foreign ministers termed a 'culture of prevention' (G8 Foreign Ministers 2000). This culture was to be created not only through the bilateral aid projects of the G8 itself, but also through 'encouraging international and regional organisations, states, NGOs and other actors to view their activities and policies from the vantage of conflict prevention, and to commit themselves to work toward this goal' (G8 Foreign Ministers 2000). This holistic treatment of conflict prevention indicated a realisation that the prevention of conflict needed to be a sustained priority that involved chronological comprehensiveness, a wide range of policy tools, and a deep understanding of the individual contexts of conflicts.

The concrete policy objectives presented in the Miyazaki Initiatives were based on three criteria developed by the conflict prevention officials and the foreign ministers:

- whether the issue has a direct relevance to conflict prevention;
- whether the G8 has a comparative advantage over other players in dealing with the issue;
- whether a joint initiative by the G8 could bear fruit (G8 Foreign Ministers 2000).

Given these criteria, the G8 foreign ministers undertook five broad conflict prevention initiatives, most of them with very tangible and concrete aims: small arms and light weapons, conflict and development, illicit trade in diamonds, children in armed conflict, and international civilian police. These initiatives are reproduced in Appendix 12.1.

Rome and Genoa 2001

Under the Italian presidency, a report card on the Miyazaki Initiatives was issued by the foreign ministers at their Rome meeting (18–19 July 2001) prior to the 2001 Genoa Summit (see Appendix D, Attachment 1). The most successful were those initiatives that had relied on other international organisations for follow-through, most notably the successful completion of the UN Conference on the Illicit Trade in Small Arms and Light Weapons in All Its Aspects and its resulting Program of Action. Likewise, the foreign ministers lauded the progress made by the Kimberley Process in developing a certification process to break the link between the illicit trade in diamonds and conflict. Work on the issue of children in armed conflict had also been successfully carried out through the UN, which had resulted in the signing of the Optional Protocol to the Convention on the Rights of the Child on Children in Armed Conflict at the 2000 Millennium Summit in New York. Further work in this area was also pursued through the International Labour Organization (ILO), which led to a convention on the worst forms of child labour.

With regard to civilian police, the G8 was gratified to see advances within the UN system with the release of the recommendations on civilian policing, published in the Brahimi report on the Panel on United Nations Peacekeeping Operations in 2000. The report suggested restructuring the Department of Peacekeeping Operations (DPKO). The comprehensive review of the DPKO was acknowledged by the G8, which noted that further work needed to be pursued on the UN's early warning capabilities.

Significantly, in the area of conflict and development — perhaps the most diffuse of all of the Miyazaki Initiatives — the foreign ministers re-emphasised that 'preventing conflict and promoting development are mutually reinforcing and pressing top priorities on the international agenda'. In their move to a more comprehensive approach, they agreed to promote 'the consideration of conflict prevention in development assistance strategies — including the HIPC Initiative — and ensure a smooth transition from relief to post-conflict development'. As an example of such a strategy, the foreign ministers lauded the guidelines on preventing conflict published by the OECD's Development Assistance Committee (DAC) (2001). These guidelines underscore the G8's consideration of conflict prevention as an issue bundle, by identifying two relatively new areas for future work: co-operative and sustainable water management and disarmament, demobilisation, and reintegration (DDR).

A second annex to the foreign ministers' communiqué examined two initiatives that were a direct result of the process leading to the Rome foreign ministers meeting (see Appendix D, Attachment 2). The first examines the role of women in conflict prevention, referring to a variety of UN reports and the DAC guidelines. The foreign ministers' document from the meeting stated that the G8 'emphasizes the importance of the systematic involvement of women in the prevention and resolution of conflicts and in peace-building, as well as women's full and equal participation in all phases of conflict prevention, resolution and peace-building' and encourages the participation of all actors of civil society. It also encourages those involved in planning for DDR programmes to consider the needs of female ex-combatants and their dependants, and supports gender-sensitive training in peace-related operations.

The document also explored the foreign ministers' consideration of corporate citizenship and conflict prevention. Noting the work done on corporate social responsibility in various other forums, such as the UN, the World Economic Forum, and the OECD, the foreign ministers isolated areas of particular regard for the G8 (see Appendix D). They stated that the G8 'recognizes that the private sector through good citizenship can play an important and positive role in conflict prevention and post-conflict reconstruction'. They also expressed their intention to work further with private and nongovernmental sectors to respond to high-risk situations, recognising that partnerships between corporations and local communities can make a valuable contribution to the development of civil society.

Whistler and Kananaskis 2002

The conflict prevention work of the G8 continued through both the ministerial and sherpa processes during the Canadian presidency. Significant strides were made at the Whistler foreign ministers meeting on 12–13 June 2002 in two key areas of conflict prevention: DDR and the sustainable management of water resources to prevent conflict.

The DDR initiative carried on from the earlier Miyazaki Initiatives on small arms and light weapons. The official document, G8 Conflict Prevention: Disarmament, Demobilisation, and Reintegration, suggests that the implementation of a culture of prevention was becoming a real priority rather than simply a good intention (see Appendix O). The foreign ministers noted that 'work on DDR is beginning to recognize that DDR not only paves the way for development, but also relies on long-term development for its own success'. Effective provisions within peace agreements for the collection, control, and destruction of arms are considered essential, as is the need for peace agreements to provide sufficient incentives for former combatants to disarm in the first place. Picking up the thread of Rome's concern for gender sensitivity in conflict prevention, the foreign ministers detailed the importance of recognising the 'special requirements' of women and child combatants, as well as victims of conflict. Overall, the foreign ministers observed that in order to be successful DDR is a long-term process that requires political will and external support: 'reintegration incentives should focus on the establishment of a visibly successful, long term reintegration programme, which goes beyond military intervention and emergency humanitarian assistance into long term development assistance'.

The foreign ministers concluded their statement on DDR with specific, action-oriented commitments. The document recognised that DDR is a multi-step process of deep intervention and highlights the important, essential role of the UN in promoting and delivering DDR programmes. At the same time, it acknowledged the importance of local participation and co-operation of NGOs and regional organisations. It notes that significant capacity building within both international institutions and NGOs is necessary to undertake the long-term requirements of the peacebuilding components of DDR.

Due to the many actors envisaged in the operation of successful DDR programmes, the G8 stressed the need for better co-ordination and the development of a 'comprehensive plan of action ... covering the political framework, military operations, economic rebuilding, public and media services, and funding as part of the process of improving coordination' (see Appendix O). All organisations involved in peacebuilding in any particular area should co-ordinate their efforts in order to prevent overlap, observe best practices, and streamline the disbursement of much needed funds.

The second major initiative promised in Rome and unveiled in Whistler was the detailed attention to sustainable water management as a key pillar in conflict prevention — especially in Africa — contained in the G8 Initiative on Conflict and Development (see Appendix N). This stand-alone document refers to Kofi Annan's Millennium Report and World Bank projections, and notes that if present trends continue, two out of every three people in the world will live in countries considered to be 'water stressed' and that by 2050, 40 percent of the global population is 'likely to face some form of water shortage, with one in five suffering severe shortages'. Recognising this problem, which has been highlighted over the past decade within the academic community,[5] the G8 declared its intention to base its approach on the principles of prevention, respect for sovereignty, co-operation, and good governance. The necessary involvement of local, regional, and international organisations, well orchestrated, is stressed. This document also highlights the important contribution that public-private partnerships can make to water management.

Although the overall, detailed approach to conflict prevention was undertaken mainly at the ministerial level while Canada was host of the G8, the 2002 Kananaskis Summit did underscore this work, primarily by focussing on 'Promoting Peace and Security' initiatives in the G8's Africa Action Plan (G8 2002). In keeping with the 'for Africans, by Africans' theme of the New Partnership for Africa's Development (NEPAD), the G8 leaders highlighted the importance of local and regional participation in all conflict prevention work and set deadlines for empowering Africa to address issues of conflict prevention. They agreed to deliver a joint plan in 2003 for building African capacity for peace support operations, and pledged to take concrete action in the Democratic Republic of Congo and Sudan. Better co-ordination of international peacekeeping training initiatives was stressed, as was the need for the G8 to provide continued support to the UN's efforts, and those of African countries, to 'better regulate the activities of arms brokers and traffickers and to eliminate the flow of illicit weapons to and within Africa' (G8 2002). The leaders reiterated the concern of their foreign ministers with supporting regional, governmental, and civil society efforts to address the link between armed conflict and the exploitation of natural resources. Most importantly, the Africa Action Plan effectively emphasised the complex nature of conflict prevention and the need for long-term support of peacebuilding activities, especially in the area of DDR.

Paris and Evian 2003

Some progress was made toward developing a comprehensive G8 conflict prevention agenda at the French-hosted 2003 Evian Summit, as the G8 followed its tradition of systematically addressing conflict prevention issues. The G8 announced a joint Africa/G8 plan to enhance African capabilities to undertake peace support operations so that by 2010, 'African partners are able to engage more effectively to prevent and resolve violent conflict on the continent, and undertake peace support operations in accordance with the United Nations Charter' (G8 Africa Personal Representatives 2003). The proposal had been made by Canada, France, the United Kingdom, and the U.S., and initiated through the Berlin process, to support the development of an African peacekeeping force. It became the leading proposal in the Implementation Report by African Personal Representatives to Leaders of the G8 Africa Action Plan. The G8 also agreed to work with its African partners to develop the institutional capacity at the continental and sub-regional levels to prevent conflict through mediation, facilitation, observation, and other strategies. The G8 also expressed its willingness to support the creation of an electronically linked, continent-wide early warning system. However, decisions regarding how these initiatives will be funded were postponed for future summits to deal with.

The G8 also returned to the issue of sustainable water management and adopted the G8 Action Plan for Water at Evian (G8 2003). The leaders agreed to promote good governance and assist with the technical and infrastructure issues that must be addressed to promote sustainable water management. The action plan also states that water will become a priority for official development assistance (ODA) and urges the international financial institutions to give the necessary priority to water issues.

The G8 and Conflict Prevention: Successes, Challenges, and Recommendations

It is worthwhile returning to the central question posed by Kirton and Stefanova in the introduction to this volume: how effective have the G8's conflict prevention efforts been? Why has the G8 succeeded and failed? And what can and should it do in the years ahead? From the self-directed report card on conflict prevention released at the 2001 G8 foreign ministers meeting in Rome, as well as the more recent documents released at the 2002 Whistler/Kananaskis ministerial and summit meetings, it is possible to draw some broad conclusions. What is most obvious from this record are the great successes that have been achieved by the G8 giving impetus to the work of other multilateral forums. The G8's overlapping membership in many of the key international bodies (the UNSC, the IMF, the World Bank, and so on) does much to assist these organisations from within and to provide political will and energy in many areas (including, for example, support for the UN Conference on the Illicit Trade in Small Arms and Light Weapons in All its Aspects, as well as their key role in supporting the Kimberley Process for certifying rough diamonds).

As Robert Fowler notes in Chapter 3, the G8 is not and should not become a 'conflict manager' or 'conflict preventer' in itself. To take on such a role would be both impossible and illegitimate. However, perhaps the most important aspect of the G8's work in the area of conflict prevention is its ability to act as a leader for other organisations, particularly the UNSC and the North Atlantic Treaty Organization (NATO), in setting the agenda for the broader international community, or, as Malone notes, as a leader in developing norms. Critically, the G8 can generate the political will necessary to compel preventive action on the part of the international community. Toscano suggests that the international community ends up 'doing and paying quite a lot' in situations where it chose not to act preventively, such as in Rwanda. This interpretation suggests that the will to act often exists. The challenge, therefore, is marshalling this will and convincing influential states to act to prevent violent conflict. This tasks appears even more daunting when one considers the divergent approaches to conflict prevention assumed by the U.S. and the European Union. As discussed in the chapters by Frank Loy and Reinhardt Rummel, and as indicated by the discord prompted by the 2003 decision to intervene in Iraq, the current approach to international peace and security of the U.S. contrasts sharply with the EU's emerging conflict prevention policy. Thus, the pivotal role that the G8 can play in bridging gaps between these key players has assumed even greater importance.

The official documents from the Whistler ministerial meeting and the Kananaskis Summit are encouraging: the G8's approach to conflict prevention is becoming ever more nuanced and largely reflects a general comprehension of the requirements for successful prevention and its place within a larger development process. That is, the G8 increasingly acknowledges the mutually reinforcing relationship between conflict prevention and development noted by Lorenzo Bini Smaghi, Marco Sarcinelli, and Umberto Triulzi and Pierluigi Montalbano elsewhere in this volume. The prevention of conflict is a necessary condition for fair and just development, and fair and just development prevents conflict. However, as Toscano remarks, economic factors in and of themselves do not cause conflicts. They often serve as the foundation or rationale for grievances between groups that are transformed, often by opportunistic political leaders, into violence. He concludes that conflict prevention 'can be attained mainly by proving that rights can be protected without violence'. It is crucial, therefore, that the G8 recognise the role played by governance and the rule of law in promoting and preventing conflict.

Moreover, particular challenges remain in the less specific areas, such as mainstreaming conflict prevention and gender. While the G8 must be praised for highlighting the importance of both these concepts, they have yet to be turned into a lens to be applied to all aspects of bilateral and multilateral development. In terms of conflict prevention mainstreaming, although the long-term nature of the commitment has been recognised, it is not clear that G8 governments have operationalised the integration of conflict prevention considerations into their aid projects. This integration might be achieved by mandating the use of frameworks for peace and conflict impact assessments (PCIAs) for evaluating development policies in conflict-prone regions. Donor agencies within G8 governments should be encouraged to engage 'conflict advisors' in their operations in actual or potential conflict zones. Likewise, the development of a system for accumulating and sharing a body of knowledge on lessons learned and best practices would also support the process of conflict prevention mainstreaming.

To underscore their intention to create a culture of prevention even more effectively, the G8 should institutionalise the previously *ad hoc* CPOM. An institutionalised working group would not only speak to the G8's sincerity and political will in this area, but would ensure that continued attention is paid to considerations of conflict prevention for summits to come. Working groups enhance the G8's ability to implement and support projects that are long-term in scope, and they direct sustained attention to areas that may be eclipsed by other international concerns. For example, in the aftermath of the terrorist attacks of 11 September 2001, the pre-existing G8 working group on terrorism proved to be invaluable in developing approaches to combating this insidious threat.[6] Similarly, an institutionalised G8 working group on conflict prevention could provide consistency and achieve a great deal toward conflict prevention mainstreaming and co-ordinating the G8's (and other international organisations') continued efforts in this area.

In terms of gender mainstreaming, it is evident from the current record — especially in light of the documents released at the Whistler foreign ministers meeting — that considerations of gender in conflict prevention are seen as important to the G8. Emphasis, especially in the area of DDR, has been placed on the special needs of women and children (both as victims and combatants). This is clearly a step forward; however, the treatment of gender in a conflict prevention process could be more nuanced. It is important that the G8 pursue a gender-sensitive approach at all stages of a conflict. Integrating a gender perspective into early warning and response is very important: 'early warning is the *sine qua non* of effective conflict prevention and peacebuilding ... A gender-sensitive approach is needed for the early identification of conflicts at the micro-level and in order to prepare adequate response options that ensure the human security of both women and men' (Schmeidl and Ismail 2001). Women make critical contributions to early warning and response, not only as providers of information but also as leaders responsible for devising and executing response options.

It is also important for G8 policy makers to recognise that women do not constitute a homogenous group; indeed, women can assume very different roles in both peace and war. Some women may promote peace, before, during, and after violence; others may be motivated, for a variety of material and emotional reasons, to encourage violence and the seizure of land. Moreover, each unique cultural context presents different challenges in terms of expected positions and aspirations. Furthermore, women of different age groups play different roles and have varying experiences in war and its aftermath. Young and adult female soldiers have unique needs and capacities coming out of war, as do elders. The conclusion to be drawn here is that gender mainstreaming, as it pertains to conflict prevention and post-conflict reconstruction, must be critically considered in order to reveal underlying assumptions of the commonalities among women as well as the appropriate roles of men and women in post-conflict societies. Awareness of the culture, context, and power relations in the community is significant. Developing this understanding requires working with local men's and women's groups.

G8 member governments should be encouraged to continue to apply a gender perspective to all their development and conflict prevention and post-conflict reconstruction projects and programmes. In order to ensure the success of these programmes from the perspective of gender, the G8 members should be encouraged to develop a streamlined monitoring and assessment system that is capable of generating long-term evaluations of the impacts of their projects from a gender perspective. This would also allow G8 members to share lessons learned and best practices.

Much had been achieved in the area of DDR through the ministerial process. As already noted, DDR was a major focus during the Canadian G8 presidency in 2002 and the resulting work has done much to advance the concept deep prevention internationally. Especially important has been the G8's emphasis on the long-term, multifaceted nature of DDR, as well as the need to involve local and regional groups in planning, executing, and maintaining all DDR projects. One continuing problem, however, is the inability of the G8 to agree on the necessity for a total ban on arms imports to conflict areas. Although there has been a great deal of attention to the illicit sale of small arms, there seems to be no political will to ban all small arms imports legal or illicit. However, in the G8 Africa Action Plan, leaders committed to supporting the efforts of African countries and the UN to regulate the activities of arms brokers and to curb the flow of illicit small arms and light weapons to and within Africa. The G8 still needs to work toward strengthening arms export controls and toward more effective enforcement of embargoes, as well as place more legal control on arms brokers.

Finally, in the area of corporate social responsibility, as Malone notes in Chapter 4, there exists a realisation on the part of the G8 (and other multilateral forums) that trade and investment can contribute significantly to the initiation and persistence of conflict. Yet the political will for compulsory regulation of trade and investment in conflict areas seems lacking. The G8's support of efforts such as the UN's Global Compact is key to advancing corporate social responsibility, yet these types of codes remain voluntary and thus not all private sector entities adhere to them systematically. The UN (2000) itself stresses that 'voluntary initiatives of the kind represented by the Global Compact are no substitute for action by governments. Effective governance is critical for the promotion of human rights, decent work, environmental protection and development'. The G8 should encourage its members to distinguish clearly between peace and conflict zones. In peace zones, the G8 should encourage its members and other OECD countries to harmonise voluntary codes of conduct for corporations. G8 and OECD members can consider offering tax cuts or other incentives to companies that commit to voluntary standards and, through their investment, contribute to building infrastructure in their host countries. The G8 should also support the creation of an independent international body of experts that can conduct fact-finding missions for corporations with foreign operations and provide context-specific advice on conflict prevention considerations that would assist with compliance to accepted voluntary codes. This international body would also assist both parent and host countries, and regional organisations, to monitor compliance with these voluntary principles, as well as the accuracy and adequacy of the codes in specific situations.

In conflict zones, the G8 should devise a set of legal regulations for the conduct of corporations already operating in zones that have become violent throughout the duration of their investment period. These regulations can be derived from the voluntary principles for corporations operating in conflict zones devised by the UK and the U.S.

Conclusion

The efforts of the G8 to contribute globally to the prevention of armed conflict are laudable and indicative of its growth as a centre for global governance. From the introduction of conflict prevention as an issue, the G8's treatment of it has increasingly moved closer to fulfilling its original promise to create a culture of prevention. Indeed, the G8 addressed conflict prevention issues at the 2003 Evian Summit and committed to building a peace support operation capacity in Africa, as well as to focussing attention on sustainable water management (G8 Africa Personal Representatives 2003; G8 2003).

A number of key challenges in this area still exist, however. Indeed, as Nicholas Bayne says in Chapter 2, the G8 has yet to determine how and at what level it will address conflict prevention. As the above discussion notes, the establishment of a permanent conflict prevention working group within the G8 structure would do much to invigorate G8 members' contributions to other multilateral organisations as well as support advances in this area within member countries' domestic bureaucracies. Although much has been done to apply conflict prevention considerations systematically, continued emphasis on the long-term complexities of conflict prevention and the need to apply a conflict prevention lens to all development policies is still essential. With progress being made in the field of conflict prevention, within the G8, as well as by other international organisations, the good intentions that prompted action in this area can be truly transformed into good practice for the future.

Notes

1 'Armed conflicts', according to Project Ploughshares (2002), includes a minimum cumulative total of combat deaths of 1000 in the current phase of the conflict.
2 For a discussion of the implications of pursuing a 'social engineering' approach to third-party involvement in post-conflict situations, see Pugh (2000).

3   Indeed, this perspective is reflected in influential work in the field, including Anderson (1999) and Lederach (1997).
4   Other authors refer to 'light prevention' as 'direct conflict prevention' or 'operational prevention', and 'deep prevention' as 'structural prevention' (see for example, Wallensteen 1998).
5   See, for example, work on environmental scarcity and armed conflict by Homer-Dixon (1994).
6   As noted by an official of Canada's Department of Foreign Affairs and International Trade in an interview, 15 March 2002.

References

Anderson, Mary B. (1999). *Do No Harm: How Aid Can Support Peace — or War*. Lynne Rienner, Boulder, CO.
Breines, Ingeborg, Robert W. Connell, and Ingrid Eide, eds. (2000). *Male Roles, Masculinities, and Violence: A Culture of Peace Perspective*. UNESCO, Paris.
Brown, Michael and Richard Rosecrance, eds. (1999). *The Costs of Conflict, Prevention, and Cure in the Global Arena*. Rowman and Littlefield, Lanham, MD.
Carment, David and Albrecht Schnabel, eds. (2001). *Conflict Prevention: Path to Peace or Grand Illusion?* United Nations University Press, Tokyo.
Cater, Charles K. and Karin Wermester (2000). 'From Reaction to Prevention: Opportunities for the UN System in the New Millennium'. Report on the international policy conference on the prevention of violent conflict, International Peace Academy, New York, 13–14 April. <www.ipacademy.org/Publications/Reports/Research/PublRepoReseUNSyPrint.htm> (July 2003).
Daudelin, Jean (2002). Personal interview. 5 March, Ottawa.
Development Assistance Committee (2001). 'The DAC Guidelines: Helping Prevent Violent Conflict'. <www.oecd.org/dataoecd/15/54/1886146.pdf> (July 2003).
Foster, Gregory D. (2001). 'Environmental Security: The Search for Strategic Legitimacy'. *Armed Forces and Society* vol. 27, no. 3, pp. 373–396.
G7 (1993). 'Tokyo Summit Political Declaration: Striving for a More Secure and Humane World'. Tokyo, 8 July. <www.g7.utoronto.ca/summit/1993tokyo/political.html> (July 2003).
G7 (1995). 'Chairman's Statement'. 17 June, Halifax. <www.g7.utoronto.ca/summit/1995halifax/chairman.html> (July 2003).
G8 (1999). 'G8 Communiqué Köln'. 20 June, Cologne. <www.g7.utoronto.ca/summit/1999koln/finalcom.htm> (July 2003).
G8 (2001). 'Conflict Prevention: Fact File'. <www.g7.utoronto.ca/summit/2001genoa/pres_docs/conflict.html> (July 2003).
G8 (2002). 'G8's Africa Action Plan'. Kananaskis, 27 June. <www.g7.utoronto.ca/summit/2002kananaskis/africaplan.html> (July 2003).
G8 (2003). 'Water: A G8 Action Plan'. 3 June, Evian. <www.g7.utoronto.ca/summit/2003evian/water_en.html> (July 2003).
G8 Africa Personal Representatives (2003). 'Implementation Report by Africa Personal Representatives to Leaders on the G8 Africa Action Plan'. 1 June, Evian. <www.g7.utoronto.ca/summit/2003evian/apr030601.html> (July 2003).
G8 Foreign Ministers (1999a). 'Conclusion of the Meeting of the G8 Foreign Ministers' Meeting in Berlin'. 16–17 December. <www.g7.utoronto.ca/foreign/fm991216.htm> (July 2003).
G8 Foreign Ministers (1999b). 'Conclusions of the Meeting of the G8 Foreign Ministers'. 10 June, Gürzenich/Cologne. <www.g7.utoronto.ca/foreign/fm9906010.htm> (July 2003).
G8 Foreign Ministers (2000). 'G8 Miyazaki Initiatives for Conflict Prevention'. Miyazaki, 13 July. <www.g7.utoronto.ca/foreign/fm000713-in.htm> (July 2003).

Geingob, Hage (2000). 'Assessing the Risks of the New Types of Conflict and Examining Ways of Dealing with Them'. Global Coalition for Africa. <www.gca-cma.org/esecurity.htm#0900> (July 2003).

Hampson, Fen Osler (2002). *Madness in the Multitude: Human Security and World Disorder.* Oxford University Press, Toronto.

Homer-Dixon, Thomas (1994). 'Environmental Scarcities and Violent Conflict'. *International Security* vol. 19, no. 1, pp. 5–40.

Landgraf, Martin (2000). 'Developing Analytical Tools for Preventive Strategies: A Practitioner's View on Conflict Impact Assessments'. In M. S. Lund and G. Rasamoelina, eds., *The Impact of Conflict Prevention Policy: Cases, Measures, Assessments.* Nomos, Baden-Baden.

Lederach, John Paul (1997). *Building Peace: Sustainable Reconciliation in Divided Societies.* United States Institute of Peace Press, Washington DC.

Lund, Michael (2000). 'Introduction and Overview'. In M. S. Lund and G. Rasamoelina, eds., *The Impact of Conflict Prevention Policy: Cases, Measures, Assessments.* Nomos, Baden-Baden.

Miall, Hugh (2000). 'Preventing Potential Conflicts: Assessing the Impact of "Light" and "Deep" Conflict Prevention in Central and Eastern Europe and the Balkans'. In M. S. Lund and G. Rasamoelina, eds., *The Impact of Conflict Prevention Policy: Cases, Measures, Assessments.* Nomos, Baden-Baden.

Panel on United Nations Peace Operations (2000). 'Report of the Panel on United Nations Peace Operations'. The Brahimi Report. <www.un.org/peace/reports/peace_operations> (July 2003).

Project Ploughshares (2002). 'Armed Conflicts Report 2002'. <www.ploughshares.ca/CONTENT/ACR/acr.html> (July 2003).

Pugh, Michael C., ed. (2000). *Regeneration of War-Torn Societies.* St. Martin's Press, New York.

Schmeidl, Susanne and Feyzi Ismail (2001). 'Implementing the United Nations Security Council Resolution on Women, Peace, and Security: Integrating Gender into Early Warning Systems'. Report on the 1st Expert Consultative Meeting, 7 May. <www.international-alert.org/women/gewreprt.pdf> (July 2003).

United Nations (2000). 'Executive Summary and Conclusion of High-Level Meeting on Global Compact'. 27 July, Press Release SG/2065 ECO/18. <www.un.org/News/Press/docs/2000/20000727.sg2065.doc.html> (July 2003).

Vayrynen, Raimo (1998). 'Environmental Security and Conflicts: Concepts and Policies'. *International Studies* vol. 35, no. 1, pp. 3–21.

Wallensteen, Peter (1998). 'Preventive Security: Direct and Structural Prevention of Violent Conflict'. In P. Wallensteen and J. Bercovitch, eds., *Preventing Violent Conflicts: Past Record and Future Challenges.* Uppsala University, Uppsala.

Appendix 12.1
Excerpts from Conflict Prevention:
Fact File

1) Small Arms and Light Weapons

The G8 underlined that the uncontrolled and illegal transfer of small arms and light weapons and the excessive proliferation of these weapons in many parts of the world pose a threat to peace and security. Emphasising the need for international institutions and individual states to improve and increase the effectiveness of their efforts by developing co-ordinated and coherent policies, the G8 decided not to authorise the export of small arms to those countries where there is a clear risk that these might be used for repression or aggression against another country. The group agreed, at the same time, to ensure that its export licensing decisions respect the ECOWAS moratorium on the importation, exportation and manufacture of light weapons approved in October 1998.

The G8 likewise urged other exporting states to adopt such a policy.

With regard to the fight against the illicit trafficking of small arms, the G8 emphasised the fundamental importance of respecting all embargoes imposed by the United Nations, and encouraged the countries and regions directly affected by illicit arms trafficking to enhance transparency in this regard by adopting measures such as the exchange of information on arms supplies and the registration of small arms. To this end, the G8 offered financial and technical assistance to support those countries that intend to take concrete steps to reduce excessive accumulations of small arms on their territory.

2) Conflict and Development

Peace and democratic stability are indispensable pre-conditions for economic growth and sustainable development. In this sense, development co-operation has a key role to play in fostering peace and stability. As the major provider of development assistance, the G8 can play a crucial role, both in terms of its own development cooperation policies and in co-ordination with the main international financial institutions, to promote democratic and legislative institutions and good governance by countries located in conflict areas, with a view to sustainable development, and human, natural and financial resources.

3) Illicit Trade in Diamonds

The G8 reiterated its concern that the proceeds from the illicit trade in commodities, such as diamonds in Africa, are aggravating international conflicts and crises. Whilst insisting that the interests of the legitimate diamond producers and traders be protected, the G8 decided to co-operate with the various actors involved (governments of diamond-producing states, neighbouring states, major marketing centres, as well as regional organisations and the private sector) in order to curb illicit diamond flows. At the same time, it calls on producers and buyers to adopt specific measures to counter such trade. The G8 in particular expressed support for the activities carried out by the United Nations in Angola and in the Democratic Republic of Congo, calling for urgent cooperation with the government of Sierra Leone on the proper control over trade in diamonds produced in that country.

4) Children in Armed Conflict

At times direct participants, and too often helpless victims, children are the social category that most directly and most dramatically suffers the harmful effects of conflicts. The G8 agreed to concert pressure in all international fora against individual governments and armed groups when access to assistance is denied to children or when children are specifically targeted as victims and/or participants in a conflict. Emphasising the importance of universal adherence to the International Labour Organisation Convention no. 182 on the elimination of [the] worst forms of child labour, the G8 is committed to promote, in close collaboration with the United Nations, the adoption of international standards for the protection of child rights, including by supporting action by those who contribute towards highlighting and raising awareness of the issue of children in armed conflict.

5) International Civil Police

United Nations civilian police forces are a critical element in conflict prevention as they help indigenous civilian police forces develop the capacity to maintain law and order. Recognising this important contribution, the G8 urged states with civilian police expertise to make a contribution. To this regard, the G8 underlined the importance of helping the United Nations develop its capacities in this sector in the framework of the peace-keeping functions conferred upon it by the Charter.

Source: G8 (2001). 'Conflict Prevention: Fact File'. <www.g7.utoronto.ca/summit/2001genoa/ pres_docs/conflict.html> (July 2003).

ANALYTICAL APPENDICES

Appendix A

Performance Assessment, Overall and by Issue, 1996–2002

G8 Research Group

	1996	1997	1998	1999	2000	2001	2002
Performance Average	B+	A–	B+	A–	B+	C	B
ECONOMIC ISSUES							
International Finance:							
Financial architecture	B	A	B+	A–	B	–	C
Financial stability	–	A	–	–	–	–	–
Macroeconomics	–	A	–	A–	A+	–	–
Microeconomics:	–	B	–	–	A	B	–
Information technology	–	–	–	–	A–	–	–
Education	–	–	–	B–	A	–	D+
Employability	–	B	A–	–	–	–	–
Ageing	–	–	B	–	–	–	–
Global Info Society	–	C	–	–	–	A	A
Trade	A+	B+	B–	A	B	B+	B+
Development:	–	B+	–	B+	B–	B–	–
HIPC/Debt relief	–	–	–	B+	B–	–	A
ODA	–	–	–	–	C	–	B
IT instrument	–	–	–	–	A–	–	–
Conflict link	–	–	–	–	A–	–	–
African development	A	–	–	–	–	–	A–
GLOBAL/TRANSNATIONAL ISSUES							
Global In General	–	–	–	C	B	–	–
Environment:	–	B+	B	C+	B–	B+	–
Climate change (Kyoto)	–	–	–	–	B	–	–
Renewable energy	–	–	–	–	B	–	–
Rio + 10 review	–	–	–	–	B+	–	–
Forests (logging)	–	–	–	–	B–	–	–
Cartagena biosafety	–	–	–	–	B–	–	–
Oceans/Maritime issues	–	–	–	–	C	–	–

Crime and drugs	–	–	–	A–	–	D	–
Nuclear safety/Ukraine	–	–	B	B+	–	–	–
Health	–	A	B+	–	A+	–	B–
Cultural diversity	–	–	–	–	C–	–	–

POLITICAL SECURITY ISSUES

Political Security in General: –	–	–	B–	B	–	–
Arms control	–	–	–	–	B	F	–
Indian nuclear explosion	–	B	–	–	–	–	–
Landmines	–	–	A–	–	–	B	–
Regional Security:	–	–	A	–	B–	–	–
Balkans/Kosovo	–	–	A	A	–	–	–
Balkan reconstruction	–	–	–	A–	–	–	–
Indonesian crisis	–	–	B+	–	–	–	–
Human Rights:						
Hong Kong/China	–	A	–	–	–	–	–
Conflict prevention	–	–	–	–	A–	–	–
Terrorism	–	–	C	–	–	–	A–

GOVERNANCE ISSUES

Global Governance:						
Globalisation	–	B+	–	–	–	–	–
UN reform	–	–	A–	–	–	–	–
G8 Governance:	–	–	–	–	A	–	–
G7/8 process reforms	–	–	–	A	–	–	–
Russian participation	–	B+	A	A	A+	–	–
Outreach	–	–	–	–	B+	–	–
Civil society	–	–	–	–	A–	–	–

Appendix B

Performance Assessment, by Country, 1996–2002

G8 Research Group

	1996 G7	1996 G8	1997 G8	1998 G8	1999 G8	2000 G8	2001 G8	2002 G8	Average
France	B	A–	A–	A–	A–	B–	B–	B+	B+
U.S.	A–	A	B+	B–	–	A–	B	B+	B+
UK	A–	A–	A–	A	A	B	C+	B–	B+
Germany	A–	B+	A–	A–	B+	B+	B	B+	B+
Japan	A	A–	A–	B	C	A–	B+	B+	B+
Italy	B–	C–	B	B	–	B	B+	A–	B–
Canada	A	B–	A–	B+	A	B–	B+	B+	B+
Russia	C	B+	A	B+	C	A	C–	B+	B
EU	B+	A–	–	B+	–	A–	B	B+	B+

Appendix C

Commitments and Significance by Issue, 1994, 2000, 2001

G8 Research Group

	Number of Commitments (significance)		
	Naples 1994[a]	Okinawa 2000	Genoa 2001
G7 statement	27	12 (43%)	10 (40%)
World economy	–		1
Trade	–		2
International financial system	–	3	5
HIPC	–	4	2
Financial abuse	–	3	0
Nuclear safety/Ukraine	–	2	0
Fatality regret	–	–	0
Regional issues	–	2 (Balkans)	2 (33%)
Middle East	–	2	0
Africa	–	2	2 (75%)
Global Information Society	–	54	
G8 communiqué	–	97 (45%; n=70)	43
World economy	–	1	0
Education	–		7
Information and communications technology	–	3	3
Development	–	15	12
Debt relief	–	5	5
Health	–	15	3
Employment	–	0	1
Trade	–	4	0
Cultural diversity	–	2	0
Crime and drugs	–	18	2
Ageing	–	6	0
Biotech/Food safety	–	3	2
Environment (Human genome/energy)	–	11	9
Conflict prevention	–	3	0
Arms control/Disarmament	–	7	0
Terrorism	–	4	0
G7 + G8 communiqué	–	82[b] (44%)	53

a. G7, without Russia.
b. 82 = 12 + 70.

DOCUMENTARY APPENDICES

.

Appendix D

Conclusions of the G8 Foreign Ministers' Meeting

Rome, 18–19 July 2001

We met in Roma on 18–19 July 2001 in order to examine the present state and the developments of the international political agenda.

We had a broad and informal exchange of views on how to enhance the dialogue between G8 and civil societies, taking into account both risks and opportunities of the present process of interdependence and globalisation. We will continue to work closely, together and with others, on this topical aspect.

We have examined the developments of the most significant political issues facing the international community, on the global as well as on the regional level. On Middle East, FYROM, Africa and the Korean Peninsula, we have agreed to submit our language directly to the G8 Heads of State and Government for their Summit in Genova on 20–22 July.

We have also reached the following Conclusions:

Global Challenges for Peace and Security

Conflict Prevention

1. We consider our commitment to conflict prevention to be an indispensable element in our international actions and initiatives. While the main responsibility for avoiding conflict lies with those directly involved, we will continue to work for effective action by the international community, primarily the United Nations, to prevent conflict. We register, and we will continue to support, progress in the five areas we identified in Miyazaki, in particular for the item of conflict and development, in the framework of which aspects such as disarmament, demobilisation and reintegration and co-operation on water management will receive our special attention. We have also decided to focus on two new initiatives: the contribution of women in the prevention of violent conflict and the role of the private sector. The relevant items are detailed in the attached documents.

Disarmament, Non-Proliferation, and Arms Control

2. With a view to maintaining and strengthening strategic stability and international security in the face of the challenges of the 21st century, we place great importance on the existing regimes of multilateral treaties and export control arrangements designed to cope with the threats that the proliferation of weapons of mass destruction and their means of delivery can pose. In this context we welcome efforts to strengthen international arms control and non-proliferation regime and reaffirm our determination to promote compliance with and the universality of the fundamental treaties related to weapons of mass destruction and to contribute to the implementation of the conclusions of the 2000 NPT Review Conference. We welcome the readiness of Russia and the U.S. to continue deep reductions in their strategic offensive arsenals and to strengthen strategic stability.

    We welcome efforts to agree on measures, including potential enforcement and compliance measures to strengthen the BTWC. We remain fully committed to pursue efforts to ensure that the BTWC is an effective instrument to counter the growing threat of biological weapons. We welcome efforts by members of the MTCR to produce an international code of conduct against missile proliferation and to promote its universalisation. So long as the Comprehensive Nuclear Test Ban Treaty has not entered into force, we urge all states to maintain global existing moratoria on nuclear testing. We reaffirm our commitment to an immediate commencement of negotiations on a Fissile Material Cut-off Treaty with a view to their conclusion within five years. We call on all States who have not already done so to conclude appropriate safeguards agreements and Additional Protocols with the International Atomic Energy Agency (IAEA).

3. We continue to attach the utmost importance to ensuring that weapon-grade plutonium no longer required for defence purposes is never used for nuclear weapons. We invite all donors intending to contribute substantially to the Russian Federation disposition program to join in completing an international financing plan and in initiating negotiations on a multilateral framework for the programme. We will also support the efforts of the Russian Federation to destroy its chemical weapons in accordance with the Chemical Weapons Convention.

4. As part of the international community's efforts to raise humanitarian standards concerning conventional weapons, including explosive remnants of war, we will work for a successful outcome to this year's Review Conference for the Convention on Certain Conventional Weapons (CCWC). We also remain concerned by the scourge of the indiscriminate use of anti-personnel landmines which have caused harm to so many innocent civilians throughout the world and by the continued existence of vast stockpiles of landmines. We are determined to support efforts, including those under the Ottawa Convention, as well as the amended Mines Protocol of the CCWC, in the areas of mine clearance, humanitarian demining, victim assistance and in the development of technologies for mine action.

Continued commitment of resources from donors will have a decisive impact on this humanitarian crisis. We commit ourselves to work actively towards achieving the goal of a practical programme at the UN Conference on the Illicit Trade in Small Arms and Light Weapons.

Terrorism

5. We renew our condemnation of all forms of terrorism, regardless of the motives, and we stress the need for enhanced international co-operation in the development of preventive and enforcement strategies. We recall and endorse the commitment expressed this year in Milan by the G8 Justice and Interior Ministers. We urge our experts to make further progress in strengthening co-operation on traditional and new terrorist threats, including High-Tech ones.
6. We underline the importance of the widest possible application of UN sectoral counter-terrorism conventions, including on the suppression of the financing of terrorism, and we reaffirm our political support for the negotiation of a comprehensive UN Convention against international terrorism. We also stress the importance of completing the elaboration of the international convention against nuclear terrorism and encourage its subsequent adoption.

United Nations

7. Restating the importance of the conclusions of last year's Millennium Summit and Assembly, we reaffirm our commitment to reform, strengthen and enhance the effectiveness of the UN system, including reform of the Security Council. We encourage the UN to further strengthen partnership, co-operation and consultation with other actors notably in the area of humanitarian and development assistance.
8. On the occasion of the 50th anniversary of the 1951 Geneva Convention on refugees, the G8 reaffirms its commitment to its provisions as well as the 1967 Protocol, and pays tribute to HCR for its action in favour of refugees.

Regional Crises

Balkans/South-Eastern Europe

9. The situation in the Balkans continues to warrant our close attention. We welcome the progress which has taken place since we met in Miyazaki, particularly in the FRY. We will continue to support reform and enhanced regional co-operation. We expect to see full compliance with international obligations including the Dayton accords and ICTY. In this respect we welcome the steps taken by the FRY

and other countries in the region. Slobodan Milosevic and other indicted war criminals are now facing trial in the Hague. We condemn all forms of ethnic nationalist and separatist violence. We support a democratic Montenegro within a democratic Yugoslavia and encourage dialogue between Belgrade and Podgorica. In Kosovo we expect the full implementation of UNSCR 1244 and Kosovo-wide elections in November conducted in a secure environment, followed by the establishment of a democratic provisional government. We encourage all ethnic communities to participate fully in the process.

10. We remain convinced that enhanced regional co-operation represents a fundamental opportunity for development and prosperity. We call on each country of the region to demonstrate its commitment to make concrete progress in this field. The EU Stabilisation and Association Process is an important factor in this regard. We welcome the assistance and initiatives by G8 members and other states concerned, as well as regional and international organisations. We reaffirm our full support for the Stability Pact and will work closely together to make the Regional Conference in Bucharest on 25–26 October a success. The respect of sovereignty and territorial integrity constitutes a solid base for long term stability and security in the region.

Cyprus

11. We recall the Okinawa statement and renew our commitment to support the efforts of the UNSG to find a just and lasting settlement that protects the fundamental interests of all parties in an undivided Cyprus giving full consideration to relevant UNSCRs. We look forward to renewed efforts by all parties and a prompt resumption of talks under the good offices of the UNSG.

Iraq

12. We call on Iraq to comply fully with the relevant UNSCRs, including the entry of UN and IAEA inspectors with the mandate of verifying the elimination of weapons of mass destruction. The resumption of co-operation with the UN is a necessary step to the suspension and eventual lifting of the sanctions and will allow for a reintegration of Iraq into the international community. To this end, we welcome the dialogue between the UN Secretary General and the Government of Iraq. We underline the responsibility of each member of the international community, in accordance with relevant UNSCRs to ensure that Iraq does not constitute again a threat to regional peace and stability. The territorial integrity and the sovereignty of every country in the region must be safeguarded in order to promote security and stability in the Gulf. We stress our continued concern about the humanitarian situation in Iraq, which calls for more ambitious measures to alleviate the suffering

of the people, and we call on the Iraqi government to fully implement the oil for food programme. Underlining UNSCRs 1352 and 1360, we call on the international community and the UN Security Council to build a new approach to Iraq.

Afghanistan

13. Recalling the need for the full implementation of UNSCRs 1267 and 1333, we reiterate our concern over the growing terrorist threat and urge the Taliban to fulfil the demands contained in those resolutions and in particular to close terrorist training camps. We call upon those having influence, including financial, on the Taliban to act responsibly. We commend and support the ban on poppy production, even though concerns remain over opium stocks and drug trafficking. We condemn the continuing violations of human rights in Afghanistan, including the worsening of conditions for women and religious minorities. We denounce the destruction by the Taliban of invaluable statues in Bamiyan. We affirm our commitment to effective assistance to relieve the disastrous humanitarian situation of the Afghan people and to effective co-operation of donor countries and implementing agencies in the framework of the Afghanistan Support Group (ASG). We support the efforts of the UN and others to advance a peace process through political negotiations between the Afghan parties or through mechanisms such as a Loya Jirga, aimed at the establishment of a broad-based, multi-ethnic and fully representative government.

South Asia

14. We welcome the Agra Summit between India and Pakistan and strongly support their intention to continue high level dialogue in order to make progress on their relationship. We encourage both countries to continue their policy of restraint and call on them to refrain from any action which could adversely affect their relations and regional stability. We reiterate the importance of UNSCR 1172 and urge India and Pakistan to participate fully in international efforts to strengthen the non-proliferation and disarmament regime. We take note of their commitment to the nuclear test moratorium.

Indonesia

15. We reaffirm our support for a democratic, stable and united Indonesia, key factor for the stability and the economic development of South East Asia, while stressing the vital importance for Indonesia to overcome the current political tension by democratic and peaceful means and in accordance with its constitution. We

encourage the Indonesian government to take forward its efforts of economic and governance reforms, and reiterate the international community's readiness to assist these endeavours. We call on the Indonesian government to increase the level of genuine dialogue among all parties, with full respect of human rights. We reiterate our support for Indonesia's territorial integrity.

East Timor

16. We welcome progress made by the East Timorese and the UNTAET towards independence and democracy for East Timor. We emphasise in this context the importance of fair and smooth implementation of the Constituent Assembly elections scheduled for the 30th August. Recognising the enormous challenges faced by East Timor we reaffirm our support for the efforts by people of East Timor to build a sustainable nation.

Colombia

17. We fully support an irreversible peace process in Colombia. We urge all parties to negotiate an end to the conflict and to respect human rights. All illegal armed groups must release their hostages. The Government of Colombia should continue its efforts to combat the activities of paramilitary groups and to take concrete action to dismantle them. We invite the international community, together with regional governments to promote initiatives to fight poverty and foster sustainable development in the Andean region, where appropriate in the framework of the support group for the peace process in Colombia, in order to combat illicit drug production and drug trafficking.

Africa

18. We welcome and support the consolidation of democracy, pluralism and electoral fairness in an increasing number of African Countries. We call for similar progress towards political openness elsewhere in Africa where democratic principles and the rule of law are undermined.
19. Horn of Africa. We welcome and support the peace process between Ethiopia and Eritrea on the basis of the Algiers Agreement and of the relevant UNSCRs as a positive example of the management of African crises by African countries with the support of the international community. We urge the parties to fulfil all their commitments, to co-operate fully with the United Nations and to move towards lasting reconciliation and regional co-operation. We consider that the end of the civil war in Sudan and the establishment of peace and national unity in

Somalia are the next essential steps for stabilisation and development in the Horn of Africa as a whole.

20. DRC and Burundi. We welcome the positive steps towards the implementation of the Lusaka and Arusha agreements and all relevant UNSCRs for peace in the Democratic Republic of Congo and in Burundi. We urge all signatories and concerned parties to co-operate fully with the United Nations and with all those engaged in the peace process and in particular to facilitate the deployment of UN peacekeepers, support the national dialogue, and undertake the process of disarming, demobilising, resettling, [and] reintegrating combatants and of complete withdrawal of foreign troops from DRC. We call on the international community to continue to support humanitarian relief activities.

21. Mano River Region. We welcome progress towards implementation of the Abuja agreement in Sierra Leone. We call on the international community to support the consolidation of the peace process and the reconstruction programme in that country. We call on all parties to co-operate fully with the United Nations and to observe the relevant UNSCRs.

22. Southern Africa. We support continuing efforts, both by the UN and by the Angolan government, to find a peaceful solution to the conflict there. We urge rapid resolution of the continuing conflict in Angola along the lines of the Lusaka Protocol. We consider that a sustainable solution to Zimbabwe's problems is essential to stability in Southern Africa.

Attachment 1:
Progress on the Miyazaki Initiatives

We have reviewed progress registered on the commitments that we took in Miyazaki in July 2000 and in particular:

- We welcome the significant developments on Small Arms and Light Weapons (SALW) since Miyazaki as part of the process leading up to the UN Conference on the Illicit Trade in Small and Arms and Light Weapons in All Its Aspects, which will conclude on 20 July 2001. These developments include relevant outcomes achieved at [the] regional level as well as the consensus reached on the UN Protocol Against the Illicit Manufacturing of and Trafficking in Fire Arms, Their Parts, Components and Ammunitions. We look to the Programme of Action to be decided at the UN Conference to set a comprehensive framework that will best facilitate support and assistance by the international community for concrete action in all regions of the world.
- The G8 welcomes the considerable progress made through the Kimberley Process to bring governments, industry and civil society together in an effort to break the link between the illicit trade in rough diamonds and armed conflict. We encourage

the continuation of the Process in a manner that will secure transparency and accountability. We also welcome UN General Assembly Resolution 55/56 of December 2000, which calls for the development of detailed proposals for a simple and workable international scheme of certification for rough diamonds primarily based on national certification schemes. We recognise the importance of this issue and look forward to a report by the Kimberley Process to the 56th Session of the General Assembly on progress achieved.

- Negotiations on the Optional Protocol to the Convention on the Rights of the Child on Children in Armed Conflict were completed and a number of world leaders signed the Protocol at the Millennium Summit in New York. We hope that the UNGA Special Session [on] Children will also give due attention to children in armed conflict and further encourage state to ratify the ILO Convention no. 182 (1999) on the Worst Forms of Child Labour. We welcome UN Security Council Resolution 1314 on measures to protect children in armed conflict and continue to support awareness raising projects on the ground.
- We note the achievements of the UN and its member states to date in implementing the Brahimi recommendations on Civilian Policing, and encourage them to maintain their commitment to implementation. Now that the Comprehensive Review of DPKO has been issued, it is essential to pursue further implementation of the Brahimi agenda. In addition to what has been achieved so far — such as beginning a reorientation of the way the UN approaches civilian policing, with the CivPol unit being taken out of military command — further effort is needed on several key issues, such as improving the UN's early warning capabilities. We will also need to give careful consideration to the financial consequences of improvements to the UN's peacekeeping mechanisms.
- We have given special attention to the issue of conflict and development. We believe that development should mean the inclusion of all countries, and all groups within countries, in the benefits of globalization, and that such inclusion constitutes the best instrument to prevent and alleviate tensions and violent conflict. We are also convinced that preventing conflict and promoting development are mutually reinforcing and pressing top priorities on the international agenda. We are promoting the consideration of conflict prevention in development assistance strategies, with a view to achieving quicker and better co-ordinated assistance strategies — including the HIPC initiative — and ensuring a smooth transition from relief to post-conflict development. A significant example of such consideration is the April 2001 OECD/ DAC Supplement to the 1997 Guidelines ('Helping Prevent Violent Conflict: Orientations for External Partners').
- We will continue to focus attention on co-operative and sustainable water management and Disarmament, Demobilisation and Reintegration as ways to prevent conflict and we call for more work to be done on these items.

Attachment 2:
G8 Roma Initiatives on Conflict Prevention

1. Strengthening the Role of Women in Conflict Prevention

The international community has increasingly recognized the positive contributions women can make to preventing conflicts and consolidating peace. For example, the role of women in conflict prevention, conflict resolution and post-conflict peace-building has been emphasized in the final document of the 23rd Special Session of the UN General Assembly 'Women 2000: Gender Equality, Development and Peace for the Twenty-First Century.' In October 2000, the Security Council adopted Resolution 1325 on women, peace and security. These efforts indicate a growing realization that in conflict situations women are more than victims requiring the protection of the international community: they are negotiators, peacemakers and advisors whose efforts are vital to sustainable peace.

Despite studies, conferences, and pledges to do so, the international community has failed to ensure women's full and equal participation in conflict prevention, peace operations and post-conflict peace-building. International efforts to address mounting political, economic and humanitarian crises can be substantially strengthened by involvement of women. Our comprehensive approach to conflict prevention is incomplete if we neglect to include women. Women bring alternative perspectives to conflict prevention at the grass-roots and community levels. We must encourage creative and innovative ways to better draw on the talents women bring to preventing conflict and sustaining peace. Furthermore, we should identify practical steps and strategies that we can support individually and collectively to advance the role of women in conflict prevention and post conflict peace building.

Building on the 1995 'Beijing Declaration and Platform for Action' adopted at the 4th World Conference on Women, the guidelines of the 1997 OECD/DAC statement on Conflict, Peace and Development Cooperation on the Threshold of the 21st Century, as well as its Supplement approved in April 2001; the 1998 Agreed conclusions on 'Women and Armed Conflict' of the UN Commission on the Status of Women Agreed Conclusions on Women and Armed Conflict; the 8 March 2000 Security Council Presidential Statement on International Women's Day; the 2000 UNIFEM report 'Women at the Peace Table: Making a Difference'; the final document of the 23rd Special Session of the UN General Assembly 'Women 2000: Gender Equality, Development and Peace for the Twenty-First Century'; the study 'Mainstreaming a Gender Perspective in Multidimensional Peace Operations' by the Lessons Learned Unit of DPKO; the Report of UN Secretariat on the implementation of the Brahimi report, G8 partners will seize the opportunity to set an example for the international community.

On the basis of these premises, the G8:

- Emphasizes the importance of the systematic involvement of women in the prevention and resolution of conflicts and in peace-building, as well as women's full and equal participation in all phases of conflict prevention, resolution and peacebuilding.
- Encourages the participation of all actors of civil society, including women's organizations, in conflict prevention and conflict resolution as well as encourage and support the sharing of experiences and best practices. In line with the 1997 OECD/DAC statement, and its April 2001 Supplement, the G-8 is confident that women's full and equal participation in all the phases of the process of conflict prevention, resolution and peacebuilding will enhance the opportunities for building a just and peaceful society. Special attention should be given, in this context, to identifying and working with local women who represent an influential voice for peace.
- Encourages those involved in planning for disarmament, demobilization and reintegration programs to consider the specific needs of female ex-combatants and to take into account the needs of their dependents, particularly in the design of reintegration approaches to education, training and resource distribution.
- Supports the provision of appropriate gender-sensitive training for participants in peace-related operations, including military observers, civilian police, human rights and humanitarian personnel.
- Encourages the appointment of more women to national and international posts, including SRSGs, Special Envoys, Resident Coordinators and other operational positions.
- Commits, where appropriate, to the integration of a gender perspective and to the participation of women in the development, design, implementation, monitoring and evaluation of bilateral and multilateral assistance programmes.

2. Corporate Citizenship and Conflict Prevention

Following the recognition contained in the conclusions of the July 2000 Miyazaki Foreign Ministers' Meeting regarding the role that corporate social responsibility (CSR) can play in conflict prevention, the G8 has identified this issue as a priority area for attention and initiative.

Although the political nature of violent conflict can hardly be doubted, economic factors frequently turn out to be highly relevant — both as objectives and instruments of conflict. With a greater number of companies selling to, investing in, and sourcing from a greater number of foreign markets, the private sector is more internationalized than ever. There is a growing awareness of the impact companies can have in conflict-prone regions.

They in turn have a direct interest shared by all in conflict prevention and peace building to ensure a stable environment for their operations.

A great deal of work is being done internationally to address CSR issues through the development of multilateral standards and norms. At the World Economic Forum in Davos in 1999, UN Secretary General Kofi Annan launched the 'Global Compact' — a call to world business leaders to adopt a set of nine principles based on existing UN instruments including the Universal Declaration of Human Rights, the Declaration on Fundamental Principles and Rights at Work and the Rio Declaration. OECD Ministers recently adopted revised Guidelines for Multinational Enterprises. International efforts to stem the illicit trade in rough diamonds from conflict zones provide a good example of areas where the private sector can make an active contribution to conflict prevention.

Based on these premises, the G8:

- recognizes that the private sector through good citizenship can play an important and positive role in conflict prevention and post-conflict reconstruction.
- welcomes the UNGA Resolution A/55/215 entitled 'Towards Global Partnership' adopted by consensus in December 2000, and takes note of initiatives such as the UN Secretary General's Global Compact, the OECD Guidelines for Multinational Enterprises and similar work in other multilateral fora, including the World Bank.
- expresses its intention to co-operate with private and non governmental sectors using these initiatives as points of reference.
- intends to work further with the private and non-governmental sectors to explore best practices to respond to specific challenges faced in high-risk environments.
- stresses the valuable contribution that partnership between corporations and local communities can make to the development of civil society.

Appendix E

Statement on Middle East: Conclusions of the G8 Foreign Ministers' Meeting

Rome, 19 July 2001

In the light of the alarming developments in the Middle East, we reaffirm that the Mitchell Report in its entirety is the only way forward to break the deadlock, to stop the escalation and to resume a political process.

The cooling off period must begin as soon as possible. This means:

- all extremism and terrorism must be opposed; they cannot be allowed to dictate the security environment;
- all the commitments given to securing a cessation of violence must be scrupulously observed;
- each party must refrain from provocation and incitement;
- no action should be taken by either party which undermines the other.

We believe that in these circumstances third-party monitoring accepted by both parties would serve their interests in implementing the Mitchell Report.

Appendix F

Statement by the G8 Leaders (Death in Genoa)

Genoa, 21 July 2001

We the leaders of the G8 express our sorrow and regret following the death in Genoa yesterday.

We have always respected people's right to legitimate protest. We recognise and praise the role that peaceful protest and argument have played, for example in putting issues like debt relief on the international agenda. But we condemn firmly and absolutely the violence overflowing into anarchy of a small minority that we have seen at work here in Genoa and at recent international meetings.

It is of vital importance that democratically elected leaders, legitimately representing millions of people can meet to discuss areas of common concern. We are firmly determined to carry on our dialogue with the representatives of civil society. For our part we will continue to focus on the issues that matter most to our people and to the wider world such as the economy, jobs, trade and help for the poorest parts of the world, devoting special attention to Africa. Yesterday evening, we dedicated a working session to Africa together with the Secretary-General of the UN and representatives of developing countries.

For all these reasons, our commitment and our work goes on.

Appendix G

G8 Communiqué

Genoa, 22 July 2001

1. We, the Heads of State and Government of eight major industrialised democracies and the Representatives of the European Union, met in Genova for the first Summit of the new millennium. In a spirit of co-operation, we discussed the most pressing issues on the international agenda.
2. As democratic leaders, accountable to our citizens, we believe in the fundamental importance of open public debate on the key challenges facing our societies. We will promote innovative solutions based on a broad partnership with civil society and the private sector. We will also seek enhanced co-operation and solidarity with developing countries, based on a mutual responsibility for combating poverty and promoting sustainable development.
3. We are determined to make globalisation work for all our citizens and especially the world's poor. Drawing the poorest countries into the global economy is the surest way to address their fundamental aspirations. We concentrated our discussions on a strategy to achieve this.

A Strategic Approach to Poverty Reduction

4. The situation in many developing countries — especially in Africa — calls for decisive global action. The most effective poverty reduction strategy is to maintain a strong, dynamic, open and growing global economy. We pledge to do that.
5. We will also continue to provide effective development assistance to help developing countries' own efforts to build long-term prosperity. Consistent with the conclusions of the LDC III Conference and the Millennium Declaration, we support a strategic approach centred on the principles of ownership and partnership. In the common interest of donors and recipients of aid, we shall ensure the efficient use of scarce resources.
6. Open, democratic and accountable systems of governance, based on respect for human rights and the rule of law, are preconditions for sustainable development and robust growth. Thus, we shall help developing countries promote:
   - accountability and transparency in the public sector
   - legal frameworks and corporate governance regimes to fight corruption
   - safeguards against the misappropriation of public funds and their diversion into non-productive uses

- access to legal systems for all citizens, independence of the judiciary, and legal provisions enabling private sector activity
- active involvement of civil society and Non Governmental Organisations (NGOs)
- freedom of economic activities.
  We, for our part, will:
- implement fully the OECD Bribery Convention
- support efforts in the UN to pursue an effective instrument against corruption
- encourage Multilateral Development Banks (MDBs) to help recipient countries strengthen public expenditure and budget management.

Debt Relief and Beyond

7. Debt relief — particularly the Enhanced Heavily Indebted Poor Countries (HIPC) Initiative — is a valuable contribution to the fight against poverty, but it is only one of the steps needed to stimulate faster growth in very poor countries. We are delighted twenty-three countries have qualified for an overall amount of debt relief of over $53 billion, out of an initial stock of debt of $74 billion. We must continue this progress.

8. In particular we look to countries affected by conflict to turn away from violence. When they do, we confirm that we will strengthen our efforts to help them take the measures needed to receive debt relief. We confirm that HIPC, in conjunction with reforms by the countries to ensure strong domestic policies and responsible lending by donors, is designed to lead to a lasting exit from unsustainable debt.

9. Beyond debt relief, we focussed our discussion on three mutually reinforcing elements:
   - greater participation by developing countries in the global trading system
   - increased private investment
   - initiatives to promote health, education and food security.

10. Open trade and investment drive global growth and poverty reduction. That is why we have agreed today to support the launch of an ambitious new Round of global trade negotiations with a balanced agenda.

11. While opening markets through global negotiations provides the greatest economic benefit for developing countries, we fully endorse measures already taken to improve market access for the least developed countries (LDCs), such as Everything But Arms, Generalised Preferences and all other initiatives that address the same objectives. We confirm our pledge made at the UN LDC III Conference to work towards duty-free and quota-free access for all products originating in the least developed countries. We support efforts made by LDCs to enter the global trading system and to take advantage of opportunities for trade-based growth.

12. Increased market access must be coupled with the capacity to take advantage of it. Thus, to help developing countries benefit from open markets, we will better co-ordinate our trade related assistance to:
    - provide bilateral assistance on technical standards, customs systems, legislation needed for World Trade Organisation (WTO) membership, the protection of intellectual property rights, and human resource development
    - support the work of the Integrated Framework for Trade-Related Technical Assistance encourage the international financial institutions to help remove obstacles to trade and investment, and establish the institutions and policies essential for trade to flourish
    - urge countries to mainstream trade expansion by including it in their poverty reduction strategies.

13. Increased private sector investment is essential to generate economic growth, increase productivity and raise living standards. To help developing countries improve the climate for private investment, we urge MDBs and other relevant international bodies to support domestic reform efforts, including the establishment of public-private partnerships and investment-related best practices, as well as codes and standards in the field of corporate governance, accounting standards, enhanced competition and transparent tax regimes. We call on the World Bank to provide additional support for programmes that promote private sector development in the poorest countries. To promote further investments in the knowledge-based economy, we call on the WTO and the World Intellectual Property Rights Organisation, in collaboration with the World Bank, to help the poorest countries comply with international rules on intellectual property rights.

14. Official development assistance (ODA) is essential. We will work with developing countries to meet the International Development Goals, by strengthening and enhancing the effectiveness of our development assistance. We commit ourselves to implement the landmark OECD-DAC Recommendation on Untying Aid to LDCs which should increase aid effectiveness and achieve more balanced effort-sharing among donors.

15. At Okinawa last year, we pledged to make a quantum leap in the fight against infectious diseases and to break the vicious cycle between disease and poverty. To meet that commitment and to respond to the appeal of the UN General Assembly, we have launched with the UN Secretary-General a new Global Fund to fight HIV/AIDS, malaria and tuberculosis. We are determined to make the Fund operational before the end of the year. We have committed $1.3 billion. The Fund will be a public-private partnership and we call on other countries, the private sector, foundations, and academic institutions to join with their own contributions — financially, in kind and through shared expertise. We welcome the further commitments already made amounting to some $500 million.

16. The Fund will promote an integrated approach emphasising prevention in a continuum of treatment and care. It will operate according to principles of proven

scientific and medical effectiveness, rapid resource transfer, low transaction costs, and light governance with a strong focus on outcomes. We hope that the existence of the Fund will promote improved co-ordination among donors and provide further incentives for private sector research and development. It will offer additional financing consistent with existing programmes, to be integrated into the national health plans of partner countries. The engagement of developing countries in the purpose and operation of the Fund will be crucial to ensure ownership and commitment to results. Local partners, including NGOs, and international agencies, will be instrumental in the successful operation of the Fund.

17. Strong national health systems will continue to play a key role in the delivery of effective prevention, treatment and care and in improving access to essential health services and commodities without discrimination. An effective response to HIV/AIDS and other diseases will require society-wide action beyond the health sector. We welcome the steps taken by the pharmaceutical industry to make drugs more affordable. In the context of the new Global Fund, we will work with the pharmaceutical industry and with affected countries to facilitate the broadest possible provision of drugs in an affordable and medically effective manner. We welcome ongoing discussion in the WTO on the use of relevant provisions in the Trade-Related Intellectual Property Rights (TRIPs) agreement. We recognise the appropriateness of affected countries using the flexibility afforded by that agreement to ensure that drugs are available to their citizens who need them, particularly those who are unable to afford basic medical care. At the same time, we reaffirm our commitment to strong and effective intellectual property rights protection as a necessary incentive for research and development of life-saving drugs.

18. Education is a central building block for growth and employment. We reaffirm our commitment to help countries meet the Dakar Framework for Action goal of universal primary education by 2015. We agree on the need to improve the effectiveness of our development assistance in support of locally-owned strategies. Education — in particular, universal primary education and equal access to education at all levels for girls — must be given high priority both in national poverty reduction strategies and in our development programmes. Resources made available through the HIPC Initiative can contribute to these objectives. We will help foster assessment systems to measure progress, identify best practices and ensure accountability for results. We will also focus on teacher training. Building on the work of the G8 Digital Opportunities Task Force (dot.force), we will work to expand the use of information and communications technology (ICT) to train teachers in best practices and strengthen education strategies. We especially encourage the private sector to examine new opportunities for investment in infrastructure, ICT and learning materials. We encourage MDBs to sharpen their focus on education and concentrate their future work on countries with sound strategies but lacking sufficient resources and to report next year to the G8. We support UNESCO in its key role for universal education. We will also work with

the International Labour Organisation (ILO) to support efforts to fight child labour and we will develop incentives to increase school enrolment.

19. We will establish a task force of senior G8 officials to advise us on how best to pursue the Dakar goals in co-operation with developing countries, relevant international organisations and other stakeholders. The task force will provide us with recommendations in time for our next meeting.

20. As the November 2001 'World Food Summit: Five Years Later' approaches, food security remains elusive. Over 800 million people remain seriously malnourished, including at least 250 million children. So a central objective of our poverty reduction strategy remains access to adequate food supplies and rural development. Support to agriculture is a crucial instrument of ODA. We shall endeavour to develop capacity in poor countries, integrating programmes into national strategies and increasing training in agricultural science. Every effort should be undertaken to enhance agricultural productivity. Among other things, the introduction of tried and tested new technology, including biotechnology, in a safe manner and adapted to local conditions has significant potential to substantially increase crop yields in developing countries, while using fewer pesticides and less water than conventional methods. We are committed to study, share and facilitate the responsible use of biotechnology in addressing development needs.

21. We shall target the most food-insecure regions, particularly Sub-Saharan Africa and South Asia, and continue to encourage South-South co-operation. We will support the crucial role international organisations and NGOs play in relief operations. We believe national poverty reduction and sectoral strategies should take due account of the nutritional needs of vulnerable groups, including new-borns and their mothers.

Digital Opportunities

22. ICT holds tremendous potential for helping developing countries accelerate growth, raise standards of living and meet other development priorities. We endorse the report of the Digital Opportunity Task Force (dot.force) and its Genoa Plan of Action that successfully fulfilled the Okinawa mandate. The direct participation of representatives from public, private and non-profit sectors, as well as that of developing countries' governments, presents a unique formula for ensuring that digital technologies meet development needs. We will continue to support the process and encourage all stakeholders to demonstrate ownership, to mobilise expertise and resources and to build on this successful co-operation. We will review the implementation of the Genoa Plan of Action at our next Summit on the basis of a report by the G8 Presidency. We also encourage development of an Action Plan on how e-Government can strengthen democracy and the rule of law by empowering citizens and making the provision of essential government services more efficient.

A Legacy for the Future

Environment

23. We confirm our determination to find global solutions to threats endangering the planet. We recognise that climate change is a pressing issue that requires a global solution. We are committed to providing strong leadership. Prompt, effective and sustainable action is needed, consistent with the ultimate objective of the UN Framework Convention on Climate Change of stabilising greenhouse gas concentrations in the atmosphere. We are determined to meet our national commitments and our obligations under the Convention through a variety of flexible means, drawing on the power of markets and technology. In this context, we agree on the importance of intensifying co-operation on climate-related science and research. We shall promote co-operation between our countries and developing countries on technology transfer and capacity building.

24. We all firmly agree on the need to reduce greenhouse gas emissions. While there is currently disagreement on the Kyoto Protocol and its ratification, we are committed to working intensively together to meet our common objective. To that end, we are participating constructively in the resumed Sixth Conference of the Parties in Bonn (COP6) and will continue to do so in all relevant fora. We welcome the recent deepening of discussions among the G8 and with other countries.

25. We reaffirm that our efforts must ultimately result in an outcome that protects the environment and ensures economic growth compatible with our shared objective of sustainable development for present and future generations.

26. We welcome Russia's proposal to convene in 2003 a global conference on climate change with the participation of governments, business and science as well as representatives of civil society.

27. We recognise the importance of renewable energy for sustainable development, diversification of energy supply, and preservation of the environment. We will ensure that renewable energy sources are adequately considered in our national plans and encourage others to do so as well. We encourage continuing research and investment in renewable energy technology, throughout the world. Renewable energy can contribute to poverty reduction. We will help developing countries strengthen institutional capacity and market-oriented national strategies that can attract private sector investment in renewable energy and other clean technologies. We call on MDBs and national development assistance agencies to adopt an innovative approach and to develop market-based financing mechanisms for renewable energy. We urge the Global Environment Facility (GEF) to continue supporting environmental protection on a global scale and fostering good practices to promote efficient energy use and the development of renewable energy sources in the developing world, and stress the need to commit adequate resources to its third replenishment. We thank all those who participated in the work of the

Renewable Energy Task Force established in Okinawa. G8 energy ministers will hold a meeting in the coming year to discuss these and other energy-related issues.

28. We are looking forward to the World Summit on Sustainable Development (WSSD) in Johannesburg in 2002, an important milestone in the Rio process. The three dimensions of sustainable development — enhancing economic growth, promoting human and social development and protecting the environment — are interdependent objectives requiring our concerted action. We will work in partnership with developing countries for an inclusive preparatory process with civil society on a forward looking and substantial agenda with action-oriented results. We welcome the recent adoption of the Stockholm Convention on Persistent Organic Pollutants (POPs) and will strongly promote its early entry into force.

29. We are committed to ensuring that our Export Credit Agencies (ECAs) adhere to high environmental standards. We therefore agreed in Okinawa to develop common environmental guidelines for ECAs, drawing on relevant MDB experience. Building on the progress made since last year, we commit to reach agreement in the OECD by the end of the year on a Recommendation that fulfils the Okinawa mandate.

Food Safety

30. Fully aware of the paramount importance of food safety to our peoples, we will continue to support a transparent, scientific and rules-based approach and will intensify our efforts to achieve greater global consensus on how precaution should be applied to food safety in circumstances where available scientific information is incomplete or contradictory. We value the ongoing dialogue between governments, scientists, consumers, regulators, and relevant stakeholders in civil society. This must be based on the principle of openness and transparency. We recognise our responsibility to promote a clear understanding by the public of food safety benefits and risks. We shall strive to provide consumers with relevant information on the safety of food products, based on independent scientific advice, sound risk analysis and the latest research developments. We believe an effective framework for risk management, consistent with the science, is a key component in maintaining consumer confidence and in fostering public acceptance.

31. We welcome the outcome of the recent Bangkok conference on new biotechnology food and crops and the ad hoc meeting of regulators from OECD countries and Russia. We encourage the relevant international organisations to follow up the conference, as appropriate, within their own respective mandates. Furthermore, we welcome the establishment of the joint FAO/WHO Global Forum of Food Safety Regulators. We also appreciate the work of the Inter-Academy Council in publicising balanced professional views on the science of food safety. All these meetings demonstrate our commitment to a process of dialogue aimed at strengthening public confidence in food safety.

Increasing Prosperity in a Socially Inclusive Society

Employment

32. In the firm belief that economic performance and social inclusion are mutually dependent, we commit to implement policies in line with the recommendations of the G8 Labour Ministers Conference held in Torino last year. We welcome the increased activity of older persons who represent, as stated in the G8 Turin Charter 'Towards Active Ageing', a great reservoir of resources for our economies and our societies.

Combating Transnational Organised Crime and Drugs

33. We reaffirm our commitment to combat transnational organised crime. To this end, we strongly endorse the outcome of the G8 Justice and Interior Ministers Conference held in Milano this year. We encourage further progress in the field of judicial co-operation and law enforcement, and in fighting corruption, cyber-crime, online child pornography, as well as trafficking in human beings.
34. Following up on the G8 ad hoc Meeting of Drug Experts held in Miyazaki last year and the recent London Conference on the global economy of illegal drugs, we will strengthen efforts to curb the trafficking and use of illegal drugs.

To the Citizens of Genova

35. We are grateful to the citizens of Genova for their hospitality, and deplore the violence, loss of life and mindless vandalism that they have had to endure. We will maintain our active and fruitful dialogue with developing countries and other stakeholders. And we will defend the right of peaceful protestors to have their voices heard. But as democratic leaders, we cannot accept that a violent minority should be allowed to disrupt our discussions on the critical issues affecting the world. Our work will go on.

Next Summit

36. We accept the invitation of the Prime Minister of Canada to meet again next year in the province of Alberta, Canada on 26–28 June.

Appendix H

G8 Foreign Ministers' Statement on Afghanistan

26 November 2001

We welcome the initiative of the Secretary General of the UN and of his Special Representative, Amb. Brahimi, to convene a meeting of Afghan representatives in Bonn this week to work towards the full implementation of UNSCR 1378 and the urgent establishment of a new, transitional administration in Afghanistan. We hope that this step will facilitate the achievement of a political solution in order to bring peace and stability to Afghanistan and to the surrounding region. In expressing our full support to Amb. Brahimi in his endeavour, we call on the Afghan participants to take full advantage of this opportunity.

We stress that the aim of this process should be to install in Afghanistan a broad-based and multi-ethnic government of national unity, ensuring the full independence and territorial integrity of the country and committed to peace with Afghanistan's neighbours.

We emphasise that respect by a new Afghan leadership of human rights, regardless of gender, ethnicity or religion, and of international humanitarian law will be a decisive factor to implement programmes of international assistance to the country's reconstruction. We welcome the recent senior officials' meeting on reconstruction assistance to Afghanistan in Washington. We look forward to the meeting, this week, organised by the World Bank, UNDP and the Asian Development Bank in Islamabad and to the larger meeting on reconstruction assistance at the ministerial level to be held in Japan in January.

We stress the urgency and gravity of the humanitarian situation and stress the necessity to continue to facilitate the urgent delivery of humanitarian assistance, particularly to refugees and displaced persons. We call for continued close coordination among governments, international institutions, and non-governmental organisations to mobilise resources and to provide humanitarian aid. In this regard, we support actions undertaken by the Afghanistan Support Group that will meet in Berlin in early December.

Appendix I

G8 Foreign Ministers' Statement on India and Pakistan

28 December 2001

We, the Foreign Ministers of the G8 Countries, express our deep concern about the tension between India and Pakistan resulting from the December 13 attack against the Indian Parliament building.

It is our firm belief that there can be no justification of terrorism. We strongly condemn terrorism in all its forms, including the attack on the Indian Parliament building. We note that the Pakistani authorities have condemned the attack and welcome the action they have announced so far against terrorist groups operating from Pakistani territory. We urge Pakistan to take further action against such groups, to arrest, to bring to justice and severely punish their leaders and to curtail their financing. We also welcome the statements by the Indian Prime Minister to the effect that a solution to the present problem is being sought through diplomatic channels and we encourage this approach.

The events of December 13 must not result in a deterioration of relations between India and Pakistan. We express our hope that both countries will avoid escalation, resume political dialogue and in the spirit of the Lahore declaration and unite their efforts in combating the global terrorist threat.

Appendix J

G8 Foreign Ministers' Statement on India and Pakistan

31 May 2002

We, the G8 Foreign Ministers, are gravely concerned about the risks inherent in the current crisis between India and Pakistan, which could destabilize the region and beyond.

We call on Pakistan, in accordance with its commitments, to take concrete actions immediately to end infiltrations across the Line of Control, and to stop terrorist groups operating from territory under its control.

We call on India and Pakistan to continue to work with the international community to ensure that there will be a diplomatic solution to the current crisis.

We encourage the resumption of dialogue between the two countries, which is the only way forward, and will remain actively engaged in contributing to the peaceful solution of the present crisis.

Appendix K

G8 Foreign Ministers' Statement on Afghanistan

Whistler, 12 June 2002

We, the G8 Foreign Ministers, reaffirm the commitment of our governments to the establishment of a sovereign, stable and prosperous Afghanistan with democratic institutions and a government representative of all Afghan people, respecting their internationally enshrined human rights.

We reaffirm our commitment to the political process set out in the Bonn Agreement of December 5, 2001, and welcome the latest step in that process, the Emergency Loya Jirga currently underway in Afghanistan. We congratulate the Loya Jirga Commission on its preparation and organization of the Emergency Loya Jirga.

This Loya Jirga is the first opportunity in decades for the Afghan people to play a decisive role in choosing their government, and is an important step on the path toward democratic elections, due by June 2004, according to the provisions of the Bonn Agreement. It is an opportunity to progress beyond the divisions and internal conflict that have devastated Afghanistan. In order for the Bonn process to succeed, it is essential that this Loya Jirga yields an effective and representative Transitional Authority truly reflective of the ethnic composition of Afghanistan. We call on the Afghan people and their leaders across the country to work together within the framework of the Bonn Agreement to build democratic institutions and prepare for national elections. The constructive engagement and support of Afghanistan's neighbours, in the spirit of the Bonn process, will be important factors in Afghanistan's recovery and reconstruction, as well as in regional stability.

We warmly congratulate Chairman Karzai and his ministers in the Interim Administration for the leadership and teamwork that have successfully brought Afghanistan to this point in the Bonn process. They have achieved a great deal in a short time, establishing foundations on which the successor Transitional Authority, endorsed by the Emergency Loya Jirga, will be able to build, to the benefit of the Afghan people.

We recognize that effective reconstruction in Afghanistan, leading to poverty eradication and social, economic, and political development, requires a stable and secure environment. For that reason, we are giving the security sector in Afghanistan a special focus in the G8 work on conflict prevention. The G8 has supported the efforts of the Afghan authorities and the UN Assistance Mission in Afghanistan (UNAMA) in devising strategies for the recovery of the security sector, and has marshalled international assistance for the task. The G8 is committed to supporting the Afghan authorities in their work to honourably demobilize former combatants and to reintegrate them into local communities, to build national armed forces, to create a national police force, to restore the justice sector, to eliminate the threat of landmines, and to help the Afghan authorities in their action — which we strongly endorse — against opium production and trafficking.

We acknowledge the importance of the extended engagement of the international community, including the International Financial Institutions, in maintaining support to Afghanistan at this critical juncture, delivering on the commitments pledged at the Tokyo Conference of January 21 and 22, 2002, and coordinating that support through the central Afghan authorities and UNAMA. We recognize the urgent need to translate pledges of support into actual programming in Afghanistan and, in that regard, acknowledge and commend the central coordinating role of the UN and its agencies, and commend UNAMA for its work to date. We continue to provide support to meet the urgent humanitarian needs of the Afghan people.

We recognize that there are many challenges ahead, and pledge our support to the Transitional Authority as it develops the capacity to provide security throughout Afghanistan and prosperity for the Afghan people.

G8 Foreign Ministers' Progress Report on the Fight against Terrorism

Whistler, 12 June 2002

We, the G8 Foreign Ministers, agreed under the Italian presidency that the heinous terrorist attacks on the United States last September 11, required a collective response. We also agreed, and continue to agree, that further attacks remain a very real danger, against which we must remain ever vigilant. For these reasons, we have been working since last fall, at the request of G8 Leaders and drawing on our quarter century of cooperation on counterterrorism, to develop concrete measures to fight terrorism. Our goal is to ensure that terrorist attacks like the one on September 11 will never happen again.

We can report progress in three main areas of this ongoing effort: strengthening security measures in our own countries and with each other; implementing and strengthening international measures against terrorism; and assisting other countries in implementing counterterrorism measures. These efforts have been coordinated with the work of G8 Ministers of Finance, the Interior and Justice.

Strengthening Security Measures in Our Own Countries and with Each Other

We have begun by putting our own houses in order first. G8 members have implemented new laws and policies strengthening our political, diplomatic, military, legal, intelligence, law enforcement and financial counter-terrorism activities. Collectively, we have invested billions of dollars in enhancing security. These domestic changes have been devised to ensure comparable levels of security in all G8 countries and to facilitate cooperation among us routinely and in times of crisis.

Police, judges and all other relevant experts of the G8 now share more information and coordinate their activities to identify and, where they exist, disrupt the linkages between drug trafficking, organized crime, smuggling of migrants and terrorism financing. This is essential as terrorists themselves are well integrated into crime networks.

We have also been implementing new standards to ensure the safety of the travelling public, nationally and internationally, whether by air, land or sea. G8 airlines have tight new security standards and demanding performance tests. We are providing substantial new voluntary contributions to the International Civil Aviation Organization

(ICAO), particularly to its aviation security program. These contributions will pay for audits of every state's aviation security system to ensure compliance with international standards and to spur the development of new safeguards.

Implementing and Strengthening International Measures against Terrorism

We are implementing UN Security Council Resolution (UNSC) 1373 along with all of the UN counter-terrorism instruments, and we are making efforts to further strengthen international obligations in this area. In particular, we are working to ensure adherence to these UN counter-terrorism instruments, which require countries to implement specific measures to prevent and combat terrorist threats, such as bombing, hijacking and hostage-taking. Together with UNSC Resolution 1373, these instruments also require states to take measures to deny safe haven and prevent terrorist financing, recruitment, supply of weapons and other support. The UN has a pivotal role in common efforts aimed at combatting terrorism. We will also persevere in our efforts to promote international consensus on the UN Comprehensive Convention on International Terrorism and on the International Convention for the Suppression of Acts of Nuclear Terrorism.

Terrorists cannot be allowed to disrupt global trade by attacking maritime, aviation or road transport. We have been developing procedures for securing these trading networks. Nor can terrorists be allowed to have access to weapons of mass destruction. We have discussed what must be done to prevent terrorists, or those who harbour them, from gaining access to chemical, biological, radiological and nuclear (CBRN) weapons and missiles. G8 members call on all countries in the world to adhere to, fully comply with, and, as necessary, strengthen multilateral instruments such as the Nuclear Non-Proliferation Treaty, the Chemical Weapons Convention and the Biological and Toxin Weapons Convention. We are exchanging information and expertise on illicit flows of sensitive materials, taking measures to protect materials and facilities, and strengthening both national and international export controls against smuggling networks. We are supporting the enhanced counter-terrorist responsibility of the International Atomic Energy Agency and promoting wider adherence to safeguards. We are also fostering international non-proliferation efforts, including an initiative to dispose of plutonium no longer required for defence purposes.

Assisting Other Countries in Implementing Counter-terrorism Measures

However, implementing measures at home and strengthening the international regime are not enough. We are committed to assisting other countries to implement their UN counter-terrorism obligations. We are helping to build their capacity to fight terrorism through training, institution-building, cooperation among law enforcement and intelligence groups, and sharing technical expertise. We have been cooperating closely with the UN Counter-Terrorism Committee in these efforts and will continue to do so. We have developed new G8 Recommendations on Counter-terrorism, which we intend to promote in our outreach to other countries. These recommendations complement the G8 Recommendations on Transnational Crime released on May 14, by G8 Justice and Interior Ministers. Foreign Ministers request further work on counter-terrorism practices and standards.

Efforts to combat terrorism do not end here. Further action is required from all nations — individually and collectively — to sustain a truly effective global offensive against terrorism. We are committed to cooperating with the international community in this continuous effort to build a safer world.

Canadian Chair's Statement, G8 Foreign Ministers' Meeting

Whistler, 13 June 2002

1. G8 Foreign Ministers met in Whistler, June 12–13, to exchange views and coordinate action on a range of important global and regional issues. Discussions focused particularly on counterterrorism; Afghanistan; tensions between India and Pakistan; the conflict in the Middle East; Non-proliferation, Arms Control and Disarmament (NACD), including weapons of mass destruction (WMD); and the Balkans. We recognized the need to go beyond simply responding to crises and to address the problems of governance and development that can give rise to them.

Counter-Terrorism

2. On September 19 last year, following the terrorist attacks in the United States, and at the initiative of the Italian Presidency, G8 Leaders asked their Ministers to develop concrete measures to fight terrorism. Yesterday, we issued a Progress Report on the Fight Against Terrorism outlining actions we have taken since September 11, 2001. These efforts have been coordinated with work by Ministers of Finance, of Interior and Justice. We rededicated ourselves to defending our values and freedoms by continuing the fight against terrorism, which we agreed will require constant vigilance and effort. We stressed the importance of increased cooperation among G8 states to prevent terrorist access to chemical, biological, radiological and nuclear (CBRN) weapons. G8 members are also committed to assisting individual states or regions to build their capacity to fight terrorism, working closely with the United Nations and relevant regional organizations, and focusing on areas where the G8 can make a value-added contribution. In offering this assistance, we will coordinate our efforts to avoid duplication and ensure the best application of our expertise.

Afghanistan

3. G8 Foreign Ministers discussed the situation in Afghanistan, on which we issued a separate statement yesterday. We expressed our strong support for the emergency Loya Jirga currently underway in Afghanistan, and offered our congratulations

to Hamid Karzai for his election today in Kabul. We commend Chairman Karzai, his cabinet, and the Afghan people for the extraordinary progress they have made in the last months in rebuilding the Afghan state. The Loya Jirga is a vital step in the creation of a representative, inclusive and effective transitional authority and a critical step towards democratic elections due in 2004. We discussed the importance of responding to the needs identified by the Afghan authorities to build the governance structures essential for continued progress. In order to create the conditions for the provision of humanitarian relief and to enable longer term reconstruction efforts, the G8 has focused attention on security sector issues in Afghanistan. We have worked with the Afghan Interim Administration, the Special Representative of the Secretary-General, Lakhdar Brahimi, and the United Nations Assistance Mission in Afghanistan (UNAMA) to support efforts to demobilize and reintegrate former combatants, build a national army, create national and regional police forces, and to restore the justice sector. Particular attention has been given to addressing the challenges of opium production and trafficking in Afghanistan. We also recognized the importance of translating without delay the pledges made during the Tokyo Conference into concrete support to reinforce the positive transition in Afghanistan and to give hope to the Afghan people for a secure and stable future.

India-Pakistan

4. G8 Foreign Ministers discussed tensions between India and Pakistan and raised continuing concerns regarding the risk of conflict between these nuclear weapons capable nations, and the threat this would pose to regional and global security and stability. We stressed the need for a continued reduction of tensions and for political dialogue between the two parties. We reiterated our May 31 call for Pakistan to put a permanent stop to terrorist activity originating from territory under Pakistani control, and for both countries to continue to work with the international community to ensure that there will be a diplomatic solution to the current crisis. We are committed to continuing to work with India and Pakistan to deal with the fundamental problems underlying the current crisis and to sustaining coordinated diplomatic efforts in the region.

The Middle East

5. G8 Foreign Ministers discussed the situation in the Middle East and called for an immediate end to terrorism and violence. We reaffirmed the vision of a region where two states, Israel and Palestine, live side by side within secure and

recognized borders. We underlined our commitment to work together, and with the parties involved, to sustain the conditions for peace, prosperity and economic rehabilitation, dignity and security in the region. G8 Foreign Ministers welcomed the Arab League initiative adopted at its Summit in Beirut and the intention of the United States to convene an international conference on the Middle East.

Non-Proliferation, Arms Control, and Disarmament (NACD)

6. G8 Foreign Ministers discussed the changed international security environment and the challenge to global stability and security posed by the proliferation of weapons of mass destruction. We exchanged views on the international non-proliferation, arms control and disarmament agenda, and welcomed the recent agreement between the United States and Russia on reducing nuclear weapons. We agreed that these positive events provide an opportunity for progress in meeting other NACD challenges. In this regard, we reaffirmed the need to use all available instruments — from multilateral mechanisms and legally binding arrangements to export controls. With respect to plutonium dispositioning, we affirmed the importance of ensuring that excess military plutonium is rendered permanently unusable for nuclear weapons. Donors are working to complete negotiations for a multilateral framework for Russia's plutonium dispositioning program in 2003.

The Balkans

7. G8 Foreign Ministers noted the progress towards peace, stability, democracy, and regional cooperation in the Balkans designed to increase the capacity for effective governance. We expressed our continued support for a strong international presence in the region. We fully supported the benchmarks presented to the Security Council by the Special Representative of the Secretary-General for Kosovo. They will be important in fulfilling the objectives of Security Council Resolution 1244 and in building a democratic, multi-ethnic Kosovo.

Conflict Prevention

8. We fulfilled our Rome commitments of last year to find new ways to contribute to the prevention of conflicts, and in this respect experts completed their work on the management of shared water resources and on Disarmament, Demobilization, and Reintegration.

Other Regional Issues

9. G8 Foreign Ministers welcomed the resumption of talks aimed at achieving a just, viable and comprehensive settlement of the Cyprus problem. We urged the two Cypriot leaders, and all others concerned, to intensify the effort to reach agreement and to bridge the remaining obstacles towards a lasting settlement. We welcomed the United Nations Secretary-General's recent visit to Cyprus and endorsed his hope that an agreement could be reached soon and that the United Nations should play a full role in facilitating this objective.

10. G8 Foreign Ministers agreed that efforts to reduce tension and establish lasting peace on the Korean Peninsula should be further encouraged. We reiterated our support for the Republic of Korea's policy of engagement. We recognized the need to continue to urge the Democratic People's Republic of Korea to respond constructively to international concerns over security, non-proliferation and humanitarian issues.

11. We agreed to meet next during the United Nations General Assembly in New York in September.

G8 Initiative on Conflict and Development, G8 Foreign Ministers' Meeting

Whistler, 13 June 2002

Promoting Co-operative and Sustainable Management of Shared Water Resources

The G8 has repeatedly stressed the conflict potential of environmental and resource issues. Meeting in March 1999, G8 Environment Ministers noted that 'environmental degradation of resources, resource scarcity and subsequent sociopolitical impact are a potential threat to security as they may give rise to or exacerbate civil conflicts and conflicts between states'. Similarly, as part of its Miyazaki initiative for conflict prevention on 'Conflict and Development', the G8 'considers ways to use economic and development assistance to address causes of conflict stemming from competition for natural resources, such as water, and to encourage regional approaches to their management'.

Water is a basic human need and a key component of development — it is a fundamental resource for food production as well as for enhancing social well-being and providing for economic growth. It is also the lifeblood of the environment. Already today, it is a scarce resource in large parts of the world. It is estimated that about one-sixth of the world population lacks access to safe drinking water and one third lacks sanitation. If present trends continue, two out of every three people on Earth will live in countries considered to be 'water stressed' (Kofi Annan, Millenium Report, para 274). According to World Bank projections, by 2050 40% of the global population are likely to face some form of water shortage, with one in five suffering severe shortages. Global climate change could further exacerbate the problem. Against this backdrop, the G8 wishes to contribute to and promote a sustainable management of shared water resources. Acknowledging significant efforts by the international community to promote cooperation in the sphere of shared water resources, the G8 offers to share its experience and expertise with interested states and organizations of regional cooperation aimed at supporting shared water resources management.

The G8's approach to this issue is based on the following principles:

Prevention

Sound water management can mean more for all and reduce the potential for water-related conflicts. Nations must be committed to integrated water resources management at the basin level that provides for a sufficient and equitable supply of water for their citizens through sound and sustainable water policies.

Respect for Sovereignty

Successful conflict prevention in this area can only be achieved on the basis of respect of sovereignty of states directly involved, and of their specific historical, cultural and economic conditions.

Co-operation

Preventing conflicts over water as well as resolving them peacefully can only be achieved through mutually beneficial cooperation. The issue of joint management of shared waters thus not only poses a challenge but also serves as a catalyst for cooperation and offers an opportunity to build confidence and foster development.

Good Governance must ensure both transparent and participatory decision making in all water management related affairs, and just pricing that integrates social considerations, in order to provide water to the poor at affordable prices. Governments bear a major responsibility to ensure an efficient, sustainable and equitable supply of water for their citizens.

The G8

- draws attention to the conflict potential of an inadequate supply and distribution of water from shared water systems, and acknowledges the need to reinforce efforts aimed at preventing water shortages;
- encourages the international community to cooperate more closely and effectively to this end on a bi- and multilateral basis, and as appropriate with international and regional organizations such as UNDP, UN regional economic commissions and takes note of activities of such fora as the Global Water Partnership and the former World Commission on Dams;
- encourages riparian states to use water and all its uses as a catalyst for peace and to develop a common vision for the sustainable use and protection of shared water resources, including mechanisms for fair and effective dispute settlement;

- notes the 1992 UN/ECE Helsinki Convention on the Protection and Use of Transboundary Watercourses and International Lakes and the 1997 UN Convention on the Non-Navigational Use of International Watercourses for beneficial cross-border cooperation and encourages the elaboration of effective regional arrangements on shared water resources management issues;
- suggests to consider elaboration of regional or bilateral agreements that build on the Conventions and further its objectives by taking into account regional and local conditions;
- acknowledges OSCE initiatives for regional approaches to joint management of shared waters, e.g., in the framework of the 1999 '7th Economic Forum on Security Aspects in the Field of the Environment';
- welcomes the decision 6/1 'Strategic approaches to freshwater management' agreed at CSD6 and the Ministerial Declaration of The Hague on Water Security in the 21st Century embraces on 22 March 2000 in the framework of the Second World Water Forum and recognizes especially the results of the International Conference on Freshwater hosted by the Federal German Government from 3 to 7 December 2001 in Bonn, notably the Bonn Recommendations for Action, which provide an important input in all aspects of the sectoral theme of water;
- condemns deliberate destruction of elements of shared water systems infrastructure;
- considers that the World Summit on Sustainable Development in 2002 offers an opportunity to promote in a cooperative spirit the issue of freshwater supply and sanitation;
- supports activities leading to the International Year of Fresh Water (2003), and expects the Third World Water Forum to be hosted by Japan in March 2003 to be a good opportunity for further discussion on the possible actions for the sustainable development of water;
- values the utility of transboundary river commissions and will continue to support states in making full use of existing and creating new commissions;
- stresses the importance of partnership (including public-private partnerships) that involve local and regional stakeholders in water management schemes;
- will use development assistance to promote integrated water resources management and good governance in the field of shared water resources development, management, protection and use within states and between states.

Appendix O

G8 Conflict Prevention: Disarmament, Demobilisation, and Reintegration, G8 Foreign Ministers' Meeting

Whistler, 13 June 2002

1. Introduction

The G8 Miyazaki initiative on 'Small arms and light weapons' (SALW), emphasised the central importance of 'Disarmament, demobilisation and reintegration' (DDR) in post-conflict situations. The initiative on 'Conflict and development' recognised that peace and democratic stability are prerequisites for economic growth and sustainable development.

DDR is an important example of how this may work in practice. Once combatants cease to be involved in conflict and are reintegrated into society, substantial progress can be made towards the creation of a safe and secure environment thereby enabling poor communities to build better lives and work their way out of poverty. DDR thus makes a key contribution to peace building and sustainable development.

But reintegration is not only the end-result of disarmament and demobilisation. It is also the key to ensuring that disarmament and demobilisation take place in the first place and are maintained in the long term. As the Brahimi report noted, demobilised fighters 'tend to return to a life of violence if they find no legitimate livelihood, that is, if they are not 'reintegrated' into the local economy'. For this to happen successfully, both ex-combatants and the local community must feel secure, and there must be opportunities for employment that can be sustained in the long term. New work on DDR is beginning to recognise that DDR not only paves the way for development, but also relies on long-term development for its own success.

2. Conditions for Successful DDR

Past experience suggests some essential pre-conditions for successful DDR: a peace agreement with genuine commitment from all parties to the conflict; proper co-ordination and clear unambiguous leadership within the group of actors involved in DDR; and the personnel, material and financial resources to make it work. DDR could take place in the context of a peacekeeping operation mandated by the UN Security Council. In this regard, the Brahimi report recommended improved co-ordination between the relevant UN agencies and a greater role for DPKO in DDR. But there may also be occasions where regional organisations and NGOs can play a valuable role in DDR as part of post-conflict peace-building.

3. DDR

The availability of weapons and the resulting insecurity can have an adverse effect (both humanitarian and socio-economic) on the stability and development of a country. A key part of any DDR process is disarmament; weapons clearly need to be under the strictest of control and where appropriate, destroyed. Previous disarmament initiatives have had varied, often limited success. As part of its Miyazaki initiative on Small Arms and Light Weapons the G8 recognised that the availability of weapons, especially small arms and light weapons is an important factor in exacerbating conflict and that disarmament is therefore a priority. Unless another form of disposition has been officially authorised and such weapons have been marked, effective provisions for the collection, control, storage and destruction of SALW should be included in peace agreements.

But it is also particularly important to ensure that peace settlements include sufficient, preferably non-cash incentives to give parties the confidence to disarm in the first place. Ideally reintegration should offer incentives to soldiers to return to civilian life, including access to health and education programmes. There is a particular need to recognise the special requirements of women and child-combatants. But many who enter post-conflict DDR processes will want to rejoin the security forces, either police or military. Therefore a broader security sector reform is often critical in enabling the development of disciplined security forces accountable to civilian authority. Provisions should also be made for the rehabilitation of victims, many of whom are women and children. Broadly speaking, reintegration incentives should focus on the establishment of a visibly successful, long-term reintegration programme, which goes beyond military intervention and emergency humanitarian assistance into long term development assistance.

4. Conclusions

Recognising that it is important to see DDR in the wider context of peace building and development, the G8 endorses the importance of DDR as a key step in the process of moving from conflict to sustainable development.

More specifically:

- The G8 strongly supports the Programme of Action adopted by the United Nations Conference on the Illicit Trade in Small Arms and Light Weapons in All Its Aspects held in July 2001 in New York. The G8 supports efforts to ensure strong commitments and concrete initiatives framed in a comprehensive approach when implementing the commitments entered into under the Programme of Action.
- The G8 recognises the need to support initiatives that are designed to improve the organisational and operational aspects of DDR programmes and to ensure that such initiatives contribute to sustainable peace, security and development.
- The G8 recognises the pre-conditions for successful DDR and support the need for better co-ordination. A comprehensive plan of action should be drawn up covering the political framework, military operations, economic re-building, public and media services, and funding, as part of the process of improving co-ordination.
- The G8 acknowledges that peacekeeping missions, where appropriate, should include a post-conflict small arms and light weapons disarmament and destruction component.
- The G8 recognises the important role which the UN can play in promoting DDR programmes given its experience and activity in the fields of peacekeeping and post-conflict rehabilitation.
- The G8 recognises the role to be played by regional organisations in supporting DDR, as part of post-conflict peace-building, based on examples which include ECOMOG in Liberia and the potential for such support by OSCE in Nagorny Karabakh.
- The G8 accepts that peace-building activities such as DDR require skilled personnel to work on the ground for long periods of time and supports capacity building within both international institutions and non-governmental organisations in order to achieve this.
- The G8 recognises that lessons have been learnt from past-peacekeeping and peacebuilding missions and undertakes to support the important research and training efforts developed by DPKO and relevant peacekeeping missions including UNTAET. Best practices in approaching the reintegration of ex-combatants include:
- Taking account of the broad spectrum of political, economic, social, media, public service, civil society, military and other issues;
- Assessing, as soon as possible, the needs of former combatants and of the conflict-torn society itself;
- Providing realistic incentives which would also benefit the citizens affected by, but not engaged in, the conflict;
- Providing better donor co-ordination on activities to support reintegration programmes, including appropriate disbursement of funds.
- The G8 undertakes to support DDR programmes, through, inter alia, calling upon international institutions involved in DDR to ensure that a coherent and

comprehensive plan for any DDR exercise is mandated and developed drawing on the above lessons.
- The G8 undertakes to offer national expertise as required to strengthen the planning and implementation of activities as part of a coherent and comprehensive DDR plan.

Appendix P

G8 Recommendations on Counter-Terrorism, G8 Foreign Ministers' Meeting

Whistler, 13 June 2002

Preamble

The G8 attaches the highest importance to preventing and combating terrorism. To assist in the effort, the G8 have defined a series of principles which provide guidance to strengthen capacities to combat terrorism. The following recommendations are the result of a revision of the Counter-Terrorism Experts Group 25 Measures, adopted in Paris in 1996. The revision was initiated by the United States, conducted by the G8 Counter-Terrorism Experts Group (Roma Group), and coordinated by the Canadian Presidency.

The recommendations update the Counter-Terrorism Experts Group 25 Measures to address new terrorist threats as well as to complement the 40 Recommendations of the G8 crime group, known as the Lyon Group (1996). The Lyon Recommendations have also been modified in order to address more effectively the challenge of transnational crime threats. The revised Lyon Group Recommendations, now entitled the G8 Recommendations on Transnational Crime, were endorsed by G8 Ministers of Justice and the Interior (Mont-Tremblant, May 13–14, 2002).

These recommendations are intended to complement the work of experts in other regional organizations and international fora. This includes other experts groups of the G8 such as the Non-Proliferation Experts' Groups which has developed Principles to prevent terrorists, or those that harbour them, from gaining access to weapons of mass destruction, radiological weapons and missiles.

The following revised G8 Recommendations on Counter-Terrorism comprise standards, principles, best practices, actions and relationships that the G8 views as providing improvements to the mechanisms, procedures and networks that exist to protect our societies from terrorist threats. They are intended as commitments by the G8, which we commend as guiding principles to all States.

States should ensure that their strategies for combating terrorism are dynamic and sufficiently flexible and innovative to respond to the constantly changing challenges. We urge all States to join the G8 in the implementation of the following measures.

Section 1: Rapid Implementation of Existing Counter-Terrorism Instruments

We commit ourselves and urge all other States to:

1. Take actions to ensure, as rapidly as possible, full adherence to the following instruments relating to the prevention and suppression of terrorism:
    a. the twelve United Nations conventions and protocols addressing counter-terrorism issues listed in the annex;
    b. all relevant United Nations Security Council Resolutions, in particular, United Nations Security Council Resolution 1373 (2001); and,
2. Become a party, if entitled, to the Council of Europe's Convention on Cybercrime (2001), ensuring full and rapid implementation of its terms, or, ensure the availability of a legal framework approximating the measures called for in the Convention, as it provides useful measures to combat attacks by terrorists and other criminals on computer systems, as well as to gather electronic evidence of terrorism and other crimes.

Section 2: Support for Additional Multilateral Counter-Terrorism Initiatives and Instruments

We commit ourselves and urge all other States to:

1. Work within the United Nations system to complete the draft UN Comprehensive Convention on International Terrorism, and coordinate our efforts in this regard.
2. Promote appropriate action in multilateral organizations of which we are members, including at the regional level, in order to usefully supplement counter-terrorism measures already taken or under development at the global level.

Section 3: Chemical, Biological, Radiological, Nuclear Weapons

We commit ourselves and urge all other States to:

1.
    a. With respect to ensuring effective action against the use of biological weapons by terrorists, make crimes the offences established in the Biological and Toxin Weapons Convention (1972), prosecute such crimes or, where appropriate, extradite individuals, in accordance with national law and bilateral extradition agreements, and work cooperatively to develop best practices to deter and detect such offences.
    b. Take measures to work cooperatively to develop effective mechanisms to track and curb the illicit possession and transfer of selected biological agents both domestically and internationally, and to explore additional measures to prevent biological agents from being used to commit terrorist attacks.

3. Work within the United Nations system to complete work on the draft International Convention for the Suppression of Acts of Nuclear Terrorism and strengthen our cooperative efforts to this end.
4. Support ongoing negotiations to strengthen the 1980 Convention on the Physical Protection of Nuclear Material and explore together potential additional international measures to advance its ends and investigate enhanced measures aimed at the problem of nuclear smuggling.
5. Work cooperatively to develop, in appropriate international fora, best practices to ensure the protection of chemical, biological, radiological, nuclear and related infrastructures against terrorist actions, and explore means to prevent sensitive information pertaining to these infrastructures from being used by terrorists for targeting purposes.
6. Coordinate efforts and encourage support in other fora where concerted CBRN prevention programs are underway, such as at the International Atomic Energy Agency (IAEA).
7. Develop best practice guidelines for contingency planning at national levels and strengthen existing arrangements for crisis response.

Section 4: Explosives and Firearms

We commit ourselves and urge all other States to:
1. Accelerate research and development of methods of detection of explosives and weapons and other harmful substances that cause death or injury, and undertake consultations on the development of standards for marking explosives in order to identify their origin in post-blast investigations, and to promote cooperation, where appropriate.
2. Adopt effective domestic laws and regulations including export controls to govern manufacture, trading, transport, and export of firearms, explosives, or any device designed to cause violent injury, damage, or destruction, in order to prevent their use for terrorists' acts.

Section 5: Financing of Terrorism

We commit ourselves and urge all other States to:
1. As rapidly as possible, ensure full implementation of the United Nations Security Council Resolution 1373, the International Convention for the Suppression of the Financing of Terrorism and the Financial Action Task Force's (FATF) Special Recommendations on Terrorist Financing (2001), and participate in the fulfilment of the FATF global action plans.

2. Adopt the steps to remove obstacles to effective common action to combat terrorist financing contained in the Report of the G8 Meeting on Legal Measures to Combat Terrorist Financing (2002), endorsed by G8 Justice and Interior Ministers (2002), and move beyond freezing to also forfeit terrorist assets in order to permanently deprive terrorists of their funds.
3. Implement the recommendations on 'Money Laundering, Related Terrorist Financing and Asset Forfeiture' contained in the G8 Recommendations on Transnational Crime (2002).
4. Facilitate, through appropriate domestic measures, the traceability of terrorist funds and ensure that mutual legal assistance is not refused on the grounds of bank secrecy or that the request involves a fiscal offence.

Section 6: Transportation Security

We commit ourselves and urge all other States to:
1. Maintain strong financial support through voluntary contributions for the International Civil Aviation Organization (ICAO) aviation security activities to fulfil its standards and recommended practices with a view to deterring and detecting terrorism.
2. Cooperate in conducting an expeditious review of aviation security conventions, international standards and recommended practices in the ICAO, with a view to updating such standards in order to deter and detect terrorism, including by applying mechanisms referred to [in] the G8 Recommendations on Transnational Crime.
3. Work as expeditiously as possible towards implementation of a common global standard for the collection and transmission of advance passenger information (API).
4. Enhance their abilities to share timely information internationally with law enforcement and other appropriate counterparts, in accordance with applicable laws, with respect to passengers concerning whom there are specific and serious reasons to consider they may engage in a terrorist act.
5. Work closely with each other and the International Maritime Organization (IMO) in order to improve the capability of governments to deter and prosecute terrorist attacks on maritime vessels or the use of such vessels to further terrorist activities.
6. Cooperate in conducting an expeditious review of maritime safety conventions, international standards and recommended practices in the IMO, with a view to updating such standards in order to deter and detect terrorism.
7. Work with relevant international organizations to develop and implement an improved global container security regime to identify and examine high-risk containers, their in-transit integrity, implement the global common standards for electronic customs reporting, and work within the World Customs Organization

(WCO) on advance information pertaining to containers as early as possible in the trade chain.

8. Urgently intensify consultations among transport security and other relevant officials to improve the capability of governments to prevent, investigate, and respond to terrorist attacks on modes of mass ground transportation, such as railway, underground and bus transport systems, and to cooperate with other governments in this regard.

Section 7: Internal Co-ordination against Terrorism

We commit ourselves and urge all other States to:
* Strengthen internal cooperation between various national agencies and services which may deal with different aspects of counter-terrorism.

Section 8: International Co-operation

We commit ourselves and urge all other States to:
1. Take all possible measures to deny safe havens to those who finance, plan, support, or commit terrorist acts, or provide safe havens.
2. Ensure, in conformity with international law and, in particular, the 1951 Convention Relating to the Status of Refugees and its 1967 Protocol, that refugee status is not abused by the perpetrators, organizers or facilitators of terrorist acts.
3. Identify and eliminate obstacles to extradition to the greatest extent possible, including those referred to in 'Part II: Enhancing International Cooperation' of the G8 Recommendations on Transnational Crime (2002).
4. Take strong measures, including relevant legislative measures if necessary, in cooperation with other countries, to prevent terrorist acts and the international movement of terrorists by strengthening, inter alia, border, immigration, and travel document control and information sharing.

   Attach special priority to mutual legal assistance and law enforcement cooperation with respect to terrorism offences in order to ensure a quick and effective response, including those referred to in the recommendations on 'Mutual Legal Assistance and Law Enforcement Channels' of the G8 Recommendations on Transnational Crime (2002).
5. Develop effective measures for obtaining the rapid freezing, seizing and confiscation of assets related to terrorist activities.
6. Ensure that claims of political motivation are not recognized as grounds for refusing requests for the extradition of alleged terrorists and, exclude or reduce to the greatest possible extent any application of the political offence exception in responding to a request for mutual legal assistance concerning terrorist offences.

Section 9: Links between Terrorism and Transnational Crime

We commit ourselves and urge all other States to:
1.
    a. Ensure that an effective framework is in place to fight against transnational crimes that can support or facilitate terrorist activity, such as that provided by the G8 Recommendations on Transnational Crime (2002).

    b. Examine and exchange information to determine the nature of links between terrorism and transnational crime, in particular, of the manner in which terrorist organizations can support their activities through the commission of other crimes, and develop strategies, as required, to enable concerted effort to disrupt and disable such activities.

2. Support the efforts of the United Nations International Drug Control Programme (UNDCP) and its donors to coordinate counter-narcotics assistance in combating the drug trade in and emanating from Afghanistan, to strengthen the 'security belts' around it and to maximize the effectiveness of UNDCP programmes in the region.

Section 10: Outreach to Non-G8 States

We commit ourselves and urge all other States to:
1. Conduct outreach, including technical assistance, to other countries, in coordination with each other and with other parts of the G8 structure as well as regional organizations, with a view to building capacity to implement UNSCR 1373, the twelve United Nations counter-terrorism conventions and protocols listed in the annex, the Roma Group counter-terrorism recommendations, and the G8 Recommendations on Transnational Crime (2002), for the purpose of combating terrorism-related activities.
2. As appropriate, develop best practices to facilitate such outreach and cooperate closely on capacity building and outreach with the United Nations Security Council's Counter-Terrorism Committee (UNSC CTC).
3. Develop additional measures, in cooperation with international organizations and civil society, to increase the awareness of all i0ndividuals that any act or threat of terrorism represents a serious crime with appropriate penalties.

Annex: United Nations Conventions and Protocols Addressing Counter-Terrorism

1. Convention on Offences and Certain Other Acts Committed on Board Aircraft, done at Tokyo, on 14 September 1963.
2. Convention for the Suppression of Unlawful Seizure of Aircraft, done at The Hague on 16 December 1970.

3. Convention for the Suppression of Unlawful Acts against the Safety of Civil Aviation, done at Montreal on 23 September 1971.
4. Convention on the Prevention and Punishment of Crimes against Internationally Protected Persons, including Diplomatic Agents, adopted by the General Assembly of the United Nations on 14 December 1973.
5. International Convention against the Taking of Hostages, adopted by the General Assembly of the United Nations on 17 December 1979.
6. Convention on the Physical Protection of Nuclear Material, adopted at Vienna on 3 March 1980.
7. Protocol for the Suppression of Unlawful Acts of Violence at Airports Serving International Civil Aviation, supplementary to the Convention for the Suppression of Unlawful Acts against the Safety of Civil Aviation, done at Montreal on 24 February 1988.
8. Convention for the Suppression of Unlawful Acts against the Safety of Maritime Navigation, done at Rome on 10 March 1988.
9. Protocol for the Suppression of Unlawful Acts against the Safety of Fixed Platform located on the Continental Shelf, done at Rome on 10 March 1988.
10. Convention on the Marking of Plastic Explosives for the Purpose of Detection, done at Montreal on 1 March 1991.
11. International Convention for the Suppression of Terrorist Bombings, adopted by the General Assembly of the United Nations on 15 December 1997.
12. International Convention for the Suppression of the Financing of Terrorism, adopted by the General Assembly of the United Nations on 9 December 1999.

Appendix Q

Co-operative G8 Action on Transport Security

Kananaskis, 26 June 2002

The terrorist attacks on September 11, 2001 illustrated the critical yet fragile nature of the international transport system. For the global economy to flourish, this system must continue to provide safe, secure, efficient and reliable services to travellers and customers in all parts of the world.

We have therefore agreed on a set of cooperative actions to promote greater security of land, sea and air transport while facilitating the cost-effective and efficient flow of people, cargo, and vehicles for legitimate economic and social purposes. The G8 will:

People

- Implement as expeditiously as possible a common global standard based on UN EDIFACT for the collection and transmission of advance passenger information (API).
- Work towards granting reciprocal bilateral access, on a voluntary basis, to departure and transit lounges, including timely implementation of a pilot project.
- Work towards agreement by October 2002 on minimum standards for issuance of travel and identity documents for adoption at ICAO, and by June 2003 on minimum standards for issuance of seafarers' identity documents for adoption at the ILO.
- Work towards developing recommendations on minimum standards for the application of biometrics in procedures and documents by the spring of 2003, with a view to forwarding them to standards organizations.
- Improve procedures and practices for sharing data on lost or stolen passports and denied entries, with a practical exercise by September 2002.

Container Security

- Recognizing the urgency of securing global trade, work expeditiously, in cooperation with relevant international organizations, to develop and implement an improved global container security regime to identify and examine high-risk containers and ensure their in-transit integrity.

- Develop, in collaboration with interested non-G8 countries, pilot projects that model an integrated container security regime.
- Implement expeditiously, by 2005 wherever possible, common standards for electronic customs reporting, and work in the WCO to encourage the implementation of the same common standards by non-G8 countries.
- Begin work expeditiously within the G8 and the WCO to require advance electronic information pertaining to containers, including their location and transit, as early as possible in the trade chain.

Aviation Security

- Accelerate implementation of standards for reinforced flight deck doors for all G8 passenger aircraft, by April 2003 wherever possible.
- Support in ICAO the rapid implementation of mandatory aviation security audits of all ICAO contracting states.
- Enhance cooperation, in a spirit of capacity-building assistance, on aviation security with other countries. The G8 will also share their information and assessments about security vulnerabilities.
- Encourage non-G8 countries to make, as we have done, proportionate contributions to the ICAO AVSEC mechanism, and encourage MDBs to consider requests to assist developing countries in this area.

Maritime Security

- Support, in the IMO, amendment of the International Convention for the Safety of Life at Sea (SOLAS) to accelerate the date of the installation of automatic identification systems (AIS) on certain ships to December 2004.*
- Support, in the IMO, amendment of the International Convention for the Safety of Life at Sea (SOLAS) to require mandatory ship security plans and ship security officers on board ships by July 2004.
- Support, in the IMO, amendment of the International Convention for the Safety of Life at Sea (SOLAS) to require mandatory port facility security plans and port facility security assessments for relevant ports serving ships engaged on international voyages by July 2004.*

Land Transportation

• Develop, in the UN and other relevant international organizations, an effective and proportionate security regime for the overland transportation and distribution of hazardous cargoes which present potentially significant security risks, with initial consultations this year.

Implementation

In order to ensure timely implementation of this initiative, we will review progress every six months, providing direction as required to G8 experts. G8 experts will pursue these priorities and will promote policy coherence and coordination in all relevant international organizations (ICAO, IMO, WCO, ILO), in partnership with industry.

* The Government of the Russian Federation supports the proposal concerning installation of AIS on certain ships by December 2004, as well as the proposal concerning availability of port facility security plans and port facility security assessments for relevant ports serving ships engaged on international voyages by July 2004. However, on grounds of technical feasibility of these proposals, the Russian Federation reserves for itself the right to extend the timeframe of their implementation by the year 2006.

Appendix R

The Kananaskis Summit Chair's Summary

Kananaskis, 27 June 2002

We met in Kananaskis for our annual Summit to discuss the challenges of fighting terrorism, strengthening global economic growth and sustainable development, and building a new partnership for Africa's development.

This was our first meeting since the terrible events of September 11. We discussed the threat posed to innocent citizens and our societies by terrorists and those who support them.

- We are committed to sustained and comprehensive actions to deny support or sanctuary to terrorists, to bring terrorists to justice, and to reduce the threat of terrorist attacks.
- We agreed on a set of six non-proliferation Principles aimed at preventing terrorists — or those who harbour them — from acquiring or developing nuclear, chemical, radiological and biological weapons; missiles; and related materials, equipment or technologies. We called on other countries to join us in implementing these Principles.
- We launched a new G8 Global Partnership Against the Spread of Weapons and Materials of Mass Destruction, under which we will undertake cooperative projects on the basis of agreed guidelines. We committed to raise up to US$ 20 billion to support such projects over the next ten years.
- We agreed on a new initiative with clear deadlines — Cooperative G8 Action on Transport Security — to strengthen the security and efficiency of the global transportation system.

We discussed the outlook for global economic growth and employment, and the challenges of poverty reduction and sustainable development. We expressed confidence in our economies and in the prospects for global growth. We agreed on the fundamental importance of strong political leadership for the success of economic reforms in our own economies. We support emerging market countries, including Brazil and others in Latin America, in their efforts to implement sound economic policies.

- We agreed to resist protectionist pressures and stressed our commitment to work with developing countries to ensure the successful conclusion of the Doha Development Agenda by January 1, 2005.

- We agreed on the importance of reaffirming the Doha Agenda and the Monterrey Consensus and to work at the upcoming Johannesburg Summit to produce meaningful partnerships for sustainable development and measurable results. We recognized that climate change is a pressing issue that requires a global solution, and we discussed the problem of deforestation.
- We will fund our share of the shortfall in the enhanced HIPC initiative, recognizing that this shortfall will be up to US $1 billion. We stressed the importance of good governance in countries benefiting from HIPC debt relief.
- We reviewed implementation of the DOT Force's Genoa Plan of Action and welcomed its initiatives to strengthen developing countries' readiness for e-development, such as the e-model to improve the efficiency of public administrations and to enhance the transparency of national budgeting.
- We adopted a series of recommendations to assist developing countries to achieve universal primary education for all children and equal access to education for girls. We agreed to increase significantly our bilateral assistance for countries that have demonstrated a strong and credible policy and financial commitment to these goals.

We met with the Presidents of Algeria, Nigeria, Senegal and South Africa, and the Secretary General of the United Nations, to discuss the challenges faced by Africa and the G8's response to the New Partnership for Africa's Development (NEPAD).

- We adopted the G8 Africa Action Plan as a framework for action in support of the NEPAD. We agreed to each establish enhanced partnerships with African countries whose performance reflects the NEPAD commitments.
- Assuming strong African policy commitments, and given recent assistance trends, we believe that in aggregate half or more of our new development assistance commitments announced at Monterrey could be directed to African nations that govern justly, invest in their own people and promote economic freedom.
- We underlined the devastating consequences for Africa's development of diseases such as malaria, tuberculosis and HIV/AIDS. In addition to our ongoing commitments to combat these diseases, we committed to provide sufficient resources to eradicate polio by 2005.
- We agreed to work with African partners to deliver a joint plan by 2003 for the development of African capability to undertake peace support operations.
- We will continue our dialogue with our African partners. At our next Summit, we will review progress on the implementation of the G8 Africa Action Plan on the basis of a final report from our Personal Representatives for Africa.

Finally, we discussed several regional issues that have significant implications for international peace and security.

- We stressed our commitment to work for peace in the Middle East, based on our vision of two states, Israel and Palestine, living side by side within secure and recognized borders. We agreed on the urgency of reform of Palestinian institutions and its economy, and of free and fair elections.
- We support the Transitional Authority of Afghanistan. We will fulfil our Tokyo Conference commitments and will work to eradicate opium production and trafficking.
- We discussed the tensions between India and Pakistan. We agreed that Pakistan must put a permanent stop to terrorist activity originating from territory under its control. Both countries should commit to sustained dialogue on the underlying issues that divide them.

We welcomed the offer of the President of France to host our next Summit in June 2003. We agreed that Russia will assume the 2006 G8 Presidency and will host our annual Summit that year.

The G8 Global Partnership against the Spread of Weapons and Materials of Mass Destruction

Kananaskis, 27 June 2002

The attacks of September 11 demonstrated that terrorists are prepared to use any means to cause terror and inflict appalling casualties on innocent people. We commit ourselves to prevent terrorists, or those that harbour them, from acquiring or developing nuclear, chemical, radiological and biological weapons; missiles; and related materials, equipment and technology. We call on all countries to join us in adopting the set of non-proliferation principles we have announced today.

In a major initiative to implement those principles, we have also decided today to launch a new G8 Global Partnership against the Spread of Weapons and Materials of Mass Destruction. Under this initiative, we will support specific cooperation projects, initially in Russia, to address non-proliferation, disarmament, counter-terrorism and nuclear safety issues. Among our priority concerns are the destruction of chemical weapons, the dismantlement of decommissioned nuclear submarines, the disposition of fissile materials and the employment of former weapons scientists. We will commit to raise up to $20 billion to support such projects over the next ten years. A range of financing options, including the option of bilateral debt for program exchanges, will be available to countries that contribute to this Global Partnership. We have adopted a set of guidelines that will form the basis for the negotiation of specific agreements for new projects, that will apply with immediate effect, to ensure effective and efficient project development, coordination and implementation. We will review over the next year the applicability of the guidelines to existing projects.

Recognizing that this Global Partnership will enhance international security and safety, we invite other countries that are prepared to adopt its common principles and guidelines to enter into discussions with us on participating in and contributing to this initiative. We will review progress on this Global Partnership at our next Summit in 2003.

The G8 Global Partnership: Principles to Prevent Terrorists, or Those That Harbour Them, from Gaining Access to Weapons or Materials of Mass Destruction

The G8 calls on all countries to join them in commitment to the following six principles to prevent terrorists or those that harbour them from acquiring or developing nuclear, chemical, radiological and biological weapons; missiles; and related materials, equipment and technology.

1. Promote the adoption, universalization, full implementation and, where necessary, strengthening of multilateral treaties and other international instruments whose aim is to prevent the proliferation or illicit acquisition of such items; strengthen the institutions designed to implement these instruments.

2. Develop and maintain appropriate effective measures to account for and secure such items in production, use, storage and domestic and international transport; provide assistance to states lacking sufficient resources to account for and secure these items.

3. Develop and maintain appropriate effective physical protection measures applied to facilities which house such items, including defence in depth; provide assistance to states lacking sufficient resources to protect their facilities.

4. Develop and maintain effective border controls, law enforcement efforts and international cooperation to detect, deter and interdict in cases of illicit trafficking in such items, for example through installation of detection systems, training of customs and law enforcement personnel and cooperation in tracking these items; provide assistance to states lacking sufficient expertise or resources to strengthen their capacity to detect, deter and interdict in cases of illicit trafficking in these items.

5. Develop, review and maintain effective national export and transshipment controls over items on multilateral export control lists, as well as items that are not identified on such lists but which may nevertheless contribute to the development, production or use of nuclear, chemical and biological weapons and missiles, with particular consideration of end-user, catch-all and brokering aspects; provide assistance to states lacking the legal and regulatory infrastructure, implementation experience and/or resources to develop their export and transshipment control systems in this regard.

6. Adopt and strengthen efforts to manage and dispose of stocks of fissile materials designated as no longer required for defence purposes, eliminate all chemical weapons, and minimize holdings of dangerous biological pathogens and toxins, based on the recognition that the threat of terrorist acquisition is reduced as the overall quantity of such items is reduced.

The G8 Global Partnership: Guidelines for New or Expanded Co-operation Projects

The G8 will work in partnership, bilaterally and multilaterally, to develop, coordinate, implement and finance, according to their respective means, new or expanded cooperation projects to address (i) non-proliferation, (ii) disarmament, (iii) counter-terrorism and (iv) nuclear safety (including environmental) issues, with a view to enhancing strategic stability, consonant with our international security objectives and in support of the multilateral non-proliferation regimes. Each country has primary responsibility for implementing its non-proliferation, disarmament, counter-terrorism and nuclear safety obligations and requirements and commits its full cooperation within the Partnership.

Cooperation projects under this initiative will be decided and implemented, taking into account international obligations and domestic laws of participating partners, within appropriate bilateral and multilateral legal frameworks that should, as necessary, include the following elements:

i.   Mutually agreed effective monitoring, auditing and transparency measures and procedures will be required in order to ensure that cooperative activities meet agreed objectives (including irreversibility as necessary), to confirm work performance, to account for the funds expended and to provide for adequate access for donor representatives to work sites;

ii. The projects will be implemented in an environmentally sound manner and will maintain the highest appropriate level of safety;

iii. Clearly defined milestones will be developed for each project, including the option of suspending or terminating a project if the milestones are not met;

iv. The material, equipment, technology, services and expertise provided will be solely for peaceful purposes and, unless otherwise agreed, will be used only for the purposes of implementing the projects and will not be transferred. Adequate measures of physical protection will also be applied to prevent theft or sabotage;

v.   All governments will take necessary steps to ensure that the support provided will be considered free technical assistance and will be exempt from taxes, duties, levies and other charges;

vi. Procurement of goods and services will be conducted in accordance with open international practices to the extent possible, consistent with national security requirements;

vii. All governments will take necessary steps to ensure that adequate liability protections from claims related to the cooperation will be provided for donor countries and their personnel and contractors;

viii. Appropriate privileges and immunities will be provided for government donor representatives working on cooperation projects; and

ix. Measures will be put in place to ensure effective protection of sensitive information and intellectual property.

Given the breadth and scope of the activities to be undertaken, the G8 will establish an appropriate mechanism for the annual review of progress under this initiative which may include consultations regarding priorities, identification of project gaps and potential overlap, and assessment of consistency of the cooperation projects with international security obligations and objectives. Specific bilateral and multilateral project implementation will be coordinated subject to arrangements appropriate to that project, including existing mechanisms.

For the purposes of these guidelines, the phrase 'new or expanded cooperation projects' is defined as cooperation projects that will be initiated or enhanced on the basis of this Global Partnership. All funds disbursed or released after its announcement would be included in the total of committed resources. A range of financing options, including the option of bilateral debt for program exchanges, will be available to countries that contribute to this Global Partnership.

The Global Partnership's initial geographic focus will be on projects in Russia, which maintains primary responsibility for implementing its obligations and requirements within the Partnership.

In addition, the G8 would be willing to enter into negotiations with any other recipient countries, including those of the Former Soviet Union, prepared to adopt the guidelines, for inclusion in the Partnership.

Recognizing that the Global Partnership is designed to enhance international security and safety, the G8 invites others to contribute to and join in this initiative.

With respect to nuclear safety and security, the partners agreed to establish a new G8 Nuclear Safety and Security Group by the time of our next Summit.

Appendix T

Statement by G8 Foreign Ministers in Connection with Terrorist Hostage Taking in Moscow

25 October 2002

We, the G8 Foreign Ministers, most resolutely condemn the hostage taking in Moscow, a terrorist act that can have no justification. We express our solidarity with the citizens of Russia and those of other countries held by the terrorists. We express support for, and sympathy with, their relatives. We call for the immediate and unconditional release of the hostages.

Terrorism openly challenges all of humanity. The Moscow hostage taking is another in a series of recent terrorist acts throughout the world. We will not allow such events to go unchecked. We are united in combatting terrorism.

As it was decided at the G8 Kananaskis Summit, we will step up our cooperation in the fight against international terrorism and will accelerate implementation of the initiatives upon which we have agreed. We stand ready to cooperate with other nations in strengthening their anti-terrorist capabilities.

We are determined to fight terrorism decisively and unconditionally in all its forms and manifestations.

Bibliography

Ackermann, Alice (2003). 'The Idea and Practice of Conflict Prevention'. *Peace Research* vol. 40, no. 3, pp. 339–347.

Ahmed, Ismail and Michael Lipton (1997). 'Impact of Structural Adjustment on Sustainable Rural Livelihoods: A Review of the Literature'. IDS Working Papers No. 62. Institute of Development Studies, Sussex. <www.ids.ac.uk/ids/bookshop/wp/wp62.pdf> (July 2003).

Ahtisaari, Martti (2001). 'EU's Civilian Crisis Management Capability: How to Make It Credible?' 4 April, Studia Generalia Fennica, Brussels. <www.ahtisaari.fi/?content=speech&id=5> (July 2003).

Alesina, Alberto and David Dollar (2000). 'Who Gives Foreign Aid to Whom and Why?' *Journal of Economic Growth* vol. 5, no. 1, pp. 33–63.

Alesina, Alberto and Beatrice Weder (1999). 'Do Corrupt Governments Receive Less Foreign Aid?' NBER Working Paper No. 7108. <papers.nber.org/papers/w7108> (July 2003).

Aliboni, Roberto, Laura Guazzone, and Daniela Pioppi (2001). 'Early Warning and Conflict Prevention in the Euro-Med Area'. Istituto Affari Internazionali Occasional Papers No. 2.

Alwang, Jeffrey, Paul B. Siegel, and Steen L. Jorgensen (2001). 'Vulnerability: A View from Different Disciplines'. Social Protection Working Paper No. 23304. World Bank, Washington DC.

Anderson, Mary B. (1999). *Do No Harm: How Aid Can Support Peace — or War*. Lynne Rienner, Boulder, CO.

Applebaum, Anne (2003). 'Here Comes the New Europe'. *Washington Post*, 29 January.

Aron, Raymond (1966). *Peace and War*. Doubleday, New York.

Ashley, Richard (1986). 'The Poverty of Neorealism'. In R. O. Keohane, ed., *Neorealism and Its Critics*, pp. 255–300. Columbia University Press, New York.

Askari, Hossein and Catherine Brown (2001). 'Water Management, Middle East Peace, and a Role for the World Bank'. *Banca Nazionale del Lavoro Quarterly Review* vol. 54, no. 216, pp. 3–36.

Attali, Jacques (1995). *Verbatim III*. Fayard, Paris.

Backhurst, Jane (2001). 'The Rapid Reaction Facility: Good News for Those in Crisis?' 18 January, Voluntary Organisations in Cooperation in Emergencies. <www.reliefweb.int/w/rwb.nsf/0/dcfc869a75eb8314c12569dc005b2128? OpenDocument> (July 2003).

Baulch, Bob and John Hoddinott (2000). 'Economic Mobility and Poverty Dynamics in Developing Countries'. *Journal of Development Studies* vol. 36, no. 5, pp. 1–24.

Bayne, Nicholas (1999). 'Continuity and Leadership in an Age of Globalisation'. In M. R. Hodges, J. J. Kirton and J. P. Daniels, eds., *The G8's Role in the New Millennium*, pp. 21–44. Ashgate, Aldershot.

Bayne, Nicholas (2000). *Hanging In There: The G7 and G8 Summit in Maturity and Renewal.* Ashgate, Aldershot.

Bayne, Nicholas (2001). 'The G7 and Multilateral Trade Liberalisation: Past Performance, Future Challenges'. In J. J. Kirton and G. M. von Furstenberg, eds., *New Directions in Global Economic Governance: Managing Globalisation in the Twenty-First Century,* pp. 23–38. Ashgate, Aldershot.

Bayne, Nicholas (2001). 'G8 Decision-making and the Genoa Summit'. *International Spectator* vol. 36, July-September, pp. 69–75.

Bayne, Nicholas (2001). 'Managing Globalisation and the New Economy: The Contribution of the G8 Summit'. In J. J. Kirton and G. M. von Furstenberg, eds., *New Directions in Global Economic Governance: Managing Globalisation in the Twenty-First Century,* pp. 171–188. Ashgate, Aldershot.

Bayne, Nicholas (2002). 'Impressions of the Genoa Summit, 20–22 July, 2001'. In M. Fratianni, P. Savona and J. J. Kirton, eds., *Governing Global Finance: New Challenges, G7 and IMF Contributions,* pp. 199–210. Ashgate, Aldershot.

Bayne, Nicholas (2003). 'Are World Leaders Puppets or Puppeteers? The Sherpas of the G7/G8 System'. In B. Reinalda and B. Verbeek, eds., *Decision Making within International Organizations.* Routledge, London.

Bayne, Nicholas (2003). 'Impressions of the Evian Summit'. <www.g7.utoronto.ca/evaluations/2003evian/assess_bayne030603.html> (July 2003).

Bayne, Nicholas (2003). 'Impressions of the Kananaskis Summit'. In M. Fratianni, P. Savona and J. J. Kirton, eds., *Sustaining Global Growth and Development: G7 and IMF Governance,* pp. 229–240. Ashgate, Aldershot.

Bergsten, C. Fred and C. Randall Henning (1996). *Global Economic Leadership and the Group of Seven.* Institute for International Economics, Washington DC.

Boone, Peter (1996). 'Politics and the Effectiveness of Foreign Aid'. *European Economic Review* vol. 40, no. 2, pp. 289–329.

Bordo, Michael D. and Harold James (2000). 'The International Monetary Fund: Its Present Role in Historical Perspective'. In A. H. Meltzer, ed., *Expert Papers.* International Financial Institution Advisory Commission, Washington DC.

Boucher, Jerry, Dan Landis, and Karen Arnold Clark, eds. (1987). *Ethnic Conflict: International Perspectives.* Sage Publications, Beverly Hills and London.

Bredel, Ralf (2003). 'The UN's Long-Term Conflict Prevention Strategies and the Impact of Counter-Terrorism'. *International Peacekeeping* vol. 10, no. 2, pp. 51–75.

Breines, Ingeborg, Robert W. Connell, and Ingrid Eide, eds. (2000). *Male Roles, Masculinities, and Violence: A Culture of Peace Perspective.* UNESCO, Paris.

Brilmayer, Lea (1989). *Justifying International Acts.* Cornell University Press, Ithaca.

Brown, Michael, ed. (1996). *The International Dimensions of Internal Conflict.* MIT Press, Cambridge, MA.

Brown, Michael and Richard Rosecrance, eds. (1999). *The Costs of Conflict, Prevention, and Cure in the Global Arena.* Rowman and Littlefield, Lanham, MD.

Budd, Colin (2002). 'G8 Summits and Their Preparation'. In N. Bayne and S. Woolcock, eds., *The New Economic Diplomacy: Decision-Making and Negotiation in International Economic Relations*, pp. 139–146. Ashgate, Aldershot.

Burnside, Craig and David Dollar (2000). 'Aid, Policies, and Growth'. *American Economic Review* vol. 90, no. 4, pp. 847–868.

Burton, John W. (1984). *Global Conflict: The Domestic Sources of International Crisis.* Wheatsheaf Books, Brighton, UK.

Burton, John W. (1990). *Conflict: Human Needs Theory.* St. Martin's Press, New York.

Burton, John W. (1990). *Conflict: Resolution and Prevention.* St. Martin's Press, New York.

Calvo, Guillermo A. and Carmen M. Reinhart (2000). 'Fear of Floating'. NBER Working Paper No. 7993, November. <papers.nber.org/papers/W7993> (January 2002).

Calvo, Guillermo A. and Carmen M. Reinhart (2000). 'Fixing for Your Life'. NBER Working Paper No. 8006. <papers.nber.org/papers/W8006> (July 2003).

Carey, Henry F., ed. (2003). 'Mitigating Conflict: The Role of NGOs'. Special Issue. *International Peacekeeping* vol. 10, no. 1.

Carment, David and Albrecht Schnabel, eds. (2001). *Conflict Prevention: Path to Peace or Grand Illusion?* United Nations University Press, Tokyo.

Carnegie Commission on Preventing Deadly Conflict (1997). 'Preventing Deadly Conflict: Final Report'. Carnegie Commission on Preventing Deadly Conflict, Washington DC.

Cater, Charles K. and Karin Wermester (2000). 'From Reaction to Prevention: Opportunities for the UN System in the New Millennium'. Report based on the international policy conference on the prevention of violent conflict, International Peace Academy, New York, 13–14 April. <www.ipacademy.org/Publications/Reports/Research/PublRepoReseUNSyPrint.htm> (July 2003).

Chandrasekaran, Rajiv (2000). 'Christian-Muslim Conflict Rages in Indonesia's East'. *International Herald Tribune*, 20 June.

Charny, Israel W., ed. (1978). *Strategies against Violence: Design for Nonviolent Change.* Westview Press, Boulder, CO.

Chayes, Abram and Antonia Handler Chayes (1996). *Preventing Conflict in the Post-Communist World: Mobilizing International and Regional Organizations.* Brookings Institution, Washington DC.

Chesterman, Simon, ed. (2001). *Civilians in War.* Lynne Rienner, Boulder, CO.

Chesterman, Simon (2001). *Just War or Just Peace? Humanitarian Intervention and International Law.* Oxford University Press, Oxford.

Cohn, Theodore H. (2002). *Governing Global Trade: International Institutions in Conflict and Convergence.* Ashgate, Aldershot.

Collier, Paul and Jan Dehn (2001). 'Aid, Shocks, and Growth'. Working Paper No. 2688. World Bank, Washington DC.

Collier, Paul and David Dollar (2001). *Globalization, Growth, and Poverty: Building an Inclusive World Economy.* World Bank and Oxford University Press, Washington DC and New York.

Collier, Paul and Anke Hoeffler (2002). 'Aid, Policy, and Growth in Post-Conflict Societies'. Working Paper No. 2902. World Bank, Washington DC. <econ.worldbank.org/files/19228_wps2902.pdf> (July 2003).

Collier, Paul, Anke Hoeffler, and Mans Söderbom (2001). 'On the Duration of Civil War'. Policy Research Working Paper WPS 2681. World Bank, Washington DC.

Commonwealth Secretariat (1991). 'The Harare Commonwealth Declaration, 1991'. 20 October. <www.thecommonwealth.org/whoweare/declarations/harare.html> (July 2003).

Conflict Prevention Network (2001). 'The Practical Guide of Conflict Prevention'. CD-ROM. Berlin/Brussels.

Conflict Prevention Network (2001). *Record of Preventive Capacities: Mainstreaming Conflict Prevention. A Survey by the Conflict Prevention Network.* Stifftung Wissenschaft und Politik, Berlin.

Cortright, David and George Lopez (2000). *The Sanctions Decade: Assessing UN Sanctions in the 1990s.* Lynne Rienner, Boulder, CO.

Cortright, David and George Lopez (2002). *Sanctions and the Search for Security: Challenges to UN Action.* Lynne Rienner, Boulder, CO.

Crawford, Beverly and Ronnie D. Lipschutz (1996). 'Economic Globalization and the "New" Ethnic Strife'. Policy Paper No. 26. Institute of Global Conflict and Cooperation.

Crawford, Beverly and Ronnie D. Lipschutz, eds. (1998). *The Myth of 'Ethnic Conflict': Politics, Economics, and 'Cultural' Violence.* University of California at Berkeley, Berkeley, CA.

Cristoplos, Ian, John Farrington, and Andrew D. Kidd (2001). 'Extension, Poverty, and Vulnerability: Inception Report of a Study for the Neuchatel Initiative'. Overseas Development Institute Working Paper No. 144. <www.odi.org.uk/publications/wp144.pdf> (July 2003).

Cross, Peter (1998). *Contributing to Preventive Action.* Nomos, Baden-Baden.

Crossette, Barbara (2000). 'UN Plan for a New Crisis Unit Opposed by Wary Poor Nations'. *New York Times,* 26 November.

Cullen, Michelle L. and Nat J. Colletta (2000). *Violent Conflict and the Transformation of Social Capital: Lessons from Cambodia, Rwanda, Guatemala, and Somalia.* World Bank, Washington DC.

Daudelin, Jean (2002). Personal interview. 5 March, Ottawa.

Davies, James (1962). 'Towards a Theory of Revolution'. *American Sociological Review* vol. 27, pp. 7.

Davies, Susanna (1996). *Adaptable Livelihoods: Coping with Food Insecurity in the Malian Sahel.* St. Martin's Press, New York.

De Gregorio, José, Barry J Eichengreen, Takatoshi Ito, et al. 'An Independent and Accountable IMF'. Geneva Reports on the World Economy. International Centre for Monetary and Banking Studies, Geneva. <www.cepr.org/press/geneva_report.htm> (July 2003).

De Silva, K. M. and S. W. R. de A. Samarasinghe, eds. (1993). *Peace Accords and Ethnic Conflict.* St. Martin's Press, New York.

Deaton, Angus (1995). 'International Commodity Prices, Macroeconomic Performance, and Politics in Sub-Saharan Africa'. Princeton Studies in International Finance No. 29. Princeton University Press.

Debiel, Tobias and Martina Fischer (2000). 'A Conflict Prevention Service for the European Union'. Berghof Research Centre for Constructive Conflict Management, Berlin.

Dehn, Jan (2001). 'Commodity Price Uncertainty and Shocks: Implications for Economic Growth'. Paper presented at the Royal Economic Society Annual Conference. April, University of Durham.

Democratic National Committee (2000). '2000 Democratic Party Platform'. 15 August. <www.democrats.org/about/2000platform.html> (July 2003).

Dercon, Stefan (2001). 'Assessing Vulnerability to Poverty'. Paper prepared for the UK Department for International Development. <www.economics.ox.ac.uk/members/stefan.dercon/assessing%20vulnerability.pdf> (July 2003).

Devarajan, Shantayanan, David Dollar, and Torgny Holmgren (2001). 'Aid and Reform in Africa: Lessons from Ten Case Studies'. World Bank, Washington DC.

Development Assistance Committee (1996). 'Shaping the 21st Century: The Role of Development Co-operation'. Organisation for Economic Co-operation and Development, Paris.

Development Assistance Committee (2000). 'New Zealand's Aid Programme to the Solomon Islands: Note by the Secretariat'. DCD/DAC/AR(2000)2/24/ADD2. 13 April. Organisation for Economic Co-operation and Development, Paris.

Development Assistance Committee (2001). 'The DAC Guidelines: Helping Prevent Violent Conflict'. <www.oecd.org/dataoecd/15/54/1886146.pdf> (July 2003).

Development Assistance Committee (2001). 'DAC Network on Conflict, Peace, and Development: Draft Programme of Work and Budget, 2001–2002'. Organisation for Economic Co-operation and Development, Paris.

Development Assistance Committee (2002). 'Countries in Conflict and Poor Performers: What Can Donors Do?' In *The DAC Journal: Development Co-operation Report 2001*, pp. 135–151. Organisation for Economic Co-operation and Development, Paris.

Dewitt, David, David Haglund, and John J. Kirton, eds. (1993). *Building a New Global Order: Emerging Trends in International Security*. Oxford University Press, Toronto.

Diamond, Larry Jay and Marc F. Plattner, eds. (1994). *Nationalism, Ethnic Conflict, and Democracy*. Johns Hopkins University Press, Baltimore.

Dinar, Ariel, Robert Mendelsohn, Robert Evaenson, et al. (1998). 'Measuring the Impact of Climate Change on Indian Agriculture'. World Bank Technical Paper No. WTP402. World Bank, Washington DC.

Dixon, L. and D. Wall (2000). 'Collective Action Problems and Collective Action Clauses'. *Financial Stability Review* June.

Dockrill, Saki (2002). 'Does a Superpower Need an Alliance?' *Internationale Politik* vol. 3 (Fall), pp. 9–12.

Dollar, David (2000). 'Has Aid Efficiency Improved in the 1990s?' Mimeo. World Bank, Washington DC.

Dollar, David and Aart Kraay (2001). 'Growth Is Good for the Poor'. Working Paper No. 2587. World Bank, Washington DC.

Donnelly, Michael (2002). 'Nuclear Safety and Criticality at Tokaimura: A Failure of Governance'. In J. J. Kirton and J. Takase, eds., *New Directions in Global Political Governance: The G8 and International Order in the Twenty-First Century*, pp. 141–166. Ashgate, Aldershot.

Dwan, Renata (2001). 'Conflict Prevention and CFSP Coherence'. In A. Missiroli, ed., *Coherence for European Security Policy: Debates — Cases — Assessments*. Institute for Security Studies of WEU, Paris.

Dwan, Renata (2003). 'Conflict Prevention'. In Stockholm International Peace Research Institute, ed., *Armaments, Disarmament, and International Security: SIPRI Yearbook 2003*, p. 107. Oxford University Press, London.

Easterley, William and Aart Kraay (1999). 'Small States, Small Problems?' Working Paper No. 2139. World Bank. <econ.worldbank.org/docs/800.pdf> (July 2003).

Edwards, Sebastian (1999). 'Crisis Prevention: Lessons from Mexico and East Asia'. NBER Working Paper No. 7233. <papers.nber.org/papers/W7322> (July 2003).

Eichengreen, Barry J. (1999). *Toward a New International Financial Architecture: A Practical Post-Asia Agenda*. Institute for International Economics, Washington DC.

Eichengreen, Barry J. and Ashoka Mody (2000). 'Would Collective Action Clauses Raise Borrowing Costs?' NBER Working Paper No. 7458. <papers.nber.org/papers/W7458> (July 2003).

'ESR News in Brief' (2002). *European Security Review* no. 10 (January), p. 5.

European Centre for Conflict Prevention (1999). *People Building Peace: 35 Inspiring Stories from Around the World*. European Centre for Conflict Prevention, Utrecht.

European Commission (1996). 'The EU and the Issue of Conflicts in Africa: Peace-Building, Conflict Prevention, and Beyond'. SEC(96) 332. Brussels. <europa.eu.int/comm/development/prevention/communication-1996.htm> (July 2003).

European Commission (2000). 'General Report 2000: Annexes'. Table II: Legislation under the Consultation Procedures (19/26). <europa.eu.int/abc/doc/off/rg/en/2000/com0601.htm#pt0745.0> (July 2003).

European Commission (2000). 'Improving the Effectiveness of European Action in the Field of Conflict Prevention'. Report presented to the Nice European Council by the Secretary General/High Representative and the Commission, Document No. 14088/00. <register.consilium.eu.int/pdf/en/00/st14/14088en0.pdf> (July 2003).

European Commission (2000). 'Santa Maria da Feira European Council: Presidency Conclusions'. 19–20 June. <europa.eu.int/european_council/conclusions/index_en.htm> (July 2003).

European Commission (2001). 'Civilian Crisis Management'. November. <europa.eu.int/comm/external_relations/cpcm/cm.htm> (July 2003).

European Commission (2001). 'Communication from the Commission on Conflict Prevention'. COM(2001) 211 final. 11 April. Brussels. <europa.eu.int/comm/ external_relations/cfsp/news/com2001_211_en.pdf> (July 2003).

European Commission (2001). 'Conflict Prevention: Commission Initiative to Improve EU's Civilian Intervention Capacities'. 11 April, Brussels. <europa.eu.int/comm/ external_relations/cfsp/news/ip_01_560_en.htm> (July 2003).

European Commission (2001). 'Council Adopts Rapid Reaction Mechanism Commission Now in Position to Intervene Fast in Civilian Crisis Management'. 26 February, Brussels. <europa.eu.int/comm/external_relations/cfsp/news/ip_01_255.htm> (July 2003).

European Commission (2001). 'Council Regulation (EC) No 381/2001 of 26 February 2001 creating a Rapid-Reaction Mechanism'. Brussels. *Official Journal of the European Communities* vol. 44 (27 February), pp. 5–9.

European Commission (2001). 'EU Programme for the Prevention of Violent Conflicts'. Göteburg, 15–16 June. <www.utrikes.regeringen.se/prefak/files/EUprogramme.pdf> (July 2003).

European Commission (2001). 'EU Support for Building Confidence in fYROM'. 4 October, Brussels. <europa.eu.int/comm/external_relations/see/news/ ip01_1368.htm> (July 2003).

European Commission (2001). 'General Budget of the European Union for the Financial Year 2001'. The 2001 Budget in Figures. <europa.eu.int/comm/budget/ pdf/budget/synthchif2001/en.pdf> (July 2003).

European Commission (2001). 'Report on the Implementation of the European Commission's External Assistance'. D(2001) 32947. <europa.eu.int/comm/ europeaid/reports/status_report_2001_en.pdf> (July 2003).

European Commission (2002). 'EU Action in Response to 11th September 2001: One Year After'. 9 September. <europa.eu.int/comm/110901> (July 2003).

European Union Operation in the Former Yugoslav Republic of Macedonia (2003). 'Operation "Concordia"'. <ue.eu.int/arym> (July 2003).

European Union Police Mission (2003). 'Bosnia and Herzegovina: EU Police Mission (EUPM)'. <ue.eu.int/eupm/homePage/index.asp> (July 2003).

Famine Early Warning System (FEWS) (1999). 'Current Vulnerability Assessment Guidance Manual'. <www.fews.org/va/cvaguide/cvaguidehome.html> (July 2003).

Farer, Tom (2002). 'The Bush Doctrine and the UN Charter Frame', *International Spectator* vol. 37, no. 3, pp. 91–100.

Feyzioglu, Tarhan, Vinaya Swaroop, and Min Zhu (1998). 'A Panel Data Analysis of the Fungibility of Foreign Aid'. *World Bank Economic Review* vol. 12, no. 1. <www.worldbank.org/research/journals/wber/revjan98/panel.htm> (July 2003).

Financial Stability Forum (2002). 'Compendium of Standards'. <www.fsforum.org/ compendium/about.html> (July 2003).

Fischer, Stanley (2001). 'Exchange Rate Regimes: Is the Bipolar View Correct?' *Journal of Economic Perspectives* vol. 15, no. 2, pp. 3–24.

Fischer, Stanley (2001). *Reducing Vulnerabilities: The Role of the Contingent Credit Line*. International Monetary Fund, Washington, DC.

Fisher, Ian (2000). 'For Central Africa, More War and Horrors: Congo's Tribal Strife Spins Out of Control'. *International Herald Tribune*, 14 February.

Food and Agriculture Organization (1998). 'Report on the Development of Food Insecurity and Vulnerability Information and Mapping Systems'. Rome, 2–5 June. <www.fao.org/docrep/meeting/W8497e.htm> (July 2003).

Foreign and Commonwealth Office, Government of the United Kingdom, (2003). 'G8 Africa Action Plan: Towards the 2003 Summit'. <www.fco.gov.uk/Files/KFile/G8africaactionplan.pdf> (July 2003).

Foster, Gregory D. (2001). 'Environmental Security: The Search for Strategic Legitimacy'. *Armed Forces and Society* vol. 27, no. 3, pp. 373–396.

Fowler, Robert (2003). 'Canadian Leadership and the Kananaskis G8 Summit: Toward a Less Self-Centred Policy'. In D. Carment, F. O. Hampson and N. Hillmer, eds., *Canada Among Nations 2003: Coping with the American Colossus*, pp. 219–241. Oxford University Press, Toronto.

Franchini-Sherifis, Rosella and Valerio Astraldi (2001). *The G7/G8: From Rambouillet to Genoa*. Franco Angelo, Milan.

Fratianni, Michele, Paolo Savona, and John J. Kirton, eds. (2002). *Governing Global Finance: New Challenges, G7 and IMF Contributions*. Ashgate, Aldershot.

Fratianni, Michele, Paolo Savona, and John J. Kirton, eds. (2003). *Sustaining Global Growth and Development: G7 and IMF Governance*. Ashgate, Aldershot.

G7 (1993). 'Tokyo Summit Political Declaration: Striving for a More Secure and Humane World'. Tokyo, 8 July. <www.g7.utoronto.ca/summit/1993tokyo/political.html> (July 2003).

G7 (1995). 'Chairman's Statement'. 17 June, Halifax. <www.g7.utoronto.ca/summit/1995halifax/chairman.html> (July 2003).

G7 (1995). 'Halifax Summit Communiqué'. 16 June, Halifax. <www.g7.utoronto.ca/summit/1995halifax/communique/index.html> (July 2003).

G7 (1995). 'The Halifax Summit Review of International Financial Institutions: Background Document'. 16 June, Halifax. <www.g7.utoronto.ca/summit/1995halifax/financial/index.html> (July 2003).

G7 (1996). 'Chairman's Statement'. Political Declaration, 29 June, Lyon. <www.g7.utoronto.ca/summit/1996lyon/chairman/index.html> (July 2003).

G7 (1996). 'Economic Communiqué: Making a Success of Globalization for the Benefit of All'. 28 June, Lyon. <www.g7.utoronto.ca/summit/1996lyon/communique/index.html> (July 2003).

G7 Finance Ministers (1996). 'Finance Ministers' Report to the Heads of State and Government on International Monetary Stability'. 28 June, Lyon. <www.g7.utoronto.ca/summit/1996lyon/finance.html> (July 2003).

G7 Finance Ministers (1999). 'Report of the G7 Finance Ministers to the Köln Economic Summit'. 18 June, Cologne. <www.g7.utoronto.ca/finance/fm061999.htm> (July 2003).

G7 Finance Ministers (2001). 'Strengthening the International Financial System and the Multilateral Development Banks: Report of the G7 Finance Ministers and Central Bank Governors'. 7 July, Rome. <www.g7.utoronto.ca/finance/fm010707.htm> (July 2003).

G8 (1997). 'Communiqué'. 22 June, Denver. <www.g7.utoronto.ca/summit/1997denver/g8final.htm> (July 2003).

G8 (1998). 'Communiqué'. 15 May, Birmingham. <www.g7.utoronto.ca/summit/1998birmingham/finalcom.htm> (July 2003).

G8 (1999). 'G8 Communiqué Köln 1999'. 20 June, Cologne. <www.g7.utoronto.ca/summit/1999koln/finalcom.htm> (July 2003).

G8 (2000). 'G8 Communiqué Okinawa 2000'. Okinawa, 23 July. <www.g7.utoronto.ca/summit/2000okinawa/finalcom.htm> (July 2003).

G8 (2001). 'Communiqué'. Genoa, 22 July. <www.g7.utoronto.ca/summit/2001genoa/finalcommunique.html> (July 2003).

G8 (2001). 'Conflict Prevention: Fact File'. <www.g7.utoronto.ca/summit/2001genoa/pres_docs/conflict.html> (July 2003).

G8 (2001). 'Genoa Plan for Africa'. Genoa, 21 July. <www.g7.utoronto.ca/summit/2001genoa/africa.html> (July 2003).

G8 (2002). 'G8's Africa Action Plan'. Kananaskis, 27 June. <www.g7.utoronto.ca/summit/2002kananaskis/africaplan.html> (July 2003).

G8 (2003). 'Water: A G8 Action Plan'. 3 June, Evian. <www.g7.utoronto.ca/summit/2003evian/water_en.html> (July 2003).

G8 Africa Personal Representatives (2003). 'Implementation Report by Africa Personal Representatives to Leaders on the G8 Africa Action Plan'. 1 June, Evian. <www.g7.utoronto.ca/summit/2003evian/apr030601.html> (July 2003).

G8 Foreign Ministers (1999). 'Conclusion of the Meeting of the G8 Foreign Ministers' Meeting in Berlin'. 16–17 December. <www.g7.utoronto.ca/foreign/fm991216.htm> (July 2003).

G8 Foreign Ministers (1999). 'Conclusions of the Meeting of the G8 Foreign Ministers'. 10 June, Gürzenich/Cologne. <www.g7.utoronto.ca/foreign/fm9906010.htm> (July 2003).

G8 Foreign Ministers (2000). 'G8 Miyazaki Initiatives for Conflict Prevention'. Miyazaki, 13 July. <www.g7.utoronto.ca/foreign/fm000713-in.htm> (July 2003).

G8 Research Group (2001). 'The 2001 G8 Compliance Report'. <www.g7.utoronto.ca/evaluations/2001compliance/index.html> (July 2003).

G8 Research Group (2002). 'Keeping Genoa's Commitments: The 2002 G8 Compliance Report'. <www.g7.utoronto.ca/evaluations/2002compliance/index.html> (July 2003).

G8 Research Group (2003). '2002 Kananaskis Interim Compliance Report'. <www.g7.utoronto.ca/evaluations/2002interimcompliance/index.html> (July 2003).

G8 Research Group (2003). 'From Kananaskis to Evian: The 2003 Compliance Report'. <www.g7.utoronto.ca/evaluations/2003compliance/index.html> (July 2003).

Gedmin, Jeffrey (2002). 'Transatlantic Ties after 9/11: An American View', *Internationale Politik* vol. 3 (Fall), pp. 13–18.

Geingob, Hage (2000). 'Assessing the Risks of the New Types of Conflict and Examining Ways of Dealing with Them'. Global Coalition for Africa. <www.gca-cma.org/esecurity.htm#0900> (July 2003).

George, Alexander L. and Jane E. Holl (1997). 'The Warning-Response Problem and Missed Opportunities in Preventive Diplomacy'. Carnegie Commission on Preventing Deadly Conflict. <wwics.si.edu/subsites/ccpdc/pubs/warn/frame.htm> (July 2003).

Ginsberg, Roy H. (2001). *The European Union in International Politics: Baptism by Fire*. Rowman & Littlefield Publishers, Lanham, MD.

Glennon, Michael J. (2003). 'Why the Security Council Failed'. *Foreign Affairs* vol. 74, no. 3, pp. 16–35.

Glewwe, Paul and Gillette Hall (1998). 'Are Some Groups More Vulnerable to Macroeconomic Shocks than Others? Hypothesis Tests Based on Panel Data from Peru'. *Journal of Development Economics* vol. 56 (June), pp. 181–206.

Gnisci, D (2000). *La vulnerabilité: Proposition d'un instroment novateur pour l'analyse des phénomènes socio-économiques*. IPALMO, Cesia, Rome.

Goldstein, Judith, Miles Kahler, Robert O. Keohane, et al. (2000). 'Legalization and World Politics'. *International Organization* vol. 54 (Summer).

Grant, James P. (1993). 'Jumpstarting Development'. *Foreign Policy* Summer, pp. 124–136.

Guillaumont, Patrick and Lisa Chauvet (2001). 'Aid and Performance: A Reassessment'. *Journal of Development Studies* vol. 37, no. 6, pp. 66–92.

Gurr, Ted Robert (1990). 'Ethnic Warfare and the Changing Priorities of Global Security'. *Mediterranean Quarterly* vol. 1 (Winter), pp. 82–98.

Gurr, Ted Robert (1993). *Minorities at Risk: A Global View of Ethnopolitical Conflicts*. United States Institute of Peace Press, Washington DC.

Gurr, Ted Robert (2002). 'Containing Internal War in the Twenty-First Century'. In F. O. Hampson and D. M. Malone, eds., *From Reaction to Conflict Prevention: Opportunities for the UN System*, pp. 41–62. Lynne Rienner, Boulder, CO.

Haas, Peter M. and Ernst B. Haas (1995). 'Learning to Learn: Improving International Governance'. *Global Goverannce* vol. 1, no. 3.

Haas, Richard (1990). *Conflicts Unending*. Yale University Press, New Haven.

Haglund, David G. and Michael K. Hawes, eds. (1990). *World Politics: Power, Interdependence, and Dependence*. Harcourt Brace Jovanovich Canada, Toronto.

Hajnal, Peter I. (1999). *The G7/G8 System: Evolution, Role, and Documentation*. Ashgate, Aldershot.

Hajnal, Peter I., ed. (2002). *Civil Society in the Information Age*. Ashgate, Aldershot.

Hajnal, Peter I. (2002). 'Partners or Adversaries? The G7/8 Encounters Civil Society'. In J. J. Kirton and J. Takase, eds., *New Directions in Global Political Governance: The G8 and International Order in the Twenty-First Century*, pp. 191–208. Ashgate, Aldershot.

Hampson, Fen Osler (2002). *Madness in the Multitude: Human Security and World Disorder*. Oxford University Press, Toronto.

Hampson, Fen Osler and David M. Malone (2002). *From Reaction to Conflict Prevention: Opportunities for the UN System*. Lynne Rienner, Boulder, CO.

Hansen, Henrik and Finn Tarp (2001). 'Aid and Growth Regressions'. *Journal of Development Economics* vol. 64, no. 2, pp. 547–570.

Harris, Peter and Ben Reilly, eds. (1998). *Democracy and Deep-Rooted Conflict: Options for Negotiators*. Institute for Democratic and Electoral Assistance, Stockholm.

Heitzmann, Karin, R. Sudharshan Canagarajah, and Paul B. Siegel (2002). 'Guidelines for Assessing the Sources of Risk and Vulnerability'. Social Protection Discussion Paper No. 0208. World Bank, Washington DC.

Hirsch, John (2001). *Sierre Leone: Diamonds and the Struggle for Democracy*. Lynne Reinner, Boulder, CO.

Holzmann, Robert (2001). 'Risk and Vulnerability: The Forward Looking Role of Social Protection in a Globalizing World'. Social Protection Working Paper No. 23161. World Bank, Washington DC.

Holzmann, Robert and Steen L. Jorgensen (2001). 'Social Risk Management: A New Conceptual Framework for Social Protection and Beyond'. *International Tax and Public Finance* vol. 8, no. 4, pp. 525–552.

Homer-Dixon, Thomas (1994). 'Environmental Scarcities and Violent Conflict'. *International Security* vol. 19, no. 1, pp. 5–40.

Hopmann, Terrence P. (2003). 'Managing Conflict in Post–Cold War Eurasia: The Role of the OSCE in Europe's Security "Architecture"'. *International Affairs* vol. 40, no. 1, pp. 75–100.

Horowitz, Donald L. (1985). *Ethnic Groups in Conflict*. University of California Press, Berkeley, CA.

'Immigrant Workers Fleeing Ivory Coast'. (2001). *International Herald Tribune*, 2 February.

International Commission on Intervention and State Sovereignty (2001). 'The Responsibility to Protect: Report of the International Commission on Intervention and State Sovereignty'. <www.dfait-maeci.gc.ca/iciss-ciise/report-en.asp> (July 2003).

International Monetary Fund (2002). 'World Economic Outlook, 2002'. Washington DC.

International Action Network on Small Arms (2003). 'IANSA Report Implementing the Programme of Action 2003'. London. <www.iansa.org/documents/03poareport/index.htm> (July 2003).

Jalan, Jyotsna and Martin Ravallion (1998). 'Transient Poverty in Postreform China'. *Journal of Comparative Economics* vol. 26, no. 2, pp. 338–357.

Jentleson, Bruce W. (1996). 'Preventive Diplomacy and Ethnic Conflict: Possible, and Difficult, Necessary'. Working Paper No. PP27. Institute on Global Conflict and Cooperation. <repositories.cdlib.org/igcc/PP/PP27> (July 2003).

Jentleson, Bruce W., ed. (2000). *Opportunities Missed, Opportunities Seized: Preventive Diplomacy in the Post–Cold War World*. Rowman and Littlefield, Lanham, MD.

Kagan, Robert (2002). 'Power and Weakness', *Policy Review* June/July, pp. 3–28.

Kaiser, Karl, John J. Kirton, and Joseph P. Daniels, eds. (2000). *Shaping a New International Financial System: Challenges of Governance in a Globalizing World*. Ashgate, Aldershot.

Kaufmann, Chaim (1996). 'Possible and Impossible Solutions to Ethnic Civil Wars'. *International Security* vol. 20, no. 4, pp. 136–175.

Kazmin, Amy (2001). 'Vietnam Bars Foreigners from Riot-Hit Areas'. *Financial Times*, 9 February.

Kenen, Peter B. (2001). *The International Financial Architecture: What's New? What's Missing?* Institute for International Economics, Washington, DC.

Kenen, Peter B. and Alexander Swoboda (2000). *Reforming the International Monetary and Financial System*. International Monetary Fund, Washington, DC.

Kenny, Charles and David Williams (2001). 'What Do We Know about Economic Growth? Or, Why Don't We Know Very Much'. *World Development* vol. 29, no. 1, pp. 1–22.

Kirton, John J. (1993). 'The Seven Power Summits as a New Security Institution'. In D. Dewitt, D. Haglund and J. J. Kirton, eds., *Building a New Global Order: Emerging Trends in International Security*, pp. 335–357. Oxford University Press, Toronto.

Kirton, John J. (2000). 'Preliminary Personal Assessment of the Kyushu-Okinawa Summit'. 23 July. <www.g7.utoronto.ca/evaluations/2000okinawa/kirtonassesment.htm> (July 2003).

Kirton, John J. (2001). 'The G7/8 and China: Toward a Closer Association'. In J. J. Kirton, J. P. Daniels and A. Freytag, eds., *Guiding Global Order: G8 Governance in the Twenty-First Century*. Ashgate, Aldershot.

Kirton, John J. (2001). 'The G20: Representativeness, Effectiveness, and Leadership in Global Governance'. In J. J. Kirton, J. P. Daniels and A. Freytag, eds., *Guiding Global Order: G8 Governance in the Twenty-First Century*, pp. 143–172. Ashgate, Aldershot.

Kirton, John J., Joseph P. Daniels, and Andreas Freytag, eds. (2001). *Guiding Global Order: G8 Governance in the Twenty-First Century*. Ashgate, Aldershot.

Kirton, John J. and Junichi Takase, eds. (2002). *New Directions in Global Political Governance: The G8 and International Order in the Twenty-First Century*. Ashgate, Aldershot.

Kirton, John J. and George M. von Furstenberg, eds. (2001). *New Directions in Global Economic Governance: Managing Globalisation in the Twenty-First Century*. Ashgate, Aldershot.

Klitgaard, Robert E. (1990). *Tropical Gangsters*. Basic Books, New York.

Knack, Stephen (2000). 'Aid Dependence and the Quality of Governance: A Cross-Country Empirical Analysis'. Working Paper No. 2396. World Bank, Washington DC. <econ.worldbank.org/docs/1151.pdf> (July 2003).

Kokotsis, Eleanore (1999). *Keeping International Commitments: Compliance, Credibility, and the G7, 1988–1995*. Garland, New York.

Krueger, Anne O. (2001). 'International Financial Architecture for 2002: A New Approach to Sovereign Debt Restructuring'. American Enterprise Institute, Washington DC, 26 November. <www.imf.org/external/np/speeches/2001/112601.htm> (July 2003).

Krueger, Anne O. (2002). 'New Approaches to Sovereign Debt Restructuring: An Update on Our Thinking'. 1 April, Institute for International Economics, Washington DC. <www.imf.org/external/np/speeches/2002/040102.htm> (July 2003).

Kühne, Winrich and Jochem Prantl, eds. (2000). *The Security Council and the G8 in the New Millennium*. Stiftung Wissenschaft und Politik, Berlin.

Lamy, Steven L. (2002). 'The G8 and the Human Security Agenda'. In J. J. Kirton and J. Takase, eds., *New Directions in Global Political Governance: The G8 and International Order in the Twenty-First Century*, pp. 167–187. Ashgate, Aldershot.

Landgraf, Martin (2000). 'Developing Analytical Tools for Preventive Strategies: A Practitioner's View on Conflict Impact Assessments'. In M. S. Lund and G. Rasamoelina, eds., *The Impact of Conflict Prevention Policy: Cases, Measures, Assessments*. Nomos, Baden-Baden.

Larus, Joel (1965). *From Collective Security to Preventive Diplomacy: Readings in International Organization and the Maintenance of Peace*. John Wiley and Sons, New York.

Lederach, John Paul (1997). *Building Peace: Sustainable Reconciliation in Divided Societies*. United States Institute of Peace Press, Washington DC.

Lombardi, Ben (2002). 'The "Bush Doctrine": Anticipatory Self-Defence and the New U.S. National Security Strategy'. *International Spectator* vol. 37, no. 4, pp. 91–105.

Lumsdaine, David H. (1993). *Moral Vision in International Politics: The Foreign Aid Regime, 1949–1989*. Princeton University Press, Princeton.

Lund, Michael (1996). *Preventing Violent Conflicts: A Strategy for Preventive Diplomacy*. U.S Institute for Peace Press, Washington DC.

Lund, Michael (2000). 'Introduction and Overview'. In M. S. Lund and G. Rasamoelina, eds., *The Impact of Conflict Prevention Policy: Cases, Measures, Assessments*. Nomos, Baden-Baden.

Lund, Michael S. and Guenola Rasamoelina, eds. (2000). *The Impact of Conflict Prevention Policy: Cases, Measures, Assessments*. Nomos Verlagsgesellschaft, Baden-Baden.

Lustig, Nora (2000). 'Crises and the Poor: Socially Responsible Macroeconomics'. Inter-American Development Bank, Washington DC. <www.iadb.org/sds/pov/publication/publication_21_1566_e.htm> (July 2003).

MacLean, George (2002). 'Building on a Legacy or Bucking Tradition? Evaluating Canada's Human Security Initative in an Era of Globalization'. *Canadian Foreign Policy* vol. 9 (Spring), pp. 65–84.

Malone, David M. (1997). 'The UN Security Council in the Post–Cold War World, 1987–97'. *Security Dialogue* vol. 28, no. 4, pp. 393–404.

Malone, David M. (1998). *Decision-Making in the UN Security Council: The Case of Haiti.* Clarendon Press, Oxford.

Malone, David M. (2000). 'The UN Security Council in the 1990s: Inconsistent, Improvisational, Indispensable?' In R. Thakur and E. Newman, eds., *New Millennium, New Perspectives: The United Nations, Security, and Governance*, pp. 21–45. United Nations University Press, Tokyo.

Manning, Robert A. (2001). 'Beware of Chinese Weaknesses before the 2008 Olympics'. *International Herald Tribune*, 18 July.

Maren, Michael (1997). *The Road to Hell: The Ravaging Effects of Foreign Aid and International Charity.* Free Press, New York.

Martin, Ian (2001). *Self-Determination in East Timor: The United Nations, the Ballot, and International Intervention.* Lynne Rienner, Boulder, CO.

Mason, John B. (1984). *Nutritional Surveillance.* World Health Organization, Geneva.

Maxwell, Daniel, Carol Levin, Margaret Armar-Klemesu, et al. (2000). 'Urban Livelihoods, Food and Nutritional Security in Greater Accra'. IFPRI Research Report No. 112. International Food Policy Research Institute, Washington DC.

McCulloch, Neil, L. Alan Winters, and Xavier Cirera (2001). *Trade Liberalization and Poverty: A Handbook.* Centre for Economic Policy Research, London.

McRae, Robert Grant and Don Hubert, eds. (2001). *Human Security and the New Diplomacy: Protecting People, Promoting Peace.* McGill-Queen's University Press, Montreal.

Mekenkamp, Monique, Paul van Tongeren, and Hans van de Veen, eds. (1999). *Searching for Peace in Africa: An Overview of Conflict Prevention and Management Activities.* European Platform for Conflict Prevention and Transformation, Utrecht.

Meltzer, Allan H. (2000). *Report of the International Financial Institutions Advisory Commission.* United States Congress, Washington DC.

Miall, Hugh (2000). 'Preventing Potential Conflicts: Assessing the Impact of "Light" and "Deep" Conflict Prevention in Central and Eastern Europe and the Balkans'. In M. S. Lund and G. Rasamoelina, eds., *The Impact of Conflict Prevention Policy: Cases, Measures, Assessments.* Nomos, Baden-Baden.

Ministry of Foreign Affairs of the Russian Federation (2002). 'Alexander Yakovenko, Official Spokesman of Russia's Ministry of Foreign Affairs, Answers a Russian Media Question about the Outcome of the Meeting of the G8 Personal Representatives for Africa in Accra'. <www.ln.mid.ru/Bl.nsf/arh/74B7F5DD7435E71F43256C90003606 FC?OpenDocument> (December 2002).

Bibliography 309

Missiroli, Antonio (2002). 'Euros for ESDP: Financing EU Operations'. Occasional Papers No. 45. Institute for Security Studies. <www.iss-eu.org/occasion/occ45.pdf> (July 2003).

Missiroli, Antonio (2003). 'EU Enlargement and CFSP/ESDP'. *European Integration* vol. 25, no. 1, pp. 1–16.

Montville, Joseph V. (1990). 'The Pathology and Prevention of Genocide'. In D. A. Julius, J. V. Montville and V. D. Volkan, eds., *The Psychodynamics of International Relationships*. Lexington Books, Lexington, MA.

Moravscik, Andrew (1999). 'Taking Preferences Seriously: A Liberal Theory of International Politics'. In C. Lipson and B. Cohen, eds., *Theory and Structure in International Political Economy*, pp. 33–74. MIT Press, Cambridge, MA.

Morgan, Theodore H. (1996). 'Trade and Investment Dimensions of International Conflict'. In C. A. Crocker, F. O. Hampson and P. Aall, eds., *Sources of and Response to International Conflict*. United States Institute of Peace Press, Washington DC.

Morrow, James D. (1990). 'When Do Power Transitions Lead to War?' Working Paper in International Studies No. I-90-15. Hoover Institution.

Nabakwe, Ruth (2002). 'France Continues Peace Keeping Initiative for Africa'. Pan-African News Agency, Dakar, Senegal, 23 January. <ww.globalpolicy.org/security/peacekpg/region/france.htm> (July 2003).

Nabulsi, Karma (2000). *Traditions of War*. Oxford University Press, Oxford.

Narayan, Deepa, Raj Patel, Kai Schafft, et al. (2000). *Voices of the Poor: Can Anyone Hear Us?* Published for the World Bank by Oxford University Press, New York.

Nielson, Poul (2001). 'Building Credibility: The Role of European Development Policy in Preventing Conflicts'. Speech delivered at the Foreign Policy Centre, 8 February, London. <europa.eu.int/comm/commissioners/nielson/speeches/index_arch_en.htm> (July 2003).

Nolan, Janne E., ed. (1994). *Global Engagement: Cooperation and Security in the 21st Century*. Brookings Institution, Washington DC.

Nye, Joseph S. (2001). 'Globalization and Discontent'. *The World Today* vol. 57, no. 8/9, pp. 39–40.

O'Hanlon, Michael (2002). 'Restraining the Growth of the U.S. Defense Budget'. Congressional Testimony, 28 February, U.S. Senate Budget Committee. <www.brook.edu/dybdocroot/views/testimony/ohanlon/20020228.htm> (July 2003).

Organisation for Economic Co-operation and Development (2001). 'Helping Prevent Violent Conflict: Orientations for External Partners'. Development Assistance Committee policy statement. <www1.oecd.org/dac/htm/conf.htm> (July 2003).

Organization of American States (2001). 'Promotion of Democracy'. 5 June. AG/RES. 1782 (XXXI-O/01). <www.oas.org/juridico/english/ga01/agres1782.htm> (July 2003).

Panel on United Nations Peace Operations (2000). 'Report of the Panel on United Nations Peace Operations'. The Brahimi Report. <www.un.org/peace/reports/peace_operations> (July 2003).

Patten, Chris (2001). 'Commission Statement on the Situation in Afghanistan'. 2 October, Strasbourg. <europa.eu.int/comm/external_relations/news/patten/sp01_429.htm> (July 2003).

Patten, Chris (2001). 'Debate on Conflict Prevention/Crisis Management'. Includes Commission statement on the situation on the border between the FRY/Kosovo and Fyrom, 14 March, Strasbourg. <europa.eu.int/comm/external_relations/news/patten/ip_01_123.htm> (July 2003).

Patten, Chris (2001). 'Rapid Reaction Force'. Remarks in the European Parliament, 17 January. <europa.eu.int/comm/external_relations/news/patten/rrf_17_01_01.htm> (July 2003).

Patten, Chris (2001). 'Sustainable Development "From Sound-Bite to Sound Policy"'. 29 November, London, Forum for the Future. <europa.eu.int/comm/external_relations/news/patten/sp01_600.htm> (July 2003).

Patten, Chris (2002). 'Developing Europe's External Policy in the Age of Globalisation'. 4 April, Central Party School, Beijing. <europa.eu.int/comm/external_relations/news/patten/sp02_134.htm> (July 2003).

Penttilä, Risto E.J. (2003). *The Role of the G8 in International Peace and Security*. Oxford University Press, Oxford.

Permanent Mission of Germany to the United Nations (2000). 'Speech by the Federal Minister for Economic Co-operation and Development, Heidemarie Wieczorek-Zeul, at the Workshop on Crisis Prevention and Development Co-operation'. New York, 19 April. <www.germany-info.org/UN/stsp_04_19_00.htm> (June 2001).

Piana, Claire (2002). 'The EU's Decision-Making Process in the Common Foreign and Security Policy: The Case of the Former Yugoslav Republic of Macedonia'. *European Foreign Affairs Review* vol. 7, no. 2, pp. 209–226.

Pomfret, John (2000). 'Miners' Riots Reveal the Pain of Change in China'. *International Herald Tribune*, 6 April.

Prime Minister of Canada (2002). 'Canada Helps Build New Partnerships with Africa'. Ottawa, 27 June. <www.pm.gc.ca> (July 2003).

Pritchett, Lant, Asep Suryahadi, and Sudarno Sumarto (2000). 'Quantifying Vulnerability to Poverty: A Proposed Measure, Applied to Indonesia'. Policy Research Working Paper No. WPS2437. World Bank, Washington DC.

Project Ploughshares (2002). 'Armed Conflicts Report 2002'. <www.ploughshares.ca/CONTENT/ACR/acr.html> (July 2003).

Pugh, Michael C., ed. (2000). *Regeneration of War-Torn Societies*. St. Martin's Press, New York.

Putnam, Robert (1988). 'Diplomacy and Domestic Politics: The Logic of Two-Level Games'. *International Organisation* vol. 423, pp. 427–460.

Putnam, Robert and Nicholas Bayne (1987). *Hanging Together: Co-operation and Conflict in the Seven-Power Summit*. 2nd ed. Sage Publications, London.

Putnam, Robert and C. Randall Henning (1989). 'The Bonn Summit of 1978: A Case Study in Coordination'. In R. N. Cooper, ed., *Can Nations Agree?* Brookings Institution, Washington DC.

Rapoport, David C. (1994). 'The Role of External Forces in Supporting Ethno-Religious Conflict'. In R. L. Pfaltzgraff and R. H. Shultz, eds., *Ethnic Conflict and Regional Instability: Implications for U.S. Policy and Army Roles and Missions.* Strategic Studies Institute U.S. Army War College, Carlisle Barracks, PA.

Rapoport, David C. (1996). 'The Importance of Space in Violent Ethno-Religious Strife'. Policy Paper No. 21. Institute of Global Conflict and Cooperation.

Reardon, Thomas and Stephen Vosti (1995). 'Links between Rural Poverty and the Environment in Development Countries: Asset Categories and Investment Poverty'. *World Development* vol. 23, no. 9, pp. 1495–1506.

'Reconstructing Post-Conflict Societies and the German Involvement' (2003). *German Foreign Policy Dialogue* vol. 4, no. 10 (24 April), pp. 1–24.

Record of Preventive Capacities: Mainstreaming Conflict Prevention. A Survey by the Conflict Prevention Network (2001). Stifftung Wissenschaft und Politik, Berlin.

Reinicke, Wolfgang and Francis Deng (2000). *Critical Choices: The United Nations, Networks, and the Future of Global Governance.* International Development Research Centre, Ottawa.

Richburg, Keith B. (1994). 'Africa in Agony: Somalia Slips Back to Bloodshed'. *Washington Post*, 4 September.

Risse, Thomas (1995). 'Democratic Peace — Warlike Democracies? A Social Constructivist Interpretation of the Liberal Argument'. *European Journal of International Relations* vol. 1, no. 4.

Robertson, Lord (2002). 'Speech at the First Magazine Dinner'. 24 January, London. <www.nato.int/docu/speech/2002/s020124a.htm> (July 2003).

Rocard, Michel (1998). 'Prévention des conflits: Une synergie d'efforts internationaux'. In P. Cross, ed., *Contributing to Preventive Action*, pp. 7–12. Stiftung Wissenschaft und Politik, Ebenhausen.

Rodrik, Dani (1996). 'Understanding Economic Policy Reform'. *Journal of Economic Literature* vol. 34, no. 1, pp. 9–41.

Rothman, Jay (1992). *From Confrontation to Cooperation: Resolving Ethnic and Regional Conflict.* Sage Publications, Newbury Park, CA.

Rouhana, Nadim N. (1995). 'Unofficial Third-Party Intervention in International Conflict'. *Negotiation Journal* vol. 11, no. 3, pp. 255–270.

Rousseau, T. K. and E. Thulow (1994). 'Regimes in Conflict: Peacemaking and Preventive Diplomacy in the New World (Dis)Order'. Working Papers Series. Centre for Foreign Policy Studies, Dalhousie University.

Rummel, Reinhardt (1996). 'Conflict Prevention in Central and Eastern Europe: Concepts and Policies of the European Union'. In S. Melnik and W. Heinz, eds., *Human Rights, Conflict Prevention, and Conflict Resolution: An Introductory Reader*. Freidrich Naumann Stiftung, Brussels.

Rummel, Reinhardt (2000). 'EU Conflict Prevention Network'. In A. Björkdahl and G. Sjösedt, eds., *Future Challenges to Conflict Prevention: How Can the EU Contribute?* Swedish Institute of International Affairs, Stockholm.

Rummel, Reinhardt (2002). 'From Weakness to Power with ESDP?' *European Foreign Affairs Review* vol. 7, no. 4, pp. 453–471.

Rummel, Reinhardt (2003). 'EU-Friedenspolitik durch Konfliktprävention: Erfahrungen mit dem Conflict Prevention Network (CPN)'. In P. Schlotter, ed., *Europa-Macht-Frieden*, pp. 240–277. AFK-Friedensschriften, Hamburg.

Rummel, Reinhardt (2003). 'How Civilian Is the ESDP?' *SWP Comments* vol. 6. <www.swp-berlin.org/english/pdf/comment/swpcomment2003_06.pdf> (July 2003).

Ryan, Stephen (1993). 'Grass-Roots Peacebuilding in Violent Ethnic Conflicts'. In J. Calliess and C. M. Merkel, eds., *Peaceful Settlement of Conflict: A Task for Civil Society*. Evangelische Aakademie, Rehburg-Loccum.

Sachs, Jeffrey and Andrew Warner (1995). 'Economic Reform and the Process of Global Integration'. Brookings Papers on Economic Activity, No. 1.

Schmeidl, Susanne and Feyzi Ismail (2001). 'Implementing the United Nations Security Council Resolution on Women, Peace, and Security: Integrating Gender into Early Warning Systems'. Report on the 1st Expert Consultative Meeting, 7 May. <www.international-alert.org/women/gewreprt.pdf> (July 2003).

Schneckener, Ullrich (2002). 'Developing and Applying EU Crisis Management: Test Case Macedonia'. European Centre for Minority Issues. <www.ecmi.de/doc/download/working_paper_14.pdf> (July 2003).

Sen, Amartya (1992). *Inequality Reexamined*. Harvard University Press, Cambridge, MA.

Sherman, Jake (2000). 'Humanitarian Action: A Symposium Summary'. International Peace Academy, New York.

Shiels, Frederick L. (1991). *Preventable Disasters: Why Governments Fail*. Rowman & Littlefield Publishers, Savage, MD.

Sriram, Chandra Lekha (2001). 'From Promise to Practice: Strengthening UN Capacities for the Prevention of Violent Conflict'. Report on a workshop held at West Point, New York, February 2001. International Peace Academy. <www.ipacademy.org/Publications/Reports/Research/PublRepoResePPUNCapacities_body.htm> (July 2003).

Sriram, Chandra Lekha and Karin Wermester (2002). 'Preventive Action at the United Nations: From Promise to Practice?' In F. O. Hampson and D. M. Malone, eds., *From Reaction to Conflict Prevention: Opportunities for the UN System*, pp. 381–398. Lynne Rienner, Boulder, CO.

Stedman, Stephen John (1995). 'Alchemy for a New World Order: Overselling "Preventive Diplomacy"'. *Foreign Affairs* vol. 74, no. 3, pp. 14–21.

Stedman, Stephen John (2001). 'Implementing Peace Agreements in Civil Wars: Lessons and Recommendations for Policymakers'. International Peace Academy, New York.

Stedman, Stephen John, Donald Rothchild, and Elizabeth Cousens, eds. (2002). *Ending Civil Wars: The Implementation of Peace Agreements*. Lynne Rienner, Boulder, CO.

Stefanova, Radoslava (1997). 'Preventing Violent Conflict in Macedonia: A Success Story?' *International Spectator* vol. 32, no. 3/4, pp. 99–120.

Stefanova, Radoslava (2000). 'Fostering Security through Regional Cooperation in South-East Europe: A Role for the EAPC'. *International Spectator* vol. 35, no. 4, pp. 97–107.

Stiglitz, Joseph (1989). 'Markets, Market Failures, and Development'. *American Economic Review* vol. 79, no. 2, pp. 197–203.

Struck, Doug (2001). 'History Rift Strains Japan's Relations with Its Neighbors'. *International Herald Tribune*, 25–26 August.

Svensson, Jakob (1998). 'Foreign Aid and Rent-Seeking'. Working Paper No. 1880. World Bank, Washington DC. <econ.worldbank.org/files/11578_wps1880.pdf> (July 2003).

Swarns, Rachel L. (2000). 'Mugabe Talks Defiance, But Is Zimbabwe Listening?' *International Herald Tribune*, 10 April.

Takase, Junichi (2002). 'The Changing G8 Summit and Japanese Foreign Policy'. In J. J. Kirton and J. Takase, eds., *New Directions in Global Political Governance: The G8 and International Order in the Twenty-First Century*, pp. 105–114. Ashgate, Aldershot.

Temple, Jonathan (1999). 'The New Growth Evidence'. *Journal of Economic Literature* vol. 37, no. 1, pp. 112–156.

Tetlock, Philip E. and Aaron Belkin (1996). *Counterfactual Thought Experiments in World Politics: Logical, Methodological, and Psychological Perspectives*. Princeton University Press, Princeton.

Thomas, Timothy S. (2003). 'A Macro-Level Methodology for Measuring Vulnerability to Poverty, with a Focus on MENA Countries'. Paper presented at the 4th Annual Global Development Conference 'Globalization and Equity', 19–21 January. Cairo.

Tobin, James (1974). 'The New Economics One Decade Older'. Eliot Janeway Lectures on Historical Economics in Honour of Joseph Schumpeter, 1972. Princeton University Press, Princeton.

Tobin, James (1978). 'A Proposal for International Monetary Reform'. *Eastern Economic Journal* vol. 4, no. 3-4 (July/October).

Tobin, James (1996). 'Prologue'. In M. ul Haq, I. Kaul and I. Grunberg, eds., *The Tobin Tax: Coping with Financial Volatility*. Oxford University Press, New York.

Tremonti, Giulio (2001). 'Pour une anti-taxe Tobin'. *Le Monde*, 12 September.

Triulzi, Umberto (2001). 'Vulnerability: The Missing Link between Conflict Prevention and Development'. Paper presented at the conference on 'Promoting Conflict Prevention and Human Security: What Can the G8 Do?', Istituto Affari Internazionali and the University of Toronto, Rome, 16 June.

Triulzi, Umberto and Pierluigi Montalbano (1997). 'Mondalizzazione degli scambi'. [Globalisation of Trade]. *Politica Internazionale* no. 3 (May–June).

Triulzi, Umberto and Pierluigi Montalbano (2001). 'Development Co-operation Policy: A Time Inconsistency Approach'. Research Report No. 2/2001. Roskilde University, Roskilde, Denmark.

Triulzi, Umberto and Pierluigi Montalbano (2001). 'Vulnerability Analysis and the Globalization Process'. *Politica Internazionale* no. 3–4.

Triulzi, Umberto, Carlo Pietrobelli, Luca De Benedictis, et al. (2003). 'Trade Shocks and Socioeconomic Vulnerability with an Application to CEECs'. Paper presented at the 4th Annual Global Development Conference 'Globalization and Equity', 19–21 January. Cairo.

Triulzi, Umberto, Pierluigi Montalbano, and Radoslava Stefanova (2001). 'New Prospects for Assessing Conflict and Development Dynamics'. Paper presented at the Second Meeting of the Development Assistance Committee Network on Conflict, Peace, and Development Co-operation, Paris, 27–28 November.

Ullrich, Heidi K. (2001). 'Stimulating Trade Liberalisation after Seattle: G7/8 Leadership in Global Governance'. In J. J. Kirton and G. M. von Furstenberg, eds., *New Directions in Global Economic Governance: Creating International Order for the Twenty-First Century*, pp. 219–240. Ashgate, Aldershot.

United Nations (1945). 'Charter of the United Nations'. <www.un.org/aboutun/charter> (July 2003).

United Nations (1992). 'An Agenda for Peace: Preventive Diplomacy, Peacemaking, and Peace-keeping'. A/47/277-S/24111. 17 June. <www.un.org/Docs/SG/agpeace.html> (July 2003).

United Nations (1999). 'The Nine Principles (of the Global Compact)'. <www.unglobalcompact.org> (July 2003).

United Nations (2000). 'Executive Summary and Conclusion of High-Level Meeting on Global Compact'. 27 July, Press Release SG/2065 ECO/18. <www.un.org/News/Press/docs/2000/20000727.sg2065.doc.html> (July 2003).

United Nations (2000). 'Report on the Panel on United Nations Peace Operations'. 21 August. A/55/305-S/2000/809. <www.un.org/peace/reports/peace_operations> (July 2003).

United Nations (2001). 'The Role of Economic Factors in Conflicts in Europe: How Can the Multilateral Security Bodies Addressing Economic Issues Be More Effective in Conflict Prevention?' Discussion paper, 19–20 November. Villars, Switzerland.

United Nations (2000). 'Secretary-General Says United Nations Stands "Ready to Help Africa, Wherever and However It Can"'. Press Release SG/SM/7485/Rev.1. 10 July. <www.un.org/News/Press/docs/2000/20000710.sgsm7485r1.doc.html> (July 2003).

United Nations (2001). 'Prevention of Armed Conflict: Report of the Secretary-General. Executive Summary'. A/55/985-S/2001/574. 7 June. United Nations, New York. <daccess-ods.un.org/TMP/7047019.html> (July 2003).

United Nations Development Programme (1994). *Human Development Report*. United Nations Development Programme, New York.

United Nations. Development Programme (1999). *Human Development Report 1999*. Oxford University Press, New York.

United States Department of State (2002). 'Bush Sends New National Security Strategy to Congress'. 20 September. <usinfo.state.gov/regional/nea/sasia/text/0920bush.htm> (July 2003).

van de Goor, Luc and Martina Huber, eds. (2002). *Mainstreaming Conflict Prevention — Concept and Practice: CPN Yearbook 2000/2001*. Nomos, Baden-Baden.

Vayrynen, Raimo (1998). 'Environmental Security and Conflicts: Concepts and Policies'. *International Studies* vol. 35, no. 1, pp. 3–21.

Volkan, Vamik D. (1985). 'The Need to Have Enemies and Allies: A Developmental Approach'. *Political Psychology* vol. 6, pp. 219–245.

von Furstenberg, George M. and Joseph P. Daniels (1992). 'Economic Summit Declarations, 1975–1989: Examining the Written Record of International Cooperation'. Princeton Studies in International Finance No. 72. Princeton University Press, Princeton.

Waldron, Arthur (2000). 'The Rumblings of an Avalanche Threaten China'. *International Herald Tribune*, 7 April.

Wallensteen, Peter (1991). 'The Resolution and Transformation of International Conflicts: A Structural Perspective'. In R. Vayrynen, ed., *New Directions in Conflict Theory: Conflict Resolution and Conflict Transformation*. Sage Publications, London.

Wallensteen, Peter (1998). 'Preventive Security: Direct and Structural Prevention of Violent Conflict'. In P. Wallensteen and J. Bercovitch, eds., *Preventing Violent Conflicts: Past Record and Future Challenges*. Uppsala University, Uppsala.

Wallensteen, Peter (2002). 'Reassessing Recent Conflicts: Direct vs. Structural Prevention'. In F. O. Hampson and D. M. Malone, eds., *From Reaction to Conflict Prevention: Opportunities for the UN System*, pp. 213–228. Lynne Rienner, Boulder, CO.

War-Torn Societies Project (1999). 'War-Torn Societies Project: The First Four Years'. Geneva.

Wood, Bernard (2001). 'Development Dimensions of Conflict Prevention and Peace-Building'. United Nations Development Programme, New York. <www.undp.org/erd/ref/undp_pb_study.pdf> (July 2003).

World Bank (1998). 'Assessing Aid: What Works, What Doesn't, and Why'. Policy Research Report, World Bank. <www.worldbank.org/research/aid/aidtoc.htm> (July 2003).

World Bank (1998). 'Building Trust to Rebuild Rwanda'. News Release No. 99/2003/AFR. <www.worldbank.org/html/extdr/extme/2003.htm> (July 2003).

World Bank (2001). 'Conflict Prevention and Reconstruction'. O.P. 2.30. <lnweb18.worldbank.org/ESSD/sdvext.nsf/67ByDocName/PoliciesandStrategies DevelopmentCooperationandConflictOP230> (July 2003).

World Bank (2001). *World Development Report 2000/2001: Attacking Poverty.* Oxford University Press, New York.

World Bank (2003). 'The Economics of Civil War, Crime, and Violence'. <econ.worldbank.org/programs/conflict> (July 2003).

Yusuf, Shahid (2001). 'Globalization and the Challenge for Developing Countries'. DECRG. World Bank, Washington DC. <www1.worldbank.org/economicpolicy/globalization/documents/wps2168.pdf> (July 2003).

Zartman, I. William (1975). *Ripe for Resolution.* Oxford University Press, New York.

Zartman, I. William (1990). 'Negotiations and Prenegotiations in Ethnic Conflict: The Beginning, the Middle, and the Ends'. In J. V. Montville, ed., *Conflict and Peacemaking in Multiethnic Societies.* Lexington Books, Lexington, MA.

Zartman, I. William (1995). *Collapsed States: The Disintegration and Restoration of Legitimate Authority.* Lynn Rienner, Boulder, CO.

Index

For Product Safety Concerns and Information please contact our EU
representative GPSR@taylorandfrancis.com Taylor & Francis Verlag GmbH,
Kaufingerstraße 24, 80331 München, Germany

Printed and bound by CPI Group (UK) Ltd, Croydon, CR0 4YY
11/04/2025
01843992-0008